NIETZSCHE AND JEWISH CULTURE

Friedrich Nietzsche occupies a contradictory position in the history of ideas: he came up with the concept of a master race, yet an eminent Jewish scholar like Martin Buber translated his *Also Sprach Zarathustra* into Polish and remained in a lifelong intellectual dialogue with Nietzsche. Sigmund Freud admired his intellectual courage and was not at all reluctant to admit that Nietzsche had anticipated many of his basic ideas.

This unique collection of essays explores the reciprocal relationship between Nietzsche and Jewish culture. It is organized in two parts: the first examines Nietzsche's attitudes towards Jews and Judaism: the second Nietzsche's influence on Jewish intellectuals as diverse and as famous as Franz Kafka, Martin Buber, Franz Rosenzweig and Sigmund Freud. Each carefully selected essay explores one aspect of Nietzsche's relation to Judaism and German intellectual history, from Heinrich Heine to Nazism.

Jacob Golomb teaches philosophy at the Hebrew University, Jerusalem, and acts as Philosophical Editor of the Hebrew University Magnes Press. His books include *Nietzsche's Enticing Psychology of Power* (1989) and *In Search of Authenticity from Kierkegaard to Camus* (1995).

NIETZSCHE AND JEWISH CULTURE

Edited by Jacob Golomb

London and New York

First published 1997
by Routledge
11 New Fetter Lane, London EC4P 4EE

Simultaneously published in the USA and Canada
by Routledge
29 West 35th Street, New York, NY 10001

© 1997 Jacob Golomb

Typeset in Garamond by
Ponting–Green Publishing Services, Chesham, Bucks
Printed and bound in Great Britain by
TJ Press (Padstow) Ltd, Padstow, Cornwall

British Library Cataloguing in Publication Data
A catalogue record for this book is available from
the British Library

Library of Congress Cataloguing in Publication Data
Nietzsche and Jewish culture / edited by Jacob Colomb.
p.   cm.
Includes bibliographical references and index.
1. Nietzsche, Friedrich Wilhelm, 1844–1900–Views on Judaism.
2. Nietzsche, Friedrich Wilhelm, 1844–1900–Influence.
3. Jews–Germany–Intellectual life.   4. Germany–Intellectual
life–20th century
I. Golomb, Jacob.
B3318.J83N54   1996
193–dc20   9542115

ISBN 0–415–09512–3 (hbk)
ISBN 0–415–09513–1 (pbk)

CONTENTS

CONTENTS

Part II Nietzsche's Jewish reception

NOTES ON
CONTRIBUTORS

Steven E. Aschheim teaches German Cultural and Intellectual History at the Hebrew University, Jerusalem. He is the author of *Brothers and Strangers: The East European Jew in German and German-Jewish Consciousness* (1982), *The Nietzsche Legacy in Germany* (1992) and *Culture and Catastrophe: German and Jewish Confrontation with National Socialism and other Crises* (1996).

Hubert Cancik teaches Classics at Eberhard-Karls-Universität, Tübingen. He is the author of *Untersuchungen zur lyrischen Kunst des P. Papinius Statius* (1965), *Grundzüge der hethitischen und alttestamentlichen Geschichtschreibung* (1976), *Nietzsches Antike* (1995) and has edited *Markus-Philologie* (1984) and *Handbuch religionswissenschaftlicher Grundbegriffe* (1988).

Stanley Corngold is Professor of German and Comparative Literature at Princeton University. He is the author of *The Fate of the Self: German Writers and French Theory* (1986), *Franz Kafka: The Necessity of Form* (1988), *Borrowed Lives* (with Irene Giersing, 1991) and *Complex Pleasure: Forms of Feeling in German Literature* (forthcoming).

Sander L. Gilman is Henry R. Luce Professor of the Liberal Arts in Human Biology at the University of Chicago. He is a cultural and literary historian and the author or editor of over forty books, the most recent in English on *Jews in Today's Germany* (1995). He is the president of the Modern Language Association.

Jacob Golomb teaches philosophy at the Hebrew University, Jerusalem and is the philosophical editor of the Hebrew University Magnes Press. Among his books are *Nietzsche's Enticing Psychology of Power* (1989), *Introduction to Philosophies of Existence* (1990) and *In Search of Authenticity from Kierkegaard to Camus* (1995).

NOTES ON CONTRIBUTORS

Peter Heller is Professor Emeritus in German and Comparative Literature at the State University of New York in Buffalo, USA. Publications on Nietzsche and Freud include *"Von den ersten und letzten Dingen": Studien und Kommentar zu einer Aphorismenreihe von F. Nietzsche* (1972) and *Studies on Nietzsche* (1980).

William J. McGrath is Professor of History at the University of Rochester, New York. He is the author of *Dionysian Art and Populist politics in Austria* (1974) and *Freud's Discovery of Psychoanalysis: The Politics of Hysteria* (1986).

Paul Mendes-Flohr is Professor of Jewish Intellectual History and Modern Jewish Philosophy at the Hebrew University. He is the author of *From Mysticism to Dialogue. Martin Buber's Transformation of German Social Thought* (1989) and *Divided Passions. Jewish Intellectuals and the Experience of Modernity* (1990), and is the co-editor of the new twenty-one volume Jewish edition of Martin Buber's *Collected Works*.

Weaver Santaniello is Assistant Professor of Philosophy at Penn State University, Berks Campus. She is the author of *Nietzsche, God, and the Jews* (1994) and is currently co-editing a collection of essays on Nietzsche and depth psychology.

Gary Shapiro is Tucker-Boatwright Professor in the Humanities and Professor of Philosophy at the University of Richmond, USA. He is the author of *Nietzschen Narratives* (1989), *Alcyone: Nietzsche on Gifts, Noise, and Women* (1991) and *Earthwards: Robert Smithson and Art After Babel* (1995).

Josef Simon is the director of philosophisches Seminar A, University of Bonn. He is the author of *Das Problem der Sprache bei Hegel* (1966), *Sprache und Raum* (1969), *Philosophie und linguistische Theorie* (1971), *Wahrheit als Freiheit* (1978), *Sprachphilosophie* (1981) and *Philosophie des Zeichens* (1989).

Yirmiyahu Yovel is Professor of Philosophy at the Hebrew University, Jerusalem and at the New School for Social Research, New York, and is chair of the Jerusalem Spinoza Institute. Among his books are *Kant and the Philosophy of History* (1980), *Spinoza and Other Heretics* (1989) and *Dark Riddle: Hegel and Nietzsche on Judaism* (1996).

INTRODUCTION

Celebrating the hundreth anniversary of the birth of Friedrich Nietzsche in Weimar on 15 October 1944, Alfred Rosenberg, the *Reichsleiter*, declared in an official speech: "In a truly historical sense, the National Socialist movement eclipses the rest of the world, much as Nietzsche, the individual, eclipsed the powers of his times."[1] Most of the essays in this volume, which was originally scheduled to appear on the occasion of the 150th anniversary of Nietzsche's birth in 1994, disapprove of such a baseless comparison. By clarifying, among others matters, Nietzsche's attitude towards Jews, and the warm reception of Nietzsche by contemporary Jews, the authors unmask the criminal falsification and manipulation of the Nietzschean corpus by the Nazis. However, fifty years after this notorious speech, there are still "powers", at least in Germany, who subscribe to Rosenberg's view. I witnessed this first-hand when invited to deliver a lecture on behalf of *Die Stiftung Weimarer Klassik*, which organized a conference in Weimar, in October 1994 on *"Jüdischer Nietzscheanismus seit 1888"*. Another invitee was Ernst Nolte, the renowned German historian who was to speak on "Nietzsche and fascism". One week before the conference was to open, he gave some interviews to Germany's leading newspaper[2] in which he made some remarks with nasty anti-Semitic connotations. In response, some Israeli and German Jewish scholars, myself among them, declined to participate in the conference if Nolte would be there. In the end, the conference was cancelled. However, its subject is far too important to let people such as Nolte have the last word. Fortunately, some of the present contributors were to participate in that conference. It is therefore our sincere hope that by explicating Nietzsche's views on Jews and presenting his Jewish legacy this volume might discourage in the future any manipulations of his writings by "movements" to which he was diametrically opposed.

Nietzsche, as is well known, encouraged his readers to shift their intellectual viewpoints and experience different, even radically incompatible perspectives. Thus by dealing with the subject matter of this collection from two different perspectives – that of Nietzsche and that of his Jewish followers or critics – we hope that the Nietzschen spirit of intellectual tolerance will be reflected in this volume. This is particularly true since no one definitive unanimous conclusion about Nietzsche's relations to Jews and Judaism is pointed to by the contributors that addressed these topics.

This volume is far from an exhaustive treatment of the reception accorded to Nietzsche by Jews. The voluminous endnotes appended to my essay and the extensive bibliography that concludes this volume highlight the fact that with regard to his reception by eminent Jewish intellectuals and writers, this collection, and indeed the literature as a whole, gives only a fraction of the possibilities for exploring Nietzsche's impact on these Jews. Thus, for example, Nietzsche's influence on Stefan Zweig, Ernst Toller, Alfred Döblin, Walter Benjamin, Karl Kraus, Jacob Wassermann, Gustav Landauer, Hermann Broch and so forth, has not as yet been adequately addressed in the literature. Consequently we believe that the appearance of this volume will contribute to promoting further investigation of this immense but little explored area.

Not only the subject matter of this collection but also its birth, has been somewhat stormy. The initial response of some of the potential contributors to the volume was quite enthusiastic, and they expressed great eagerness to help in shaping it. However, after deciding upon their subjects, some of those who had promised to write seem to have had second thoughts, for they simply disappeared. No fax, e-mail or courier mail could persuade them to react and respond and finally they withdrew from the project by default. One of the more honest, however, wrote to me that when it came to matters concerning Judaism he often experienced "an unexplained block". I am referring to both scholars of Jewish and non-Jewish origin who, as I said, initially went out of their way to help me in this project, but when it came to the delivery date – and afterwards – refrained from submitting the promised contributions. The experience was enlightening, though, of course, I do not intend to psychoanalyse these scholars' ambivalence to the project. I address the matter indirectly in my contribution below. Thus, I am afraid that some reasons for their peculiar behaviour had to do with their reluctance to come out of the closet and to be identified as Jewish scholars or as German scholars appearing in a collection on predominantly Jewish issues. The first group, perhaps, is still suffering from the phenomenon of "Jewish self-hatred" which, as I tried to show, Nietzsche's psychological teaching helped such scholars as Theodor Lessing to articulate and elucidate. Briefly, many of the human-all-too-human aspects of our psyche and behaviour which were so masterfully exposed in Nietzsche's writings, are also poignantly reflected in the various reactions the subject evoked among ambivalent scholars, Jewish and non-Jewish alike. This in turn reflects very positively upon the present contributors, especially those from Germany, who did not fall prey to these emotional barriers, but courageously dared to express their own original perspectives.

To repeat, this volume does not intend to provide a definitive solution to the complicated and emotion-laden topics covered here. My main intention is only to present this complexity as comprehensively and honestly as possible. As in other matters concerning Nietzsche's thought, and especially that pertaining to his views on the Jews, there is no final, definitive exposition. Indeed, a number of the essays in this volume clash on how we are to interpret his views on these matters. The interpretations vacillate from regarding him as a racist to seeing in him a great thinker with a profound sympathy for the Jewish people, who opposed any anti-Semitic or Nazi sentiment in his thought and life. This broad range seems, I believe, to attest once more to the unfathomed richness of Nietzsche's thought and to the vital importance of his legacy for our times.

Credit for this collection must go to Routledge's Richard Stoneman and his staff, in particular: Ruth Schafer and Patricia Stankiewicz. Their unwavering support, generous assistance and boundless patience made the rather taxing job of editing into a pleasurable assignment.

J.G.

NOTES

1 Quoted in the *Marbacher Katologe: "Das 20. Jahrhundert: Von Nietz-sche bis zur Gruppe 47"*, ed. B. Zeller (Marbach a. N.: Deutsche Schillergesellschaft, 1980), p. 20 (my translation). Cf. A. Rosenberg, *Friedrich Nietzsche: Ansprache bei einer Gedenkstunde anlässlich des 100. Geburtstages Nietzsches am 15. Oktober 1944* (Weimar, Munich: Zentralverlag der NSDAP).
2 One appeared, for example, in *Der Spiegel* 40 (1994): 83–103.

Part I

NIETZSCHE'S RELATIONS TO JEWS, JUDAISM AND JEWISH CULTURE

1

NIETZSCHE, ANTI-SEMITISM AND THE HOLOCAUST

Steven E. Aschheim

Each generation, I suggest, constructs its own, most appropriate Nietzsche – or Nietzsches. During the years of the Third Reich (and immediately after) Nietzsche appeared to be paradigmatically Nazi (while National Socialism seemed best understood as a kind of Nietzschean project).[1] Both National Socialists and their opponents tended to agree that Nietzsche was the movement's *most* formative and influential thinker, visionary of a biologized *Lebensphilosophie* society, fuelled by regenerationist, post-democratic, post-Christian impulses in which the weak, decrepit and useless were to be legislated out of existence. For those interested in making the case any number of prophetic themes and uncannily appropriate quotes were available. "From now on", Nietzsche wrote in *The Will to Power*,

> there will be more favourable preconditions for more comprehensive forms of dominion, whose like has never yet existed. And even this is not the most important thing; the possibility has been established for the production of international racial union whose task it will be to rear a master-race, the future "masters of the earth." The time is coming when politics will have a different meaning.[2]

The paradigmatic Nietzsche of the 1930s, 1940s and early 1950s was then the Nietzsche who was regarded as the thinker most crucially and intimately definitive of the Nazi order. To be sure there were always dissenting voices (both within and without the Nazi camp) but the prevailing wisdom held that Nietzsche was proto-Nazi, that he uncannily prefigured and, indeed, in some way even "caused" National Socialism and that in fundamental ways the movement itself had to be regarded as "Nietzschen".[3] This perception began to shift in about the mid-1950s and, although there have always been

3

counterchallenges, it has so proceeded apace that, for many younger people educated from about the 1970s on, the identification seems virtually incomprehensible. Nietzsche's de-Nazification – and the de-Nietzscheanism of Nazism, I would argue, has become close to a *fait accompli* within western culture (at least in English-speaking countries and France). This, in the main, has been the product of two, quite different, intellectual forces that – in consonance with wider political changes – have rendered the only other early major competitor and counterinterpretation, Georg Lukács's *Destruction of Reason* with its guiding thesis that "Hitler ... was the executor of Nietzsche's spiritual testament and of the philosophical development coming after Nietzsche and from him",[4] if not downright quaint, then certainly a little anachronistic.

I am not sure if it is an exaggeration to claim that the basic aim of Nietzsche's most insistent and influential post-war expositor, translator and popularizer, Walter Kaufmann, was casuistically to rid Nietzsche of these sullied associations and to provide him with the kind of liberal-humanist face consistent with American academic values of the time. His 1950 masterwork portrayed the Nazified Nietzsche as a pure, virtually inexplicable distortion. Essentially a good European, he was a thinker who had to be grasped in terms of his emphases on creativity, culture and critical individualism and whose dismissal of nationalism, racism and anti-Semitism could not have been more apparent.[5]

Kaufmann was, of course, a more or less systematic philosopher who insisted upon pressing Nietzsche's thought into a comprehensible and comprehensive system. Such systematization is, of course, anathema to those who since, in a different, less liberally certain and determinate age, have most dominantly colonized Nietzsche (and at the same time been crucially shaped by him!) – those various exponents of what, for lack of a better name, we call post-modernism and deconstructionism (Foucault, Deleuze, de Man, Derrida and so on). For them – as distinct from Kaufmann – the issue by and large goes quite unmentioned, unnoticed; the very need to refute the putative Nietzsche–Nazi link has been obliterated! Theirs is a Nietzsche that is quite dissimilar to Kaufmann's. Here he is the radically sceptical perspectivist, the anti-totalizing prophet of heterogeneity, *différance*, fragmentation and discontinuity.[6] But like Kaufmann, they have also fashioned a rather sterilized Nietzsche[7] whose project appears as the diametrical opposite, even therapeutic answer to, National Socialism. With one exception (to be dealt with a little later) they usually elide the more compromising aspects of his thought, those that sit less comfortably with their hero of ironic indeterminacy.

It may not be at all surprising that the post-war de-Nazification of Nietzsche occurred above all in France and the USA, where, given not only the brilliance but the remarkable elasticity of Nietzsche's *ouvre*, he could be harnessed to new cultural and political agendas. In Germany, of course, loosening him from these moorings was a different matter. In the land where Nazism had arisen and flourished and where Nietzsche had become so identified with the regime, it should perhaps not surprise us that, for upholders of the new liberal-democratic regime, resistance to his renewed influence was perhaps the greatest. It is no coincidence therefore that the most vociferous contemporary critic of Nietzsche – as well as post-modernism and what he considers to be its parallel irrationalist, anti-Enlightenment thrust – is Jürgen Habermas.[8] There are signs, I believe, that – perhaps with the slow demise of deconstructionist thinking – not only in Germany but elsewhere there has begun to occur another shift, or a rethinking, that, on a more sophisticated, qualified basis, will be able seriously to grapple with this question. The present chapter is an attempt to contribute to this renewed conversation.

Of course, particular readings and judgements of Nietzsche will determine whether we believe him to be implicated in Nazism. And, on the other hand, particular interpretations of National Socialism will influence our readiness to include him within its contours. But the very range and complexity of opinion is also related to the exceedingly charged nature of the issue. After all, both Nietzsche and National Socialism remain central to the twentieth-century experience and our own defining cultural and ideological landscape and sense of self.[9] And this chapter, of course, deals with the entwinement in its most explosive dimension: not the general question of the interrelationship of Nietzsche and the Third Reich (this I have done in detail elsewhere[10]) but the connections between the philosopher and radical Jew-hatred as well as the possible connections between his thought and the genocidal project (and the other major mass murderers) that stood at the dark heart of the Third Reich.

How may the historian deal with such vexed questions and what are the assumptions and materials that must be brought to bear? Anyone even vaguely acquainted with the history of Nietzsche's political and cultural influence and reception will know how manifold, pervasive and contradictory it has been. It is clear that no

5

"unmediated", causally direct relationship can be inferred or demonstrated. It would be an error to reduce Nietzsche's – exceedingly ambiguous, protean, elastic – work to an essence possessed of a single, clear and authoritative meaning and operating in a linearly determined historical direction. There should be no set portrait of the "authentic" Nietzsche, nor dogmatic certainty as to his original intent. Clearly the essentialist representations of both Kaufmann and Lukács – Nietzsche's thought as either *inherently antithetical to or the prototypical reflection, the ideational incarnation, of the Nazi project* – prejudge precisely the question at hand. What needs to be sifted out, and analysed as precisely as possible, are the concrete mediating links, the transmission belts that demonstrate conscious appropriation, explicit acknowledgments of affiliation and influence, the recognized thematic parallels and (more speculatively) the preconditions, the creations of states of mind and sensibility that render such events conceivable in the first place.

Let us first turn to the question of Nietzsche and anti-Semitism and, most importantly, his annexation – or, perhaps, rejection – by German anti-Semites from the Second Reich on. As always, Nietzsche's texts themselves provide a positive goldmine of varied possibilities, filled with ambiguities that his followers – and critics – could scavenge and turn in numerous, very often quite contradictory, directions (this was typical of Nietzsche's reception in virtually every area). What is clear is that Jews and Judaism are complexly central to Nietzsche's work; in both his hostile and friendly deliberations, he insisted upon their absolutely fateful historical role within European civilization. Who else could have written in such a simultaneously affirmative and ominous tone: "Among the spectacles to which the coming century invites us is the decision as to the destiny of the Jews of Europe. That their die is cast, that they have crossed their Rubicon, is now palpably obvious: all that is left for them is either to become the masters of Europe or to lose Europe."[11] From our point of view it does not really matter whether Nietzsche's views on Jews and Judaism are to be regarded as a unified and coherent element of a larger systematic outlook or as disparate and self-contradictory.[12] For the historian of culture what is important are the interpretive spaces open to those who selectively read and receive the texts. There are clearly sufficient allusions, hints and themes to satisfy virtually all comers. Jew and anti-Semites alike were aware that both could find Nietzsche's work useful (and spent much of their time in casuistically explaining away those passages that were not compatible with their own particular outlook). *Völkisch* anti-Semites interested in annexing Nietzsche had to contend with the knowledge that he was no nationalist, indeed was perhaps the most pronounced critic of his contemporary Germans, and above all the most outspoken opponent of the anti-Semitic "swindle". Turning around the very basis of his notion of *ressentiment* he even branded the herd, mass movement of anti-Semitism as itself a kind of slave revolt.[13] To make matters worse, more than any other European thinker he lavished extravagant praise on "The *Old* Testament – all honour to [it]! I find in it great human beings, a heroic landscape, and something of the very rarest quality in the world, the incomparable naïveté of the *strong heart*; what is more I find a people. In the New one, on the other hand, I find nothing but petty sectarianism, mere rococo of the soul, mere involutions, nooks, queer things"[14] – and the comparative virtues of the European Jews of his own time: "Jews among Germans are always the higher race", he wrote, – "more refined, spiritual, kind. *L'adorable* Heine, they say in Paris."[15]

Those inclined to pick up and disseminate these positive Nietzschean Jewish messages could easily do so (this is precisely what many in the Jewish community consistently did[16]) and this, indeed, was the reason that many anti-Semites from the Second Reich through the Nazi period either rejected Nietzsche entirely (Theodor Fritsch, Dietrich Eckart and Ernst Krieck are only the best-known of many examples) or, if they did so, appropriated him in qualified, selectively harnessed fashion (for instance Adolf Bartels, Wilhelm Schallmeyer, Heinrich Härtle).[17] Even those many anti-Semites and Nazis who were wholeheartedly Nietzschean (Franz Haiser, Ernst Wachler, Alfred Schuler, Ludwig Klages, Alfred Bäumler among others) were aware that casuistic explanation of Nietzsche's proJewish comments and his biting contempt for political anti-Semitism was needed. Variations on this theme were offered in abundance: the true "Germanic", indeed, racist, Nietzsche had been consistently hidden by his Jewish mediators who had maliciously transformed him into a libertarian, nihilist internationalist.[18] Anyone familiar with Nietzsche, wrote Alfred Bäumler, knew how opposed to the Jews he actually was. His philo-Semitic comments were simply an attention-getting device – playing the Jews against the Germans was part of his strategy to get the Germans to listen to him![19] But the most important claim argued that in recasting the terms of the debate, by infinitely radicalizing the question and going beyond all its conventional forms, Nietzsche was in fact "the most acute anti-

Semite that ever was".[20] He had, so the argument went, only opposed its traditional nineteenth-century varieties and its Christian versions because he stood for a newer and more radical form, one whose anti-Christian and biological sources pushed it far beyond the limited confessional, economic and social domains.[21]

No matter how selective an exercise this was, these anti-Semites were basing themselves upon, and finding inspiration in, particular readings of some of Nietzsche's most powerful – and extreme – texts. (Their reading, incidentally, was shared by Nietzsche's close friend and confidant, Franz Overbeck, who remarked that although "Nietzsche has been a convinced enemy of anti-Semitism as he had experienced it. . . . That does not exclude that his opinions about the Jews, when he spoke frankly, had a sharpness which surpassed by far every anti-Semitism. His position against Christianity is primarily founded in anti-Semitism."[22]) The philosopher had, after all, endowed the Jews with a world-historical stain, the stain that his entire philosophy sought to uncover, diagnose and overcome. It was *On the Genealogy of Morals* that held the "priestly people" responsible for nothing less than beginning "the slave revolt in morality: that revolt which has a history of two thousand years behind it and which we no longer see because it has been victorious".[23] And as Nietzsche put it in *The Antichrist*, the Jews, with their desire to survive at any price, were nothing less than "the *most catastrophic* people of world history". Their sin was inconceivably heinous for they had radically falsified.

> all nature, all naturalness, all reality, of the whole inner-world as well as the outer . . . out of themselves they created a counterconcept to *natural* conditions: they turned religion, cult, morality, history, psychology, one after the other, into an *incurable contradiction to their natural values* . . . by their aftereffect they have made mankind so thoroughly false that even today the Christian can feel anti-Jewish without realizing that he himself *is the ultimate Jewish consequence*.[24]

It is true that Nietzsche was in the main referring to the priestly period but the force of the texts themselves submerged this somewhat and interested appropriators were certainly not going to bother themselves with such scholastic qualifications! (It may also be that Nietzsche's distinction between the Hebrews and – priestly – Judaism matched the same opposition between vitality and decadence that he posited between pre and post-Socratic Greece. That may or may not have been the case but in terms of reception, history and political consequences, Greeks in late nineteenth-century Europe did not constitute a politically vulnerable and threatened minority nor did Athens possess the same negative emotional valence that surrounded the question of Jews and Judaism in the Germany of that time. No comparable Nietzschean ethnic anti-Alexandrian movement can be identified.)

It was these radical themes that were picked by extreme anti-Semites and certain Nazi supporters and that informed their everyday rhetoric. Nazism, wrote Heinrich Römer in 1940, was indebted to Nietzsche's pivotal insight that Israel had de-naturalized natural values. The clear implication was that National Socialism had to be regarded as the countermovement leading to renaturalization.[25] For such commentators the significance of Nietzsche's anti-Christian posture consisted in its anti-Jewish basis. His demonstration that Christianity was the ultimate Jewish consequence and that it engendered the spread of Jewish blood poisoning (Nietzsche's words)[26] made the Jews the most fateful people of world history. As one acolyte, Hans Eggert Schröder, put it, Judaized Christianity represented racial decline and decadence, "the antiracial principle applied against the racial".[27] It was in this way, according to these Nietzschean Nazis, that Nietzsche found his way to the race problem and then toward the solution of racial hygiene in an attempt "to break the degeneration of a thousand years".[28]

This kind of rhetoric was awash at every level of Nazi discourse and if it was not the only source it certainly served to canalize, reinforce and significantly radicalize already pre-existent anti-Semitic impulses. To be sure, it is almost certain that Hitler either never read Nietzsche directly or read very little.[29] Nevertheless his thought, sayings and speeches clearly espoused a popularized Nietzscheanism as it had percolated down to him during and after World War I – after all, a certain brutalized Nietzschean coin had become the basic currency of the radical right during that period. It was this that he selectively applied and melded into the *mélange* that constituted his own peculiar mode of thinking.[30]

Historical transmission belts – the ways in which thought, ideas, moods and sensibility become translated into policy – are complex indeed and all this is not meant to draw a causally straight line between Nietzsche, his epigones and the destruction of European Jewry. As we have already point out, Nietzsche's influence was like his writings, always multivalent and never simplistically reducible to any single political or cultural current or direction.[31] Nevertheless, I would argue that these texts and the mediated sensibility they could embody possess a relevance to the problem at hand. They formed an explicit ingredient of – and particularly radical way of canalizing – this kind of anti-Semitic consciousness, an influence that (for many, though obviously not for all) was openly acknowledged, and which constituted a crucial element of a radicalized mind-set that was a kind of precondition for what was to come.

This at any rate is how some recent historians have viewed the matter. Thus, as Conor Cruise O'Brien has argued, it was Nietzsche who was the decisive force in the fateful switch from a "limited" Christian theological Jew-hatred to an unlimited, secular brand and who thus concretely paved the way to the Holocaust. Hitler, he writes, learned from Nietzsche "that the traditional Christian *limit* on anti-Semitism was itself part of a Jewish trick. When the values that the Jews had reversed were restored, there would be no limits and no Jews."[32] (We do not know if Hitler knew of the following Nietzschean passage but his utterances certainly echoed such senti-ments: "Decadence is only a *means* for the type of man who demands power in Judaism and Christianity, the *priestly* type: this type of man has a life interest in making mankind *sick* and in so twisting the concepts of good and evil, true and false, as to imperil life and slander the world."[33]) And, as George Lichtheim would have it, only when Nietzschean ideas antithetical to the Judeo-Christian inheritance and its humanist offshoots had slowly percolated through and success-fully gripped certain German minds did Auschwitz become possible:

> It is not too much to say that but for Nietzsche the SS – Hitler's shock troops and the core of the whole movement – would have lacked the inspiration which enabled them to carry out their programme of mass murder in Eastern Europe.[34]

Before going on with the argument and trying to clarify some particular historical distinctions some general remarks would be in order. While here, and elsewhere, I insist that for the cultural historian interested in grasping the role, dynamics and effects of ideas within a political culture, the question of "valid" or "invalid" interpretations and applications must be set aside, this does not, of course render irrelevant the role of the text – and here the Nietz-schean text – within this process. Even if, for a moment, we retain the language of "distortion" or "misinterpretation", approaches such as Kaufmann's leave us oblivious to the possibility that, as Martin Jay has put it,

> the potential for the specific distortions that do occur can be understood as latent in the original text. Thus, while it may be questionable to saddle Marx with responsibility for the Gulag Archipelago or blame Nietzsche for Auschwitz, it is nevertheless true that their writings could be misread as justifications for these horrors in a way that, say, those of John Stuart Mill or Alexis de Tocqueville could not.[35]

Jacques Derrida, so much a part of the "new" Nietzsche that we discussed at the beginning of the chapter, has nevertheless similarly argued for a certain complicated complicity – "one can't falsify just anything . . . " – and notes the need

> to account for the possibility of this mimetic inversion and perversion. If one refuses the distinction between unconscious and deliberate programs as an absolute criterion, if one no longer considers only intent – whether conscious or not – when reading a text, then the law that makes the perverting simplification possible must lie in the structure of the text "remaining". . . . There is nothing absolutely contingent about the fact that the only political regime to have *effectively* brandished his name as a major and official banner was Nazi.
>
> I do not say this in order to suggest that this kind of "Nietzschean" politics is the only one conceivable for all eternity, nor that it corresponds to the best reading of the legacy, nor even that those who have not picked up this reference have produced a better reading of it. No. The future of the Nietzsche text is not closed. But if, within the still-open contours of an era, the only politics calling itself – proclaiming itself – Nietzschean will have been a Nazi one, then is necessarily significant and must be questioned in all of its consequences.
>
> I am also not suggesting that we ought to reread "Nietzsche" and his great politics on the basis of what we know or think we know Nazism to be. I do not believe that we as yet know how to think what Nazism is. The task remains before us, and the political reading of the Nietzschean body or corpus is part of it.[36]

To be sure, other historians and thinkers – Berel Lang is the most recent example – have claimed the very opposite, arguing that while ideas *are* central in grasping the genocidal impulse of Nazism,

> for Nietzsche's historical aftermath, what is at issue is an instance of misapproriation, not of deduction and not even . . . of affiliation. Far from being entailed by the premises underlying Nietzsche's position, the conclusions drawn are inconsistent with them. To reconstruct in the imagination the events leading up to the Nazi genocide against the Jews without the name or presence of Nietzsche is to be compelled to change almost nothing in that pattern.[37]

This, it seems to me, is entirely unpersuasive. Of course, Nietzsche's influence permeated many – contradictory – political and cultural tendencies but an exceptionally wide range of historical actors themselves (many Nazis and their adversaries) as well as any number of later critics have, at different levels of complexity, identified a profound affinity and a thematic complicity of Nietzschean impulses (always selectively mediated) in Nazism's definitive taboo-defying, transgressive core and its programmatic, murderous drives. To be sure, distinctions and not just commonalities need to be noted. It is remarkable that numerous victims of National Socialism have similarly intuited such a relationship and that a survivor of Auschwitz, Primo Levi, sought (whether successfully or not) to identify the commonalities as well as the defining differences. It is worth quoting him in full. "Neither Nietzsche nor Hitler nor Rosenberg", he wrote, as if the connections between them were entirely obvious,

> were mad when they intoxicated themselves and their followers by preaching the myth of the Superman, to whom everything is permitted in recognition of his dogmatic and congenital superiority; but worthy of meditation is the fact that all of them, teacher and pupils, became progressively removed from reality as little by little their morality came unglued from the morality common to all times and civilisations, which is an integral part of our human heritage and which in the end must be acknowledged.
>
> Rationality ceases, and the disciples have amply surpassed (and betrayed) the teacher, precisely in the practice of useless cruelty. Nietzsche's message is profoundly repugnant to me; I find it difficult to discover an affirmation in it which is not contrary to what I like to think; his oracular tone irritates me;

yet it seems that a desire for the sufferings of others cannot be found in it. Indifference, yes, almost on every page, but never *Schadenfreude*, the joy in your neighbour's misfortune and even less the joy of deliberately inflicting suffering. The pain of *hoi polloi*, of the *Ungestalten*, the shapeless, the not-born-noble, is a price that must be paid for the advent of the reign of the elect; it is a minor evil, but still an evil; it is not in itself desirable. Hitlerian doctrine and practice were much different.[38]

(Other intellectual survivors did not necessarily agree with this view. Thus another Auschwitz survivor, Jean Amery, viewed the philosopher quite differently to Levi. Nietzsche, he wrote, was "the man who dreamed of the synthesis of the brute with the superman. He must be answered by those who witnessed the union of the brute with the subhuman; they were present as victims when a certain humankind joyously celebrated a festival of cruelty, as Nietzsche himself expressed it . . . . "[39])

At any rate, what I am proposing here is that both in its overall bio-eugenic political and medical vision, its programmatic obsession with degeneration and regeneration, whether in parodistic form or not, there are clear informing parallels with key Nietzschean categories and goals. From one perspective, as Robert Jay Lifton has recently persuasively argued, Nazism is about the "medicalisation of killing". Its genocidal impulses were implicit within a bio-medical vision and its vast, self-proclaimed programmatic task of racial and eugenic hygiene. On an unprecedented scale it would assume control of the human biological future, assuring health to positive racial stock and purging humanity of its sick, degenerative elements. Its vision of "violent cure", of murder and genocide as a "therapeutic imperative", Lifton argues, resonates with such Nietzschean themes.[40]

While every generation may emphasize their particular Nietzsche, there can be little doubt that in the first half of this century various European political circles came to regard him as *the* deepest diagnostician of sickness and degeneration and its most thoroughgoing regenerative therapist. "The sick", he wrote, "are man's greatest danger; not the evil, not the 'beasts of prey'."[41] To be sure, as was his wont, he employed these notions in multiple, shifting ways, as metaphor and irony (he even has a section on "ennoblement through degeneration"[42]) but most often, most crucially, it was represented (and understood) as a substantial literal danger whose overcoming through drastic measures was the precondition for the urgent re-creation of a "naturalized", non-decadent humankind. Although he was not alone in the wider nineteenth-century quasi-bio-medical, moral, discourse of "degeneration"[43] – that highly flexible, politically adjustable tool that cut across the ideological spectrum, able simultaneously to locate, diagnose and resolve a prevalent, though inchoate, sense of social and cultural crisis through an exercise of eugenic labelling and a language of bio-social pathology and potential renewal[44] – he formed an integral part in defining and radicalizing it. He certainly constituted its most important conduit into the emerging radical right. What else was Nietzsche's *Lebensphilosophie*, his reassertion of instinct and his proposed transvaluation whereby the healthy naturalistic ethic replaced the sickly moral one (a central theme conveniently ignored or elided by the current post-structuralist champions of Nietzsche). "Tell me, my brothers", Zarathustra asks, "what do we consider bad and worst of all? Is it not *degeneration*?"[45] In this world, the reassertion of all that is natural and healthy is dependent upon the ruthless extirpation of those anti-natural *ressentiment* sources of degeneration who have thoroughly weakened and falsified the natural and aristocratic bases of life. Over and over again, and in different ways, Nietzsche declared that "The species requires that the ill-constituted, weak, degenerate, perish".[46]

The Nazi bio-political understanding of, and solution to "degeneration", as I have tried to show here and elsewhere, was in multilayered ways explicitly Nietzsche-inspired. From the World War I through its Nazi implementation, Nietzschean exhortations to prevent procreation of "anti-life" elements and his advocacy of euthanasia, of what he called "holy cruelty" – "The Biblical prohibition 'thou shalt not kill'", he noted in *The Will to Power*, "is a piece of naïveté compared with the seriousness of the prohibition of life to decadents: 'thou shalt not procreate!' . . . Sympathy for decadents, equal rights for the ill-constituted – that would be the profoundest immorality, that would be antinature itself as morality!"[47] – both inspired and provided a "higher" rationale for theorists and practitioners of such measures.[48]

The translation of traditional anti-Jewish impulses into genocide and the murderous policies adopted in different degrees to other labelled outsiders (Gypsies, physically and mentally handicapped, homosexuals, criminals, inferior Eastern peoples and Communist political enemies) occurred within the distinct context of this medico-bio-eugenic vision. There were, to be sure, many building-blocks that went into conceiving and implementing genocide and mass murder but I would argue that this Nietzschean framework of thinking provided a crucial conceptual precondition and his radical sensibility a partial trigger for its implementation.

Related to but also going beyond these programmatic parallels and links we must raise another highly speculative, though necessary, issue: the vexed question of enabling preconditions and psycho-logical motivations. Clearly, for events as thick and complex as these no single theoretical or methodological approach or methodology will suffice. Yet, given the extraordinary nature of the events, more conventional modes of historical analysis soon reach their limits and demand novel answers (the study of Nazism has provided them in abundance, some more, some less convincing[49]). I am not thus claiming exclusiveness for the Nietzschean element at this level of explanation, but rather arguing for his continued and important relevance. To be sure, of late, many accounts of the ideas behind, and the psychological wellsprings enabling, mass murder have been, if anything, anti-Nietzschean in content. For Christopher Browning it was hardly Nietzschean intoxication, the nihilistic belief that "all is permitted", that motivated the "ordinary killers" – but rather prosaic inuring psychological mechanisms such as group conformity, defer-ence to authority, the dulling powers of alcohol and simple (but powerful) processes of routinization.[50] For George L. Mosse, far from indicating a dynamic anti-bourgeois Nietzschean revolt, the mass murders represented a *defence* of bourgeois morality, the attempt to preserve a clean, orderly middle-class world against all those outsider and deviant groups that threatened it.[51]

These contain important insights but, in my view, leave out crucial experiential ingredients, closely related to the Nietzschean dimen-sion, which must form at least part of the picture. At some point or another, the realization must have dawned on the conceivers and perpetrators of this event that something quite extraordinary, un-precedented, was occurring and that ordinary and middle-class men were committing radically transgressive, taboo-breaking, quite "un-bourgeois" acts.[52] Even if we grant the problematic proposition that such acts were done in order to defend bourgeois interests and values, we would want to know about the galvanizing, radicalizing trigger that allowed decision-makers and perpetrators alike to set out in this direction and do the deed. To argue that it was "racism" merely

pushes the argument a step backward, for "racism" on its own –
while always pernicious – has to be made genocidal.

We are left with the issue of the radicalizing, triggering forces.
These may be many in number but it seems to me that Nietzsche's
determined anti-humanism (an atheism that, as George Lichtheim
has noted, differs from the Feuerbachian attempt to replace theism
with humanism[53]), apocalyptic imaginings and exhortatory visions,
rendered *such a possibility, such an act, conceivable in the first place*
(or, at the very least, once thought of and given the correct selective
readings easily able to provide the appropriate idealogical cover).
This Nietzschean kind of thought, vocabulary and sensibility constitutes an important (if not the only) long-term enabling precondition
of such radical elements in Nazism. With all its affinities to an
older conservatism, it was the radically experimental, morality-
challenging, tradition-shattering Nietzschean sensibility that made
the vast transformative scale of the Nazi project thinkable. Nietzsche, as one contemporary commentator has pointed out, "prepared
a consciousness that excluded nothing that anyone might think,
feel, or do, including unimaginable atrocities carried out on a
gigantic order".[54]

Of course, Nazism was a manifold historical phenomenon and its
revolutionary thrust sat side by side with *petit-bourgeois*, provincial,
traditional and conservative impulses.[55] But surely, beyond its doc-
trinal emphases on destruction and violent regeneration, health and
disease, the moral and historical significance of Nazism lies precisely
in its unprecedented transvaluations and boundary-breaking extrem-
ities, its transgressive acts and shattering of previously intact taboos.
It is here – however parodistic, selectively mediated or debased – that
the sense of Nazism, its informing project and experiential dynamic,
as a kind of Nietzschean Great Politics continues to haunt us.

NOTES

1 I have discussed all this in great detail in my *The Nietzsche Legacy in
  Germany: 1890–1990* (Berkeley: University of California Press, 1992).
2 *The Will to Power*, ed. Walter Kaufmann (New York: Vintage Books,
  1968), 960 (1885–6), p. 504.
3 There are no end of supporting contemporary examples of this. At the
  "higher" levels of discourse this was best illustrated by Heidegger, who
  initially viewed Nazism (and facism) as essentially Nietzschean projects,
  the most radical attempts to overcome western nihilism. "The two men",
  he proclaimed in his 1936 lectures on Schelling,

who each in his own way, have introduced a counter-movement to nihilism – Mussolini and Hitler – have learned from Nietzsche, each in an essentially different way. But even with that, Nietzsche's authentic metaphysical domain has not yet come into its own.

(quoted in Thomas Sheehan, "Heidegger and the Nazis", *New York Review of Books*, 16 June 1988.)

4 *The Destruction of Reason*, tr. Peter Palmer (Atlantic Highlands, NJ: Humanities Press, 1981), p. 341. The work was completed in 1952 but based on essays written in the 1930s and 1940s.

5 *Nietzsche: Philosopher, Psychologist, Antichrist* (Princeton: Princeton University Press, 1950).

6 Our culture is awash with this Nietzsche. All the above-named authors' works should be consulted. For typical examples of this genre amongst many see Clayton Koelb (ed.), *Nietzsche as Postmodernist: Essays Pro and Con* (Albany: SUNY Press, 1990); and David B. Allison (ed.), *The New Nietzsche: Contemporary Styles of Interpretation* (Cambridge, Mass.: MIT Press, 1985).

7 On Kaufmann's denaturing of Nietzsche's power-political dimensions see Walter Sokel, "Poltical uses and abuses of Nietzsche in Walter Kaufmann's image of Nietzsche", *Nietzsche-Studien* 12 (1983).

8 The most relevant text in this regard is Jürgen Habermas, *The Philosophical Discourse of Modernity*, tr. Frederick Lawrence (Cambridge, Mass.: MIT Press, 1987). Habermas declared prematurely in 1968 that Nietzsche was "no longer contagious" but subsequently spent a considerable amount of time combating the epidemic! For his mistimed proclamation see his "Zur Nietzsches Erkenntnistheorie", in Friedrich Nietzsche, *Erkenntnistheoretische Schriften* (Frankfurt am Main, 1968).

9 "Nietzsche and National Socialism", *Michael* XIII (1993): Steven E. Aschheim, 11–27. See esp. p. 11.

10 See Aschheim, *Nietzsche Legacy*, esp. chs 8–10 and the Afterword.

11 The full passage is filled with ambiguities, combining awe, and fear. See *Daybreak: Thoughts on the prejudices of Morality*, tr. R.J. Hollingdale (Cambridge: Cambridge University Press, 1982), 205, pp. 124–5.

12 For some recent attempts to examine Nietzsche's views on Jews and Judaism in the relation to his whole philosophy see Arnold M. Eisen, "Nietzsche and the Jews reconsidered", *Jewish Social Studies* 48(1) (Winter 1986); M.F. Duffy and Willard Mittlemen, "Nietzsche's attitude toward the Jews", *Journal of the History of Ideas* 49(2) (April–June 1988); Jacob Golomb, "Nietzsche's Judaism of power", *Revue des études juives* 147 (July–December 1988).

13 See for example, *On the Genealogy of Morals, Ecce Homo*, ed. Walter Kaufmann (New York: Vintage, 1969), III 14, pp. 123–4. See too Yirmiyahu Yovel, "Nietzsche, the Jews and *ressentiment*", in Richard Schacht (ed.), *Nietzsche, Genealogy, Morality: Essays on Nietzsche's On the Genealogy of Morals* (Berkeley: 1994), pp. 214–36. See esp. p. 224.

14 Nietzsche, *Genealogy of Morals, Ecce Homo* 22, p. 144.

15 Prior to this quote the paragraph – a discarded draft for a passage from

Ecce Homo – reads: "Whoever reads me in Germany, has first de-Germanized himself thoroughly as I have done: my formula is known 'to be a good German means to de-Germanize oneself'; or he is – no small distinction among Germans – of Jewish descent" (ibid., p. 262, n. 1).

16 I have outlined all of this in "Nietzsche and the Nietzschean moment in Jewish life (1890–1939)", in *Leo Baeck Institute Yearbook* 37 (1992).

17 All these variations are treated in Aschheim, *Nietzsche Legacy*.

18 This too was a common line. For just one example see "Friedrich Nietzsche und die Modernen", *Deutsche Zeitung* 10294, 28 August 1990.

19 Alfred Bäumler, *Nietzsche als Philosoph und Politiker* (Leipzig: Reclam, 1931), p. 157.

20 Heinrich Römer, "Nietzsche und das Rasseproblem", *Rasse: Monatschrift für den Nordischen Gedanken* 7 (1940).

21 Again, for just one source, see Kurt Kassler, *Nietzsche und das Recht* (Munich: Ernst Reinhardt, 1941), pp. 74ff.

22 Franz Overbeck, *Kirchlexicon, Nietzsche und das Judentum* (Nachlass Basel A 232), in R. Braendle and E. Stegemann (eds), *Franz Overbecks underledigte Anfragen an das Christentum* (Munich, 1988). I thank Hubert and Hildegard Cancik for this source.

23 Nietzsche, *Genealogy of Morals* 7, pp. 33–4.

24 *The Antichrist*, in Walter Kaufmann (ed.), *The Portable Nietzsche* (New York: Viking, 1968), p. 593.

25 Römer, "Nietzsche und das Rasseproblem", p. 61.

26 As Nietzsche wrote of the Jewish

> world-historic mission. The "masters" have been disposed of; the morality of the common man has won. One may conceive of this victory as at the same time a blood poisoning (it has mixed the races together) – I shan't contradict; but this intoxication has undoubtedly been *successful*. The "redemption" of the human race (from the "masters", that is) is going forward; everything is becoming visibly Judaized, Christianized, mobilized (what do the words matter!).
>
> (*Genealogy of Morals* 9, p. 36)

27 See his *Nietzsche und das Christentum* (Berlin and Lichter felde: Widulind, 1937), p. 75.

28 Römer, "Nietzsche und das Rasseproblem", p. 63.

29 Hitler's youthful companion August Kubizek, in his memoir, *The Young Hitler I Knew*, tr. E.V. Anderson (Boston: Houghton Mifflin, 1955), claims that the young Hitler did read Nietzsche but no work by the philosopher was found in his library (although it did contain a slim volume dedicated to him by Himmler entitled *Von Tacitus bis Nietzsche*). See Robert L. Waite, *Hitler: The Psychopathic God* (New York, 1977), p. 62.

30 Even if one disregards the many Nietzsche-inspired Hitler quotations from the now rather discredited works of Hermann Rauschning, this is patently obvious in *Hitler's Table Talk 1941–1944*, ed. and tr. Norman Cameron and R.H. Stevens (London, 1953), esp. pp. 720–2.

31 The entire thrust of my *Nietzsche Legacy* is to establish the multiple,

often contradictory, nature of Nietzsche's influence and the impossibility of reducing it to an "essential" political direction or position.
Clearly, this should be kept in mind here. This article obviously deals
with only *one* strand of influence.

32 See his *The Siege* (London, Weidenfeld & Nicholson, 1986), p. 59. See
   generally pp. 57–9, 85.
33 Nietzsche, *The Antichrist* 24, pp. 593–4.
34 See his *Europe in the Twentieth Century* (London: Cardinal, 1974), pp.
   185, 186.
35 Martin Jay, "Should intellectual history take a linguistic turn? Reflections on the Habermas–Gadamer debate", in *Fin-de-siècle Socialism*
   (New York: Routledge, Chapman & Hall, 1988), p. 33.
36 Jacques Derrida, "Otobiographies: the teaching of Nietzsche and the
   politics of the proper name", in *The Ear of the Other: Otobiography
   Transference Translation*, ed. Christie V. McDonald, tr. Peggy Kamuf
   and Avital Ronell (New York: Schocken, 1985), pp. 30–1.
37 Berel Lang, *Act and Idea in the Nazi Genocide* (Chicago and London:
   University of Chicago Press, 1990), pp. 197–8.
38 Primo Levi, "Useless violence", in *The Drowned and the Saved*, tr.
   Raymond Rosenthal (London, 1988), pp. 84–5.
39 See the whole chapter entitled "Resentments" in his stunning *At the
   Mind's Limits: Contemplations by a Survivor on Auschwitz and its
   Realities*, tr. Sidney Rosenfeld and Stella P. Rosenfeld (Bloomington:
   University of Indiana Press, 1980). The quote appears on p. 68. Amery,
   we should note, recast Nietzsche's theory of *ressentiment* into a *positive*
   virtue for the maintenance of ethical consciousness over the "natural"
   processes of time and forgetfulness of crimes committed but not
   acknowledged.
40 *The Nazi Doctors: Medical Killing and the Psychology of Genocide*
   (London: Papermac, 1987), esp. pp. 15–27, ch. 21 and p. 486.
41 *Genealogy of Morals* III 14, p. 122.
42 "Tokens of higher and lower culture", in *Human All Too Human: A
   Book for Free Spirits*, tr. R.J. Hollingdale (Cambridge: University of
   Cambridge Press, 1986), 224, pp. 107–8.
43 On this see my "Max Nordau, Friedrich Nietzsche and *Degeneration*",
   Journal of Contemporary History 28(4), (October 1993).
44 See Daniel Pick, *Faces of Degeneration: A European Disorder, c.
   1848–1918* (Cambridge: University of Cambridge Press, 1989) for a sense
   of the politically diverse annexation of the notion and its wide dissemination.
45 "On the gift-giving virtue" 1, *Thus Spoke Zarathustra*, in *Portable
   Nietzsche*, p. 187, italics in the original.
46 *Will to Power* 246 (January–Fall 1888), p. 142.
47 Ibid., p. 389. These kinds of sentiments are dotted throughout Nietzsche's works. See *Will to Power*, pp. 141–2, 391–3; *Zarathustra*, pp. 183–6
   (although here *freedom* to die is stressed); *Twilight of the Idols*, in
   Portable Nietzsche, pp. 536–8; *Genealogy of Morals*, pp. 120–5.
48 For examples see Aschheim, *Nietzsche Legacy*, pp. 161, 163, 243–4.

STEVEN E. ASCHHEIM

49 I am presently undertaking a study on "Nazism and Western Consciousness, 1933–1993" which will seek to investigate and place into
contextual and conceptual order these diverse analyses.

50 See his *Ordinary Men: Reserve Police Batallion 101 and the Final
Solution in Poland* (New York: HarperCollins, 1992).

51 See his *Nationalism and Sexuality: Respectability and Abnormal Sexuality in Modern Europe* (New York: Howard Fertig, 1985).

52 This has recently been interestingly explored by Saul Friedlander, in
"'The Final Solution': on the unease in historical interpretation", in
Memory, History, and the Extermination of the Jews of Europe (Indiana:
University of Indiana Press, 1993); see esp. p. 110.

53 *Europe in the Twentieth Century*, p. 186. Too often this has been
exclusively and ideologically linked to the downfall supposedly inherent
in Nietzsche's "atheism", thus enabling unlimited powers to man in
which, given the fact that nothing is sacred, he has total licence to kill.
This is not the position upheld here for it, I would argue, is the anti-
Enlightenment, anti-humanist impulse, not secularization *per se*, that is
linked to these events.

54 Kurt Rudolf Fischer, "Nazism as a Nietzschean experiment", *Nietzsche-
Studien*, 6 (1977): 121.

55 For a good evaluation of these different sides see Hans Sluga, *Heidegger's
Crisis: Philosophy and Politics in Nazi Germany* (Cambridge, Mass.:
Harvard University Press, 1993).

2

A POST-HOLOCAUST RE-EXAMINATION OF NIETZSCHE AND THE JEWS

Vis-à-vis Christendom and Nazism

Weaver Santaniello

INTRODUCTION

Much recent scholarship and the appearance of previously un-published material has made possible a more accurate post-World War II evaluation of Nietzsche's views toward Judaism and the Jews, especially in connection to Christianity and his analysis of turbulent Jewish–Christian relations in nineteenth-century Germany.

Throughout the past twenty years, numerous histories of anti-Semitism, the Holocaust and those addressing the intellectual origins of Nazism have shown that, contrary to Nazi propaganda and thus the widespread popular view, Nietzsche was not an anti-Semite; that the Germanic ideology was formed well before Nietzsche's works appeared; and that Nietzsche, during his own lifetime, actually opposed many intellectual forerunners of the Third Reich.[1] These proto-fascists that surrounded Nietzsche include his sister Elisabeth, a virulent Christian anti-Semite who later became a staunch sup-porter of Hitler and the Nazis decades after her brother's death; her husband Bernard Förster, the son of a Protestant pastor who, along with Elisabeth in 1886, cultivated a human breeding colony in Paraguay devoted to Aryan racial purity which excluded Jews; Nietzsche's mentor and then foe, Richard Wagner, whom Nietzsche broke with partly because of his conversion to Christianity and mainly because of his anti-Jewish racism; Adolf Stöcker, the promin-ent court pastor and leader of the Lutheran state church in Germany; the anti-Christian anarchist Eugen Dühring, who was the first to

21

preach Jewish extermination and is now regarded by historians as the first "proto-Nazi"; and the Christian theologian, Ernst Renan, who was a prominent advocate of the Aryan myth in France and later became an almost official ideologist of the Third Reich. As will be shown, these and other (Christian and anti-Christian) anti-Semites appear as Nietzsche's major religious and political opponents throughout Nietzsche's writings, particularly in his later works, *Thus Spoke Zarathustra, Toward the Genealogy of Morals* and *The Antichrist*. An almost centuries-long propaganda campaign beginning with Elisabeth's tampering with and censorship of Nietzsche's works, notes and documents immediately after his insanity in 1889, has served to suppress these texts.[2] And the enduring World War II propaganda generated by Elisabeth and Hitler's continuing distortion and manipulation of Nietzsche's works and words has further confused interpreters writing after the Nazi era who have sought to discern Nietzsche's intricate critique of Christianity, Judaism and anti-Semitism during the time in which he wrote. The 1976 release of Cosima Wagner's previously unpublished diaries, as well as the public reopening of the Nietzsche Archive in Weimar in 1991, wherein Elisabeth's papers have been kept under lock and key throughout the duration of the Third Reich and then the Cold War, will also aid scholars who want further to investigate her and the Wagner families' prominent role in the formation of Nazi Germany. Their roles and racist ideologies are not only central for placing Nietzsche's views in their proper biographical, historical and intellectual context, but also for understanding his empathy with the Jews of his time; his elitist contempt for Christianity as the religion of mass *ressentiment*; and then his alleged association to Nazism decades after his death. Nietzsche was repulsed by anti-Semitism because of its hostility toward spiritual and cultural values: "The struggle against the Jews has always been a symptom of the worst characters, those more envious and more cowardly. He who participates in it now must have much of the disposition of the mob."[3] And it was Nietzsche's firm contention that "when Christianity is once destroyed, one will become *more appreciative of the Jews*."[4] It is therefore crucial at the outset to recognize that Nietzsche's critique of Christianity is intertwined with his contempt for anti-Semitism.

It is my conviction that Nietzsche, an original member and then "apostate" of the nationalistic and viciously anti-Semitic Wagner circle, had something very important to say about his culture's revolt against European Jewry during the latter third of the nineteenth century – something that religious and political authorities did not – and still *do* not – want the world to hear. One should therefore attempt to resist the tremendous amount of myths, massive propaganda and hermeneutical conundrums that have traditionally (and conveniently) surrounded Nietzsche in an effort to analyze historically his incisive critique of religion and politics *before* he was turned into a brutal (anti-Christian and anti-Semitic) "Nazi" in the 1930s.

That Nietzsche opposed anti-Semitism, German nationalism and the Germanic Aryan race, the three doctrines crucial to National Socialism, is now common knowledge in Nietzsche studies. But initially in the 1940s when Nietzsche scholars, such as Walter Kaufmann, quoted Nietzsche's published works to refute Nazi claims that Nietzsche supported these doctrines, the Nazis retorted that Nietzsche's published works were "masks of ideas" and that the "true Nietzsche" was not to be found in his publications.[5] Hence, one should ask *why* the Nazis "wanted" Nietzsche and why they went to the trouble of misquoting, distorting and ripping his texts out of context, which they undeniably did. One should also ask why Elisabeth, from 1892 onward, heavily censored and controlled Nietzsche's published works, *why* she rushed to compile and promote a collection of notes entitled *The Will to Power* (1901) as Nietzsche's last great "synthesizing" work, why she falsified the story of the Wagner/Nietzsche break in her skewed biography on her brother, and why she forged, altered or destroyed Nietzsche's documents to cover up his negative remarks concerning Wagner, herself, Christianity and anti-Semitism. Methodologically, for almost a generation now, some interpreters have continued to assume that because the Nazis used Nietzsche they "liked" him and/or that Nietzsche's philosophy somehow "led to" or "influenced" Nazism. The stark historical evidence, however, points to the contrary. Instead of assuming that Nazi leaders liked Nietzsche, one should assess his texts to see what Elisabeth and the Nazis did *not* like. I will expound on the relevance of Elisabeth's myth-making of Nietzsche at the conclusion of this essay. However, prior to what would fast become Nietzsche's erratic rise to fame in Germany after his breakdown, the subtle eye will nonetheless see two dominant traditions initially in conflict, represented by Elisabeth and Nietzsche's Jewish ally, Georg Brandes, who was one of Nietzsche's rare readers during the last few years of his prolific life. One tradition goes from Wagner to Elisabeth and then to Hitler, the other from Nietzsche to Brandes and the *émigrés* such as Kaufmann who, like other Nietzsche scholars, refused to relinquish Nietzsche in whole or in part to Nazi manipulations. Other commentators in the English-speaking world, such as Crane Brinton, who theorized (in the 1940s) that Nietzsche was "half a Nazi and half an anti-Nazi", fell into a middle position.[6] The first (Nazi) tradition claimed a few of "Nietzsche's" (1901) notes on "race and breeding" as authentic, stating that Nietzsche really did not mean what he said in his texts. The second tradition appealed to the corpus of Nietzsche's writings, and has used the *Nachlass* responsibly. The third tradition, over time, failed to recognize that the Nazis demeaned Nietzsche's works, thus confusing issues by lifting random quotes from his publications to "show" Nietzsche was compatible with Nazism. Regardless, since the turn of the century in Germany, the general strategy of Elisabeth and then the Nazis was to divert readers *away* from Nietzsche's publications. This crucial point is almost always overlooked.[7]

As stated, today, Nietzsche's opposition to anti-Semitism and his high regard for his Jewish contemporaries is rarely in question by Nietzsche scholars. However, these scholars have grappled with Nietzsche's complex view toward ancient Judaism which are both positive and negative. Nietzsche's stance has led most commentators to interpret his negative evaluation of Judaism in light of the fact that Judaism gave birth to Christianity, which is his major enemy; others simply to dismiss his views as contradictory; and yet others to grossly distort Nietzsche's texts.[8]

In recent years, closer evaluations of Nietzsche's texts reveal a threefold distinction of Jews: Nietzsche favors original Israel and contemporary Jewry, he is ambivalent toward priestly-prophetic Judaism which he believes gave rise to Christianity.[9] Paradoxically, these threefold distinctions, which fully emerge in Nietzsche's later writings, are not key to understanding Nietzsche's views toward ancient Judaism *per se*, but for grasping the logistics of his opposition to anti-Semitism as manifest in nineteenth-century Christian theology. Succinctly put, Nietzsche's threefold position is the exact reverse of the Christian anti-Semites he opposed. Whereas Elisabeth and other Christian anti-Semites generally demeaned original Israel and contemporary Jewry, claiming the priestly-prophetic strand of Judaism for professing Jesus as the Messiah, Nietzsche overturns that position. He elevates original Israel and contemporary Jewry, deriding Judeo-Christianity as that tradition rooted in *ressentiment*.[10] When approaching Nietzsche's texts, it is thus *extremely* important to place his views in their proper political and theological contexts, and in dialogue with the views of his major religious and political opponents, such as his sister and her husband Förster. This will not only demonstrate that Nietzsche's views are coherent when interpreted in light of the theological and political categories that pre-existed in Germany, but also that Nietzsche, a solitary eccentric who had virtually no social standing whatsoever, was nailing and incensing some of the most powerful and prominent anti-Semitic leaders of his time, such as the widely respected pastor and state church leader, Adolf Stöcker, as well as other popular authors such as Eugen Dühring, who spoke of Jewish extermination as a viable "solution" to the Jewish "problem."[11]

CHRISTIAN AND ANTI-CHRISTIAN
ANTI-SEMITISM

Anti-Semitism in nineteenth-century Germany was generally expressed in two forms: Christian anti-Semitism and anti-Christian anti-Semitism. The former, rooted in Christian theology, usually distinguished some positive element in ancient Judaism which was carried on and perfected in Jesus, from a deformed Israel which is made antithetical to Jesus and Christianity. The latter was found in French philosophies such as Voltaire and Holbach. It consisted in an attack on Jews and Judaism as well as Christianity itself, including its biblical Jewish sources, its eschatological conception and its ethical theological elements.[12] Broadly speaking, Christian anti-Semites, such as Stöcker, sought to convert "stubborn" contemporary Jews to Christianity and usually distinguished "noble" Jews of the priestly-prophetic era from corrupt scribal/rabbinic Judaism (original Israel). Anti-Christian anti-Semites, such as Dühring, abhorred the whole of Judaism and disdained Christianity as well. Even so, Stöcker and Dühring's respective positions were not incompatible. Both groups viewed Jews as morally inferior despite their opposing views toward Christianity.[13]

Nietzsche firmly opposes both forms of anti-Semitism. But he despises the concepts of election and the notion of justice via eternal vengeance that he regards as originating with Judaism. He believes Christians adopt these ideas; regard themselves as God's chosen people; and then apply against the Jews that which the Jews previously applied against their enemies – the Last Judgement.[14] Thus, while Nietzsche derides certain elements of Judaism as a religion, particularly those elements that Christian anti-Semites honored, he

25

nonetheless remains steadfast in his praise for contemporary Jewry, as demonstrated biographically and throughout his texts.[15]

The defense of the Christian state was a high priority for the anti-Semitic court preacher and pastor Adolf Stöcker, who was Förster's ally and perhaps the most well known among German Protestants. Stöcker, who represents Christian anti-Semitism, preached that the Jewish "problem" could not be solved unless the Jews renounced their faith and ceased to "live in the flesh".[16] His popularity soared in the 1880s, as he opened his ultra-conservative, anti-Semitic campaign to the economically strapped middle classes and began distributing anti-Semitic propaganda. He denounced the capitalistic power of modern Jewry; publicly expressed his feat that "the cancer from which we suffer" (the German spirit becoming Judaized) would impoverish the German economy and pleaded for a return to Germanic rule in law and business.[17] His fundamental political theology was that because the Jews rejected the message of salvation in Christ, Christian Germans were the true inheritors of God's election. Because the Jews crucified Christ, they committed the "unpardonable sin" and brought upon themselves the curse of everlasting abhorrence.[18] Stöcker, whose rhetoric was often clothed beneath the guise of piety and "equality," claimed that his intention was to deal with the Jewish question "in full Christian love but also in full social truthfulness."[19] And the "truth," Stöcker held, was that Israel had to give up its desire to become master in Germany or a catastrophe was ultimately unavoidable.[20] In this fashion, Stöcker exploited the existing hatred of the Jews to shore up the authority of the Christian state.

Nietzsche makes occasional reference to Stöcker in his notes and in his writings (the most famous is his made note that he wants "Wilhelm, Bismarck, and Stöcker shot").[21] In the early 1880s, Nietzsche became disturbed by Stöcker's anti-Jewish sentiments and regarded the Christian Social Workers' movement as one which grew out of resentment and cowardice.[22] By the late 1880s, Nietzsche is even more alarmed and preoccupied with Stöcker's rhetorical revival of the Christian state.[23] He writes of the homeopath of Christianity, "that of the court chaplains and anti-Semitic speculators."[24] Regarding Christian anti-Semites as "little, good-natured, absurd sheep with horns" who posed as judges and possessed "little herd animal virtues", Nietzsche, while grieving the death of Friedrich III, announced in a personal letter in the summer of 1888 that "the age of Stöcker had begun."[25]

26

The most radical representative of anti-Christian anti-Semitism during the 1880s was the anarchist Eugen Dühring, whom Nietzsche refers to as the "Berlin apostle of revenge" and who appears as Nietzsche's political opponent in *Zarathustra* and in the second and third essay of the *Genealogy*.[26]

Dühring, whom historian Peter Gay describes as a "bombastic, shallow, and confused writer," was most famous for his general will or "equal wills" theory which was rooted in the notion of altruistic human nature.[27] On the one hand, morality is based on the notion of equal wills who abstain from hurting each other; this, Dühring says, is the ground of all ethics. On the other hand, history begins with force and consists of oppression and slavery; it does not begin in the economic system. Contradictions between force (oppression) and will (freedom) must be resolved to reshape history, and this will come in the "socialitary system." Because the Jews manipulate the economy, they oppose the common good and must thus be eliminated.

In the second essay of the *Genealogy*, Nietzsche seeks to repudiate attempts such as Dühring's in order to seek the "origin of justice in the sphere of *ressentiment*."[28] After condemning Dühring's notion of human nature and of justice as products of *ressentiment*, Nietzsche concludes that Dühring's principle of equal will is a principle hostile to life, "an agent of the dissolution and destruction of man, an attempt to assassinate the future of man, a sign of weariness, a secret path to nothingness."[29]

Dühring opposed the Christian state and sought a new state that would serve a free and individualistic society.[30] As a favourite author of the members of the Executive Committee of the People's will in the 1880s, he preached a particular and peculiar democratic socialism, drawing upon John Stuart Mill's *Utilitarianism* in attempting to establish the doctrine of punishment upon the instinct of retaliation.[31]

Dühring sought national self-sufficiency in a controlled economy. He wanted this limited national socialism to be based on the enthusiasm of the masses and on a general will of the Germanic *Volk*.[32] His central position was that the *Volk* possessed a unity of interests that were engaged in the struggle against the Jews who opposed the "common good" and the *Volk*'s general will.[33] His theological position was that the Germans should reject the Old Testament, that the Jews were not people of God and that Christ was an Aryan and an anti-Semite.[34] He opposed mixed marriages in order to protect the German people from blood contamination, and assailed Christianity as incompatible with the Nordic spirit.[35]

According to historians, Dühring went farther than most in his fundamental stance to deny the right of Jewish existence. He is therefore regarded as the first proto-Nazi, a "sinister and embittered figure" whose obscure followers later became prominent members of the SS after his death in 1921. The year after Wagner's death, Dühring's convert and pupil, Heinrich von Stein, visited Nietzsche and tried to coax him back into the Wagner circle. Nietzsche refused. He instead attempted to lead the young academician out of the "morass" into which Dühring and Wagner had plunged him – to no avail.[36]

The intellectual and cultural background of anti-Semitism, particularly Christian anti-Semitism, which deeply affected Nietzsche via his immediate family, provide the proper framework in which his critique of ancient Judaism can be understood. This is especially the case during his last productive years, as his writings generally become more fierce and political in tone and in temperament. Jewish––Christian relations have been neglected in Nietzsche studies and are central to his thought.

THE MATURE WRITINGS

Zarathustra

Historical clues reveal that Nietzsche also encounters Dühring in the highly poetic and autobiographical *Zarathustra*, wherein Nietzsche sets up his infamous eternal return in contrast to Dühring's scientific theory, and his *übermensch* in contrast to the "masses of barbarian force," as exemplified by Dühring. So that Nietzsche's *übermensch* would not be confused with the savage masses, the philosopher locked his *übermensch* in conflict with his ultimate antagonist, the *Untermensch* of mass society, *the last man*.[37] In the 1880s, Nietzsche returned to Dühring's works to "comprehend the mysteries of the new terrorism."[38]

Throughout *Zarathustra*, Nietzsche derogatorily refers to the Lutheran state church (the "hypocritical fire hound"),[39] and attempts to replace the wrathful notion of the Last Judgement with the joyful advent of the Great Noon.[40] He continues to defile his sister and Wagner, as well as a host of other anti-Semitic enemies whom he frequently regards as the preachers of equality, the preachers of death, the good and the just, the tarantulas, the poison-mixers and the grave-diggers, to name a few. Autobiographical sections describing the pain of his "break" with Elisabeth and the Wagner circle include "On apostates" and "Upon the blessed isles," the latter which refers to Nietzsche's days at the Wagners' Swiss villa in Tribschen, which Nietzsche regarded as the isle of the blessed. Specific references to Wagner are also found in the "The magician," and it is most likely that the infamous jester (the devil) who trips up and thus kills the tightrope walker in the Prologue to Book I is in reference to Wagner.[41] Specific passages concerning the *ressentiment* of Nietzsche/Zarathustra's "vicious enemies" are recorded in a string of four consecutive sections in Book II; namely, "On priests," "On the virtuous," "On the rabble" and "On the tarantulas." In "On priests," Zarathustra makes his famous announcement that there has never yet been an overman, and that even the greatest he found all too human. If it is assumed that Nietzsche is writing against Christian anti-Semites, it is probable that this passage on the overman is a bold political statement which upheld the Jews' traditional contention that the Messiah had *not* come, as Christianity claimed, and that Jesus was human, not divine. (In *Human, All Too Human*, Nietzsche regards Jesus as the "noblest human being."[42]) In the following three sections, Zarathustra writes against the concept of hell, and proclaims instead that the "bridge to the highest hope is that man be *delivered* from revenge." And he regards the "preachers of equality" as the slanderers of the world and the burners of heretics, advising his friends to mistrust them:

> But thus I counsel you, my friends: Mistrust all in whom the impulse to punish is powerful. Mistrust all who talk much of their justice! And when they call themselves the good and the just, do not forget that they would be pharisees, if only they had – power.[43]

Elsewhere, in an extremely interesting passage, the prophet Zarathustra encounters a "foaming fool" at the gate of the "great city," which the fool regards as a hell for hermit's thoughts: "Don't you smell the slaughterhouses and ovens of the spirit even now? Does not this town steam with the fumes of slaughtered spirit?", says the fool. Wanting to be rid of the prophet, the fool (similar to the jester) warns Zarathustra, telling him to spit on the city and turn back. Zarathustra puts his hand over the fool's mouth and replies:

> "Stop at last ... your speech and your manner have long

29

nauseated me ... For all your foaming is revenge, you vain fool; I guessed it well."

"But your fool's words injure me, even where you are right. And even if Zarathustra's words *were* a thousand times right, still *you* would always *do* wrong with my words."

Thus spoke Zarathustra; and he looked at the great city, sighed, and long remained silent.[44]

According to Theodor Lessing, a controversial German Jewish philosopher who was a Nietzschean scholar in the early 1920s, *Zarathustra's* "foaming fool" *is* Dühring.[45] Lessing, in 1933, was one of the first victims of Nazism.

Perhaps the dark prophetic tinges these sections convey can be linked to the fact that Nietzsche had access to an inner Wagner circle that is now regarded as the root of National Socialism. Upon leaving the circle in 1876, he wrote that Wagnerites were leading "the Jews to the slaughterhouse" as scapegoats for Germany's misfortunes.[46] Utterances, images and metaphors concerning Jews and their extermination are recorded on several occasions throughout Nietzsche's works. These include a passage in *Daybreak* where – immediately prior to expressing concern for the destiny of European Jewry – Nietzsche writes of the "inhumaneness" of former times in which "Jews, heretics and the extermination of higher cultures" was done out of lust for power and with a good conscience: "The means employed by the lust for power have changed, but the same volcano continues to glow ... what one formerly did for the 'sake of God' one now does for the sake of money."[47] Passages also occur in the *Genealogy*, wherein Nietzsche writes of Dühring's attempt to "assassinate the future of man";[48] in *Zarathustra*, "The good are *unable* to create ... they sacrifice the future to *themselves* – they crucify all man's future. The good have always been the beginning of the end";[49] and in the *Antichrist*, wherein Nietzsche, battling his enemies, writes that the concept of immortality has been the greatest, and

> most malignant attempt to assassinate *noble* humanity ....
> The *ressentiment* of the masses forged its chief weapon against *us*, against all that is noble, gay, high-minded on earth....
> And let us not underestimate the calamity which crept out of Christianity into politics.[50]

Thus, painstaking historical analyses of Nietzsche's texts are crucial not only for discerning why Elisabeth and the Nazis frightened (well-intentioned) people away from Nietzsche's works, but why "the powers that be" have traditionally tried to perpetuate the nonsense that *Nietzsche's* writings are "dangerous" to read – for they could lead to social anarchy!

Toward the Genealogy of Morals

In spite of the numerous pro-Semitic passages prevalent throughout the corpus of Nietzsche's works, *due to* Nazi distortions decades later, perhaps no passage reverberates in contemporary minds more than his notorious attribution of the slave revolt in morality to priestly Judea recorded in section 7 of the first essays in the *Genealogy of Morals*. Here, in tones bordering on a tantrum, Nietzsche ascribes the slave revolt as stemming from the root of [priestly] Jewish hatred, "the sublimest kind of hatred."[51] Although this one segment has traditionally evoked hasty charges that Nietzsche himself was an anti-Semite, it is seldom noted that Nietzsche is not attacking contemporary Jewry but priestly Judea, which he believes gave rise to (anti-Semitic) Christianity. Nor is frequently noted that elsewhere throughout the *Genealogy's* three essays, Nietzsche – in no less tyrannical tones – reiterates that the psychological disposition of *ressentiment* lurks within the "antisemites where it has always bloomed";[52] that he contrasts the superior Old Testament with the New;[53] and that his overall wrath is unleashed upon the entire history of Christianity, especially its visions of hell and the psychic pleasures, the "cellar rodents of vengefulness and hatred" derived from imaging pagans perishing in the wrath of God's fire at the Final Judgement.[54] Throughout the *Genealogy*, Nietzsche rants against "the antisemites who today roll their eyes in a Christian-Aryan bourgeois manner," and at the conclusion of the work, explodes mercilessly against the whole of modern Germany, including Dühring, Renan and the contemporary Lutheran state-church. He crucifies the "worms of vengefulness and rancor" that swarm on the soil of modern Europe, describing anti-Semites as "moral masturbators," "hangmen" and as those who represent the "will to power of the weakest": "They are all men of *ressentiment*, physiologically unfortunate and worm-eaten ... inexhaustible and insatiable in outbursts against the fortunate and happy."[55] Thus, more in-depth evaluations of the *Genealogy* – aside from isolated readings of the (priestly) Jewish slave revolt as briefly recorded in the first essay – are necessary for discerning whether Nietzsche himself was of sound mind, and also for grasping why the most vicious anti-Semites of his time were offended by, and in fact retaliated against, Nietzsche's treatise.[56]

With all due respect to the intricacies, details and complexities of the *Genealogy*, on the whole, the text should be compared and contrasted with other Germanic-Aryan mythologies prevalent during Nietzsche's time which were based on the exclusion of Semites.

When viewed in its entirety, the structure of the *Genealogy* is a treatise on the "genealogy of morals" in a somewhat literal sense. The first essay, from the original Aryan race to Napoleon, places the slave revolt and the Judeo-Christian tradition at the center. The second goes from the origin of bad conscience and its expression in the state to the atonement (Christianity) and ends with the announcement that the Antichrist and anti-nihilst must triumph over God and nothingness. And the third begins with a discussion of Nietzsche's former heroes Wagner and Schopenhauer, and ends with the claim that Christian morality and the ascetic ideal must be overcome: "And, to repeat in conclusion what I said at the beginning; man would rather will *nothingness* than *not* will."[57]

In the infamous section 7, in contrast to the Greek barbaric nobles, Nietzsche attributes the slave revolt in morality to the priestly caste of Judea that reaches its fruition with Christianity: "That with the Jews there begins *the slave revolt in morality*: that revolt which has a history of two thousand years behind it and which we no longer see because it – has been victorious."[58] The moral revolt which "has two thousand years behind it" is an allusion to the Christian religion; the "victorious" morality of modern-day Germany that Nietzsche abhors is the priestly morality of Judea that is continued in Christianity. The point here is simply that Nietzsche is describing Christianity's inheritance of priestly Judea, as distinct from original Israel. And he expounds this point in section 9.

After describing the slave revolt (section 7) and stating that the Judeo-Christian morality of modern Germany has triumphed over the masters, "everything is becoming Judaized, Christianized, and mob-ized (what do the words matter!)" (section 9), Nietzsche does not use the term "Israel" or "Jews" again in the essay unless he is referring specifically to Christians. There is one exception to this (section 16), which I will address shortly. The language in the first essay borders on wrath, particularly when he uses the word Jew: "everywhere that man has become tame or desires to become tame: *three Jews*, as is known, and *one Jewess* (Jesus of Nazareth, the

fisherman Peter, the rug weaver Paul ... Mary)."[59] However, he
adopts the rhetoric not to fuel secular or Christian anti-Semites, who
were his enemies. He is attempting to annoy Christians who denied
their Jewishness, as well as create conflict between anarchists and
Christians over the sole ingredient which separated them: Christianity's relationship to Judaism. By attacking priestly Judea, Nietzsche is denigrating that strand of Judaism that Christian anti-Semites
claimed as their ancestor, which allegedly professed the coming
Messiah – as represented by Jesus Christ. This serves to explain the
logistics of why Nietzsche derided priestly Judea, all the while
upholding contemporary Jewry and original Israel. Conversely, it
also illuminates why prominent (Christian and anti-Christian) Aryan
racial supremacists, such as Renan, Dühring and Förster, retaliated
against Nietzsche's *Genealogy*.

Historically, the myth of the Germanic-Aryan race was formed
and promoted by racial theorists such as Gobineau, Wagner and
Renan well before the *Genealogy* appeared. In the *Genealogy*,
Nietzsche was entering the political dialogue of his time, presenting
an alternative version of the Aryan master race; a version that would
have inflamed anti-Jewish racists. In the texts, Nietzsche severs the
Germanic bloodline *from* Aryan humanity ("between the old Germanic tribes and us Germans there exists hardly a conceptual
relationship, let alone one of blood"),[60] proclaims mixed races
instead (the blond beast is at the bottom of all "noble races,"
including "the Roman, Arabian, Germanic, Japanese nobility, the
Homeric heroes, and the Scandinavian Vikings")[61] and exalts the
Jews over the Germans ("one only has to compare similarly gifted
nations – the Chinese or the Germans, for instance – with the Jews,
to sense which is of the first and which of the fifth rank").[62] Although
decades later the Nazis uplifted terms like the "blond beast" to create
the illusion that Nietzsche supported Aryan racial supremacy,
Nietzsche was, in fact, opposing the actual precursors of the Third
Reich, of which Nazi leaders were well aware. Initially, Nietzsche
used the term "blond beast" when referring to the state and the
Christian church of the Middle Ages.[63]

The Antichrist

Nietzsche's war against the proto-Nazis continues in the *Antichrist*,
wherein he opposes the Christian theologian Ernst Renan, whose
anti-Semitic biography, *The Life of Jesus,*was a bestseller throughout

Europe. Renan demeaned original Israel and contemporary Jewry, locating the spiritual development of Christianity with the priestly-prophetic strand of Judaism, especially the prophet Isaiah. Thus, again, although surface readings of the *Antichrist* could suggest that Nietzsche demeans priestly-prophetic Judaism for no apparent reason, placing his stance in dialogue with that of his anti-Semitic opponent Renan reveals that Nietzsche's prime motive was not a capricious assault on Judaism (or the Jews), but was geared to reverse Renan's anti-Semitic Christian theology.

For instance, in Chapter 10, "The Preachings on the Lake," Renan writes that Jesus's preaching, in his early ministry, "was gentle and pleasing, breathing Nature and the perfume of the fields."[64] After meeting with opposition from his "enemies," Jesus eventually comes to regard himself as the violent judge who would return to condemn the world and judge his opponents.[65] By Chapter 20, Jesus is beset even more with bitterness, resentment and reproachfulness toward those who would not believe in him. Renan writes:

He was no longer the mild teacher who delivered the "Sermon on the Mount," who had met with neither resistance nor difficulty. . . . And yet many of the recommendations which he addressed to his disciples contain the germs of a true fanaticism. . . . Must we reproach him for this? No revolution is effected without some harshness . . . . The invincible obstacle to the ideas of Jesus came especially from orthodox Judaism, represented by the Pharisees. Jesus became more and more alienated from the ancient Law.[66]

In regards to this evolvement, Nietzsche jests: "[T]here is a gaping contradiction between the sermonizer on the mount, lake and meadow ... and that fanatic of aggression, that mortal enemy of theologians and priests whom Renan's malice has glorified as *le grand maître en ironie*."[67]

Renan writes that Jesus increasingly "came to think of himself" as "the destroyer of Judaism"; he "completely lost his Jewish faith," and "far from continuing Judaism, Jesus represents the rupture with the Jewish spirit": "The general march of Christianity has been to remove itself more and more from Judaism. It will become perfect in returning to Jesus, but certainly not in returning to Judaism."[68] Renan concludes that the Old Jewish party, the Mosaic Law, was responsible for Jesus's death; therefore, nineteenth-century Jews are responsible for Christ's: "Consequently, every Jew who suffers today for the murder of Jesus has the right to complain. . . . But nations, like individuals have their responsibilities, and if ever crime was the crime of a nation, it was the death of Jesus."[69]

Renan's book, released in 1864, was not only popular within the academy; it sold like a "Waverly novel" among the populace from the first hour of its publication. Five months after its release, eleven editions (100,000 books) had been exhausted and it was already translated into German, Italian and Dutch, rapidly to be followed by additional translations. In 1927, the book, which is now regarded as one of the two anti-Semitic bestsellers throughout Europe in the nineteenth century, was still read more widely than any other biography on Jesus.[70]

In the *Genealogy*, Nietzsche refers to Renan in connection with Dühring and the Aryan myth; in the *Nachlass* (1884) he regards him a weak-willed representative of "herd animal" democratic Europe; and in *Twilight*, he names him as one among the family of Rousseau and derogatorily calls him a democrat:[71]

> With no little ambition, he wishes to represent an aristocracy of the spirit: yet at the same time he is on his knees before its very counter-doctrine, the *évangile des humbles* – and not only on his knees. To what avail is all free-spiritedness . . . if in one's guts one is still a Christian, a Catholic – in fact, a priest! . . . This spirit of Renan's a spirit which is enervated, is one more calamity for poor, sick, will-sick France.[72]

In the *Antichrist*, Nietzsche addresses Renan's notion of the Last Judgement. He connects what he regards as the "propaganda" of the early Christian community which "created its god according to its needs and put words into its Master's mouth" to "those wholly unevangelical concepts it now cannot do without: the return, the 'Last Judgment,' every kind of temporal expectation and promise."[73] Nietzsche traces anti-Semitism from the early Christian community to Rousseau to contemporaries such as Renan and Dühring, whom Nietzsche regards as those needing to be reckoned with.[74]

Nietzsche not only opposes Renan's preference for the Christian God to that of the powerful Yahweh, he opposes Renan's notion of Jesus as a genius and a hero. When Renan regards Jesus as a genius, it is in reference to Jesus's initial coming to self-consciousness that he would be a violent judge ushering in the apocalyptic kingdom, which would consist of a "sudden renovation of the world."[75] According to Renan, Jesus applied to himself the title "Son of Man" and affirmed the "coming catastrophe" in which he was to figure as judge, clothed with full powers which had been delegated to him from the Ancient of Days. Renan writes: "Beset by an idea [the Kingdom of God], gradually becoming more and more imperious (*impérieux*) and exclusive, Jesus proceeds henceforth with a kind of fatal impassability in the path marked out by his astonishing genius."[76] In the *Antichrist*, Nietzsche is responding to that passage:

> To repeat, I am against any attempt to introduce the fanatic into the Redeemer type; the word *impérieux*, which Renan uses, is alone enough to annul the type. The "glad tidings" are precisely that there are no longer any opposites; the kingdom of heaven belongs to the *children*. . . . Such a faith is not angry, does not reproach, does not resist; it does not bring "the sword".[77]

Renan located the origin of Christianity with the prophet Isaiah, discarded original Israel and held nineteenth-century Jews, Israel's remnants, responsible for the death of Jesus.[78] Nietzsche's position is the exact reverse. Although Nietzsche concurs with Renan that Christianity originated with the prophet Isaiah, he disagrees that this represents spiritual *progress*, but rather, the origin of Israel's demise which has culminated in the (anti-Semitic) Christianity of *ressentiment*.[79] The slave morality of *ressentiment*, Nietzsche insists, began with the death on the cross; it reached its most profound form of vengefulness when the disciples totally misunderstood Jesus's message concerning the kingdom of God, and instead opted for the apocalyptic Last Judgement.[80] "What are the glad tidings?" Nietzsche repeatedly asks. The glad tidings Jesus brings are that the concepts of guilt, sin and punishment are abolished. Sin, that which separates humans from God, is destroyed. The kingdom of God is nothing that one expects; it has no yesterday or today; it will not come in the future or in a thousand years: "The kingdom of God is *in you*."[81] Thus, although shallow readings of Nietzsche's *Antichrist* have led to erroneous claims that Nietzsche was "anti-Semitic" for "attacking" Judaism; it is crucial to recognize that Nietzsche's position serves to refute the fundamental position of anti-Semitic Christian theology. And it is also crucial to realize that much confusion regarding Nietzsche's position stems *not* from any lack of clarity or coherence of Nietzsche's part, but *because* Elisabeth and the Nazis misquoted his words and used them against the Jews decades later. That tactic created havoc and has successfully confused interpreters to this very day. It has made sorting out Nietzsche's views toward Judaism and the Jews extremely difficult, to the point where the topic itself has become an emotionally sensitive issue; an issue that has led many well-meaning persons to "blame" Nietzsche for his fierce rhetoric, and thus for providing "anti-Semitic fuel" for the Nazis, who allegedly "learned" from him. Moreover – perhaps to the less well-intentioned – the tactic also serves to protect Elisabeth's type of Christendom: whereas many writing after the Nazi era have been quick to point out Nietzsche's negative critique of ancient Judea, works addressing Nietzsche's critique of Christian anti-Semitism are virtually *non-existent*.

CONCLUSION

That anti-Semitism played such a major role in Nietzsche's break with Wagner, his sister and even his publisher, that he urged those closest to him to renounce anti-Semitism and suffered personal sacrifice for doing so; that his later writings show increased pre-occupation with contemporary Jews, Christianity and German nationalism; and that he raved against anti-Semites during the hours of his transition to insanity, make clear that the issue of anti-Semitism – and Nietzsche's almost pathological response to it – was not a passing phase nor peripheral to his existence. However, the question as to why Nietzsche identified with the Jews, who only composed 1 per cent of the population, remains unclear.

It is evident that there was nothing in Nietzsche's upbringing that steered him away from anti-Semitism; if anything, the reverse is true. In his youth, although anti-Semitism was commonplace throughout Germany, the Jews were simply not an important issue in Nietzsche's family; his exposure to anti-Semitism, and his own casual anti-Semitism tendencies, began in college and were strengthened during his association with Wagner (1869–76).[82]

The first notion of a positive attitude toward contemporary Jews occurs in a personal letter written in 1872.[83] Although this predates his encounter with his Jewish friend Paul Rée, whom Nietzsche met in 1873, Nietzsche's friendship with Rée was instrumental in changing his stance. The Nietzsche–Rée friendship corresponds with Nietzsche's growing discontent with Wagner's prejudices; and the Wagners' disapproval of Rée and Nietzsche's disregard for their opinions was central in his decision to sever his ties with them.[84] After the break, and with the appearance of *Human, All Too Human*

(1878–1880), Nietzsche's attitude toward the Jews abruptly changes. It is here that Nietzsche begins to express a concern for the dangerous national hostilities that scapegoated Jews for Germany's misfortunes.[85]

From this point on (including *Daybreak* and the *Gay Science*, 1881–2), although Nietzsche is not wholly uncritical of contemporary Jewry, he consistently displays an enthusiastic and positive attitude toward modern Jews; his views toward ancient Judaism are both positive and negative; the features he condemns are almost always connected to his criticisms of Christianity.[86] Although *Zarathustra* (1883–5) contains sparse references to Jews, and does not mention the term "Christianity" once, the work abounds in Judeo-Christian themes, and was written in the throes of turmoil surrounding the loss of the holy trinity (Nietzsche, Rée and Lou Salomé), Wagner's death and also Elisabeth's newfound relationship with the anti-Semitic Förster.[87]

Nietzsche's exit from the Wagner circle and Elisabeth's continuing association with Wagnerites had caused tension between them for years. However, her marriage to Förster in 1885 was the major incident that Nietzsche regarded as a personal betrayal: "You have gone over to my antipodes ... I will not conceal that I consider this engagement an insult – or a stupidity – which will harm you as much as me."[88]

Elisabeth's marriage marks the beginning of Nietzsche's political involvement, perhaps because he realized that he had to come to grips with a cultural phenomenon that had deeply affected his own life. A few weeks after the wedding, Nietzsche began writing *Beyond Good and Evil* (1886), in which he announced that he "never met a German who liked the Jews," regarding the Jews as the "purest race". Nietzsche elects the Jews to partake in his "new caste that would rule Europe" and bring about the much-needed revaluation.[89]

In light of the fact that Nietzsche emerges as an advocate for contemporary Jews, his ambivalent views toward priestly-prophetic Judaism, especially the bitter and shrill tone in section 7 of the *Genealogy* (1887), have been described by modern scholars as unequivocal, careless, unguarded and irresponsible.[90] Essentially, they are none of these. Nietzsche's views were formed by, and should be interpreted within, the theological and political categories that pre-existed in Germany. It must be remembered that anti-semitism in nineteenth-century Germany was the rule; Nietzsche, an exception. As a minority who was an obscure author, Nietzsche was essentially a powerless voice opposing very prominent leaders. That anti-Semites themselves regarded Nietzsche as an "insolent" enemy and attacked his later works, is evidence that they did not view his texts to be as ambivalent as do modern-day readers.

Whereas Christian theology tended to demean ancient Hebrews and modern Jews, claiming the prophets as their ancestors, Nietzsche took the opposing stance (*The Antichrist*, 1888). Nietzsche's ambivalence toward the priestly-prophetic strand was not driven by any profound contempt for historical Judaism *per se*, nor was it soley designed to attack its offspring. Rather, Nietzsche's position was a logical consequence arising from his opposition to both Christianity and anti-Semitism. The Hebrew prophets were necessary to the Christian tradition; both liberal and conservative Christians cut off the Jews precisely on the basis that they had rejected Jesus the Messiah, whom the prophets had foretold. Hence, if Nietzsche were completely to affirm priestly-prophetic Judaism, he would basically be affirming Christian anti-Semitism. This is why the *übermensch* is central: he represents the Messiah who has yet to come. In short, Christianity, not Nietzsche, created the terms; he was simply reversing its dominant theology. As a result, the threefold distinction of Jews is a necessary weapon as Nietzsche becomes more politically involved. Affirming ancient Hebrews and contemporary Jews, while deriding Judeo-Christianity as that tradition rooted in *ressentiment*, serves two primary functions. First, it flips anti-Semitic Christian theology upside down (in Nietzsche's scheme, Christians are "not the *true* people of Israel"; Jesus is a Jew but not a Christian).[91] Second, it opposes anti-Christian anti-Semitism which derided original Israel (and the entire Judeo-Christian tradition as well). In a word, one could say that if one were to oppose anti-Semitism in nineteenth-century Germany in both its Christian and anti-Christian forms, one would end up with the exact position that Nietzsche has. Nietzsche's language is indeed violent and *excessive*, but not uncalculated, careless or irresponsible:[92] "Now a comic fact ... I have an 'influence,' very subterranean, to be sure. ... I can even abuse my outspokenness ... perhaps they 'implore' me, but they cannot escape me. In the *Anti-Semitic Correspondence* ... my name appears in almost every issue."[93]

Nietzsche's elevation of "genuine philosophers" and contemporary Jews as those harbingers of the new aristocratic culture he sought to bring about, as well as his desire to resurrect the heroic qualities of ancient pre-Christian cultures, was not formed in an historical vacuum. In large measure, his aristocratic radicalism was also a logical consequence which arose from opposing the dominant political ideologies of his time which, in their socialist, democratic and Lutheran forms, were predominantly nationalistic; opposed to the assimilation and emancipation of Jews; and/or based on the masses' Christian spiritual elitism. Regardless of one's opinions toward Nietzsche's alternative position as to who the spiritual elites really were, or to his alternative political visions, it is relevant to point out that Nietzsche did not win.

That the Jews were becoming affluent citizens in German society obviously did not provoke Nietzsche's growing concern; the expanding national resentment did: "The anti-Semites do not forgive the Jews for possessing 'spirit' – and money. Anti-Semites – another name for the 'underprivileged.'"[94] It is out of this national conflict, which is now regarded as the incubation period of anti-Semitism, that Nietzsche's critique of culture arose. During the 1880s, the mounting racist propaganda prompted Nietzsche to rebut Aryan mythologies, as evidenced in the *Genealogy* and in personal notes written during that time. Nietzsche was well acquainted with the works of Renan, Gobineau and Paul de Lagarde; his language reflects the political climate created by theorists who advocated racial supremacy: "*Aryan influence*," Nietzsche wrote, "has corrupted all the world."[95] *Zarathustra* is primarily concerned with the psychology of Christianity in relation to revenge and eschatology; the *Genealogy* with Germany's political climate and Aryan mythologies; and the *Antichrist* with anti-Semitic Christian theology. Although most commentators regard the *Antichrist* as key to understanding Nietzsche's stance toward the Judeo-Christian tradition, it is the least profound of the three texts.

In short, Nietzsche's connection with Jews, including his early relationship with Rée; his encounter with the Austrian Jew, Paneth, in which they discussed the possibility of regenerating the Jewish masses (in the early 1880s); and his association with Brandes, who was responsible for Nietzsche's initial popularity, illustrates that Nietzsche's affinity with the Jews was not an indifferent or abstract argument constructed to scorn the Christian tradition and/or Wagnerites; it arose from a genuine concern for the future of European Jews, a concern Nietzsche expresses early on in *Daybreak*:

> Among the spectacles to which the coming century invites us
> is the decision as to the destiny of the Jews of Europe. That their

die is cast, that they have crossed their Rubicon, is now palpably obvious: all that is left for them is either to become the masters of Europe or lose Europe as they once a long time ago lost Egypt, where they had placed themselves before a similar either-or.[96]

Nietzsche's identification with his Jewish contemporaries thus includes personal, religious, political, cultural and not least of all, prophetic elements. The question as to why Nietzsche strongly aligned himself with the Jewish people is almost impossible to discern – it is difficult to establish anyone's motives for anything, let alone Nietzsche's. However, it is accurate to say that his concerns were ethically grounded, and unfortunately, justified. The question itself is at least tremendous advance from the Nazi myth perpetuated by Brinton and others, who sought to portray Nietzsche as one who derided the Jews of his time as "parasites and decadents"; the Antichrist who was the true forerunner of Hitler's ideology.[97]

This brief sketch of Nietzsche's life and writings has shown that Nietzsche's assault on Christianity was motivated by his contempt for Wagner's and Elisabeth's religiopolitical views and by a genuine empathy for the Jewish people, as manifest in his resistence to the rampant anti-Semitic movement of his time. As a recluse, Nietzsche chose to be an outcast of German society. Perhaps this is another reason he sided with the Jews, who were branded as such without having a choice.

In regards to ancient Judaism, analyzing Nietzsche's later writings demonstrates that Nietzsche's views are coherent when placed in their proper historical and political context. I have shown that Nietzsche upholds original Israel, and that paradoxically, Nietzsche's wrath against priestly-prophetic Judea was actually directed at Christian anti-Semitism. Even so, this is not to suggest that Nietzsche was wholly uncritical of historical Judaism, for he particularly abhorred the concepts of election and the Last Judgement, which, he believed, originated with Judaism and were developed in Christianity and the modern Germanic notion of the *Volk*. In regards to modern Jewry, placing Nietzsche's texts in dialogue with the religious and political ideas of his major opponents has proven that Nietzsche was fighting against the social persecution that was being launched against the Jews in the latter third of the nineteenth century.

Overall, Nietzsche was an outspoken cultural critic of Christianity, anti-Semitism and Wagnerism; Elisabeth professed allegiance to the Christian religion, Aryan racial supremacy and, decades after her brother's death, to Hitler and the Nazi party. It is thus no mystery as to how Nietzsche ended up in Hitler's hands. And the bitter strife concerning anti-Semitism that originated between Nietzsche and Wagner, and was then taken up after Wagner's death by Nietzsche and Elisabeth, should not be undermined. Hitler probably never read a word of Nietzsche; however, he was a Wagner enthusiast since youth and was undoubtedly aware of Nietzsche's sentiments toward Wagner, the Wagner family, Elisabeth and contemporary Jewry. It is very doubtful that Hitler approved. Historically, two irreconcilable facts are at work. One fact is that Nietzsche was not an anti-Semite. The other is that the Nazis claimed that he was, all the while knowing he was not. That Nazi leaders uplifted terms such as the "superman" and the "blond beast" to deceive millions into thinking that Nietzsche hated the Jews, that they frightened people *away* from his works and virtually destroyed his reputation while committing their monstrosities in his name, should thus be *highly* suspect.

Without belaboring the obvious, my position is contrary to those positions which assume that the Nazis "liked" Nietzsche, that they learned from him and/or that they "misunderstood" him. I rather hold that the Nazis understood Nietzsche extremely well and that is precisely why they sought to destroy him – and sever a vital part of Jewish history. The Nazis did not "like" Nietzsche, they were repulsed and enraged by him precisely *because* he upheld the Jews and dared to defy many intellectual forerunners of the Third Reich: namely, Richard and Cosima Wagner, Renan, Dühring, Lagarde, Chamberlain, Gobineau, Stöcker, Förster and Elisabeth Förster-Nietzsche.[98] The Nazis' use of Nietzsche was not based on any "misinterpretation" or "selective appropriation," it was based on a twisted sense of spite and was an act of retaliation. Alfred Rosenberg's odd inscription on a wreath that he placed on Nietzsche's grave, "To the great fighter," gives testimony to this, for it makes little sense when viewed apart from its sinister context. The Nazi appropriation of Nietzsche, however, was not solely rooted in revenge, it was also a means of silencing him, a technique that began with Elisabeth. If one imagines that in Nietzsche's time, Wagnerites had strong intentions to annihilate all or part of European Jewry – and to cover their traces in the process – Nietzsche's writings, initially made popular by a Jew, would be an obstacle. As Nietzsche started to become popular, Elisabeth clearly saw this, as evidence by her immediate

42

panic to suppress or destroy Nietzsche's documents, writings and ideas – especially regarding anti-Semitism. Later, as master propagandists, the Nazis continued Elisabeth's question to confuse matters and to suppress his views in precisely the manner in which they did. On the one hand, they heralded Nietzsche as an anti-Semitic ally to cover their tracks and to discredit his opposition to anti-Semitism. On the other hand, they realized that if their crimes were discovered, Nietzsche would *still* serve as a scapegoat, which he indeed has. The fact that Nietzsche, among other things, wrote about and against Jewish extermination, coupled with the fact that Elisabeth immediately set out to mythologize her brother and to destroy or alter his documents, leads one to strongly suspect that the intent to destroy the Jews was already formulated during Nietzsche's time. I concede that Nietzsche, as a former member of an inner Wagner circle who had access to their "secret" correspondence sheet, knew of that design, was frightened to death, and that Elisabeth and then the Nazis sought to silence, disempower and destroy him. One does not forge documents, destroy letters, write skewed biographies, censor publications, create "books" out of scribbled notes and cover up bitter strife regarding anti-Semitism for *no reason* at all, and Elisabeth's mere bigotry does not appear to be a sufficient motive. The process of manipulating Nietzsche, which began with Elisabeth and culminated with Hitler, was no "selective appropriation" or "misinterpretation"; it was based on the plain fact that they sought to silence an obnoxious foe, which they indeed did. The Nazis may have fooled the world, but they did not fool the Jews. According to Steven Aschheim, German Jewish leaders looked to Nietzsche and Nietzschean folk wisdom for consolation while suffering under the Nazi regime, often quoting Nietzsche's famous phrase: "What does not destroy me makes me stronger."[99]

In summary, even if we were to assume with the most radical anti-Nietzsche interpreters today that Nietzsche, in whole or in part, *caused* Hitler's Germany; it is still the case that Nietzsche's writings provide insight into the Wagner circle, anti-Semitism in both its religious and political forms, German nationalism and Aryan racial supremacy – all of which he opposed. It was precisely those elements of his philosophy that Elisabeth and the Nazis sought to suppress and that this essay has attempted to highlight. The point here is not to elevate Nietzsche as a hero, a saint or a saviour – that was one of his greatest fears – but only to stress that his writings are very important to the study of anti-Semitism and to the history of the European Holocaust.[100]

The post-World War II challenge for serious Nietzsche scholars is not to engage in fruitless debates as to which, if any, elements of Nietzsche are compatible with Nazism, for that would be playing right into their hands. We should not assume that the Nazis "learned" from Nietzsche; for if this were true, they certainly would have renounced anti-Semitism – and spared us the bloodshed of six million innocent Jews. Today, the challenge for historians and Nietzsche scholars is painstakingly to investigate, with the aid of Nietzsche's texts, what the nineteenth-century state church, Elisabeth, the Wagner family and finally, the Nazis themselves, were trying to hide.

ABBREVIATIONS

AC   Nietzsche, Friedrich, *The Antichrist*, in *The Portable Nietzsche*, tr. Walter Kaufmann, New York: Viking Press, 1968.

BT   Nietzsche, Friedrich, *The Birth of Tragedy*, tr. Walter Kaufmann, New York: Vintage Books, 1967.

BGE Nietzsche, Friedrich, *Beyond Good and Evil*, tr. Walter Kaufmann, New York: Random House, 1966.

D   Nietzsche, Friedrich, *Daybreak*, tr. R.J. Hollingdale, Cambridge: Cambridge University Press, 1982.

EH   Nietzsche, Friedrich, *Ecce Homo*, tr. Walter Kaufmann, New York: Random House, 1967.

GM Nietzsche, Friedrich, *On the Genealogy of Morals*, tr. Walter Kaufmann and R.J. Hollingdale, New York: Random House, 1967.

GS   Nietzsche, Friedrich, *The Gay Science*, tr. Walter Kaufmann, New York: Random House, 1974.

HU   Nietzsche, Friedrich, *Human, All Too Human*, tr. Marion Faber, Lincoln: University of Nebraska Press, 1984.

L   Nietzsche, Friedrich, *The Selected Letters of Friedrich Nietzsche*, ed. and tr. Christopher Middleton, Chicago: University of Chicago Press, 1969.

SL   Nietzsche, Friedrich, *The Selected Letters of Friedrich Nietzsche*, ed. Oscar Levy, tr. A.N. Ludovici, London: Soho Book Company, 1985.

TW Nietzsche, Friedrich, *Twilight of the Idols*, in *The Portable Nietzsche*, tr. Walter Kafumann, New York: Viking Press, 1968.

WP Nietzsche, Friedrich, *The Will to Power*, ed. Walter Kaufmann, tr. Walter Kaufmann and R.J. Hollingdale, New York: Random House, 1967. Selections from Nietzsche's unpublished notebooks (1883–8).

Z Nietzsche, Friedrich, *Thus Spoke Zarathustra*, tr. Walter Kaufmann, New York: Viking Press, 1966.

NOTES

1 For further reading on the intellectual origins of fascism, see Hans Kohn, *The Mind of Germany* (New York, 1960); George Mosse, *The Crisis of German Ideology* (New York, 1981); Fritz Stern, *The Politics of Cultural Despair* (Berkeley, 1973); Peter Viereck, *Metapolitics* (1941; New York, 1961) and David Weiss, *The Fascist Tradition* (New York, 1967). Kohn insists that Nietzsche was no intellectual forerunner of National Socialism, but does note (what he views as) the "dangerous implications" of his violent language and his praise of heroic greatness during his last productive years, pp. 207ff.; Mosse describes how Nietzsche, in spite of Bäumler's misinterpretation and Nietzsche's ridicule of Lagarde's works, was nonetheless appropriated as a Nordic prophet, pp. 204ff.; Stern insists that Nietzsche "had nothing to do with the birth of Germanic ideology," that he had nothing but contempt of its intellectual forebears (e.g., Wagner, Dühring and Lagarde), and that he would have continued his battle against the collective tyranny of the Germanic community, pp. 283ff.; Viereck, acknowledging an intellectual debt to Nietzsche, writes how "uncannily Nietzsche had predicted the Nazi future" through experiencing Wagner and his "proto-Nazi" sister: "It is in no way Nietzsche's fault that *The Will to Power* . . . fell into German nationalist hands," pp. xxff; and Weiss flatly refuses to entertain Nietzsche's alleged affinity to fascism, stating that intellectual historians who do so have confused the issue by an outmoded method that regards a handful of theorists as major carriers of the intellectual tradition:

> Such esoteric and brilliant thinkers as . . . Nietzsche have no real influence on large groups or classes of men, and thus no direct influence on that great abstraction we call history. They are altogether too complicated and subtle to be heard beyond a few. (p. 3).

2 For further discussion of the problems surrounding the *Nachlass*, see Walter Kaufmann's appendix "Nietzsche's 'suppressed' manuscripts," in *Nietzsche: Philosopher, Psychologist, Antichrist*, 4th edn (1950; Princeton: Princeton University Press, 1974). The issues are complicated and center on Elisabeth's tampering and suppression of her brother's notebooks and letters at the Nietzsche Archive in Weimar. Elisabeth suppressed some remarks directed against herself, her husband, Wagner, anti-Semitism, the Germans, Jesus and Christianity. Although the suppressed remarks indirectly bear on the primary concerns of this work,

I regard the notes and letters as secondary to Nietzsche's texts, wherein his ideas are sufficiently presented.

3 Quoted in Alfred D. Low, *Jesus in the Eyes of the Germans: From the Enlightenment to Imperial Germany* (Philadelphia, 1979), p. 386. Cf. *D* 205; *GS* 136; *BGE* 248; *EH*, "Clever" 4; *WP* 832.

4 Quoted in Kaufmann, *Nietzsche*, pp. 361–2.

5 See ch. 10 in Kaufmann, *Nietzsche*, esp. p. 289.

6 Cf. ch. 8 in Crane Brinton, *Nietzsche* (1941; New York: Harper & Row, 1965) and "The National Socialists' use of Nietzsche," *Journal of the History of Ideas* 1 (1940): 131–50.

7 The notes that Elisabeth arranged under the title *Zucht und Züchtung* (Discipline and Breeding) better suited her own ideas, not her brother's (*WP*, Book IV). They were derived from thousands of random scribblings, jottings and notes that Nietzsche had written down over an extended period of time. In the passages on breeding, it is unclear as to whether the term has cultural or biological connotations. In other words, one can speak of well-bred children, in a cultural or biological sense. Cf. *WP* 397 (biological) and 462, 862, 1053 (cultural). Considering that the notes on breeding were meager in proportion to Nietzsche's many other concerns and that he specifically condemned the "morality of breeding" and the morality of taming in *Twilight* as "immoral", it was preposterous for Elisabeth and the Nazis to lift the drafts out of context, cf. *TW*, "Improvers" 5. Elisabeth's Paraguay experiment to breed German families was explicitly condemned by Nietzsche; it appears that she and the Nazis tried to create the illusion that "Nietzsche's" thoughts on breeding informed their racism. It should be stressed, once again, that preoccupation with the notes serves to divert readers *from* Nietzsche's texts in which his alternative view on an ideal "future Aryan race" is formulated (see the section on the *Genealogy*, below). Overall, the *Nachlass* is invaluable for supplementing Nietzsche's publications, but the notes should not be read in isolation from his texts, which was precisely Elisabeth's, and then Bäumler's strategy. For further discussion of the *Nachlass* and posthumous material, see Kaufmann's Prologue and ch. 2 in *Nietzsche*, esp. pp. 76ff.

8 Both Kaufmann (*Nietzsche*, pp. 290–2) and Jacob Golomb, "Nietzsche's Judaism of power," *Revue des Études juives* 146–7 (July–December, 1988): 353–85 (p. 353), point to Crane Brinton as the culprit in the English-speaking world largely responsible for perpetuating distortions of Nietzsche's treatment of the Jews. Kaufmann exposes Brinton's unfamiliarity with Nietzsche – and his incompetent scholarship – when critiquing Brinton's *Nietzsche*. Brinton claims that "most of the stock of professional anti-Semitism is represented in Nietzsche," and that Nietzsche "held the Jews responsible for Christianity, Democracy, Marxism" (p. 215). Brinton then cites six references to substantiate this claim. Kaufmann discovers that out of the six references two of Nietzsche's quotes do not even mention the Jews; two speak against anti-Semitism; one is a reference that does not even exist; and none mention the "triad" of Christianity, Democracy and Marxism. Kaufmann also discovers that the "triad" comes from the Nazi scholar, Heinrich Härtle, as do all six

references, and that Brinton copied the references from Härtle's work without checking them himself. The results are embarrassing; however, even after reading Kaufmann's findings Brinton refused to correct the bogus references in the new edition published in 1965. Brinton's book includes a picture of Hitler staring at a Nietzsche bust at the Nietzsche Archive in Weimar (interestingly, only half of Nietzsche's face is shown and Hitler is frowning); throughout the entire work, the widely respected Harvard historian erroneously attributes sections from *Beyond Good and Evil* to *The Genealogy of Morals*.

9 Michael Duffy and Willard Mittleman, "Nietzsche's attitudes toward the Jews," *Journal of the History of Ideas* 49 (1988): 301–17 are to be credited with recognizing these sharp distinctions chronologically, beginning with *Beyond Good and Evil* (which are assumed here). Golomb also recognizes these distinctions, although his primary approach is not chronological, but designed to situate Nietzsche's views toward Jews and Judaism within the framework of Nietzsche's overall psychology and philosophy.

10 See for instance, *AC* 24.

11 According to historians such as Joseph Tennenbaum, *Race and Reich* (New York: Twaine, 1956), p. 12, Dühring's *The Jewish Question as a Problem of Race, Morals, and Culture* (1881) presented an almost complete Nazi program. Adolf Stöcker's speech, "Our demands on modern Jewry", is printed in Richard S. Levy, *Antisemitism in the Modern World* (Lexington: D.C. Heath and Company, 1991).

12 See ch. 5 in Uriel Tal, *Christians and Jews in Germany: Religion, Politics and Ideology in the Second Reich, 1870–1904* (Ithaca: Cornell University Press, 1975), for a complete discussion of Christian and anti-Christian anti-Semitism.

13 Jacob Katz, *From Prejudice to Destruction: Anti-Semitism, 1700–1933* (Cambridge, Mass.: Harvard University Press, 1980), p. 267. Although the term anti-Christian anti-Semitism signifies an opposition to Christianity, this does not mean that anti-Semites such as Dühring disdained Christianity to the degree that they abhorred Judaism and the Jews, or that anti-Semitism *derived* from an opposition to Christianity. Thus, Dühring and Stöcker could reach a common ground in their disdain for modern Jewry.

14 *AC* 25ff., 31, 40; *GM* I 14ff.; *WP* 197 and 186:

> The profound contempt with which the Christian was treated in the noble areas of classical antiquity is of a kind with the present instinctive aversion to Jews. . . . The New Testament is the gospel of a wholly ignoble species of man; their claim to possess more value, indeed to possess *all* value, actually has something revolting about it – even today.

15 "The accursed anti-Semitism is ruining all my chances for financial independence, pupils, new friends, influence; it alienated Richard Wagner and me; it is the cause of the radical break between myself and my sister etc., etc., etc." Letter to Overbeck, 2 April 1884, quoted in Peter

Bergmann, *Nietzsche: "The Last Antipolitical German"* (Bloomington: Indiana University Press, 1987), p. 157.

16 John E. Groh, *Nineteenth Century German Protestantism* (Washington: University Press of America, Inc., 1982), p. 569. Stöcker was elected to the Prussian House of Deputies in 1879, where he served uninterruptedly until 1898. In 1881 Stöcker was also elected to the national *Reichstag*, where he held a seat until 1893, and was then re-elected in 1898. For further discussion on Stöcker see Peter Pulzer, *The Rise of Political Anti-Semitism in Germany and Austria* (Cambridge, Mass.: Harvard University Press, 1988), ch. 10: "Stöcker and the Berlin Movement."

17 Stöcker, in Levy, *Anti-Semitism*, p. 66.

18 Tal, *Christians and Jews*, p. 257.

19 Stöcker, in Levy, *Antisemitism*, p. 59.

20 Stöcker, in Levy, *Antisemitism*, p. 66.

21 Quoted in Kaufmann's *Nietzsche*, p. 46.

22 Bergman, *Nietzsche*, p. 144. Bergmann, whose fine historical work primarily focuses on biography and Nietzsche's letters – not his texts – writes that even though Nietzsche was not an anti-Semite, when his "Caesarism and anti-Christian atheism were inflamed, harsh invective would flow toward the Jews." As will become evident, however, the reverse is the case. Nietzsche's harsh invective toward ancient Judaism (especially in *The Genealogy of Morals*) was directed toward Christian anti-Semitism. And alluding to Nietzsche's alleged "atheism" is irrelevant to the issue under discussion.

23 Bergmann, *Nietzsche*, pp. 172–3.

24 *WP* 89.

25 *WP* 203; letter to Peter Gast, Sils-Maria, 20 June 1888, in *SL*, p. 231. After announcing the age of Stöcker, Nietzsche adds: "I draw conclusions and know already that my 'Will to Power' will be suppressed first in Germany." The phrase from *The Will to Power* concerning "the sheep with horns" mentions the "court chaplains", which would allow readers to identify Stöcker as the object of Nietzsche's dig. The term "court chaplains" is found only in 1911, p. 502.

26 *GM* II 11, III 14, III 26.

27 Peter Gay, *The Dilemma of Democratic Socialism* (New York, 1952), p. 95; Mosse regards Dühring's view of equal wills as "mythical". It can be described as mythical not in the sense that Dühring posits an initial beginning of the world, but rather an original "essence" of human wills. Although Dühring was, according to Katz, a remarkable scholar who possessed a high degree of intelligence, he was nonetheless imbued with a "morbid mental constitution", *Prejudice to Destruction*, p. 265. Nietzsche concurs with Katz. He regards Dühring as a "clever and well-informed scholar," but one who has a "petty soul" and is "tormented by narrow, envious feelings", *WP* 792. See also *Z* II, "On the land of education" ("You are sterile: that is why you lack faith. You are half-open gates at which the gravediggers wait. And this is *your* reality: 'Everything deserves to perish'"), and *Z* II, "On scholars": "And yet I live *over* their heads with my thoughts . . . . For men are *not* equal: thus speaks justice."

28 *GM* II 11.

29 *GM* II 11; Z III, "On old and new tablets" sec 26. Compare the section in *The Genealogy of Morals* with *BGE* 259, which is most likely further commentary on Dühring's equal wills theory.

30 Gay, *Dilemma*, p. 97.

31 Georg Brandes, *Friedrich* , "An essay on aristocratic radicalism" (1889; London: William Heinemann, 1914), p. 31. In *BGE* 253, Nietzsche regards the "mediocre Englishmen" as Darwin, John Stuart Mill and Herbert Spencer. He is most likely referring to Mill's utilitarianism at the beginning of *The Genealogy of Morals*.

32 Pulzer, *Rise of Political Anti-Semitism*, pp. 50–1.

33 Mosse, *Crisis*, pp. 131–2. Gay, *Dilemma*, p. 95.

34 Katz, *Prejudice to Destruction*, pp. 268ff. For a succinct discussion of Dühring as Nietzsche's intellectual nemesis, see Peter Bergmann's *Nietzsche*, pp. 121–2 and 124–5.

35 Tennenbaum, *Race and Reich*, p. 12.

36 *EH*, "Wise" 4; Bergmann, *Nietzsche*, pp. 124–5. For a discussion of Nietzsche and von Stein, see R. Stackelberg, "The role of H. v. Stein in Nietzsche's emergence as a critic of Wagnerian idealism and cultural nationalism," *Nietzsche-Studien* 5 (1976): 178–93. Wagner was skeptical of Dühring because he was not Christian; however, Dühring approved of von Stein's role in the Wagner household as Siegfried's tutor because Wagner and he shared a hatred of the Jews. Von Stein became "Nietzsche's substitute" in the Wagner household after the break in 1878.

37 Bergmann, *Nietzsche*, p. 136; *WP* 130. The Nazis, of course, later flipped these terms upside down. They regarded themselves as *Übermenschen*, and the Jews as *Untermenschen*, subhuman beings.

38 Bergmann, *Nietzsche*, p. 145.

39 Z II, "On great events;" Z I, "On the new idol."

40 Z, III, "On the three evils."

41 Z, Prologue 6. This passage is strikingly similar to the story of a tightrope walker that Wagner conveys in his autobiography, *Mein Leben* (2 vols, Munich, 1911) that Nietzsche had edited and was thus familiar with. For an excellent study of references to Wagner throughout *Zarathustra*, see Roger Hollinrake, *Nietzsche, Wagner, and the Philosophy of Pessimism* (London: George Allen & Unwin, 1982), p. 12.

42 *HU* 475.

43 Z II, "On the tarantulas."

44 Z III, "On passing by." For further passages on the 'language of silence' see the Preface to *Human, All Too Human* ("one remains a philosopher only by – keeping silent"), and an interesting passage which occurs after Nietzsche attacks the state church (*GM* 19): "For at this point I have much to be silent about."

45 Theodor Lessing, *Untergang der Erde am Geist* (Hanover, 1924) p. 429; Bergmann, *Nietzsche*, p. 150. Lessing (1872–1933) was a Zionist who wrote several general works on Nietzsche and applied many Nietzschean themes in analyzing, and providing solutions for, the contemporary Jewish condition. Cf. Steven E. Ashheim's cultural history,

The Nietzsche Legacy in Germany 1890–1990 (Berkeley: University of California Press, 1992), pp. 107–8.

46 *HU* 475.
47 *D* 204. Compare with *GS* 9, and *Z* II, "On the tarantulas."
48 *GM* II 11; *BGE* 204, 259.
49 *Z* III, "On old and new tablets" 26. See also *EH*, "Destiny" 4 for an important commentary on sections 26 and 15 of "Tablets."
50 *AC* 43.
51 *GM* I 8.
52 *GM* II 11.
53 *GM* III 22.
54 *GM* I 14ff.
55 *GM* III 14, III 26.
56 In 1887, Nietzsche's works were attacked in the *Antisemitische Correspondenz* (an anti-Semitic newsletter), depicted as "eccentric," "pathological" and "psychiatric." Cf. letter to Paul Deussen, Nice, 3 January 1888, in *Sämtliche Briefe*, 8 vols (Berlin: de Gruyter, 1975–84), vol. 8; 939, p. 220. The philosopher welcomed the small, but growing number of negative reviews of his last two works (*Beyond Good and Evil* and *The Genealogy of Morals*), for the public disapproval appeared to him a sign that he was becoming somewhat of an "influence" in Germany: "You can guess that [Dr Förster] and I have to exert ourselves to the uttermost to avoid treating each other openly as enemies.... The anti-Semitic pamphlets shower down wildly upon me (which pleases me a hundred times more than their earlier restraint)," letter to Franz Overbeck, Nice, 3 February 1888, in *L* 162, p. 282.
57 *GM* III 28.
58 *GM* I 7.
59 *GM* I 16.
60 *GM* I 11.
61 *GM* I 11.
62 *GM* I 16, *BGE* 251.
63 The term "blond beast" occurs five times throughout Nietzsche's writing (three times in the first section of the *Genealogy*, once in the second section, and once in *Twilight of the Idols*).
64 Ernst Renan, *The Life of Jesus* intro. John Haynes Holmes (New York: Random House, 1927), p. 186.
65 *Ibid.*
66 *Ibid.*
67 *AC* 31. Renan, *Jesus*, p. 295.
68 Renan, *Jesus*, pp. 224, 235, and 391. The last passage echoes Renan's remark in his *Histoire générale des langues Sémitiques* (Paris, 1878): "Once this mission [monotheism] was accomplished, the Semitic race rapidly declined and left it to the Aryan race alone to lead the march of human destiny," quoted in Léon Poliakov, *The Aryan Myth*, tr. Edmund Howard (Chatto: Sussex University Press, 1975), p. 207.
69 Renan, *Jesus*, p. 358.
70 As the author's introduction to the English translation of the 1927 edition notes, Renan's *La Vie de Jésus* sold like a Waverly novel among

the academy and the populace alike, highly esteemed for its "beautiful style" which flourished throughout Renan's "brilliant" retelling of Jesus's story. Renan, the introduction continues, was a "supreme figure" among the scholars of his time, a simple, sincere, courageous saint, "even if judged by the teachings of the Galilean lake."

To Holocaust scholars and historians of anti-Semitism, however, Renan's storytelling is neither beautiful not brilliant. Renan's *Vie de Jésus*, together with Edouard Drumont's *La France juive*, the latter of which paved the way for large-scale anti-Semitic propaganda in France, were the two anti-Semitic bestsellers in the latter half of the nineteenth century. Cf. Léon Poliakov, *A History of Anti-Semitism*, vol. 4 (New York: Vanguard Press, 1985), pp. 39–40; Poliakov, *Aryan Myth*, p. 208.

Incredibly, that which outraged Nietzsche (and these historians) about Renan is overlooked – or disregarded – even today. In a 1968 English-speaking biography on Renan, Richard Chadbourne, *Ernst Renan* (New York: Twaine Publishers, 1968), p. 153, writes of Renan's "valiant" attempt to base an ethic largely on Christian principles without believing in its supernatural teachings: "A simple criterion guiding Renan is his testing of Christian works: 'How much they contain of Jesus.' He is far from the scandalous simplicity of Nietzsche's 'the last Christian died on the cross.'" For further discussion on Renan's racial views, see Shmuel Almog, "The racial motif in Renan's attitude toward Judaism and the Jews," *Zion* 32 (1967): 175–200.

71 *GM* III 26: *WP* 128. Cf. Letter to Peter Gast, Nice, 24 November 1887, in *SL*, p. 206.

72 *TW*, "Skirmishes" 1. Renan was, in fact, an ex-Catholic whom the Catholic Church denounced because of his non-divinization of Jesus. He was suspended from his professorship at the Collège de France in 1862, declined a position as an Assistant Director of Department of Manuscripts in the Imperial Library in 1864, in order to devote himself to his studies, but in 1871 was restored to his professorship. In 1879 he became a member of the Academy. From 1884 onward he was adminis-trator of the Collège de France. Renan regarded himself as a Liberal Protestant, but like Nietzsche, had no use for institutional religion or dogmatic Christianity. Unlike Nietzsche, Renan nonetheless viewed Christianity as an exemplary spiritual discipline, Katz, *Prejudice to Destruction*, p. 133.

73 *AC* 31.

74 For a brief comparison of Renan and Dühring, see Katz, *Prejudice to Destruction*, pp. 265ff.

75 Renan, *Jesus*, pp. 125, 160ff.

76 Renan, *Jesus*, p. 160 (ch. 7).

77 *AC* 32.

78 See the Preface to vol. 7: *Marcus-Aurelius* in Renan's multi-volume work, entitled *Origins of Christianity*, for a summary of his position concerning Christianity's origins with Isaiah; his negativity regarding original Israel prevails throughout his writings. Nietzsche read Renan's *Origins* in the winter of 1887, "with much spite and – little profit", Letter to Overbeck, Nice, 23 February 1887, in *L* 149, p. 261.

79 *AC* 17, 25, 26.

80 *AC* 40.
81 *AC* 29. Cf. *TW* "Errors" 7 in which Nietzsche writes that the priests at the head of ancient communities invented the doctrine of free will in order that they – or God – might punish and find others guilty: "Christianity is a metaphysics of the hangman."
    Situating the origin of Christianity with the prophet Isaiah was crucial for Christian anti-Semites. They used the raging words of Isaiah ("Hear and hear, but do not understand; see and see, but do not perceive. Make the heart of this people calloused" *Isaiah* 6: 9–10) against German Jewry for rejecting salvation and the Savior. Isaiah is repeated and used against the Jews in the New Testament (*Mark* 4: 12, *Acts* 28: 26). According to the Gospels, because Israel rejected salvation in Christ, it forfeited its election to the "new Israel," the Gentiles: "This salvation of God has been sent to the Gentiles," says Paul, "they will listen" (*Acts* 28: 28).
82 Low, *Jews*, p. 383; Duffy and Mittelman, "Nietzsche's attitudes," p. 302. At Leipzig (1866) Nietzsche placed an ad in the *Leipziger Tageblatt* for rooms in a "non commercial area" because he wanted to get away from the Jews. Cf. Ronald Hayman, *Nietzsche: A Critical Life* (New York: Penguin Books, 1984), p. 78.
83 Duffy and Mittelman, "Nietzsche's attitudes," p. 303; cf. the letter to Rohde on 7 December 1882 (*Briefe, Kritische Gesamtausgabe*, ed. Giorgio Colli and Mazziono Montineri (Berlin, 1975ff.), 11/3 #277, p. 97) which is cited in *L*.
84 "The Wagners also corroborate Nietzsche's account of the break, rightly attributing it to the Wagners' anti-Jewish racism. Cosima wrote to a friend: "In the end, Israel took over in the shape of a Dr. Rée, very slick, very cool ... representing the relationship of Judea to Germania .... It is the victory of evil over good," quoted in Erich Heller's Introduction to *Human, All Too Human*, tr. R.J. Hollingdale (Cambridge: Cambridge University Press, 1986), p. xi. Cf. Robert Gutman, *Richard Wagner* (1968; San Diego: Harvest, 1990), p. 360; and Nietzsche's letter to Peter Gast, Basle, 31 May 1878, in *L* 80, p. 166, p. xi. Traditionally, like Elisabeth, commentators (for whatever reason) have tended to ignore Nietzsche's account of the break, attributing the rupture *not* to Wagner's anti-Semitism, but to secondary factors, such as Wagner's conversion to Christianity, or to the fact that Wagner offended Nietzsche beyond repair when he wrote to Nietzsche's doctor, suggesting that Nietzsche's "odd behavior" was caused by habitual masturbation – and so on.
85 The *Birth of Tragedy* (1872) is silent about Jews.
86 "Every nation, every man has disagreeable, even dangerous character-istics; it is cruel to demand that the Jew should be an exception," *HU* 475. For Nietzsche's occasional comments on ancient Judaism see *D* 38, 68, 72, 205; *GS* 135–9.
87 Cf. *Z* I "On the thousand and one goals" and *Z* IV, "Conversation with the kings," in which Nietzsche uses the term Jew in reference to Christ. As noted, although the *terms* Jew and Christians are sparse or non-existent, the text flourishes with Judeo-Christian imagery and viciously polemicizes against anti-Semitic enemies. Werner Dannhauser, in *Nietzsche's View of Socrates* (New York: Ithaca, 1974) is to be credited with

the observation that the term Christianity is not mentioned in *Zarathustra*, p. 241.

88 Quoted in Low, *Jews*, p. 383.

89 Prior to *Beyond Good and Evil*, although Nietzsche consistently praises contemporary Jews, he was not totally uncritical of them (e.g. in *GS* 135 he states that the Jew did not have an appreciation for tragedy as did the Greeks, "in spite of all his poetic gifts and his sense of the sublime"). With *Beyond Good and Evil*, he virtually has nothing but exaggerated praise for his Jewish contemporaries, often contrasting the Jews with decadent Germans, and the superior Old Testament with the New: to have glued the New Testament to the Old "is perhaps the greatest audacity and sin against the spirit that literary Europe has on its conscience," *BGE* 52. Cf. 348 in Book V of *The Gay Science* (which Nietzsche added and published in 1887); *BGE* 250; *GM* I 16, III 22; *EH*, "Clever" 7, "Wagner" 4, and Appendix 3 and 4a; *WP* 49, etc. Nietzsche's elevation of the Jews during this time-period is obviously not due to a conviction that Jews were perfect or racially pure; it simply served to rebut his political enemies who scorned his Jewish contemporaries. Cf. *EH*, "Books" 2 (n. 1).

90 Cf. Arthur Danto, *Nietzsche As Philosopher* (New York: Columbia, 1965). "If he was not an anti-Semite, his language is misleading to a point of irresponsibility," pp. 166–7; Duffy and Mittelman, "Nietzsche's attitudes," pp. 313, 317; and Arnold M. Eisen, "Nietzsche and the Jews reconsidered," *Jewish Social Studies* 48(1) (1986): 7.

91 *D* 84; Golomb, "Nietzsche's Judaism of power," p. 379. Nietzsche's infamous phrase in *AC* 39, "There was only *one* Christian and he died on the cross," is key here.

92 Duffy and Mittelman attribute Nietzsche's purely negative attack on prophetic Judaism in the *Genealogy* to his failed relationship with Rée, and to a "temporary diversion" to the early vestiges of his anti-Semitism ("Nietzsche's attitudes," p. 314), thus failing to recognize Nietzsche's political maneuver against Christian theology. They recognize however, that his vehement attack against priestly Judaism (in *The Genealogy of Morals*) is directly connected to the Christian culture of his time. The Rée hypothesis is untenable mainly because it remains unclear as to why Nietzsche would attack priestly-prophetic Judaism and not contemporary Jewry, to which Rée belonged.

93 Letter to Franz Overbeck, Nice, 24 March 1887 in *L* 151, p. 264. Tal clearly sees Nietzsche's strategy:

> Friedrich Nietzsche, wielding his mother tongue with unrivaled vigor, sought to arouse his generation to the evils of the time, to the sterility of contemporary culture, ethics, and religion and to the ominous rise of political and spiritual depotism. He warned against attempts to find simple solutions for the existential problems of those days by stretching them on the procrustean bed of racial and political anti-Semitism as formulated by Paul de Lagard, Richard Wagner, and Professor Adolf Wahrmund. (*Christians and Jews*, p. 47)

94 *WP* 864.
95 *WP* 142; 145.
96 *D* 205. According to Low, on the eve of the appearance of cultural and political Zionism in Europe, Nietzsche and Paneth discussed the question of the rebirth of Palestine, *Jews*, p. 388. Nietzsche sent many of his early works, and works he had just completed, to Brandes in 1888, cf. *L* 164, pp. 283–4. Brandes and Nietzsche, who never had a chance to meet in person, began exchanging letters, photographs and ideas the previous year; the former coined the term "aristocratic radicalism" to describe Nietzsche, which delighted him. Brandes was also an elitist who was disgusted with Germans.
97 Brinton, *Nietzsche*, p. 215.
98 According to de Lagarde, one ought

> to despise those who – out of humanity! – defend these Jews or who are too cowardly to trample this usurious vermin to death. With trichinae and bacilli one does not negotiate, nor are trichinae and bacilli to be educated: they are exterminated as quickly and thoroughly as possible. (quoted in Yehuda Bauer, *A History of the Holocaust* (New York: Franklin Watts, 1982), p. 43)

99 Aschheim, *Nietzsche Legacy*, p. 97; *TW*, "Maxims" 8.
100 See *EH*, "Destiny" 1: "I have a terrible fear that one day I will be pronounced *holy*: you will guess why I publish this book *before*; it shall prevent people from doing mischief with me."

Historically, anti-Nazi commentators who later defended Nietzsche against the Nazis include Georges Bataille, *Sur Nietzsche* (Paris, 1945), Thomas Mann, *Nietzsche's Philosophy in the Light of Contemporary Events* (Washington: Library of Congress, 1948) and Albert Camus, *The Rebel* (1956; New York, 1958), pp. 65ff. The most extreme radical members who "nazified Nietzsche" are George Lichtheim, who states that if not for Nietzsche, Hitler's troops "would have lacked inspiration to carry out their programme of mass murder in Eastern Europe," *Europe in the Twentieth Century* (New York, 1972), p. 152; Georg Lukács, who writes from a Marxist perspective, *The Destruction of Reason*, tr. Peter Palmer (1962; London, 1980); and William McGovern, *From Luther to Hitler* (New York, 1941). The Nazi appropriation of Nietzsche clearly has not gone unchallenged or undiscussed; yet it is firmly embedded within much of the world's consciousness – and always will be. That does not mean, however, that it will always reflect a negative judgement upon Nietzsche; the reverse could actually prove to be the case.

3

"MONGOLS, SEMITES AND THE PURE-BRED GREEKS"

Nietzsche's handling of the racial doctrines of his time.[1]

Hubert Cancik

GREECE AS MODEL

"Something Mongolian" – "Semitic elements"

In his "Notes to 'We philologists'", which he intended one day to become the fourth "Untimely meditation", Nietzsche had gathered material on educational reform, on the criticism of classical philology and on German culture in general.[2] In addition, there are a great many notes concerning the emergence and construction of Greek culture – a process also seen here by Nietzsche as the means and paradigm for any education or culture. The Greeks are "the genius among the peoples" (p. 169 = 5[70]): "Child's nature. Credulous. Passionate. They live for the creation of genius unconsciously." Their creativity – or so Nietzsche assumed – was due to the fact that the conquerors who had fallen upon what was to become Greece had preserved their aggressive energy and had thereby founded their "cultural state" (*Culturstaat*) upon a "robber state" (*Raubstaat*).[3] From the Greek model, Nietzsche derived the basic principle of his *Lebensphilosophie* (p. 114 = 5[188]): "We must desire that life retains its violent character, that wild power and energy be called forth. The judgement concerning the value of existence[4] is the highest result of the most powerful tension in chaos." Such a chaos of races and cultures, a chaos put in order by a "master race", shows up in Nietzsche's vision of the early history of Greece. It also serves as a model for the future of Europe and its races, including the Aryans

55

and the Jews. Consequently, it is necessary and fruitful to comment in detail upon these "Notes".

Nietzsche's notes about the "original inhabitants of Greek soil" read as follows:[5]

> Mongolian extraction with tree and snake cult. The coast garnished with a Semitic strip. Here and there Thracians. The Greeks took all these components into their blood – including all the gods and myths (in the Odysseus legends, some Mongolian). The Doric migration is a *follow-up*, for everything had already been gradually inundated earlier. What are "pure-bred Greeks"? Is it not sufficient to accept that Italians with Thracian and Semitic elements have been coupled to *Greeks*?

This little "racial history of Greece", as Nietzsche called it elsewhere,[6] was put together from many sources. Using gross examples, Nietzsche wants to show that the "original inhabitants" were very heterogeneous. There were, in any case, no "pure-bred Greeks", but rather Mongolians, Semites and Thracians instead. All three names were intended to shock the philhellenic admirer of quiet dignity and white marble. The suggestion of a tree and snake cult set the beliefs of the Hellenes on the level of "savages". Material from ethnology and the history of religion lay ready at hand in the works of Mannhardt, Tylor, Caspari and Lubbock. Nietzsche knew these and other works on the origin of civilization and religion: he owned some, others he borrowed from the University of Basel's library, as the records of books checked out show.[7] In his lectures about the "Worship of the Greeks" (GdG), he used Carl Boetticher's "Tree cults of the Hellenes" (1856).[8] For the unusual combination "Tree and snake cult", Nietzsche used a title by J. Fergusson.[9] Even in Homer, the patriarch of Hellenic education, Nietzsche found "some Mongolian" elements. But one had also "found", in Nietzsche's time, that a "branch of the Mongolian race" had inhabited Northern and Middle Europe during the Stone Age.[10] J.A. de Gobineau even claimed that the "yellow race" had been the primitive population of Europe and that Mongolian elements were present in Greece, too. He identified eight components in the Greek population which, for their part, were composed of the three primitive elements of the human race, namely the black, the yellow and the white.[11] Nietzsche's formulation that "the coast [of Greece was] garnished with a Semitic strip" seems to echo Gobineau's statement that Semites settled "along the coast of Greece".[12]

In the revised form of these notes about the "original inhabitants" of Greece, Nietzsche even sees "the mainland in its interior [covered] with a race of Mongolian origin".[13] Because the Greeks themselves had made numerous observations and speculations about the history of their own origins – about migration and autochthony – the new racial researchers found a rich field of activity.[14] There were the Lelegians, the Karians – who were strongly mingled with the Phoenicians – and the Pelasgians, who were also even supposed to have been a Semitic people. A single pure race was nowhere to be found. The scholarly debate about how many Phoenician tribes might have settled upon Greek soil[15] or about how many oriental religions might have been "imported" to Greece was still undecided in Nietzsche's time. In his lectures, Nietzsche had also rated the Phoenician influence upon Greece very high, attributing the alphabet, the polis, the goddess Aphrodite and various myths to them.[16] Nietzsche's source was Franz K. Movers, whose work was the standard one at that time for the history of the Phoenicians.[17] Nietzsche's colleague Heinrich Nissen went further, even speaking of a "semitising of the Hellenes".[18]

Thus, in the view of Nietzsche and his colleagues, the original inhabitants of Greece were already very "mixed". And the immigrants who then gradually "inundated" Greece were also no "pure-bred Greeks": even the conquerors had their "Thracian and Semitic elements" – remarkably enough, the very same elements as those of the original inhabitants. The Greeks – according to Nietzsche's hypothesis of their racial history – did not in fact, migrate into "Greece": their ethnic identity first originated in the land of immigration itself.[19] There, they took all the garishly evoked Mongolian, Thracian and Semitic "components into their blood" – including even the "gods and myths". From this "coupling", the true Greeks emerged. Only after this can one speak of a "Greek race". Such a hypothesis excluded, above all, any sort of "Indo-Germanic[20] heritage" that might have been used to explain the specific cultural feats of the Greeks in Greece by reference to the biological predisposition or the cultural achievements of the Aryans alone.[21] On the other hand, Nietzsche thoroughly accepted the biological discourse of his contemporaries: history was supposed to be explained through the "mixing of blood", the "coupling" of heterogeneous elements, "extraction" (in a biological sense) and, finally, "collisions" and "waves" of "immigrants". The genesis of the Greeks in Greece, where they "became Greeks", is the point of his notes on the "original inhabitants". This point owes a debt to a particular biological (see "Nietzsche's Greeks, Jews and Europe", below) and political (see "A higher caste", below) theory of Nietzsche's.

"A higher caste"

Nietzsche's notes jump from the prehistoric "original inhabitants" to the historical period of Greece: from the conquerors came the rulers; from the original inhabitants came the slaves; from the battle of races came the battle of the "castes". Politics built itself upon the previous "racial history". Together, all of these components formed the Greek model that was supposed to mediate between antiquity and the European future. Immediately following upon his racial history of Greece, Nietzsche continued with these words:[22]

> If one considers the enormous number of slaves on the mainland, then *Greeks* were only to be found sporadically. A higher caste of the idle, the statesman, etc. Their *hostilities* held them in physical and intellectual tension. They had to ground their superiority upon quality – that was their spell over the masses.

Now then, there are "Greeks". The conquerors "had taken into their blood", consumed and digested the Semitic, Mongolian and Thracian components.[23] Something new had come into existence. Yet the "wild energy" through which the conquerors had taken possession of the land and its inhabitants remained preserved up into the earlier period of antiquity – or so Nietzsche thought. It was, indeed, essential in order to keep the "enormous number of slaves" suppressed. This same energy drove the Greeks both to rivalry with each other and to the highest cultural achievements:[24] "The intellectual culture of Greece [was] an aberration of the tremendous political drive toward distinction." The highest achievements of culture were necessary; they were not some lovely but superficial decoration. They engendered the cohesion of the higher caste of the "idle" – the political class and the creators of culture: in the musical and the athletic contests, aggression was channelled and sublimated.[25] Moreover, the supreme achievements of culture cast a spell over the "masses", who obviously had to care for each one of those belonging to the "idle", whose rule, in this manner, was justified aesthetically.

Consequently, Nietzsche believed that he had proven through

historical methods that the wild power and energy belonging to a conquering people has to be "bred great" (groß gezüchtet), a cultivation process by which such achievements as those the Greeks once produced would also be brought forth in Europe in the future.[26] Neither peace, luxury, socialism, the ideal political state, welfare, nor short-term educational reform are preconditions for the engendering of genius – whether of a people or of an individual; rather, genius should arise from conditions "as malicious and ruthless" as those in nature itself:[27] "Mistreat people – drive them to their limits" ("Mißhandelt die Menschen, treibt sie zum Außersten").

Nietzsche's considerations about race and caste as well as rule and culture for the Greeks were aimed at his present. "The Greeks", he thought, "believed in differences among the races". Nietzsche approvingly recalled Schopenhauer's opinion that slaves were a different species, and in addition, he cited the image of a winged animal in contrast to that of an unmoving shellfish.[28] In such a generalization as this one, the statement is incorrect, and in a more narrowly defined sense, it is racist. Neither the study of the origin of populations – their tribes, dialects and customs (through such fields as anthropology, ethnology and folklore) – nor the analysis and critical evaluation of differences in language, law and religion, on the one hand, and of peoples and cultures on the other hand, constitutes racism; however, the political use of these findings for generating and propagating narcissistic self-images, destructive caricatures of enemies and stereotypes that raise fear and disgust *does* constitute racism. Accordingly, the following statements by Nietzsche are to be characterized as racist:[29]

1 "The new problem: whether or not educating[!] *a part* of humanity to a higher race must come at the cost of the rest. Breeding . . ." (1881).
2 "We would as little choose 'early Christians' as Polish Jews to associate with us: not that one would need to have even a single [i.e., rational] objection to them. . . . Both of them simply do not smell good."

Nietzsche tested his racial teachings within the framework of classical studies. The aphoristic formulation that he gave to his "Notes" on the original population of Greece in September 1876 forms a connection to the racial teachings of his critical writings.[30] In his "Plowshare", Nietzsche excluded the Doric migration and avoided the word "caste" as well as such peculiarities as the tree and snake cult, or the Mongolian elements in the Odyssey or the Italians who had become Greeks. Purified of offensive, concrete, verifiable details, a more refined, polished, dashing aphorism emerged, one that suggested, in more pleasing language, the necessary connection of racial differences to the rule of "higher beings" – thus "the idle, the political class, etc." are now called – and to cultural superiority.

NIETZSCHE'S GREEKS, JEWS AND EUROPE

Inheritance of acquired characteristics

Not only a political but also a biological theory stood behind Nietzsche's notes on the racial history of Greece. His thoroughly legitimate doubts about an autochthonous people, a pure origin or an Indo-European heritage found support, for their part, in biological hypotheses and the application of these to history. He writes:[31]

> It is a completely unclear concept to talk about Greeks who do not yet live in Greece. The typical Greek is much less the result of a predisposition than of the adapted institutions – and also, among other things, of the adopted language.

Once that "typical Greek" has been created, however, it must be kept "pure", best of all through a rigid, steep hierarchy of "castes".[32] In any case, the "purity" of the race is also a positive, basic concept of biology for Nietzsche.

Nietzsche constructed a little racial history of ancient Europe upon concepts he had borrowed from biology.[33] "Blood mixing", skull shape and skin and hair color are the main terms of his anthropology. Nietzsche coupled the biological to social characteristics and to moral values: the blond-haired is better than the black-haired, and the short-haired is worse than the long-skulled. Some fearless etymologies suggested by the erstwhile philologist make this chapter from the *Genealogy of Morals* into a prize exhibit of philo-Aryan prose[34] because for Nietzsche, the long-skulled blond – the good, noble, pure conqueror – was the Aryan, of course: they were the master race in Europe.

Nietzsche's little racial history of ancient Europe aimed at the present. In the social and political movements of the Democrats, the

Anarchists and the Socialists of his time, he saw, namely, the instincts of the "pre-Aryan population" breaking through again. Nietzsche related these political programs explicitly to biology. He feared that "the conquering and master race – that of the Aryans – is also being defeated physiologically".[35] According to Nietzsche, the Jews had begun this slave revolt:[36] they led the slaves – the mob, the herd – to this victory over the aristocracy. This victory meant "blood poisoning", "intoxication" – this pastor's son and classical philologist loved to adorn himself with medical jargon. Nietzsche identified the reason for the poisoning:[37] "It [i.e., the victory] had mingled the races promiscuously." The pre-Aryan population was thus in league with the Jews and against the Italians, the Greeks, the Celts, the Germans – and generally speaking, all Aryans everywhere.

The biological – even physiological – claim, the rejection of the theories of inheritance and the demand for the purity of the ruling castes forced Nietzsche to a biological hypothesis that presupposed the inheritance of acquired characteristics. Nietzsche writes:[38] "No reflection is so important as that upon the inheritance of characteristics."[39] The "character of the Greeks" is "acquired"; nothing is "given" to them.

In 1881, Nietzsche published a general draft of his racial ideas under the title "The becoming-pure of a race".[40] What he had previously scattered about in notes concerning classical studies and in various other hints is here summarized in twenty-five lines of print covering five points:

1 The races are not originally pure but, at best, become pure in the course of history.
2 The crossing of races simultaneously means the crossing of cultures: crossing leads to "disharmony" in bodily form, in custom and in morality.
3 The process of purification occurs through "adapting, imbibing, [and] excreting" foreign elements.
4 The result of purification is a stronger and more beautiful organism.
5 The Greeks are "the model of a race and culture that had become pure".

All historical details have now been suppressed. The blueprint of Nietzsche's thinking, however, which he had already structured in his early classical notes, has here become undisguisably clear. We can connect every single "note" with this blueprint, as we will shortly see in what follows.

Those who were to become Greeks imbibed the Mongolian, Semitic and Thracian elements, excreting what could not be assimilated. After this process, these elements were no longer specific components of the now-existent Greek race, for it was now a new race, stronger and more beautiful than any single, previous one. Nietzsche's metaphorical language suggests the intake, digestion and excretion of food occurring in an organism. This image of a "battle among the disharmonious characteristics" within impure organisms reminds one of the "battle of the parts within an organism", as Wilhelm Roux, the founder of developmental mechanics,[41] had described it. Nietzsche had already copied down passages from Roux's major work in the year it had appeared – 1881.[42] The significance of this text for Nietzsche has been shown by W. Müller-Lauter.[43]

The "model" for the breeding of a European ruling caste was the Greeks:[44] "it is to be hoped that a pure European race and culture will also one day succeed [in coming into being]." In such a race and culture – as the model prepared by Nietzsche has instructed us – the foreign elements (those bred in) will be imbibed for digestion or excretion.

Nietzsche's sources

Nietzsche drew his biological and medical concepts, methods and materials from many different sources. Some clues are provided by the authors he himself named, others by the reading lists he jotted down in his notebooks, still others from the University of Basel's book-loan lists of books he and his friends checked out and the remainder, finally, by the books he kept in his library.[45] Nietzsche used physiological texts as well as popularized scientific writings but also anonymous treatises with striking titles: *Die Aristokratie des Geistes als Lösung der sozialen Frage: Ein Grundriß der natürlichen und vernünftigen Zuchtwahl in der Menschheit* (The Aristocracy of Intellect as the Solution to the Social Question: An Outline for the Natural and Reasonable Selective Breeding of Humanity) (Anon., Leipzig, n.d.). Nietzsche mentions Thomas Robert Malthus and Jean Baptiste Lamarck,[46] Rudolph Virchow,[47] Wilhelm Roux and the founder of Social Darwinism, Herbert Spencer, from whom he may possibly have learned the term "cull out" (German translation:

Ausmerze).[48] Spencer had transferred theorems from biological evolution to the historical process. He complained that a policy of social reform hindered "natural selection". For this reason, Nietzsche advised, one must "eliminate the continuance and effectiveness" of bad, sick and uneducated people.[49] From Sir Francis Galton, one of the original founders of eugenics, he took over the formula of "hereditary genius", which Galton had used in his study of the families of criminals.[50] He had already as a student informed himself about Charles Darwin's theories by reading F. Albert Lange's *History of Materialism*.[51] In the scholarship upon Nietzsche, it is debated as to whether he is to be understood as a Darwinist or an anti-Darwinist. Werner Stegmaier, who has demonstrated the minor significance of anti-Darwinian passages in Nietzsche's later writings, considers him a convinced Darwinian "in every phase of his work".[52]

Nietzsche's utterances about acquired character, the purity of races, the inheritance of characteristics, the degeneracy of half-breeds[53] and the cultivation of drives over long periods of time[54] could – for this branch – suggest an unorthodox (Neo-)Lamarckianism. Still, it is unclear whether or not Nietzsche would have recognized any difference between the Lamarckian and the Darwinian ideas within Darwin's own writings. The following formulation – gained with help from Wilhelm Roux's formulation of his teachings on the inheritance of acquired characteristics and habits – is typical of Nietzsche:[55] "Thus are peoples who have grown old more explicit about what is typical of them, and it is clearer to recognize [it then] than in the prime of their youth."[56]

By Nietzsche's time, the knowledge, terminology and manner of formulating questions that were characteristic of the fields of demographics, biology and medicine had long entered into the various branches of the humanities, even if to various degrees. Comparative linguistics had already recognized the connections among the Indo-European languages stretching from Asia all the way to the Celtic north-west of Europe. The overhasty connection made between a people and a language led to the search for the original home of the Aryans. Comparative mythology[57] found the remnants of a pre-historic religion common to all of the Aryan peoples. As early as 1868, Nietzsche became acquainted with the philosopher, all-round publicist and anti-Semite Eugen Dühring.[58] In 1875, he wrote down passages from Dühring's work *On the Value of Life* (1865), adding his own, critical remarks.[59] Dühring published in a verbose, self-conscious and vulgar manner about religious *ersatz* in modern culture, about the supposed necessary correspondence of race, character and religion, about whether or not Jesus had been a full-blooded Jew and about whether or not Christianity carried features of the "Jewish race" and therefore posed the frightening danger of Judaizing the various European peoples.[60] Nietzsche made great efforts to distance himself from his threatening proximity to this philosophizing university lecturer.

In historical scholarship as well – and even in classical philology – racist teachings had penetrated.[61] Within Nietzsche's racial teachings, Jews and Aryans had a special position. In his first monograph (1872), Nietzsche had already arrayed the "Aryan character" against the Semitic one, Prometheus against Eve, the creative man against the lying woman, the tragic wantonness in battle for higher culture against lascivious sin.[62] This argumentative structure is still present in *The Antichrist* (1888): against the philhellenic hyperboreans and what Nietzsche called "Aryan humanity" stood denatured Judaism and Judaism "raised to the second power", Christianity.[63] The Jews – as Nietzsche had indicated with the Eve myth – are not creative; in contrast to the Aryan peoples, they are mere "intermediaries", merchants: "they invent nothing." Even their law is from the Codex of Manu – copied from an "absolutely Aryan creation".[64]

One typical product of this kind of racial history is the "Contribution to historical anthropology" by Theodor Poesche, in which he wished to treat only a single race but nevertheless bind together natural and cultural history. The unity of this field was to be established through the concept of "race". Poesche defined this physiologically, through the size and form of the skull and through the color of the skin and hair, rather than linguistically, for language would be transmissible from one group to another. On the other hand, Poesche believed in an "original concordance of physical constitution and language": "the blond peoples speak Indo-Germanic."[65] Greeks and Romans, on the one hand, and Persians and Indians, on the other hand, were already a mixed people – completely homogeneous peoples had not existed for thousands of years.[66] His history covered human development from the beginning up to his present day. The Aryan settling of both Americas, of Siberia and of the Russian part of America was forming the concluding high point of this process. The last sentence of this work praised the Aryans as "the master race of the earth". Nietzsche made the breeding of a European master race somewhat more difficult.

Breeding a pure European race

"Imbibed and absorbed by Europe"

Nietzsche only grudgingly accepted the Aryan myth, for it competed with his Hellenic myth. He found surprising the fact that Christianity could have forced a Semitic religion upon the Indo-Germans.[67] For this reason, he fought both Judaism and Christianity, and he created for himself a pagan, Indo-Germanic alternative with his new, Hellenic Dionysos and the Iranian Zarathustra. He finished this battle in autumn of 1888 with his "A curse on Christianity".[68] and his "War to the death against Christianity".[69]

The Christian was "only a Jew of a 'freer' confession of faith" – Christians and Jews were "related, racially related",[70] and Christianity was a form of Judaism raised "yet one time" higher through negation.[71] Nietzsche wrote:[72]

> Christianity is to be understood entirely in terms of the soil from which is grew – it is *not* a countermovement to the Jewish instinct; it is the successor itself, a further step in its [i.e., the Jewish instinct's] frightening logic.

Nietzsche's fight against the "denaturalization of natural values",[73] his "transvaluation of all values" was directed against Jews and Christians. Because Nietzsche argued against both, Christian anti-Semitism was especially offensive for him. The Jews, Nietzsche maintained, were nevertheless guilty:[74] They had "made humanity into something so false that, still today, a Christian can feel anti-Semitic without understanding himself as the last stage of Judaism".

The Antichrist was Nietzsche's last word on Judaism which he himself intended to be published. It is precisely with respect to supposed or truly "positive" utterances on Jews and Judaism that this fact should never be forgotten.[75]

A short essay (section 251) in Nietzsche's "Philosophy of the Future" – *Beyond Good and Evil* (1885/6) – belongs to the "positive" parts. Here, "the breeding of a new caste to rule over Europe" – definitely a current "European problem" according to Nietzsche – is discussed. The breeding of this caste follows the "Greek model": the foreign elements are "imbibed" and either assimilated or "excreted" – thus does a "pure European race and culture come into being". With the Jews, however, Germany was going to have difficulty, for Germany had "amply enough Jews" (so wrote

Nietzsche in 1885/6): "that the German stomach, the German blood, is having difficulty (and for a long time yet will continue to have difficulty) finishing even this quantity of 'Jews'." Other European countries had finished with the Jews "because of a more strenuous digestion"; in Germany, however, there were simply too many. Nietzsche demanded what all anti-Semites demanded at that time: "Allow no more Jews in! And, especially, close the gates to the east (including the one between Germany and Austria!" Nietzsche praised the Jews so much that he appeared to confirm the fears of anti-Semites about Jews striving to rule the world. He writes:[76] "That the Jews, if they wished ... could already have the pre-dominance – yes, literally the dominion over Europe – is certain; it is equally certain, however, that they are not working upon this or making plans." Nietzsche speculated, though, that the vulgar anti-Semites might provoke the Jews into seizing "power over Europe" for themselves. For anti-Semitism itself, Nietzsche had complete understanding; he was simply – like "all careful and judicious people" – against the "dangerous extravagance" of this feeling,[77] "especially against the tasteless and scandalous expression of this extravagant feeling". Nietzsche had a measured and tasteful manner of expressing this "feeling". And his solution to the problem was also mild: the Jews are to be bred in. They even desire it themselves, "to be in Europe, to be imbibed and absorbed". As for the "anti-Semitic complainers", those who might hinder this gentle final solution with their radical words, Nietzsche wanted to have them expelled from the country. And then, he thought, one could – "with great care" and "with selectivity" – cross an intelligent Jewish woman with an "aristocratic officer from the Mark" (i.e., a Prussian aristocratic officer). In this manner, one could "breed in" some intellect to the "already strongly molded character of the new Teutonic". The valuable elements of Judaism, which Nietzsche was able to praise generously in this context, would be absorbed and assimilated in the new Europe; whatever disturbed would be "excreted".

In this manner, the new European race would be purified and a new caste ruling over Europe cultivated. The "Greek model" that Nietzsche had developed in his classical studies was proving its value for planning the racial, cultural and political future of Europe. The programmatic anti-Semitism was to be surpassed through Nietzsche's tasteful solution of the problem, precisely that solution acceptable to an intellectual aristocracy.

A tasteful gentle anti-Semitism

Among those belonging to the "careful and judicious" category of the ones who could support a gentle solution were Schopenhauer and Wagner. Nietzsche had known Schopenhauer's "theory of inheritance" ever since his student days.[78] Nietzsche wanted to sharpen the social and political distinctions between Greeks and barbarians, lords and serfs, geniuses and breadwinners by identifying the races to which people belonged. For this, he cited Schopenhauer, who had been surprised that "nature had not chosen to invent two separate species".[79] On the other hand, Schopenhauer had wanted "to solve in the gentlest way in the world" the Jewish question – through marrying them to Christians.[80] Wagner had, at the close of his early essay "Judaism in music", challenged the Jews to become human beings. To do this, they would have to stop being Jews and destroy themselves:[81]

> Participate without restraint in this self-destroying, bloody battle, and we will be one and indivisible! But consider – you have only one salvation from the curse remaining upon you, the salvation provided for Ahasver – destruction!

Despite this bloody language, Wagner had later rejected the vulgar, primitive anti-Semitism that was partially even inspired by motives of social criticism. Wagner did not support the anti-Semitic petition to the Kaiser organized by Bernhard Förster, Max Liebermann von Sonnenberg, Ernst Henrici and others.[82] In this elevated, fine, tasteful, gentle anti-Semitism, a thematic communality between Wagner and Nietzsche reveals itself, one going deeper than any disagreement in other areas, whether personal, musical or religious.

SUMMARY

Nietzsche's antiquity

In the picture of antiquity that Nietzsche drew for himself, race and contemporary racial teaching played a substantial role. Because Nietzsche combined the expressions "procreation, rearing, and breeding", his early statements on educational reform also had a biological tint. His research in the history of religion was influenced by contemporary theories about Aryans and a supposed Indo-Germanic heritage in Greco-Roman culture. Exhaustive considerations upon the connection between race and religion centered especially on the question of what it had meant "to put the sacred book of a Semitic people into the hands of a people of the Indo-Germanic race".[83]

Nietzsche construed the demographic history of Greece and Italy as a model for "racial history". In agreement with his particularly biological manner of viewing things, he emphasized not the cultural heritage but rather the biological origin of the Greek nation within the country, the gradual "cleaning" of the racial chaos – Mongols, Semites, Thracian – that had resulted in a caste: only in Greece did the Greeks become Greek.[84] That was the Greek model for Nietzsche's ideas about how a new, pure European "race and culture" should be bred.

Nietzsche's concept of antiquity is determined by the sterile antithesis "Greek/Jew". His philhellenism, from his early notes in Basel to his *Antichrist*, is anti-Jewish.[85] As early as 1869/70, he feared the "destruction of Greek culture through the Jewish world".[86]

"Pure European race and culture" (Nietzsche)

Nietzsche had a comparatively broad knowledge of contemporary biology, evolutionary theory and Darwinism as well as of racial teachings in the humanities, in comparative linguistics and comparative history of religion and in ethnology. The assumption that acquired characteristics could be passed on and the related claim that the "purity" of a race was a late, hard-achieved result rather than a gift of inheritance are important, special hypotheses for Nietzsche's racial history.

The analysis of the Greek model makes easier an understanding of Nietzsche's views on the place of Jews in the racial history of Europe. Just as "pure-bred Greeks" were the high point of a long development in the process of which foreign elements had been "digested", so would the Jews have to be "imbibed" in Europe – and especially in Germany – by a gradual, intelligent, careful crossing that would serve to "breed in" their good characteristics. In this manner, a new, pure European race and culture would come into being.

The vulgar anti-Semitic propaganda with its anti-capitalist, even social-critical components, hindered, according to Nietzsche, this process of the "digesting" of the Jewish population; instead, it drove them to resistance and isolation. Much as did Schopenhauer, Wagner and Wolzogen in the 1870s and 1880s, Nietzsche set himself against the programmatic anti-Semitism: to this extent, Nietzsche was an "anti-anti-Semite". He developed, however, a measured and – through the incorporation of Christianity – a sharpened, tasteful, aristocratic anti-Semitism. To this extent, Nietzsche improved upon the anti-Semitism of his times and thereby made it more acceptable for the highbrow public.

NOTES

1 Translation from German by Horace Jeffrey Hodges (Berkeley/ Tübingen). I am very indebted to Hubert Treiber (Hanover) for kindly indicating and commenting on many sources Nietzsche might have consulted: this paper owes much to his stimulating and competent criticism.

2 The "Notizen zu 'Wir Philologen'" (WPh) are to be found in manuscript *UB* II 8; they were written in 1875. Our quotations follow the pagination of the archives in the manuscript; when necessary, the numbering of the edition by M. Montinari in *KGW* IV, resp. *KSA*, vol. 8 has been added.

3 *GM* I 5. For the concepts of "cultural state/robber state", cf. H. Cancik and H. Cancik-Lindemaier, "Das Thema 'Religion und Kultur' bei Friedrich Nietzsche und Franz Overbeck", in D. Thofern, S. Gabbani and W. Vosse (eds), *Rationalität im Diskurs: Rudolf Wolfgang Müller zum 60. Geburtstag* (Marburg: Diagonal, 1994) pp. 49–67.

4 The formula "value of life" was coined by Eugen Dühring, whom Nietzsche read in 1875; there are extracts with critical annotations in *UB* III 1 = *KSA* vol. 8, pp. 131ff.

5 *UB* II 8, p. 110 = *KSA* p. 96: 5[198].

6 Encyc 21 (*KGW* II 3, pp. 427ff.).

7 Cf. "Nietzsche's sources", below; Otto Caspari, *Die Urgeschichte der Menschheit: Mit Rücksicht auf die natürkliche Entwickelung des frühesten Geisteslebens*, 2nd edn (Leipzig: Brockhaus, 1877), p. 59; John Lubbock, *Die Entstehung der Zivilisation und der Urzustand des Menschengeschlechtes* (Jena: Castenoble, 1875), pp. 222f., 240; Edward Tylor, *Die Anfänge der Cultur: Untersuchungen über die Entwicklung der Mythologie, Philosophie, Religion, Kunst und Sitte* (Leipzig: Winter, 1873) II, pp. 218ff.; cf. W. Mannhardt, *Wald- und Feldculte: Erster Theil: Baumcultus der Germanen und ihrer Nachbarstämme* (Berlin, 1875).

8 The conference entitled GdG (winter term 1875/6) is in GA 19, pp. 1–124 (not complete). Boetticher is used in MS N I 6, p. 72 (summer 1875; cf. GdG, pp. 36f., 69f., 73f., *et al.*

9 James Fergusson, *Tree and Serpent Worship* (London: W.H. Allen & Co., 1868), used by Lubbock, *Die Entsehung der Zivilisation*, pp. 187ff.; Nietzsche quotes Fergusson in GdG, pp. 34f. Cf. Tylor, *Anfänge*, pp. 222ff.: tree worship in Siberia.

10 Cf. *Das Ausland*, 1873, pp. 270ff.: "Prof. Friedrich Müller's anthropological researches" (Prof. Friedrich Müller's ethnologische Forschungen), esp. p. 310: "The race of the Hyperboreans"; "Original home of the so-called Mongolian or better High-Asiatic race".

11 M.A. de Gobineau, *Essai sur l'inégalité des races humaines* (Paris: Didot, vols. 1–2 1853, vols. 3–4 1855). For the dissemination of the yellow race see vol. 3, p. 17; cf. the fantastic etymologies, ibid., p. 43. For different racial elements in the population of Greece see vol. 2, p. 416: "La gloire de la Grèce fut l'oeuvre de la fraction ariane, alliée au sang sémitique; tandis que la grande prépondérance extérieure de ce pays résulta de l'action des populations quelque peu mongolisées du nord." Cf. the list of eight components, ibid., pp. 421f.

12 Gobineau, *Essai*, vol. 1, p. 393: "le long du litoral de la Grèce." Cf. E.J. Young, *Gobineau und der Rassismus*, (Meisenheim am Glan, 1968).

13 There is a new version of WPh 3[198] in "Die Pflugschar" 143 (*KSA* vol. 8, p. 327).

14 One classical passage is Thucydides 1, 2–3; cf. the annotations by Wahrmund; cf. Thucydides 1, 8 (the Carians); 2, 2 (the Thracians).

15 Ernst Curtius, *Die Ionier vor der ionischen Wanderung* (Berlin: Hertz, 1855), p. 50.

16 Encyc, pp. 428f., 410; *UB* II 8, p. 168 = 5[65]; GdG, pp. 22f.

17 Franz Karl Movers, Die Phönizier (Bonn: Weber, 1841).

18 H. Nissen, "Über Tempelorientierung", *Rheinisches Museum* 28 (1873): 513–57, p. 525.

19 It is impossible to present here the contemporary theories upon a common prehistory of the Greco-Italians and upon the various immigrations to Greece; but, see Theodor Poesche, *Die Arier: Ein Beitrag zur historischen Anthropologie* (Jena: Costenoble, 1878), pp. 155ff.; p. 162: "the Greeks, at any rate, bear a frequent Semitic element within themselves"; pp. 181f.: "black, roundheaded, ugly Pre-Aryans in Europe" ("Mongoloids"); pp. 184ff.; p. 186: "Italy in the earliest times totally occupied by a dark population."

20 Although the normal translation for *indogermanisch* would be "Indo-European", the various writers cited in this article in fact stressed the *Germanic* part of the term, and the translation used here reflects this stress.

21 Cf. *UB* II 8, p. 206 = 2[5].

22 *UB* II 8, p. 206 = 5[199].

23 For this imagery, see "Nietzsche's sources", below.

24 *UB* II 8, p. 118 = 5[179].

25 Cf. e.g. the piece from December 1872 on: "Homer's Wettkampf" (not published by Nietzsche): *KSA* vol. 1, pp. 783–92.

26 *UB* II 8, p. 116 and 114 = 5[185] and [188].

27 *UB* II 8, p. 112 = 5[191] and [194].

28 *UB* II 8, p. 112 = 5[72] and [73].

29 (1) *KSA* vol. 9, p. 577 12[10]; (2) *AC* 46 (*KSA* vol. 6, p. 223).

30 "Die Pflugschar" 143 (*KSA* vol. 8, p. 327). It is proved by the version of "Pflugschar" that the passages numbered 5[198] and [199] in *KGW* are not separated "fragments" but rather a unity.

31 *UB* II 8, p. 206 = 2[5].

32 Friedrich Nietzsche, "Der griechische Staat" (1872): *KSA* vol. 1, p. 764–77, here p. 775; cf. B. von Reibnitz, "Nietzsches 'Griechischer Staat' und das Deutsche Kaiserreich", *Der altsprachliche Unterricht* 30 (3)

(1987): 76–89. Nietzsche evidently did not care that there never had been a caste system in Greece; he combined what seemed useful to him. In his later work, the main source was L. Jacolliot, *Les Législateurs religieux: Manou–Moïse–Mahomet* (Paris, 1876), see his extracts in *KSA* vol. 13, p. 284 and, e.g., *GD* (*KSA* vol. 6, pp. 100f.) and *AC* 57. Nietzsche had this completely unreliable book in his library, and he should have recognized its dubious nature: cf. A. Etter, "Nietzsche und das Gesetzbuch des Manu, "*Nietzsche-Studien* 16 (1987): 340–52 and Vasudha Dalmia-Lüderitz, "Die Aneignung der Vedischen Vergangenheit: Aspekte der frühen deutschen Indien-Forschung", *Zeitschrift für Kulturaustausch* 37 (3) (1987): 434–43. Cf., further, L. Dumont, "Caste, racisme et stratification", *Cahiers Internationaux de Sociologie* 29 (1960): 91ff.

33 *GM* I 5 (1887). Note that Nietzsche had read Tocqueville – see his letter to Overbeck, 23 February 1887.
34 Some examples: ἐσθλός ("noble") to εἶναι ("to be"), *malus* ("bad") to μέλας ("black").
35 *GM* I 5.
36 *GM* I 7.
37 *GM* I 9. For the mixture of races considered as an evil, cf. *JGB* 208, 200.
38 *KSA* vol. 8, p. 301: 17 [28].
39 *VM* 219.
40 *M* IV 272.
41 Wilhelm Roux, *Der Kampf der Teile im Organismus: Ein Beitrag zur Vervollständigung der mechanischen Zweckmäßigkeitslehre* (Leipzig, 1881), *BN*.
42 *KSA* vol. 9, pp. 487f.: 11[130].
43 W. Müller-Lauter, "Der Organismus als innerer Kampf. Der Einfluß von Wilhelm Roux auf Friedrich Nietzsche", *Nietzsche-Studien* 7 (1978): 189–223; cf. "Nietzsche's sources", below.
44 *JGB* 251 (last sentence) and *M* IV 272 (last sentence).
45 Max Oehler, *Nietzsches Bibliothek* (Weimar, 1942). The list compiled by Oehler is unreliable, probably not even complete. There is no information in Oehler as to when Nietzsche first came to possess the books indicated or as to which copies might possibly have been supplied later. As to the lists of Romundt's book loans, cf. H. Treiber, "Wahlverwandschaften zwischen Nietzsches Idee eines 'Klosters für freiere Geister' und Webers Idealtypus der puritanischen Sekte", *Nietzsche-Studien*, 21 (1992): 344; "Zur Genealogie einer 'science positive de la morale en Allemagne'", ibid. 22 (1993): 196ff.; "Zur 'Logik des Traumes' bei Nietzsche", ibid. 23, (1994): 35ff.
46 Malthus: *KSA* vol. 6, p. 120; vol. 8, pp. 167ff.; *FW* II 99 (*KSA* vol. 3, p. 454); cf. *KSA* vol. 9, p. 397; vol. 11, p. 442.
47 Cf. *GM* I 5 (*KSA* vol. 3, p. 263).
48 H. Spencer, *Die Thatsachen der Ethik*, tr. B. Vetter (Stuttgart, 1879), *BN*; cf. *KSA* vol. 9, p. 10 (1880).
49 *KSA* vol. 9, p. 10 (1880); cf. ibid., pp. 27f., 454f.
50 Letter to Strindberg, 8 December 1888.; cf. letter to Overbeck, 4 July 1888. Cf. Marie Louise Haase, "Friedrich Nietzsche liest Francis Galton", *Nietzsche-Studien*, 18 (1889): 633ff.
51 Letter to Gersdorff, 16 February 1868; cf. *UB* I 7 (*KSA* vol. 1, pp. 194ff.);

KSA vol. 7, p. 267 (1870/1–fall 1872): "Bell quoted by Darwin upon the expression of emotions (concerning the genesis of language!)."

52 W. Stegmaier, "Darwin, Darwinismus, Nietzsche", *Nietzsche-Studien* 16 (1987): 269.

53 *JGB* 208 (*KSA* vol. 5, pp. 138). Cf. Peosche, *Arier*, p. 10 concerning the sterility of mixtures: a mixed race can persist only "if supplied with fresh blood". Cf. *JGB* 200: "The man belonging to an epoch of dissolution, which mixes up the races".

54 *KSA* vol. 9, 11[130].

55 *KSA* vol. 10, p. 273: 7[90] (summer 1883); from Wilhelm Roux, *Der Kampf der Teile im Organismus: Ein Beitrag zur Vervollständigung der mechanischen Zweckmäßigkeitslehre* (Leipzig: Engelmann, 1881), pp. 62ff.

56 Cf. H. Ottmann, *Philosophie und Politik bei Nietzsche* (Berlin and New York: de Gruyter, 1987), pp. 245ff., 262ff.

57 Encyc, *KGW* II 3, p. 389, 397, 410ff. (for Creuzer, O. Müller, Max Müller, A. Kuhn, *et al.*).

58 Letter to Gersdorff, 16 February 1868.

59 *KSA* vol. 8, pp. 129, 131–81.

60 These keywords come from E. Dühring, *Der Ersatz der Religion durch Vollkommeneres und die Ausscheidung alles Judäerthums durch den modernen Völkergeist* (Berlin, 1897). Cf. Aldo Venturelli, "Asketismus und Wille zur Macht, Nietzsches Auseinandersetzung mit Eugen Dühring", *Nietzsche-Studien* 15 (1986): 107–39.

61 Cf. e.g. letter to T. Fritsch, 29 March 1887, where Adolf Wahrmund is mentioned, whose translation of Thucydides Nietzsche used; cf. A. Wahrmund, *Das Gesete des Nomadentums und die heutige Judenherrschaft* (March, 1887).

62 *GT* 9. In German, the word *Frevel* ("wantonness") is masculine in gender; the word *Sünde* ("sin") is feminine. For the theme "Aryans and Semites" in general, cf. M. Olender, *Les Langues du paradis: Aryens et Sémites: un couple providential*, Paris: Gallimard, 1989.

63 Cf. *GD The 'correctors' of mankind" KSA* vol. 12, p. 501.

64 Letter to Köselitz, 31 May 1888; cf. n. 31.

65 Poesche, *Arier*, pp. 4, 7f.; language: p. 41.

66 Ibid. VII: "The Aryan half-breeds".

67 *KSA* vol. 9, pp. 21f.

68 Subtitle of *The Antichrist*, 1888.

69 *KSA* vol. 6, p. 254.

70 *AC* 44.

71 *AC* 27: "the small rebellious movement, which is baptised in the name of Jesus of Nazareth, is the Jewish instinct *once more*." Cf. H. Cancik and H. Cancik-Lindemaier, "Philhellenisine et antisémitisme en Allemagne: le cas Nietzsche", in D. Bourel and J. Le Rider (eds), *De Sils-Maria à Jérusalem: Nietzsche et le judaïsme – les intellectuals juifs et Nietzsche* (Paris: Editions du Cerf, 1991) and H. Cancik, "'Judentum in Zweiter Potenz'": Ein Beitrag zur Interpretation von Friedrich Nietzsche, 'Der Antichrist', in *"Mit unserer Macht ist nichts getan": Festschrift Dieter Schellong* (Frankfurt am Main: Haag & Herchen Verlag, 1993).

72 *AC* 24.
73 *AC* 25.
74 *AC* 24.
75 In the enigmatic utterances Nietzsche sent to several persons after his breakdown the anti-Semites to be shot appear among Dionysus and Ariadne, the crucified, the pope, Bismarck, the *Hohenzollern* etc.; see *KSB* 8, pp. 570–79.
76 *JGB* 251; cf. *M* 205 (*KSA* vol. 3, p. 182): "They [i.e., the Jews] themselves know best that they cannot think of conquering Europe and of whatsoever an act of violence: they know, however, that someday Europe might fall into their hands like a fully ripe fruit." Cf. *KSA* vol. 10, p. 251 (1883): "Thus a temporary reign of the Jews is the only means to ennoble them."
77 By asking moderation in the expression of anti-Semitism, which he considers as principally justified, Nietzsche takes the same position as the later Wagner and Wolzogen. The anti-capitalist and anti-bourgeois potential of anti-Semitism was then already frightening the "educated middle class". That is why they tried to channel it.
78 Letter to E. Rohde, 8 October 1868.
79 *UB* II 8, p. 112 = 5[72].
80 Cf. Schopenhauer, *Parerga und Paralipomena* II 132. For the reception of Schopenhauer in German anti-Semitism, cf. Maria Groener, *Schopenhauer und die Juden*, (Munich: Deutscher Volksverlag, n.d., about 1920); Micha Brumlik (1991), "Das Judentum in der Philosophie Schopenhauers", in Marcel Markus, *et al.* (eds), *Israel und die Kirche heute*: 256–72.
81 R. Wagner, "Das Judentum in der Musik", *Neue Zeitschrift für Musik* 19–20 (1850): 101–12; new edition with commentary by Tibor Kneif (Munich, 1975), the quotation is on p. 77.
82 Cf. Paul W. Massing (German edn, 1959), *Vorgeschichte des politischen Antisemitismus* (American edn, 1949), Ch. 3: "Conservative state and social demagogy".
83 *KSA* vol. 9, pp. 21–3: 1[73].
84 Cf. *HL* 10 (*KSA* vol. 1, p. 333).
85 Further evidence in Cancik and Cancik-Lindemaier, "Philhéllenisme".
86 *KSA* vol. 7, p. 83.

BIBLIOGRAPHY

Friedrich Nietzsche, writings: editions and abbreviations

AC   *Der Antichrist* (*KSA* vol. 6)
BN   To be found in Nietzsche's library, cf. Max Oehler, *Nietzsches Bibliotek*, Vierzehnte Jahresgabe der Gesellschaft der Freunde ders Nietzsche-Archivs, Weimar, 1942. The data are not complete and are often unreliable.
Encyc "Encyclopädie der klassischen Philologie", lecture (1871/4), in *KGW* II 3, pp. 339–437.

FW   *Die fröhliche Wissenschaft* (*KSA* vol. 3)
GA   "Großoktav-Ausgabe": *Fr. Nietzsche, Werke*, Leipzig: Naumann/ Kröner, 1894ff.
GD   *Götzendämmerung* (*KSA* vol. 6)
GdG   "Der Gottesdienst der Griechen", lecture (1875/6), in GA 19, 99. 1–124 see *KGW* II 5, pp. 355–520.
GM   *Zur Genealogie der Moral* (*KSA* vol. 5)
GT   *Die Geburt der Tragödie aus dem Geiste des Musik* (*KSA* vol. 1)
HL   *Vom Nutzen und Nachtheil der Historie für das Leben* (= *UB* II) (*KSA* vol. 1)
JGB   *Jenseits von Gut und Böse* (*KSA* vol. 5)
KGW   Friedrich Nietzsche, *Werke Kritische Gesamtausgabe*, ed. Giorgio Colli and Mazzino Montinari, Berlin: de Gruyter, 1967.
KSA   Friedrich Nietzsche, *Sämtliche Werke Kritische Studienausgabe*, ed. Giorgio Colli and Mazzino Montinari, Berlin: de Gruyter and Munich: dtv, 1980.
KSB   Friedrich Nietzsche, *Sämtliche Briefe Kritische Studienausgabe*, ed. Giorgio Colli and Mazzino Montinari, Berlin: de Gruyter and Munich: dtv, 1986.
M   *Morgenröthe* (*KSA* vol. 3)
MA   *Menschliches, Allzumenschliches* (*KSA* vol. 2)
UB   *Unzeitgemäße Betrachtungen* (*KSA* vol. 1)
VM   *Vermischte Meinungen und Sprüche* (*KSA* vol. 2)
WPh   "Notizen zu 'Wir Philologen'" (*KSA* vol. 8)

Some writings concerning biology, culture-history and race-history in Nietzsche's library

Biology and medicine

Bagehot, Walter, *Der Ursprung der Nationen: Betrachtungen über den Einfluß der natürlichen Zuchtwahl und der Vererbung auf die Bildung politischer Gemeinwesen*, Leipzig: Brockhaus, 1874.
Bain, Alexander, *Geist und Körper*, Leipzig: Brockhaus, 1874.
Dreher, Eugen, *Der Darwinismus und seine Konsequenzen in wissenschaftlicher und sozialer Beziehung*, Halle: Pfeffer, 1882.
Foster, Michael, *Lehrbuch der Physiologie*, Heidelberg: Winter, 1881.
Galton, Francis, *Inquiries into human faculty and its development*, London: Macmillan, 1883.
His, Wilhelm, *Unsere Körperform und das physiologische Problem ihrer Entstehung*, Leipzig: Engelmann, 1874.
Nägeli, C. von, *Mechanisch-physiologische Theorie der Abstammungslehre*, Munich and Leipzig, 1884 (with many marginals, probably by Nietzsche, according to Oehler).
Rolph, W.H., *Biologische Probleme zugleich als Versuch zur Entwicklung einer rationellen Ethik*, 2nd edn, Leipzig: Engelmann, 1884.
Roux, Wilhelm, *Der Kampf der Teile im Organismus: Ein Beitrag zur*

Vervollständigung der mechanischen Zweckmäßigkeitslehre, Leipzig: Engelmann, 1881.
Schmidt, Oscar, *Deszendenzlehre und Darwinismus*, Leipzig: Brockhaus, 1873.
Thomassen, J.H., *Bibel und Natur*, 4th edn, Cologne: Mayer, 1881.

Cultural history

Caspari, Otto, *Die Urgeschichte der Menschheit: Mit Rücksicht auf die natürliche Entwickelung des frühesten Geisteslebens*, 2nd edn, Leipzig: Brockhaus, 1877 (1st edn 1872; according to Oehler Nietzsche possessed the second edition).
Lubbock, John, *Die Entstehung der Zivilisation und der Urzustand des Menschengeschlechtes*, tr. A. Passow, introductory preface R. Virchow, Jena: Costenoble, 1875, English edn 1870.
Poesche, Theodor, *Die Arier: Ein Beitrag zur historischen Anthropologie*, Jena: Costenoble, 1878.

Borrowed by Nietzsche:
Tylor, Edward B., *Die Anfänge der Cultur: Untersuchungen über die Entwicklung der Mythologie, Philosophie, Religion, Kunst und Sitte*, Leipzig: Winter, 1873.

Literature

Cancik, H., "'Judentum in zweiter Potenz': Ein Beitrag zur Interpretation von Friedrich Nietzsche, 'Der Antichrist'" in *"Mit unsrer Macht ist nichts getan": Festschrift Dieter Schellong*, Frankfurt am Main: Haag & Herchen Verlag, 1993, pp. 55–70.
Cancik, H., *Nietzsches Antike*, Stuttgart: Metzler, 1995.
Cancik, H. and Cancik-Lindemaier, H., "Philhellénisme et antisémitisme en Allemagne: le cas Nietzsche", in D. Bourel and J. Le Rider (eds), *De Sils-Maria à Jérusalem: Nietzsche et le judaïsme – les intellectuels juifs et Nietzsche*, Paris: Editions du Cerf, 1991, pp. 21–46.
Henke, D., "Nietzsches Darwinismuskritik aus der Sicht der gegenwärtigen Evolutionsforschung", *Nietzsche-Studien* 13 (1984): 189–210.
Müller-Lauter, W., "Der Organismus als innerer Kampf. Der Einfluß von Wilhelm Roux auf Friedrich Nietzsche", *Nietzsche-Studien* 7 (1978): 189–223.
Olender, M., *Les langues du paradis: Aryens et Sémites: un couple providentiel*, Paris: Gallimard, 1989.
Römer, Ruth, *Sprachwissenschaft und Rassenideologie in Deutschland*, Munich: Wilhelm Fink, 1985.
Stegmaier, W., "Darwin, Darwinismus, Nietzsche", *Nietzsche-Studien* 16 (1987): 246–87.

4

HEINE, NIETZSCHE AND THE IDEA OF THE JEW

Sander L. Gilman

THE PROBLEM

Nietzsche's works are full of false dichotomies. Of these, the most problematic politically has been his distinction between the Greek and the Jew. Indeed, if this is a polarity, his labelling of Plato as the quintessential anti-Hellene and Semite must force the reader to ask exactly what Nietzsche understood by the generalized terms "Jews" or "Semite" or "Hebrew."[1] Since the *fin-de-siècle* world was dominated by a discourse on race in which the Jew served as the central marker of difference, it is important to understand the "meaning" of the Jew for the formation of Nietzsche's sense of self.

Nietzsche perceived three moments in the natural history of the Jew: the Jew as the prophet of the Old Testament, serving the angry and holy *Jehovah*; the Jew as the archetypal wandering Christian (Saul/Paul), weak and destructive; and the Jew as contemporary, the antithesis of all decadence, self-sufficient and incorruptible.[2] These stages in a real way reflect the dichotomy of Nietzsche's identification with Heine, since they separate the "good" Jew (with whom Nietzsche identifies) from the "bad" Jew, against whom Nietzsche (still his pastor father's son) defines himself. For all three of these images serve as stereotypes of difference which are, in the last analysis, negative in that they reduce the perception of a group of single individuals to the generalities of a class. The search for the source and structure of these images of Otherness forces the reader of Nietzsche to the foundation of Nietzsche's own sense of self, for it is in terms of his sense of Otherness that the boundaries of his own self were drawn.

The most evident place of departure for an examination of Nietzsche's understanding of the Jew is that oft-quoted passage from *Beyond Good and Evil* – oft-quoted, at least, by a number of Jewish writers and anthologizers of the *fin-de-siècle* who wished to see Nietzsche as the ultimate philo-Semite, in contrast to Elisabeth Förster-Nietzsche's propagation of his image as the philosopher of proto-fascist anti-Semitism.[3] In the chapter on "Nations and fatherlands" Nietzsche praises the Jews as the purest race in Europe.

I have not met a German yet who was well disposed toward the Jews; and however unconditionally all the cautious and politically-minded repudiated real anti-Semitism, even this caution and policy are not directed against the species of this feeling itself but only against its dangerous immoderation, especially against the insipid and shameful expression of this immoderate feeling – about this, one should not deceive oneself. That Germany has amply *enough* Jews, that the German stomach, the German blood has trouble (and will still have trouble for a long time) digesting even this quantum of "Jews" – as the Italians, French, and English have done, having a stronger digestive system – that is the clear testimony and language of a general instinct to which one must act. "Admit no more new Jews! And especially close the doors to the east (also to Austria)!" Thus commands the instinct of a people whose type is still weak and indefinite, so it could easily be blurred or extinguished by a stronger race. The Jews, however, are beyond any doubt the strongest, toughest, and purest race now living in Europe: they know how to prevail even under the worst condition (even better than under favourable conditions), by means of virtues that today one would like to mark as vices – thanks above all to a resolute faith that need not be ashamed before "modern ideas", they change, *when* they change, always only as the Russian Empire makes its conquests – being an empire that has time and is not of yesterday – namely, according to the principle, "as slowly as possible."[4]

This passage is clearly linked to Nietzsche's later statement in *The Antichrist[ian]* that the Jews are the antithesis of all decadence:

Psychologically considered, the Jewish people are a people endowed with the toughest vital energy, who, placed in impossible circumstances, voluntarily are out of the most profound prudence of self-preservation, take sides with all the instincts of decadence – *not* as mastered by them, but because they divined a power in these instincts with which one could prevail against "the world." The Jews are the antithesis of all decadents: they have had to *represent* decadents to the point of illusion; with a *non plus ultra* of historic genius they have known how to place themselves at the head of all movements of decadence (as the Christianity of *Paul*), in order to create something out of them which is stronger than any *Yes-saying* part of life.[5]

Nietzsche wrote both of these seemingly positive passages about the Jew at a very special moment in the history of the Eastern European Jew. After the assassination of Tsar Alexander II in 1881, extensive anti-Semitic pogroms drove literally millions of Eastern European Jews toward the West. They spilled through Central Europe on their way to England and the United States. Their presence was viewed as a threat to the false sense of cultural homogeneity felt both by the European nationalists and by those communities of westernized Jews who had already been assimilated (at least in their self-perception) for a number of generations. Thus the influx of Eastern Jews became the enemy, *in nuce*, threatening to disrupt the fabric of European society as had the Turks centuries before.

It was not only within the popular mind that the Jew was categorized as the degenerate Other. Here Nietzsche's comments on the nature of the Jew as the anti-decadent can be understood. For the common ground of all Nietzsche's examples of decadence (and decadence is but a subclass of the concept of degeneracy) is the morose, mad figure – Poe, Kleist, Leopardi, Gogol, the madman as degenerate.[6] Late nineteenth-century medicine certainly supported Nietzsche in his linking of exactly such figures with degenerate madness, but it also saw the decadence of the Jew in a very special light: the Jew, more than any other outsider in the West, was perceived as having a special tendency toward madness. The giants of nineteenth-century German psychiatry – Emil Kraepelin, Richard Krafft-Ebbing and Theodor Kirchhoff – all agreed that the Jew was inherently degenerate.[7] Theodor Kirchhoff's view is representative:

Perhaps the Jews exhibit a comparatively greater predisposition to insanity, but this may be explained by another peculiarity apart from race, viz, the fact that the Jews intermarry very often in close family circles, the crossing is insufficient, and heredity thus gives rise, by in-breeding, to a rapidly increasing predisposition to insanity.[8]

The Western European (read: Christian or secularized Christian) mind needed to create a mental structure through which to cope with the movement of the Eastern Jews. Here was a class of individuals readily recognizable not only through their dress and appearance, but also through their language and rhetoric. This was the Other *par excellence*, the reification of the anti-Semitic caricature of the Jew in the West. Indeed, they were living proof of one of the basic tenets of late nineteenth-century popular thought. These Eastern Jews were clearly degenerate: one could sense it in their dirty, smelly, barbaric essence; one could hear it in their decayed mock-German and their crude, loud and boisterous love of argument. For the Western mind this was proof enough of the true nature of all Jews as degenerate, as overt or covert forms of the Eastern Jew; the Westernized Jew, on the other hand, was presented with the fearful specter of that which he feared he had been – the Eastern Jew seemed to be the embodiment of the image of the Jew fossilized in the bedrock of Western myth.

Kirchhoff's etiology for the prevalence of insanity among the Jews is inbreeding. But Nietzsche, as with his understanding of the nature of the physiology of the black, inverts this accepted wisdom concerning the Other.[9] For the very condemnation of the Jew as degenerate by the accepted authorities of Western society gave fulcrum he needed to move the world: he simply turned it on its head. If the anti-Semites need to see the Jew as the essence of decay, Nietzsche, placing himself in the role of the opposition *per se*, must see in the imposed isolation of the Jew a source of strength. Nietzsche is thus not a philo-Semite but rather an anti-anti-Semite. His sense of the contemporary Jew is colored by his personal opposition to the self-assumed role of the anti-Semite (including his brother-in-law Bernard Förster) as the guardian of the truths of Europe in opposition to the invading Eastern hordes. Nietzsche's anti-establishment view could never accept this; as he became more and more alienated from this view he came to identify himself with the outsider: the Pole in Germany, the Easterner in the West.

And yet there is a complex subtext to this glorification of the "mad", degenerate Jews. Nietzsche's own life-long fear of madness and collapse, a fear triggered as a 5-year-old child, laying in bed, hearing the mover's horses and wagon preparing to take him, his mother and his sister from the parsonage in Röcken where his father died. The howling of the dog which Nietzsche heard on that occasion – or which he dreamt – haunted his nightmares as an adult. Indeed, after the initial syphilitic infection (which probably occurred during his student years), the unceasing migraine headaches and the long dissociative episodes which he recounts prefigured for him the madness which had claimed his father. But there is yet another aspect of Nietzsche's sense of identification. For not only was the model of "degenerative" madness present within Nietzsche's fictive self – his sister finds it absolutely necessary to argue against this view in her writing about his illness since she, too, would thus be at risk – but the potential contextualization for this madness, the transgression against the incest taboo, was also present. (The implicit charge of incest stood as the center of the understanding of the pathology of the Jew.) The relationship between Nietzsche and his sister Elisabeth was a highly cathectic one. His opposition to her marriage was keyed to Bernard Förster's attitude toward the Jews, but it represented a basic confusion between the sexualized focus which his sister would have had to have had for him as a child. With the absence of the father she became the only possible figure upon whom to transfer his attraction for his mother. The Jews became Nietzsche and Nietzsche became the Jews – potentially mad, degenerate, opposed to political anti-Semites such as Förster. The function of the "Jews" in all of their stereotypical representation within Nietzsche's world was to externalize many of the qualities associated with Nietzsche's psychic life.

NIETZSCHE'S READING OF HEINE

Nietzsche, the 24-year-old Professor of Classical Philology at the University of Basel, saw Heine very much through his mentor Richard Wagner's anti-Semitic rhetoric as the antithesis of an Aryan/Germanic view of the world. For it was not solely the content of Heine's works which attracted the interest and opprobrium of the younger Nietzsche. In the spring of 1876 Nietzsche can still observe that:

> The influence of Hegel and Heine on German style! The latter destroyed the barely finished work of our great writers, the barely achieved feeling for the uniform texture of style. He loves the variegated fool's cloak. His inventions, his images, his observations, his *sentiments*, his vocabulary are not compatible. He controls all styles like a virtuoso, but uses this mastery only to confuse them totally. With Hegel everything is an unworthy gray: with Heine, an electric fountain of color, which however, attacks the eye as much as the gray dulls it. As a stylist Hegel is a *factor*, Heine, a *farceur*.[10]

Heine's style appears to Nietzsche as the formal equivalent to the placid sensualism of his classical world. It is the "real" world of color as opposed to the "gray" world of the photograph and yet the photograph here seems more "real". Nietzsche used specific references to Heine as an actor: he wears his style like a clown's cloak, he is a superficial *farceur*. This encoding of Heine's Jewish identity as the verbal equivalent to Wagner's Meyerbeer is clear. And yet we must ask why Nietzsche cares about this *farceur*, this comic actor. Nietzsche's approach to Heine reveals the underlying problem which haunts much of Nietzsche's antipathy towards Heine. For as early as Franz Schubert's musical interpretations of Heine's poetry, the importance of the mask in Heine's aesthetic vocabulary had been known and appreciated.[11] Nietzsche, in the period reflected in the above quotation, assumed that Heine was but a *poseur*, putting on that mask which struck his fancy at any given moment. But Nietzsche himself was evolving a complex set of theories concerning the psychological mask, theories which would dominate his view of the nature of human psychology for the nest decade. In *The Birth of Tragedy* he begins to evolve this theory of the defenses of the ego represented by the Romantic concept of the mask. (Schubert owes his idea of the mask to earlier Romantic writers such as Jean Paul Friedrich Richter.) The illusion of the mask implied, on the one hand, that the ego of the poet, his inner being, was not present in his work. This was, of course, the image of Heine as the Jewish poet merely abusing the purity of Greece for his own sensuous purposes. On the other hand, Nietzsche himself relies on the idea of the mask, taken from the theater of Sophocles, as one of the core concepts of the manner by which the inner forces of the Will are transmuted into ritual. Again it is this damn Jew, Heinrich Heine, who appears on the popular horizon, bells a-jingle, his collected works found in every middle-class drawing room, having present in debased form the pure truths of the Greco-Germanic spirit.

Heine defines the boundary for the fictive personally of the young Nietzsche. Heine is not merely one of these young writers who do not have control over their own discourse. He writes in a fragment from the fall of 1873 about Berthold Auerbach. Originally known as Moishe Baruch, Auerbach was an acculturated German Jewish writer who had written a spirited attack on the anti-Semitism of Wolfgang Menzel in 1836, but who had gone down in the annals of German culture as the author of a popular series of "Village Tales from the Black Forest" (1843–53):

Where Heine and Hegel both have had influence, as, for example, in the works of Auerbach (if not directly), and where a natural estrangement to the German language exists out of a national feeling, a "jargon" develops, which is despicable in every word, every turn of phrase.[12]

Auerbach is thus little more than a Yiddish-speaking Jew, for "jargon" is one of the pejorative terms for Yiddish. And the reason for this is that he is an inbreed result of the crossing of two perverted discourses – one, that of Hegel, because is misunderstands the basis for philosophy, the other, that of Heine, for it, like that of Auerbach, reveals an inborn inability to be anything but the language of the Jew. And this language has merely the ability to "mimic" true style, as Nietzsche notes in a fragment from the spring of 1884. What the Jews can do is to "accommodate themselves to literary forms," thus their uncanny ability as actors and the existence of writers such as Heinrich Heine.[13] Here is the boundary between Heine and Nietzsche – the difference between true command of literary form and the mere ability to mimic it.

WHERE IS GREECE?

Nietzsche's vocal and persistent condemnation of Heine tends to force a reassessment of the implications of the "meaning" of Greece for both poets. But the parallels between their world-views, at least their world-views of the classical world of ancient Greece, that utopia which defined human potential for both of them, extend into the core of their work. Nietzsche is popularly held to be the promulgator of the concept of the death of God. In *The Gay Science* he presents the often quoted anecdote of the madman who, seeking God, finds him not, but rather becomes aware of the death of the deity: "Don't we smell the divine decay? – even gods rot! God is dead! God remains dead! And we have killed him! How can we comfort ourselves – the murderers above all murderers."[14] For the madman, the symbol of the dead God is the fossilized institution of religion: "It is said that the madman broke into various churches on the same day and sang his *Requiem aeternam deo*. Led out and asked to explain, he only answered: "What are these churches, if not the tombs and monuments of God?"[15] While the madman uncovers the death of God, accusing mankind as his murderers, it is only in *Thus Spoke Zarathustra* that Nietzsche fixes the actual cause of death: "God is dead:

he died through his sympathy with man."[16] The death of God is, for Nietzsche, a direct result of the human situation. His death, however, makes little impression on the forms of human action, such as religion, for mankind is, by nature, self-contained. The forces of this world transcend the death of God, as Zarathustra proclaimed: "I even love the churches and tombs of God, when the sky shows its pure eye through their broken roofs. I enjoy sitting, like the grass and the red poppies, in destroyed churches."[17]

Nietzsche's indebtedness to Heine's image of the death of God has been widely acknowledged, as Georg Siegmund observed: "It was Heine who translated the philosophical speculation of his time into visual images in order to make the ideas more easily comprehensible."[18] Indeed, Heine's images are most striking, as in his lyric cycle *Homeward*:

> My heart is sad and filled with longing
> I think of the past;
> the world was then so comfortable
> and everyone lived so peacefully
> And everythnig is now as if displaced.
> Such crowding! such need.
> Lord God is dead above,
> and below the devil is dead.
> And everything looks so peevishly sad,
> so confusing, so rotten, so cold,
> and if it were not for the bit of love,
> there would not be a foothold anywhere.[19]

"Time past," the antiquity of his own myth of Greece, was, for Heine, the age of the gods; modern philosophy and theology sounded its death knell. The confrontation began with the confrontation between Hebrew and Hellene, between Christ and the pagan gods as described in *the City of Lucca*:

> Then suddenly a pale Jew, dripping blood, enters panting, a crown of thorns on his head and a large wooden cross on his shoulder. He threw the cross on the high table of the gods, so that the golden cups trembled and the gods became silent. They grew pale and then even paler until they vanished into a mist.[20]

Christianity is a somber replacement for the gods of Greece, and the temples of the new religion a source of superstition (as in Heine's depiction of the Cologne cathedral in *Germany: A Winter's Tale*) and morbidity, as in Heine's answer to Schiller's *the Gods of Greece*:

It is the gods who conquer you,
the new ruling, sad gods,
who, maliciously, in a sheepskin of modesty –
O, a melancholy anger appears within me,
I wish to destroy the new temple,
and fight for you, you ancient gods,
for you and your good, ambrosian law.[21]

Nietzsche's vision of the churches in which the madman reads his memorial masses, his placing of natural forces above the artificialities of religion both find their presentations in Heine's works. If Heine stands as the promulgator of the death of God in the nineteenth century, he felt that its roots were to be traced back to Kant. In Heine's *On the History of Religion and Philosophy in Germany*, published in 1834, it is Kant who is made responsible for the death of the murderer of the ancient gods:

We shall speak of this catastrophe, the January 21st of Deism, in the next chapters. A strange dread, an unusual piety will not allow us to write any further today. Our heart is full of overwhelming pity – it is the old Jehovah who is preparing himself for death. We know him so well, from the cradle in Egypt, as he was born among the divine calves, crocodiles, holy onions, ibixes and cats . . .

Don't you hear the bells ringing? Kneel, they are bringing the sacrament to a dying God.[22]

Heine and Nietzsche rejected the intrusion of the concept of the omnipotent deity into the human sphere. Emphasizing a religion of this world (a "worldly religion" of "love" or "grass and red poppies"), they relegated the role of the conventional representation of God to a negative position. For Heine, however, the death of the gods was a continual process. With the advent of Christianity the "gods" underwent a series of metamorphoses. These changes merged them into the development of Western religious thought. Such a dynamic view of the "gods" is an extraordinary view to ascribe to a Jew, especially the arch-Jewish thinker (in Nietzsche's and Wagner's view), Heinrich Heine. For the "Jew's" major contribution to the West is monotheism, according to every major thinker of the nineteenth century from Hegel through Renan to Ratzel. It is not a Jew's business to chronicle the rebirth of paganism or the death of Christianity and the rise of nationalism, for the Jew is emblematic of the origin of the first in their killing of God and excluded from the latter because of their congenital inability to be rational.

Nietzsche positions himself against Heine's view of the death of God, a view that appears in that other arch-Jew, Karl Marx, in the psychic pantheon of the anti-socialist Nietzsche. For Nietzsche, the death of God in modern times is an absolute. There is no question of the perpetuation of the religious tradition of the past for it no longer has any validity in the contemporary sphere. Thus Heine's image of the death of the gods and Nietzsche's view of the death of God, while similar in overall structure, are radically different in their final conclusions. Heine is able, at the conclusion of his life, to find solace in a simplified version of the Judaeo-Christian God; Nietzsche ends his philosophy, which strives for the realization of a world without the need for God, in the unfulfillable desire for God:

> What binds you
> with the chains of your wisdom?
> What tempts you
> into the paradise of the ancient snake?
> What steals into you from you – to you? . . .
>
> But recently so proud,
> On all the stilts of your pride!
> But recently a hermit without a God, a compatriot of the devil
> the scarlet prince of pride . . .
>
> O Zarathustra! . . .
> Self-knowing
> Self-destroying![23]

What an oriental point of view! The seeking for a temporal God, a God of this world, an answer within history! The challenge of the "external return of the same," the Schopenhauer-Vico amalgam which places human history and individual fate within the same system is precisely the view ascribed to the materialistic religion of the Jews by Ludwig Feuerbach. And Nietzsche is forced to take this position to isolate his world of ideas from that of Heine.

NIETZSCHE'S HEINE AND
HEINE'S HEINE

Heinrich Heine's own fictive personality, as embedded in his work, sets the stage for Nietzsche's response. S.S. Prawer, in what is without a doubt the best modern book on Heine, illustrates this subtlety by comparing two passages in *Atta Troll*. This is evident in Heine's attempt to introduce himself into the poem as the sick man he really was:

> This took place on the second of July
> Eighteen hundred and forty-one
> As a sickly German poet
> who, from a secure balcony
> this great . . .

At this point Heine broke off, crossed out the last two and half lines and substituted:

> And a German poet
> who observed the great spectacle
> (from a secure balcony) sighed heavily: O Fatherland . . .[24]

With this glimpse into the author's working method, it becomes quite clear that the "ironic" mask does not merely disguise the poetic ego but serves to mitigate it. Thus the pathos of the "sickly German poet" is altered to that of the ironic "great German poet" so that the immediacy of the effect is avoided. This avoidance creates an ambiguity concerning the reference to the irony. Does it stem from the ego of the poet, from yet a second mask (the poet as ironist), or merely from the most superficial and immediate use of irony as a rhetorical device?

It was only with Nietzsche's own development of the understanding of the role of the mask in all personality that he was able to come to terms with Heine. He became aware that the relationship between mask and ego was not merely one of armor to the defenseless spirit, or religious form to the inchoate forces of the Will. The mask and the ego are so closely intertwined as to make them inseparable. This fact has its clearest presentation in the preface to the second edition of *The Gay Science*:

> Those who could, would attribute to me more than foolishness, exuberance, "gay science," – for example the handful of poems which have been added to the present edition of the book – poems in which the poet mocks, in a manner which is difficult to forgive, all poets. Oh, it is not merely poets and their pretty "lyrical emotions" against which this resurrected one vents his

malice; who knows what monster of parodic material will tempt him in the future? *"Incipit tragoedia!* – thus reads the end of this thoughtful-thoughtless book – take care! Something extraordinarily evil and malicious is being announced: *incipit parodia*, without a doubt![25]

It is Nietzsche himself who serves as the object for the parody of the poems, the *Poems of Prince Free-as-a-Bird*. The mask he presents of the parodist as "malicious" and his ironic defense of lyric emotionality shows that he has come to an awareness of the omnipresence of the mask and its necessity in self-reflective art. For, like Heine's, Nietzsche's mask now serves not to conceal but to reveal. He has come to the realization of the falsity of his earlier statement that "[Eduard von] Hartmann and Heine are unconscious ironists, rogues against themselves."[26] On the contrary, Nietzsche comes to see Heine as a conscious parodist, with his parodic source, like his own, his mask and ego.[27] The role of the parodist, one which Nietzsche plays with from his earliest schoolboy versions of poems from the classical German tradition, becomes a model for his complex understanding of the interplay between the past and the present through the world of texts. For it is in the self-conscious nature of the rhetoric of expression, in the nature of words as their own world, a classical world of the book, in which Nietzsche discovers a new Heine, who looks and sounds very much like Friedrich Nietzsche. This new Heine becomes part of the internal definition of the poet rather than his boundary. And the basis for this community of spirits is Nietzsche's identification of Heine (or at least Heine's persona) as not only the exemplary Jewish (read: decadent and sensualist) poet but as the figure who defined the sick poet within the tradition of German letters. Like Keat's tuberculosis, Heine's chronic illness became of the public image of the poet.[28] The image of the sick poet is part of the public definition of Heine. (Ironically, while Nietzsche separates the image of the Jew and the image of the sufferer, Heine tropes being Jewish as being ill, seeing the stigma of race as parallel to the stigma of illness.)

In the *Poems of Prince Free-as-a-Bird* Nietzsche set a monument to his new-found understanding for Heine as the chronically ill poet. Written after Nietzsche's serious illness of 1879, the poem, "Rimus remedium," subtitled "or, how poets comfort themselves" compares his illness to Heine's "mattress tomb," the bed on which the crippled poet was trapped:

From your mouth
you salivating witch, time,
hour drips on hour,
Needlessly I cry with revulsion:
"Damn, damn the abyss
of eternity!"

"The world is made of brass:
a glowing steer,
which hears no cries of anguish.
With flying daggers pain inscribes on my limb:
"The world has no heart.
And it would be foolish to be angry with it for that reason."

Pour opium,
pour fever
poison into my brain!
And you who have been checking pulse and brow
What do you ask?
What? "For what – reward?"
Ha! Whore's curse
as well as her mockery!

No! come back!
Outside it is cold, I hear rain –
I should approach you more gently?
"Here! Here is gold: how the coins glisten! –
To call you "joy"?
To please you, fever? –

The door springs open!
Rain sprays towards my bed!
Wind extinguishes the light – disaster *en masse*!
He who does not have at least a hundred rhymes,
I would wager,
that he would come undone.[29]

While this is evidently a dramatic monologue, it is in no way clear exactly who is speaking; the striving after "happiness" is no more a leitmotif of Nietzsche's poetic fantasy than it is of Heine's. But it is the disease itself which haunts the poet. For the disease of Nietzsche's poem is syphilis, the figure of Madam Time, the whore who infects and causes the suffering of the male poet. The figure of "fever", as

early as in the poetry of Ulrich von Hutten, one of the first generation
of syphilitics in sixteenth-century Germany, is the literary icon of
the disease. Hutten again became a figure of cultural interest during
the mid-nineteenth century through the scholarship of Nietzsche's
bête noire, David Friedrich Strauss. Indeed, Nietzsche makes a clear
reference in his notes for the summer of 1877 to his reading of
Strauss on Hutten and makes that note in conjunction with the
following aphorism: "I have learned my good opinion of myself from
others and, as I think about it, I am constantly subtracting from it
when I am ill."[30] Illness causes the philosopher to restructure his
sense of self – why? Because the illness is a socially stigmatizing one,
one which he believed himself to share with his poetic *alter ego*.
There is one specific, if encoded, reference within the poem to
venereal disease. The image of the "salivating" source of the disease,
the witch Time, is a reference to one of the most public signs of the
syphilitic, the uncontrollable salivation which results from the
treatment of the disease with mercury.[31] Nietzsche, who suspects
that he (as he suspects that Heine) suffered from this unmentioned
and unmentionable disease, presents his parodic reading of Heine's
lyric within the model of the image of the syphilitic.

Nietzsche incorporates the image of the poet suffering from
venereal disease, the disease of women and time, into the model of
his relationship with Heine. Heine had given him sufficient material
for this parallel in his poem "Madam Sorrow":

> In the sunny glow of my joy
> the dance of the mosquito buzzing
> lingers happily.
> Loving friends loved me
> And in brotherhood shared with me
> my best roasts and my last ducats.
>
> Joy is past, my wallet empty
> And I have no friends anymore;
> The sunny glow has disappeared,
> vanished has the mosquito dance,
> vanished, the friends, like the mosquito, with the joy.
>
> Sorrow, my attendant, watches
> at my bedside during the winter nights.
> She wears a white undershirt,
> a black cap and dips snuff.

SANDER L. GILMAN

The snuff box squeaks dreadfully,
the old woman nods so grotesquely.

Sometimes I dream,
that joy and May have returned
And friendship and the swarms of mosquitos
the snuff box squeaks – God have mercy.
The bubble vanishes – the old woman blows her nose.[32]

The social world is now past, a world of purchased friends and lovers. Heine had actually speculated on the nature and implication of syphilis for the West in "*Vitzliputzli*," his very late evocation of the world of the sixteenth-century conquistadors.[33] In this poem, unnamed, this disease reappears in the feminized figure of the waiting death. She is blowing her nose, the displaced reference to the salivating witch of Nietzsche's text. For the "nose" is the iconic representation of the Jew's phallus throughout the nineteenth century. Indeed, Jewish social scientists such as Joseph Jacobs spend a good deal of their time denying the salience of "nostrility" as a sign of the racial cohesion of the Jews.[34] It is clear that for Jacobs (as for Sigmund Freud's friend, Wilhelm Fliess in Germany[35]) the nose is the deplaced locus of anxiety associated with the marking of the male Jew's body through circumcision, given the debate about the "primitive" nature of circumcision and its reflection on the acculturation of the Western Jew during the late nineteenth century.[36] Heine's "witch" has a dripping nose, a sign of her (his) sexuality and race.

Socially stigmatizing, syphilis shared a "classical" origin with many of the other images in Heine's and Nietzsche's common poetic vocabulary. It was part of the repertoire of Renaissance images which were incorporated into the nineteenth-century image of the classical world. "Syphilis," the eponymous Arcadian shepherd whose defiance of the gods caused him to be struck down with the disease which came to bear his name, had been created in a long Latin poem by the poet-physician Girolamo Fracastoro of Verona in 1530.[37] Drawing on the depiction of the plague in Lucretius, and prefiguring his own theory of contagion, Fracastoro created a mythic origin for the disease in the confrontation between man and the classical gods. Syphilis is a shepherd who chooses to offer sacrifices to his master, Alcithous, rather than the sun-god. The scorned god inflicts the entire countryside, including Syphilis and his master, with a new disease. Nietzsche's madman bemoaning the death of the gods and Pan's announcement of the death of the gods in Heine both incorpor-

90

ate as a source of their power the image of Syphilis and his punishment. In the Renaissance this myth was eventually understood in terms of Fracastoro's "germ" theory. For in his essay "*De Contagoine*" of 1546, Fracastoro argued that disease, including syphilis, had its origins in the transmission from humans and objects of *seminaria* (literally "germs"), a term from the vocabulary of conception and reproduction.[38] Fracastoro's association of the idea of germs (with all of the sexual connotations of that term) with the sexual origin of the disease was masked in the mythology in his *Syphilis* but quite evident in the discussion on contagion. The image of the contagious disease, as Roy Porter has noted, is one of the basic paradigms for understanding the power disease has to invade and conquer.[39] The female as the muse becomes the female as the source of contagion. And thus Fracastoro's text becomes a standard means of depicting the idea of sexually transmitted disease within the confinement and control of the literary work. It is no surprise, therefore, that Fracastoro's text had a remarkable renaissance in the late nineteenth century, that age of fascination for the world of the classical text and the age of intense syphilophobia. *Syphilis* appeared in a widely-read French translation by August Barthelemy in 1840.[40] The title page vignette of this edition presented the image of the source of infection, the image of the corrupting, aged women within the beautiful seductress. It is the image of Kakia, the classical seductress of Hercules. Such images are also part of the fictive representation of the poet which Nietzsche takes as part of his new self-definition as the chronically ill writer.

The desire for the world of health, a world outside of the image of the sick poet, becomes a *topos* about which the poet writes. Like Heine, Nietzsche, too, converted his sense of his own illness, with its "classical" origin, into the stuff of his poetry. A parallel to Nietzsche's poem may be found in the *pointe* in the last verse of Heine's "Bad dreams," in which the poet awakes from an ironically idyllic dream to find himself still chained to his bed:

> What she answered, I don't know
> For I awoke suddenly – and was
> once again an invalid, having lain
> without solace in a sickroom for many a year.[41]

The role of the ill poet permits Heine (and later Nietzsche) to achieve distance from the reality of suffering. It permits him to contain the reality of his own pain in the confines of a world of words, a world created by the poet and, therefore, always (he hopes) within the poet's control. All illness and torment are transferred to the fictive mask, which becomes a separate reality in which the ego is mirrored. This division of personality, the escape from the role of the ill poet which is present in both of the Heine quoted above, is revealed in the *pointe* to be but a mask for the "reality" of suffering. Nietzsche takes over this structure in *"Rimus remedium,"* with, however, a substantial alteration. "Madam Sorrow" becomes transmuted into the image of time, the cause of the poet's suffering. The passage of time, the naturalness of entropy, replaces the fear of contagion. Disease becomes a "natural" process. The dialogue between time and the poet, like the dream sequences in both Heine poems, merges one fictive mask with another. The culmination of Nietzsche's poem, the presence of death in the form of the intrusion of the external world into the sickroom as the aged, corrupt, indeed, syphilitic woman awaiting his death for her own gain. It is the rhymes of the poet which protect him from ultimate dissolution.

Indeed, Nietzsche's Wagnerian attack on Heine's style is here reversed. For Nietzsche, inscribing his own fictive persons within the conventions of the representation of the classical world of his (and Heine's) disease, presents the fantasy, the mask, through which all sick poets desire to comfort themselves. They view themselves as immortal through their works. They wish to control and distance their disease, their mortality, through the presumed immortality of their verse. Nietzsche is quite aware that this is but a mask, and thus the final parodic *pointe* establishes the nature of the mask as mask, without negating its vital role in the expression of the poet's ego.[42] In doing so he incorporated his image of Heine, that arch-poet, here not the Jew but the syphilitic, as the internalized model for the stance which the poet must take suspended between the inchoate realities of his suffering and his need to articulate this suffering, to give it form, in order also to give it meaning.

Nietzsche's identification with Heine reached its height in his final major work *Ecce Homo*. In the section "Why I am so clever" Nietzsche confesses:

> Heinrich Heine gave me the highest concept of the poet. I have looked in vain in all of the kingdoms of the centuries for an equivalently sweet and passionate music. He possessed that divine malice without which I cannot conceive of perfection. – I regard the value of men of races in the light of how much they do not isolate the god from the satyr. In the future it will be said that Heine and I are by far the primary artists of the

German language – and inconceivable distance from everything created by mere Germans.[43]

Here the "malice," which Nietzsche attributed to his own parodic attempts in *The Gay Science* forms the bridge between his fictive personality and that he ascribes to (and, indeed, finds in) Heine. Nietzsche, who emphasized the Slavic source of his family, isolates himself, with the Jew Heine, from the stylistically banal camp of the Germans. It is the power of disease which links all outsiders. It is the awareness of that godly "malice," as represented in Fracastoro's image of the classical world, which forms the bond between the fictive personalities of these two men which is incorporated in Nietzsche's final judgement of Heine.

He becomes aware that Heine's greatest talent was the use of his parodic, linguistic facility to probe and present his own fictive personality. It is precisely this quality which had been denied Heine by Wagner. Nietzsche sought, and found in Heine, a poet whose prime consideration was the presentation of the internal self-image of the writer in self-consciously artistic form. This preoccupation extended even to the presentation of a classical world which mirrors the basic human desires and faults of the poet. The masks that Heine created in search of the classical myth, those of Hellene and Hebrew, of the exile and death of the gods, are but extensions of the sick poet's ego. Thus Nietzsche began his debate with the shadow of Heine by rejecting an ego-oriented image of the past. As he came more and more to the awareness that his image, too, was determined by his own desires, his internalization of Heine also altered. By the end of his creative period, Nietzsche assumed a sense of modified autoscopy, in which Heine became his historical *Doppelgänger*, a figure in which he found himself recapitulated. His awareness of the parallels between his fate and that of Heine led to this identification with the poet. Nietzsche knew Heine's work well even when, under the influence of Wagner, he sought to reject him. When, in the course of his break with Wagner, he begins to read Heine's image of the sick poet as the mirror of his (Nietzsche's) own literary biography, his image of the poet becomes more and more autobiographical. Nietzsche's Heine thus becomes the image of the philosopher as poet, and less and less that of the Jew. No longer Jew, no longer *farceur*, Heine becomes, for the older Nietzsche, the one socially acceptable vision of himself as diseased. He is the ill poet – Heine – the image which he had so long denied. And yet as Nietzsche rejects

Wagner and transvalues Heine, his condemnation of Wagner is that he learned his trade at the feet of the Jews.[44] And these two "Jews" – Heine the convert to Christianity out of convenience and Wagner the anti-Semite with a putative Jewish father – *Doppelgänger* and father – became in the summer of 1888: "the two greatest confidence men, which Germany has given Europe."[45] In this final transvaluation, Nietzsche's ability to separate the two categories, the Jew as mimic from the Jew as diseased poet, collapses, and Heine becomes, as he was a decade earlier, merely a Jew, with all of the negative connotations of that concept for the Teuton hidden within Friedrich Nietzsche, the diseased poet.

JEWS AND CHRISTIANS

If Nietzsche found that he must defend the contemporary Jew from the attacks of the anti-Semites in the West, he had no such compunction about the Christian, for the Christians were the powerful majority against which he wished to defend himself. They were Bernard Förster incarnate. However, Nietzsche saw the softness and weakness of Christianity, its degeneracy, as lying specifically in its Jewish roots. The strength of the Old Testament became the smothering "love" of the New Testament. Nietzsche was writing about texts, about books, about language. This becomes clear when, in *The Antichrist[ian]*, he contrasts the primitive law of Manu with the New Testament:

> Ultimately, it is a matter of the end to which one lies. That "holy" ends are lacking in Christianity is my objection to its means. Only *bad* ends: poisoning, slander, negation of life, contempt for the body, the degradation and self-violation of man through the concept of sin – consequently its means too are bad. It is with an opposite feeling that I read the law of Manu, an incomparably spiritual and superior work: even to mention it in the same breadth with the Bible would be a sin against the spirit. One guesses immediately: there is a real philosophy behind it, in it, not merely an ill-smelling Judaine of rabbinism and superstition; it offers even the most spoiled psychologist something to chew on. Not to forget the main point, the basic difference from every kind of bible: here the *noble* classes, the philosophers and the warriors, stand above the mass; noble values everywhere, a feeling of perfection, an affirmation of life, a triumphant delight in oneself and in life –

the *sun* shines on the whole book. All the things on which Christianity vents its unfathomable meanness – procreation, for example, woman, marriage – are here treated seriously, with respect, with love and trust.[46]

The laws of Manu are positive, strengthening the nature of man in the world; the New Testament is destructive of life. But all relate to the idea of the female and the image of the sexual. The incest taboo, violated by the Jews, becomes the hidden context for the glorification of the East, the truth of the "real" Orient, the fantasy East to be found in the world of words of Arthur Schopenhauer, a world of "India," without the "crudity" of Judaism.[47] Thus the world of the Christian represents the false world of the East. Sexuality and corruption, the idea of the woman, form the centerpiece for Nietzsche's understanding of the Jew in his (yes: his) manifestation as the Christian.

Nietzsche's understanding of the nature of the New Testament is important, for he sees it as an "ill-smelling Judaine of rabbinism and superstition" ("Judaine" is Nietzsche's neologism for the evil essence of Jewishness). The entire phrase points not to an image of the Jews of the New Testament, but to the rhetoric of late nineteenth-century anti-Semitism with its stress on the false logic, the rabbinical sophistries, and the superstitions of the Jews linked to their appearance and smell. The latter was associated by anti-Semites such as Theodor Fritsch with "their uncleanliness and use of garlic."[48] The synesthesia of smelling the illogic, of dirty sophistry, reappears in *The Antichrist[ian]* in a much more specific context:

> *What follows from this?* That one does well to put on gloves when reading the New Testament. The proximity of so much uncleanliness almost forces one to do this. We would no more choose the "first Christians" to associate with than Polish Jews – not that one even required any objection to them: they both do not smell good.[49]

The first Christians were really just Eastern Jews. They contaminated through their very presence. Their presence, however, is felt through the word, through their language, through their rhetoric. And these external signs and symptoms reflected the inherent sexual corruption.

It is the mode of discourse of the New Testament the Nietzsche is attacking, as much as its contents. The common ground of the

SANDER L. GILMAN

New Testament and contemporary rabbinic tradition lies in their shared lying and corrupting rhetoric. But Christianity is the rhetoric of power with which, whether he wishes it or not, Nietzsche is condemned to be linked. His attempt at exorcizing the Christian demons that lurk within his self-perception, his violent parodies of the style of the New Testament in *Thus Spoke Zarathustra*, only heighten his self-awareness of his existence as a representative of the most dominant of all groups, the most powerful, the most frightening: the German Christians.[50] For they are the "healthy," the norm which defines the diseased, and he possesses within himself the hidden Jew, the stigma of disease and madness which marks the Jew. This is an impossible position in which to be placed. Nietzsche must project this sense of marginality into the world he has created within the text. And he must do it in a way which is acceptable to the consistence of the fictive universe which he has constructed. Thus the "Jews," because they are the primary referent for disease and sexuality in his time, must be idealized, for they represented, within his world, the boundaries of his own personality. It is the "Christian," the Jew at one remove, who can serve as the "new Jew" in this system. But he cannot escape the representation of difference which he has so completely internalized. When he attempts to vilify that which he hates most within himself, he uses the German Christian rhetoric that labels the Eastern Jew as the epitome of Otherness. Nietzsche acknowledges, if but as a reflex, his role as a member of the dominant society in condemning that society. He is, for the moment, the self-conscious Antichrist damning the Christians as merely Eastern Jews.

Thus, Nietzsche invests with the most anger those otherwise inarticulate hatreds that reflect his inner fears. To no little extent these fears are associated with Christianity. We might speculate that his concept of Christianity is loaded with the anger and disappointment felt by the young Nietzsche at the death of his father, who not only represented the Church in his role as a minister but also held the same patriarchal position in the youthful Nietzsche's world as does the Church in the philosopher's mental universe. When Nietzsche addresses the question of Jews in the contemporary world, Jews as the object of hatred, he sees a problem that is the direct result of this paternalism and he is able to condemn anti-Semitism as a social evil; when he strives to characterize the inconstant nature of Christianity, he falls back upon that rhetoric which for him (as a German Christian) and his time possessed the greatest force, the rhetoric of anti-Semitism. Thus the Jews can be both a positive and a negative image within Nietzsche's system: positive, when seen as the objects of Christian anti-Semitism (a fact that reveals the true nature of Christianity as evil and destructive); negative, when used as the most accessible analogue for that which Nietzsche feared most within himself – the German Christian. The result is a complex form of self-hatred, a self-hatred that draws upon anti-anti-Semitic rhetoric as well as anti-Semitic rhetoric for its articulation. Yet his rhetoric is not unique even in this very specific context: it has an analogue and its justification in the verbal representation of the image of the Eastern Jew within the work of Heinrich Heine, a writer with whom Nietzsche identified and who made the use of this image acceptable because he was himself publicly identified as the arch-Jew.

NOTES

1 All references to Nietzsche's works in this chapter are to the only complete critical edition, Friedrich Nietzsche, *Sämtliche Werke: Kritische Studienausgabe*, ed. Giorgio Colli and Mazzino Montinari (Berlin: de Gruyter and Munich: dtv, 1980), here vol. 13, p. 114. All translations are by the author; some of these translations have been modified from those by Walter Kaufmann. Hereafter this edition will be referred to as *KSA*. The question of the false dichotomy between the Hebrew and the Hellene may rest on the reading of Nietzsche's thought in the light of "Max Stirner's" faulty distinction between *"Die Alten"* and *"Die Neuen,"* which is itself riddled with anti-Semitic references. In general on the question see Werner J. Dannhauser, *Nietzsche's View of Socrates* (Ithaca: Cornell University Press, 1974).

2 *KSA* vol. 3, pp. 45–6; vol. 6, pp. 246–7; vol. 6, pp. 192–3. The following titles are of interest for the present chapter: Gerd-Günter Grau, *Christlicher Glaube und intellekuelle Redlichkeit: Eine religionsphilosophiche Studie über Nietzsche* (Frankfurt am Main: Schulte-Bulmke, 1958), pp. 201–39; Hermann Wein, *Positives Antichristentum: Nietzsches Christusbild im Brennpunkt nachchristlicher Anthropologie* (The Hague: Nijhoff, 1962), pp. 89–93; Wiebrecht Ries, *Friedrich Nietzsche: Wie die "wahre Welt" endlich zur Fabel wurde* (Hanover: Schlüter, 1977), pp. 62–4; J.P. Stern, *A Study of Nietzsche* (Cambridge: Cambridge University Press, 1979).

3 Of the early attempts to categorize Nietzsche as a philo-Semite the most interesting works are: Josef Schrattenholz (ed.), *Anti-Semiten Hammer* (Düsseldorf: E. Lintz, 1894); Anon., "Friedrich Nietzsche über die Juden," *Allgemeine Israelitische Wochenschrift Teschurim*, 29 March 1895; Anon., "Friedrich Nietzsche über die Juden!" *General-Anzeiger für die gesamten Interessen des Judentums*, 30 October 1902; Achad Ha'am, "Nietzscheanismus und Judentum," *Ost und West* 2 (1902): 145–52, 242–54; Samuel Jankolowitz, "Friedrich Nietzsche und der Antisemitismus," *Israelitisches Wochenblatt* (Zurich), 13 November 1908; Anon., "Wie klein mancher Große ist . . .", *Deutsche Sociale*

Blätter, 12 December 1908; Josef Stolzing, "Friedrich Nietzsche und Judentum," *Deutsche Tageszeitung* (Berlin), 10 January 1909; Eberhard Kraus, "Wie Friedrich Nietzsche über das Judentum urteilte," *Deutsche Zeitung* (Berlin), 1 January 1909; and Gustav Witkowsky, "Nietzsches Stellung zum Zionismus," *Jüdische Rundschau*, 2 May 1913. An extraordinary book by an exiled German Jew appeared in Sweden during the Nazi period. It is an example of a "Jewish" reading at a time during which Nietzsche had become one of the cultural idols of the Nazis. See Richard Maximilian Lonsbach (i.e. Richard Maximilian Cahen), *Friedrich Nietzsche und die Juden* (Stockholm: Bermann-Fischer, 1939; reprinted Bonn: Bouvier Verlag Herbert Grundmann, 1985). Of the recent scholarship the best attempts to understand Nietzsche's image of the Jew are Harry Neumann, "The case against apolitical morality: Nietzsche's interpretation of the Jewish instinct," in James C. O'Flaherty, Timothy F. Sellner and Robert M. Helm (eds), *Studies in Nietzsche and the Judaeo-Christian Tradition* (Chapel Hill: University of North Carolina Press, 1985), pp. 29–46; Gert Mattenklott, "Nietzscheanismus und Judentum," *Jahrbuch: Archiva Bibliographia Judaica E. V.* 1 (1985): 57–71; Léon Poliakov, *The History of Anti-Semitism*, vol. 4: *Suicidal Europe, 1870–1933*, tr. George Klin (Oxford: Oxford University Press, 1985), pp. 8–11; Jacob Golomb, "Nietzsche on Jews and Judaism," *Archiv für Geschichte der Philosophie* 67 (1985): 139–61; George Steiner, Robert Boyers and Taylor Stochr, *Jewish Themes: Holocaust, Dispersal, Preservation* (Saratoga Springs, NY: Skidmore College, 1985); Arnold M. Eisen, "Nietzsche and the Jews reconsidered," *Jewish Social Studies* 48 (1986): 1–14; Jacob Golomb, "Nietzsche's Judaism of power," *Revue des études juives* 147 (1988): 335–85; Michael F. Duffy and Willard Mittelman, "Nietzsche's attitudes towards the Jews," *Journal of the History of Ideas* 49 (1988): 301–17; Sigrid Bauschinger, Susan L. Cocalis and Sarah Lennox (eds), *Nietzsche haute: die Rezeption seines Werks nach 1968* (Berne: Francke, 1988); Dominique Bourel and Jacques Le Rider (eds), *De Sils-Maria á Jerusalem: Nietzsche et le judaisme, les intellectuels juifs et Nietzsche* (Paris: Cerf, 1991); Eva M. Knodt, "The Janus face of decadence: Nietzsche's genealogy and the rhetoric of anti-Semitism," *The German Quarterly* 66 (1993): 160–78; Janet Lungstrum, "In Agon with Nietzsche: studies in modernist creativity" (Dissertation, University of Virginia, 1993); Sarah Kofman, *Le Mépris des juifs: Nietzsche, les juifs, l'antisémitisme* (Paris: Editions Galilee, 1994). On Elisabeth Förster-Nietzsche's anti-Semitism see H.F. Peters, *Zarathustra's Sister: The Case of Elisabeth and Friedrich Nietzsche* (New York: Crown, 1977) and Roderick Stackelberg, "Nietzsche and the Nazis: the *völkisch* reaction to Nietzschean thought," *Research Studies* 51 (1983): 36–46. See also Alfred D. Low, *Jews in the Eyes of the Germans: From the Enlightenment to Imperial Germany* (Philadelphia: Institute for the Study of Human Issues, 1979).

4   *KSA* vol. 5, p. 193.

5   *KSA* vol. 6, pp. 192–3, cf. Vol. 12, p. 532.

6   *KSA* vol. 5, p. 224. See especially Sander L. Gilman and J. Edward Chamberlin (eds), *Degeneration: The Dark Side of Progress* (New York: Columbia University Press, 1985) pp. 72–95.

7 A detailed survey of the nineteenth-century literature on this topic was undertaken by Alexander Pilcz, "Geistesstörungen bei den Juden," *Wiener klinische Rundschau* 14 (1901): 888–908. That this was not merely a question of esoteric medical interest can be seen in a popular essay on this topic, "Einfluß der Rasse auf pathologische Erscheinungen," *Proschaskas illustrirte Monatsbände* 8 (1896): 198–201, which contains much the same information about Jews and insanity. On the background see Sander L. Gilman, *Difference and Pathology: Stereotypes of Sexuality, Race, and Madness* (Ithaca: Cornell University Press, 1985), pp. 150–74.

8 Quoted from the contemporary English translation, Theodor Kirchhoff, *Handbook of Insanity for Practitioners and Students* (New York: William Wood and Co., 1893), p. 23.

9 See Sander L. Gilman, *On Blackness without Blacks: Essays on the Image of the Black in Germany* (Boston: G.K. Hall, 1982), pp. 93–118.

10 *KSA* vol. 8, p. 281; cf. vol. 7, p. 595.

11 Jeffrey L. Sammons, *Heinrich Heine, the Elusive Poet*, Yale Germanic Studies 3 (New Haven: Yale University Press, 1969).

12 *KSA* vol. 7, p. 598.

13 *KSA* vol. 11, p. 84.

14 *KSA* vol. 12, p. 157.

15 *KSA* vol. 13, p. 157.

16 *KSA* vol. 13, p. 114.

17 *KSA* vol. 13, p. 193.

18 Georg Siegmund, *Nietzsches Kunde vom Tode Gottes* (Berlin: Morus, 1964), p. 128.

19 Heinrich Heine, *Sämtliche Schriften*, ed. Klaus Briegleb, 12 vols (Berlin: Ullstein, 1981), vol. 1, pp. 127–8. Where volumes of the new critical editions exist, the texts have been checked against them; except where otherwise noted, the translations are my own.

20 Heine, *Sämtliche Schriften*, vol. 3, p. 394.

21 Heine, *Sämtliche Schriften*, vol. 1, p. 188.

22 Heine, *Sämtliche Schriften*, vol. 5, p. 543.

23 *KSA*, vol. 6, pp. 391–2.

24 S.S. Prawer, *Heine, The Tragic Satirist* (Cambridge: Cambridge University Press, 1961), p. 65.

25 *KSA* vol. 3, p. 346. On the idea of parody in Nietzsche see Sander L. Gilman, *Nietzschean Parody: An Introduction to Reading Nietzsche* (Bonn: Bouvier, 1976).

26 *KSA* vol. 7, p. 659.

27 Cf. Beda Allemann, *Ironie und Dichtung* (Pfullingen: Neske, 1969) and Charles I. Glicksberg, *The Ironic Vision in Modern Literature* (The Hague: Nijhoff, 1969).

28 *KSA* vol. 3, p. 647.

29 *KSA* vol. 8, p. 391.

30 W.J. Brown, *Syphilis and Other Venereal Diseases* (Cambridge, Mass.: Harvard University Press, 1970).

31 Heine, *Sämtliche Schriften*, vol. 11, p. 114.

32 Heine, *Sämtliche Schriften*, vol. 11, pp. 56–75. See the discussion in David

Hobbs, "Heine's *Ludwig Börne: Eine Denkschrift*: a literary analysis" (Dissertation, Cornell University, 1976).

33 Joseph Jacobs, *Studies in Jewish Statistics, Social, Vital, and Anthropometric* (London: D. Nutt, 1891), pp. xxxii–xxxiii.

34 See Frank J. Sulloway, *Freud: Biologist of the Mind* (New York: Basic Books, 1979), pp. 147–58.

35 See the discussion in Sander L. Gilman, *Disease and Representation: Images of Illness from Madness to AIDS* (Ithaca: Cornell University Press, 1985), pp. 182–201.

36 Geoffrey Eatough (ed. and tr.), *Fracastoro's Syphilis* (Liverpool: Francis Cairns, 1984). See also John E. Ziolokowski, "Epic conventions in Fracastoro's poem Syphilis," *Altro Polo* (1984): 57–73.

37 See Hieronymous Fracastoro, *Drei Bücher von den Kontagien, den kontagiösen Krankheiten und dren Behandlung (1546)*, tr. and intro. Viktor Fossel (Leipzig: Johann Ambrosius Barth, 1910), specifically the section on "Syphilis" (pp. 67–70) in which he stresses the sexual origin of the disease.

39 Roy Porter, "Ever since Eve: the fear of contagion," *Times Literary Supplement*, 27 May–2 June 1988, p. 582.

40 August Barthelemy (tr.), *Syphilis: Poeme en deux chants* (Paris: Béchet junior et Labé & Bohaire, 1840).

41 Heine, *Sämtliche Schriften*, vol. 11, p. 118.

42 See Sander L. Gilman, "'Braune Nacht': Friedrich Nietzsche's Venetian poems," *Nietzsche-Studien* 1 (1972): 247–60 and "Incipit parodia: the function of parody in the poetry of Friedrich Nietzsche," *Nietzsche-Studien* 4 (1975): 52–74.

43 *KSA* vol. 6, p. 286.

44 *KSA* vol. 11, p. 472.

45 *KSA* vol. 12, p. 500.

46 *KSA* vol. 6, p. 240.

47 See Poliakov, *History* vol. 4, p. 6.

48 Fritsch was a contemporary of Förster. Cited here from Theodore Fritsch, *Handbuch der Judenfrage*, 38th edn (Leipzig: Hammer, 1935), pp. 27–8.

49 *KSA* vol. 6, p. 223.

50 See Donald F. Nelson, "Nietzsche, Zarathustra and *Jesus redivivus*," *Germanic Review* 48 (1973): 175–88.

5

NIETZSCHE ON JUDAISM AND EUROPE

Josef Simon
Translated by John Stanley

When Nietzsche speaks of truth, he is concerned with the problem of a "subjective" access to an "objective" truth. The philosophical tradition had two solutions to this problem. The first one was the "invention of the philosopher": this was a person who, unlike everyone else, had the unique capacity to "perceive" "the" truth and "comprehend the eternal unchangeable being."[1] His only remaining problem was how to "communicate" the truth to the others, who were unable to comprehend it in the same way for themselves. This implies that the problem of language is subordinate to epistemology. The other, later solution to this problem was seen in the participation of human thinking in *divine* cogitation. In this context human thinking considered itself to be a "derivative" (*Ektypus*) of a divine archetype (*Archetypus*). This approach *necessarily* assumes that God's *existence* must be *thought*. As the all-powerful and benevolent God, he should mediate the truth to humanity "down below." One then finds in Descartes's philosophy the next logically consistent step: he transplaced this act of mediation into his "proof of God's existence," which every rational being should be able to follow.

These two approaches, the invention of the philosopher and the mediation of truth by God, work in collaboration in European thinking. Nietzsche attributes this invention of the philosopher – which is distinguished conceptually from the sophist – to Socrates. Socrates is for Nietzsche the first "theoretical man," i.e., the first person who understood truth in an absolute sense in spite of all the *peculiarities*[2] of individual perception. This thought did not exist in polytheistic religions such as that of the Greeks. Rather, here the mediation of the *one* truth is a task to be accomplished by the "Logos." It must convince everyone of a certain proposition's truth: thus, by definition this conception of the "Logos" presupposes that every individual is in principle willing to have himself proved wrong. On the other hand, Nietzsche sees the notion of a *divine* mediation of the *one, single* truth as one originating in Judaism. Judaic monotheism does not gain access to truth by way of a "mediating" Logos or a "convincing" conversation. Rather, it is certain of its truth as revealed by its people's God – the one and only God, who has adjoined himself with a particular folk and therewith provided this people with their unity.

GOOD AND EVIL – THE "ABSOLUTE" PERSPECTIVE

Nietzsche's confrontation with *both* of these attempted solutions to the problem of truth defined his thinking: at first glance, both approaches seem to accomplish the same thing for the European intellectual spirit (*Geist*). Yet – though historically closely intertwined – conceptually, they are fundamentally different. The *idea of the Logos* as such implies a-historicity: any rational being is capable – fundamentally and at any particular time – of participating in the "Logos" and, in so doing, of shedding his own particularities and peculiarness. On the other hand, mediation through this one and only personal God is something special. It is valid only for this one people that God has gathered around himself, i.e., for the Jews. In its own view, this people had always inhabited this place of truth due to their ancestry, for God has made a covenant with their forefathers. And in Christianity it is the community of Christians – which is also considered to be something special, something mediated by God's grace – that takes the place of truth. The Jewish God is the *one* God of justice, whereas the Greeks had a special goddess or, respectively, their special gods of justice. Consequently, justice was no more a virtue that served to unite the Greek gods than was truthfulness. For this reason, these could become for the Greeks topics of "logical" discussions. Contrarily, the often "logically" incomprehensible justice of the Jewish God stands directly *for* the truth, and Christians have retained this notion in spite of their close association with the Platonic and Aristotelian philosophies.

The covenant between God and his people is understood to be something special: it has a delimiting function. Everyone *within* this delimitation is equal before the law of God. Nietzsche responded to the question "For what should Europe be thankful to the Jews?" with the answer:

For a lot, for good and bad, and most of all for that one thing that is simultaneously of the worst and the best: for the great moral style, for the awe-fulness and majesty of the absolute demands, of the absolute interpretations, for the whole romanticism and sublimity of the moral dubiousness. Thus, Europe should be grateful for precisely the most attractive, treacherous and exquisite part of this kaleidoscope of colors and seduction to life, in whose afterglow the heavens[3] – the evening heavens – of our European culture shimmer today, or, perhaps, are shimmering out. We artists among the observers and philosophers are, well, grateful to the Jews for that.[4]

This "great moral style" is a consequence of an individual's *certitude* that he participates in God's justice. The individual gains this certitude through the covenant, yet it is already mediated to each individual through his affiliation with a people.[5] Of course, Nietzsche also sees in Judaism the "priestly people of resentment *par exellence*."[6] "The priests" are indeed "mediators" between God and the people, but only as custodians of the pure immediacy which was actually already present in a natural way due to this affiliation with a people. The priests make decisions concerning purity and impurity and thereby concerning a given immediacy to God or, in the opposing cases, a lack of immediacy that has to be re-established through rituals. For this reason, Nietzsche named the *Jewish people as a whole* priestly, and, in light of the fact that purity and impurity serve as the criteria for the level of one's affiliation with this people and, thus, of justice, this description seems to fit. By contrast, Socrates argued that this criterion is to be found in the Logos, which should be able to mediate *logically* the *idea* of justice to everyone – even to those who are not philosophers. The Socratic idea of justice contains as an essential element the notion that it extends beyond Attic particularness, or any particularness whatsoever for that matter.

In Nietzsche's view, this "great moral style" that had shaped Europe comes from Judaism. Thus, Europe did not develop this lifestyle "logically"; on the contrary, this style shaped Europe's intellectual spirit. The question: 'What is the distinguishing element of this style?' is itself one that inquires about this style as something *peculiar*. For Nietzsche, its peculiarness is characterized by two facts: (1) that evaluating is done according to the opposing concepts "good and evil," and (2) that this way of evaluating is not considered to be

103

"anything special." An alternative to this peculiarity would be to evaluate according to the "distancing"[7] opposites "good or bad." Although it refers to the "highest" value in both cases, the word "good" can mean radically different things depending upon whether its devaluing counterpart is "bad" or "evil." This difference in the meaning of "good" permeates from the historical linguistic usage into the highest value. Thus, the meaning is *dependent* upon the reigning linguistic usage, which declares itself to be good and proper.

When Nietzsche speaks of a "genealogy" of morals, his linguistic, historical hypothesis is that the value "good" as defined in a semantic opposition to "bad" is actually "older" than this value in the semantic pair "good and evil." According to this hypothesis, it was those who *reigned over* the then current linguistic usage that characterized themselves as "good."[8] However, when those who are called "bad" in this reigning perspective see themselves from their own perspective as being "good," this leads to a struggle over the *power* to evaluate. The people that up until now had considered themselves to be "bad" gain thereby a perspective in which they appear to be better than and superior to those who are *actually ruling*. They considered their own view as one opposed to *any* particular, ruling view; they thought of their own perspective as an "absolute" view, as the one that no human being had, as one not originating from a particular person. But, in actuality, this is *no longer* a "view"; rather, it is more of a lifestyle that is subject to *divine* law, or, perhaps one could say, a life in justice devoid of any *perspectival* values that would have to be defended against other ways of evaluating.

The usage of the word "good" as the semantic opposite to "evil" can be defended in spite of this factual inferiority, for the words "good" and "evil" *ought* to retain their "meaning" above and beyond any factually existing "usage." These words are thought to have an "absolute" meaning, one derived from an "absolute" point of view that no person really holds. The "internal" solidity of this linguistic usage is, then, tantamount to its "justification." According to Nietzsche, the European intellectual spirit was formed by this "morality," one which believes of itself that it no longer needs to defend itself against other ways of living – in spite of its own particularity. It removes itself from its particular origin by claiming to be unconditional. (Hegel calls "morality" "the intellectual spirit (*Geist*) which is certain of itself."[9]) In its evaluating spirit (*Geist der Wertung*), it is simultaneously the absolute determination of values for "the intellectual spirit" (*des Geistes*). The course of worldly events in no way weakens the virtue of this morality, and, thus, in keeping with the Kantian concept of the sublime, Nietzsche can speak of the "romanticism and sublimity of moral dubiousness."

This "romanticism" lies in the "absoluteness" of meanings found in the *language* of morality. Instead of a language with the usual meanings formed by speaking individuals, this is considered to be a language of "absolute" meanings. It is first with these "meanings" that the language is capable of grasping something "spiritual" (*etwas Geistiges*) which is not in need of a defense. The "sublimity" comes from the self-certitude of this moral usage of language in the face of the reigning powers. As Nietzsche understood it, post-Socratic Greek philosophy had a similar intention. But here a "logic" was developed in order to ground this absolute claim. It was not until Kant that the issue of founding a morality in "pure reason" becomes a *problem* for moral thinking once again. As is well known, he sees the solution to this problem in the categorical imperative of pure reason: the imperative demands that one act only according to those maxims which could simultaneously serve as "a rule for general legislation."

However, this restricts the function of pure *practical* reason to examining those *given maxims* that are themselves – even if only provisionally and within the particular framework of their "subject-ive" validity – already "oughts." Thus, this line of reasoning is devoid of all "dubiousness" that would result from the naturalistic fallacy of proceeding from "is" to "ought." It is in order to preserve its rational foundation that the domain of morality is restricted to the maxims. Yet this results in a certain ambiguity: of all those concepts for the different types of actions named in the maxims, which is applicable to a given, concrete ethical case? We find ourselves faced once again with the issue of determining linguistic usage: is it the subject that is speaking from his *own* contemporary perspective that determines this usage, or are we dealing here with the presumption that there are "absolute meanings," independent from all perspectives?

According to Kant's critical position, the acting individual must determine and know (*wissen*) for himself (in his own conscience (*Gewissen*)), if – in light of the underlying *concepts* – what he is planning to do is the type of thing that a rationally examined maxim would *generally* command or prohibit. As a result of this "critique" of the domain of *pure* practical reason, *reason* demands a legal system. The law serves as an authority that limits the sphere of freedom of each acting individual in order to preserve the freedom of all individuals. The legal system reserves for itself the right to name deeds under "finite" conditions via the person of a judge. When Nietzsche writes that "the evening heavens" of "our European culture" are shimmering in "the afterglow" emanating this "moral dubiousness," he initially sees this "dubiousness" with reference to its consequences in a favorable light. According to Kant, it is impossible to live without the rights of humans – rights that take the place of this "heaven" of "absolute meanings" whose sun set with the "critique" of reason; thus, these rights are the "holiest entity" that "God has on this earth."[10] For Kant, "life" refers to the capacity to "act based upon one's own [subjective] ideas" [or "representations" (*Vorstellungen*[11])], which entails that one be able to determine and defend one's own perspective. Clashes are, however, unavoidable when everyone lives according to their own ideas, especially since this includes their ideas concerning what is "good" and "evil." "In life," the moral self-certitude of one person invariably comes into conflict with the moral self-certitude of others, and what one person might describe using the "hard name of a lie" could very well be seen by another as well-mannered, polite behavior,[12] as conduct that preserves communicability. Different persons cannot live *together* when the legal system does not delegate – and with an "authorization to coerce" according to positive laws – how "the arbitrary freedom of one person" can *actually* "co-exist with the freedom of everyone else."[13]

Nietzsche sees in these moral clashes (and in this moral dubiousness) an artistic refinement of opposites, a shift to a "spiritual realm" that results in this "kaleidoscope of colors" – and in this seductiveness. This "kaleidoscope of colors" – produced by the moral controversies and projected upon the area where acts are *named* – is something for which only the "artistes among the observers and philosophers" could be, "well, grateful to the Jews."[14] The "artistes" are masters of disguises and masks. "Every deep intellect (*Geist*) requires a mask";[15] it appears only in masks. To converse with one another while conceding, on the one hand, that signs have *different* meanings and simultaneously assuming, on the other, that their meanings are also "absolute" – this is the *art* of speaking as the production and culture of style and illusion. This is the "great style" of the intellectual spirit (*Geist*) as formed under these moral conditions.

Europe is grateful to Judaism for *this* "intellectual spirit"; the "genealogy of morals" is simultaneously the genealogy of that which

Europeans call "the" intellectual spirit. This spirit was born out of the self-awareness of a type of inferiority, out of the power of a language in which a people – while still considered to be inferior – did not characterize themselves as "bad," but as "good" – although with another meaning, namely as "the" people of God. This people even considers "natural" living conditions to be bound up with a life within God's justice; this people lives literally "in" this justice inasmuch as they take their nourishment from those foodstuffs that *God* allows. Thus, even the natural nourishment becomes a part of the larger issue of how – in the "name" of the God who himself *cannot* be named – properly to name everything.

According to Nietzsche, the "artistes" among the philosophers – and not the moralists – are grateful to the Jews. This is the statement that best describes his orientation to the Jews. But, as is common knowledge, one does not find only gratitude towards the Jews in Nietzsche's writings. The capacity "to assert oneself in spite of the worst conditions (better, perhaps, than under favorable conditions),"[16] leads to a resentment against those who have a better life. In order to live under these conditions, the disadvantaged group must be *more cunning* than the nobility, for they must defend their values against this *appearance*, i.e., they defend themselves "intellectually" (*geistig*). Thus, the source of their power is to be found precisely in this resistant resentment. Whereas the resentment of the "good" nobility exhausts itself "in an immediate reaction,"[17] the Jews must "retain" their resentful energy without being able to communicate their self-certitude concerning their "intellectual" superiority to outsiders. Resentment is a self-certitude that has been "internalized"; it is the consciousness of a superiority over *all* circumstance, a superiority which nevertheless has a *particular* basis. This consciousness is unarticulable and – because it never gains general recognition – "sublime."

Anyone who attempts to experience this particularity as an outsider inevitably finds that he has no access to this intellectual spirit. Rather, the experience that one has here is of the *other*, of an alienating way of behaving that calls forth a counterresentment. Even Nietzsche understood that he himself was not free of resentment: that would contradict his own concept of understanding. The eternal return of the same can be seen as the affirmation of everything above and beyond all *time*. When viewed in this light, "this *most difficult* thought" has "presumptions that also must be true when the thought itself is true."[18] Nietzsche takes into consideration that all understanding – including, of course, his own – is necessarily perspectival. He thus calls the Jews, and not without resentment, "the strongest, most resilient and purest race that is currently living in Europe."[19]

This characteristic is a consequence of the Jews' resolute faith, one which need not be ashamed in the face of "modern ideas." "A thinker who has Europe's future on his conscience" – Nietzsche obviously means himself –

> can count on the Jews just like he can count on the Russians while making his drafts of the future: they will be, at least at first, the most dependable and probable factors in the great battle and interplay of powers.

This comment was made from Nietzsche's perspective one hundred years ago, in the age of the European nation-states. Yet, Nietzsche's thinking is not "nationalistic." Rather, here he is much more interested in criticizing the questionable claim of the Europeans that they have "nations" in the first place. For, in Nietzsche's view, that

> which is called a "nation" in Europe today is really more a *res facta* than a *res nata* (indeed, it looks so much like a *res ficta et picta* that it could be mistaken for one); it is something young, something in a process of becoming, something easily transposed from place to place – by no means a race, and certainly nothing like an *aere perennius* such as that found with the Jews.

The European "nations" (notice that the concept appears here only in quotation marks) should therefore "certainly watch out for all forms of hot-headed rivalry and hostility" against one another – especially against the Jews! For Nietzsche it is "definitely the case" that the Jews "*could* dominate Europe" if they only wanted to, but it is just as clear "that they are *not* working towards this end." Their lifestyle is not (or no longer) based upon the values "good" and "bad", but upon the values "good" and "evil"; they no longer wish to haggle over a certain perspective that might exemplify and prescribe to others what is "good." Thus,

> they desire much more, indeed, they are somewhat intrusive with this wish, to be taken up and in by Europe; they thirst for stability, for a place where they are accepted and respected; they would like to give their nomadic life – that of the "eternal

Jew" – a destination. We should take note of and try to accomodate . . . this compelling, pressing trend: this end would perhaps be best served and supported by the decision to banish all raving anti-Semites from the country.[20]

The Jews no longer form their self-consciousness through an *opposition* (*Gegensatz*) to other peoples. They are not a people in *this* sense, nor do they want to be. They have, as "the one" people chosen by God, their self-certitude in and of themselves and are "the one" true people. All the other peoples would like to form "nations," but they in no way constitute nations as "*rest facta*"; instead, they make their appeal "nihilistically" with reference to nothing other than their "nationality," which they then demarcate with traits that can be exchanged for others when new political interests so demand. Such determinations can never be complete or definitive; they can only be viewed subjectively as being adequate. Different traits serve at different times as the primary criterion for the identity of a nation: a language, a religion, perhaps a common history, the beginning of which, of course, must be (arbitrarily) determined. By contrast, the Jews are as a people cosmopolitan. If they did want to "settle down" "somewhere," then this would only be in Europe, which, even if it is not Jewish "soil" (*Boden*), is nevertheless Judaic in its way of evaluating, due to the Christian heritage. "Salvation," i.e., passing judgement before God, would still be constituted by being good as opposed (*Gegensatz*) to "evil" (instead of to "bad") (*als "das Heil" gilt das Gutsein*).

This "being good" does *not* consist in *evaluating oneself* with reference to others who, in accordance with the reigning linguistic usage, would then have to characterize themselves as "bad" – until the thought occurs to them that they do not have to continue playing this linguistic game. Then, in their revolt, this weaker group would designate themselves as "good," only now in a framework defined by the "absolute" meaning of a "spiritual" opposition (*Gegensatz*) to "evil." By wanting to become nations that assert themselves, Europeans show that they have not yet grasped this: thus, their "national consciousness" is nihilistic.

This "nihilistic" will to become a nation is dangerous; instead of having (in a transcendental sense) its own identity, this will must *define* itself by delineating itself from others. Such delineations must be asserted and defended; they are genuinely "polemic" and can never be "absolutely" certain. By contrast, Judaism is peculiar in

Nietzsche's eyes because it seeks to negate every peculiarity that it might define for itself and assert "externally." As the political power of Christianity diminishes, European nations find themselves more and more concerned with precisely this type of peculiarity, which can then be asserted to fill the vacuum. Thus, the Jews become somewhat offensive to those "nations" that are searching for their identity, for the Jews make it clear with their example that these attempts to "become" a nation can lead only nowhere.

THE TENSION BETWEEN "TRUTH" AND TEMPORALITY

According to Nietzsche, Judaism can only be compared to Rome with reference to its importance for Europe. "The Romans" were for him the prototype of "the strong and noble, as there was never a stronger, more noble people on the face of the earth; indeed, no one had ever even dreamed of such a group."[21] Nietzsche contrasts typologically the two ways of evaluating something as "good" using the names "Rome and Judaea." It is, however, important to Nietzsche that Judaea was superior to Rome – *not vice versa*; this implies that the resentment born by the prerogative of the majority was actually superior to the noble prerogative of the minority.

Nietzsche's primary concern is with the *historical* appearance of this Roman style that transcended all "dreams," i.e., all powers of the imagination. He is concerned with a nobility that finds its self-consciousness in its own factually existing reign, one that takes its bearings (*orientiert sich*) from the reigning values. Here, the opposing concepts "good" and "bad" do not gain their meaning with reference to "spiritual" or "absolute" values; rather, the defining values are those set and defended by this reigning group itself. The fact that the "intellectual spirit" of Judaism has *actually* been able successfully to assert itself – especially in the form of Christianity – has for Nietzsche nothing to do with truth; rather, it is a matter of strength. It was the *actual* demise of Rome that demonstrated the truth of the way of evaluating which this name (Rome) signifies. As the "intellectual spirit" that was unwilling to measure and assert itself against others, the "intellectual spirit" of Judaism proved to be stronger than Rome, and precisely within Rome's own system of values. Nietzsche is rather ambivalent in his evaluation of Judaism. The reason for this ambivalence is that neither of the two perspectives can be viewed as being higher in an absolute sense. Neither perspective is more true

110

than the other. The truth of the Roman perspective is demonstrated (*ziegt sich*) precisely in the *actual* superiority of the Jewish perspective, which negates its *own* "will to power." Yet everything which "reveals" itself (*zeigt sich*) (as an aesthetic phenomenon) has "its time."[22]

Of course, Nietzsche is aware that even his own orientation (*Orientation*) to these two opposing pairs, i.e., "good and bad" and "good and evil," is a perspectival *interpretation*, and, like every doctrine – including the "will to power" – has "its time." According to Nietzsche, only when viewed from an "exoteric" vantage point "is" there such a thing as a "will," and only in the actual polemics that ensue when one viewpoint clashes with another is it possible to have one will "standing in opposition to another will." When viewed "esoterically," there is "no such thing as a will";[23] even the designation "will" is only a "name," a "false reification" with a "morally questionable" meaning.[24] His reflections on the fact that even the philosopher could have neither an extramundane "standpoint," i.e., one participating in a "*visio dei*," nor a language consisting of "absolute meanings" had a determining, enduring influence on Nietzsche's own philosophical style. Yet the metaphysical style of philosophy, in which one writes as if there were such a standpoint, has nonetheless left its mark on our language, going even so far as to give "grammar" its form. According to Nietzsche, to want to reason apart from "this schema" (and no longer under the *assumption* that there are "absolute meanings") would mean the "cessation of thinking."[25] Yet to continue to reason in this schema "uncritically" and without interruption, as if it were "the one" form of truth, would also mean to cease to think.

"Rome" stands for the "right" to determine *for itself*, divide and actually rule its own territory. When viewed in this light, the Roman Empire was not a "moral" state. Kant argued that "something other than a people" must be the legislator in an "ethical" – as opposed to a merely "juridical" – "commonwealth." This legislator must be able to enact laws with a divine "overview" and in a language of "absolute meanings." The concept of ethical commonwealth is the concept of the one people of God living under ethical laws."[26] When *understood* as divine, these laws *per se* would have everyone's approval. On the other hand, the laws in a "juridical" commonwealth remain dependent upon the external force used to execute these laws in the fact of the most diverse ideas, even, sometimes, in the face of differing ideas concerning what is "good."

According to Kant, the law is intrinsically connected with the authorization to coerce"; thus, the law necessarily has a limited range. Its validity rests upon the actual control over a region: this region forms a legal domain only inasmuch as it stands under *legal dominion*. The legal system is also the counterpart to morality. A moral lifestyle cannot prescribe a set of rules that could be used to judge individual acts in accordance with the current demands "of a particular time"; rather, it rests upon the "sublime" self-certitude that it has the proper set of rules for "all times." For this reason, an internal tension exists between morality and the law, between the "intellectual spirit" and "life". However, according to Nietzsche, the "intellectual spirit" is itself – contrary to its own self-consciousness – an historical "lifestyle." This intellectual spirit has already had, in conjunction with the legal system that sheltered this same intellectual spirit in its apathy from all "external," "exoteric" elements – and, thus, even from itself – its great moment (*große Zeit*/great time).

It is in essence the desire to overcome this opposition that Nietzsche expresses when he has Zarathustra say:

> I care not for your cold justice; nothing other than an executioner with his cold irons stares at me through the eyes of your judges. Tell me, where is this justice which is said to be love with perceiving eyes? Conjure up for me this love which brings not only punishment but also is able to carry guilt! Conjure up for me this justice which acquits everyone – except the judges![27]

A "love with perceiving eyes" would be a love that really "perceives" another human being, recognizes in an*other* a human being, even when it is unable to understand this other person from its own point of view. It no longer wishes to reduce this person to its own concepts, to notions about this person that it cannot "understand" from its own perspective. "*Comprendre c'est égaler*"[28] – this does the other person an injustice. Nietzsche saw "something insulting about being understood."[29] – Emmanuel Lévinas claims, like Nietzsche, that a recognizing "love" must be "perceptive" beyond any ability to "understand" (using logic and concepts). Nietzsche knows how "hard" Zarathustra's "teachings" (*Lehre*) are. He has Zarathustra ask: "Do you want to hear something else? The lie will be become something that can be humane and kind in the face of that person who has a deep, fundamental desire to be just" In order to avoid hurting others, this person would refrain from referring to this locution with "the hard name of a lie" (Kant);[30] he would understand that the type of things that might deserve this "hard name" could not have been intended when viewed "from the vantage point" from which the locution was made. He would *view* this from the other's vantage point without wanting to understand it from his own viewpoint: the world would become for him an aesthetic phenomenon (instead of a conceptual object). "However," continues Zarathustra, "how could I possibly want to be fundamentally just? How could I give to each what is his? This is enough for me: I will give to each what is mine!"[31]

Here lies Zarathustras's limit. He enters the scene as a "teacher," for example, of the "doctrine" (*Lehre*) of the "will to power,"[32] of the "superhuman"[33]or of the "eternal return of the same."[34] To be a "teacher" – he is told that this is to be his "destiny." A "teacher" wishes to tell "the truth"; he wants to "communicate" *his* thoughts to others as *the* truth. The others, however, will understand him according to their *own* capacities, i.e., using their own concepts. Nietzsche is expressedly not Zarathustra. He conjured up this figure who then speaks of "conjuring up" a love "with perceiving eyes" in order to distance himself from a philosophy understood as a "doctrine." He uses this figure "artistically" as a "mask," for he knows that he, too, can only speak "from his own perspective" – and he embraces this "destiny" ("*amor fati*") as well.

Nietzsche never loses sight of the fact that everything that he says – including everything about Judaism – remains determined by *his* way of understanding. Judaism taken *for what it is* would be for Nietzsche, at least as he understands it, much too much of a "doctrine" dependent upon the "dominating notion" of a "sublime" self-certitude which is derived from its covenant with God. When seen in this light, this great moral style is a result of the period of exile: it was able to avoid the dialectical process of being understood *in life* due to its moral delineation and separation from those powers that, even though they preserved the "external" *status quo*, remained "internally" foreign. Yet it is precisely here that this style becomes problematic for Nietzsche. How might Nietzsche himself be able to avoid this problem? He certainly does not "know", nor can he claim to know and remain true to his own thinking.

Instead, Nietzsche speaks of "good and bad days." "It is difficult to be understood. One should be deeply grateful merely for a good will towards the *subtlety* of an interpretation." "On good days" one can "grant one's friends a great deal of leeway for misunderstandings."[35] This leeway is for the viewpoints of the *others* for a way of understanding that simply cannot be understood from one's own vantage point. One demands on such "days" to have absolutely no more "interpretations"; one understands "without having to mediate with an interpretation," i.e., "aesthetically." By contrast, "resentment" holds sway on bad days. Everything has "its" time.

Nietzsche calls understanding without a "mediating" interpretation, without a "translation" into one's own language, "the latest" and "scarcely possible" "form of 'inner experience.'"[36] That this is scarcely possible means that it is currently possible only "on good days" – not at all times and not whenever one wishes. "Good" and "bad" are terms still used to describe the various conditions that one and the same person is in. The rift runs through one's own identity. It is only on "bad days" that one searches for the certitude found in one's "self"-"identity," hoping to drive away this internal opposition. One searches for safety in a worldly knowledge gained through one's "participation" in a "divine," "undivided" view of everything. Nietzsche's own evaluation of Judaism vacillates depending on his own condition. These vacillations result from Nietzsche's own reflections on evaluating himself: he is well aware that his own thinking cannot completely remove itself from the temporal shifts in perspectives. This has been grasped in the "intellectual spirit"; "in the intellectual realm (*im Geistigen*) nothing is ever completely annihilated."[37] Something passes away after it has had its time; in this way, something *other* can come to be. It is *time* that provides for this justice.

NOTES

1 Plato, *Politics* 484 b.
2 Translator's note: the German word that is translated here as "pecularities" is *Besonderheiten*. In German, *besonders* is the conceptual opposite of common, general or universal and, depending upon the context and meaning being stressed, can be translated with one of three words: "special," "particular" or "peculiar." Josef Simon exploits all three meanings in this essay, making it necessary to use all three English words in this translation. So that the play on words is not completely lost, the words "special," "particular" and "peculiar" will only be used when translating the German word *besonders* or some form thereof, i.e., when any of those three words appear, the counterpart to universal is implied.
3 Translator's note: the German word translated here as "heavens" is *Himmel*. This term has in German two different meanings: the first one refers to firmament or sky, i.e., the physical expanse above the earth; the second meaning has a spiritual character, i.e., it refers metaphorically to the celestial regions as a revered place, as the "adobe" of God. Even

though it is sometimes somewhat awkward, I have decided to use "heavens" here because it is conceptually closer than any of the other options to *Himmel*.

4 Friedrich Nietzsche, *Jenseits von Gut und Böse*, "Völker und Vater-länder" *Kritische Studienausgabe (KSA)*, ed. Giorgio Coli and Mazzino Montimari (Berlin: de Gruyter, 198), vol. 5, p. 192. See also with reference to this topic Werner Stegmaier, "Nietzsches 'Genealogie der Moral'," in *Werkinterpretation*, ed. Horst Enders, 2nd edn (Darmstadt: Wissen-schaftliche Buchgasellschaft, 1978).

5 Translator's note: instead of "affiliation with," a more literal translation of the German *Zugehörigkeit* would be "belongingness to" – but there is not such a word in English.

6 Feidrich Nietzsche, *Zur Genealogie der Moral*, "Gut und Böse," "Gut und Schlecht" 16, *KSA* vol. 5, p. 286.

7 See Nietzsche, *Genealogie*, "Gut und Schlecht" 2, *KSA* vol. 5, p. 259.

8 Das Herrenrecht, Namen zu geben, geht so weit, daß man sich erlauben sollte, den Ursprung der Sprache selbst als Machtäußerung der Herr-schenden zu fassen: sie sagen "das *ist* das und das", sie siegeln jegliches Ding und Geschehen mit einem Laute ab und nehmen es dadurch gleichsam in Besitz. (*Nietzsche, Genealogie*, "Gut und Böse", Gut und Schlecht" 2, *KSA* Vol. 5, p. 259).

9 Hegel, *Phänomenologie des Geistes* (Hamburg: Felix Meiner Press, 1952), pp. 423f.

10 Immanuel Kant, *Zum ewigen Frieden*, in *Kants gesammelte Schriften*, Akademieausgabe (*AA* (Berlin: Georg Reimer Press, 1913), vol. 8. p. 352n.

11 Kant, *Metaphysik der Sitten*, *AA* vol. 6, p. 211.

12 See Kant's "casuistry" concerning the concept of lying in ibid., p. 429.

13 See ibid., p. 231 (also p. 230).

14 Nietzsche, *Jenseits*, "Völker und Vaterländer" 250, *KSA* Vol. 5, p. 192.

15 Nietzsche, *Jenseits*, "Der freie Geist" 40, *KSA* vol. 5, p. 58.

16 Nietzsche, *Jenseits*, "Völker und Vaterländer" 251, *KSA* vol. 5, p. 193.

17 Nietzsche, *Genealogie*, "Gut und Böse," "Gut und Schlecht" 10, *KSA* vol. 5, p. 273.

18 Nietzsche, *Nachlaß* VIII 26 [284], *KSA* vol. 11, p. 225.

19 Nietzsche, *Jenseits*, "Völker und Vaterländer" 251, *KSA* vol. 5, p. 193.

20 Ibid., pp. 193f.

21 Nietzsche, *Genealogie*, "Gut und Böse," "Gut und Schlecht" 16, *KSA* vol. 5, p. 286.

22 Bible, *Ecclesiastes* ("Qoheleth"), 3: 1.

23 Nietzsche, *Nachlaß* VIII 5 [9], *KSA* vol. 12, p. 187.

24 Nietzsche, *Nachlaß* VIII 1 [62], *KSA* vol. 12, p. 26.

25 "*[W]ir-hören auf zu denken, wenn wir es nicht in dem sprachlichen Zwange thun wollen*, wir langen gerade noch bei dem Zweifel an, hier eine Grenze als Grenze zu sehen" (*Nachlaß* VIII 5 [22], *KSA* vol. 12, p. 193). See also Josef Simon, "Grammatik und Wahrheit," *Nietzsche-Studien* 1 (1972): 1.

26 Kant, *Die Religion innerhalb der Grenzen der bloßen Vernunft*, AA vol. 6, pp. 98f.

27 *Nietzsche, Also Sprach Zarathustra, KSA* vol. 4, p. 88.
28 Translator's note: Understanding is tantamount to leveling off.
29 Nietzsche, *Nachlaß* VIII 1 [182], *KSA* vol. 12, pp. 50f.
30 Kant, Metaphsik der Sitten, *AA* vol. 6, p. 429.
31 Nietzsche, *Zarathustra, KSA* vol. 4, p. 88.
32 Ibid., p. 149.
33 Ibid., p. 14.
34 Zarathustra entschließt sich, zu den Menschen hinabzugehen und ihnen
    seine Weisheiten mitzuteilen. Die Tiere sprechen aus, was ihm dabei
    geschieht: Er stellt sich ihnen als "Fürsprecher des Lebens" dar – in der
    Tat hat man ja Nietzsche zum "Lebensphilosophen" erklärt – und
    schließlich ist er für sie der *"Lehrer der ewigen Wiederkunft."* Diese
    "Lehre" wird als sein "abgründigster Gedanke" bezeichnet. Darin liegt
    schon der Widerspruch. Eine "Lehre" dürfte nicht "abgründig" bleiben.
    Zugleich damit sagen die Tiere ihm, weil sie glauben, "die Zeit sei
    gekommen, mit ihm zu reden": "Denn deine Tiere wissen es wohl, oh
    Zarathustra, wer du bist und werden musst: siehe, *du bist der Lehrer der
    ewigen Widerkunft* – das ist nun *dein* Schicksal!" (*KSA* vol. 4, p. 275).
35 Nietzsche, *Nachlaß* VIII 1 [182], *KSA* vol. 12, pp. 50f.
36 Nietzsche, *Nachlaß* VIII 15 [90], *KSA* vol. 13, p. 460.
37 "Nicht ein Kampf um Existenz wird zwischen den Vorstellungen und
    Wahrnehmungen gekämpft, sondern um Herrschaft: – *vernichtet* wird
    die überwundene V[orstellung] *nicht,* nur *zurückgedrängt* oder *sub-
    ordinirt. Es giebt im Geistigen keine Vernichtung …*" (*Nachlaß* VIII
    7 [53], *KSA* vol. 12, p. 312).

6

NIETZSCHE AND THE JEWS

The structure of an ambivalence

Yirmiyahu Yovel

This chapter is based on a forthcoming study[1] which examines the image of Judaism as offered by the two most important philosophers of the nineteenth century, Hegel and Nietzsche. One was active in the first and the other in the second half of the century, one was a major philosopher of reason and the other one of its severest critics. I confine myself to treating both of them *as philosophers*, which means concentrating on their own philosophical ideas rather than on their various users and abusers, and understanding their image of the Jews in its relation to each philosopher's ideas and overall philosophical project.

Hegel's philosophical project was a vast and ambitious one. It included the attempt to reach a philosophical understanding of the modern world, its essence and genesis, and thereby to shape modernity still further and lead to its climax. Hegel saw European culture as the core of world history, and as being essentially a Christian culture – which the philosopher must translate and elevate into concepts; Judaism was a necessary background for understanding the Christian revolution and era.

According to the Hegelian dialectic, every cultural form makes some genuine contribution to world history (and the world Spirit), after which it is sublated (*aufgehoben*) and disappears from the historical scene. Yet the Jews continued to survive long after their *raison d'être* had disappeared – indeed, after they no longer had a genuine history in Hegel's sense, but merely existed as the dead corpse of their extinguished essence. Now, with the French Revolution, the Jews were entering the modern world and claiming their rights and place within it. Hegel, despite his anti-Jewish bias, was perfectly disposed to grant these rights, but did not know what to do with the Jews in modernity *as Jews*, nor how to explain their survival in terms of his system.

117

Nietzsche too had an ambitious philosophical project, in many ways opposing Hegel's. A radical cultural revolutionary, his goal was not to bring the process of modernity to culmination but rather to subvert and reverse it or, more precisely, to *divert* it into a totally different course. The process which had started with Socrates, Moses and Jesus, and which Hegel saw as creating truth, civilization, spirit and even God himself (the Absolute) was to Nietzsche a story of decadence and degeneration. Nietzsche attributed this decadence to two main sources – rationalistic metaphysics and Christianity: the first stemming from the Greeks, the second from the ancient Jews. He therefore needed an interpretation of Judaism (and also of Socratism, as offered in the *Birth of Tragedy*) in order to expose and upset the decadent culture of the present. Given these projects, Hegel had seen the merit of ancient Judaism in its discovery – which led to Christianity – that God was spirit and that spirit is higher than nature; whereas for Nietzsche this was the great falsification which the ancient Jewish priests had brought about. However, as my analysis shows, Nietzsche did not recognize a single, permanent Jewish essence. He distinguished three different modes or phases in Judaism, and expressed admiration for two of them: for biblical Judaism, and for the Jews of the latter Diaspora.[2] His harsh critique pours exclusively on the middle phase, the second-temple "priestly" Judaism (as he calls it) which had started the "slave revolution" in morality – namely, Christianity. Nietzsche's true target is Christianity: so much so that often he reads the ideas and even the phrases of the New Testament directly into what he derogates under the name of Judaism.

On the emotional level, Hegel, especially in maturity, had lost interest in the Jewish theme, whereas Nietzsche's interest in it was increasingly passionate and burning. And this links into another aspect of my study: to what extent did each philosopher overcome the anti-Jewish feelings imbued in his upbringing and milieu? Those feelings were of a different kind in each case. Nietzsche came to maturity in the second half of the nineteenth century amidst a wave of nationalistic and racist anti-Semitism raging in Germany, which had already a distinct secular feature. For a short time, Nietzsche says, he too "had resided in the zone of the disease" (meaning his association with Wagner), but later he performed a powerful overcoming of that "disease" and became opposed to the anti-Semites with particular energy and passion.

It has become a commonplace to say Nietzsche was "ambivalent" about the Jews. Yet the word "ambivalent" itself is ambiguous and often creates an impression of depth where there is but confusion. My aim is to analyze the *precise structure* of Nietzsche's ambivalence about the Jews and bring to light its ingredients in their mutual relations. On the one hand Nietzsche sees ancient Judaism as one of the main sources of European decadence, and on the other he assigns modern Jews, whom he admires, a leading role in creating the non-decadent, de-Christianized Europe he wishes for the future. As for modern anti-Semitism, Nietzsche repudiates it with the same passion he reserves for the proto-Christian Jewish "priests" – and for similar reasons. These two human types, apparently so opposed to each other – the anti-Semite and the Jewish priest – are actually genea-logical cousins: they share the same deep-psychological pattern of *ressentiment* which Nietzsche's philosophy diagnoses at the basis of human meanness and degeneration.

METHODOLOGICAL ELEMENTS

The following are the main methodological elements of this study: (1) I examine Nietzsche's views of the Jews in relation to his actual philosophy, not as casual reflections that any intellectual, artist or scientist may have about the Jews. (2) Taking an immanent approach, I deal with Nietzsche's own thought and not – despite their interest for the historian or sociologist – with its many popular and politically motivated usages, or with what is vaguely called "Nietzscheanism". (3) In addition to their philosophical meaning, I try also to listen to Nietzsche's words in their *rhetorical context*. (4) To a limited extent I have taken his psychological career into account – both his struggle with close anti-Semitic intimates, and his last twilight letters before he went mad, which carry a special hermeneutic value. (5) Above all, I am looking for the underlying structure of Nietzsche's complex position as indicated above.

This search has led me to distinguish, first, between Nietzsche's attitude toward *anti-Semitism* and toward *Judaism*. Second, within Judaism I had to further distinguish between three periods or modalities: (1) biblical Judaism; (2) second-temple "priestly" Juda-ism; (c) Diaspora and contemporary Jews.

JUDAISM AND ANTI-SEMITISM

When Nietzsche attacks the anti-Semites or defends the Jews, he aims at real people: the actual community of the Jews, and anti-Semitism as a contemporary movement. By contrast, when dealing with ancient priestly Judaism Nietzsche treats it as a psychocultural *category* which is latent in the current (Christian) culture and which Nietzsche, as the "genealogist" of this culture, has to expose. Contrary to many anti-Semites – and also to many Jewish apologetics – Nietzsche does not project his view of ancient Judaism into a political attitude toward the Jews of today. This break allowed him to be at the same time – and with the same intense passion – both an anti-anti-Semite and a critique of ancient priestly Judaism – the fountain of Christianity.

THE ANTI-ANTI-SEMITE: QUID FACTI[3]

A selection of four kinds of texts allows us to recognize the fact of Nietzsche's fierce and univocal opposition to contemporary anti-Semitism. These texts are drawn from (1) his published writings; (2) his intimate letters (to his sister, his mother, his close friends); (3) his "twilight letters" written on the verge of madness; (4) "The Fritsch Affair" – a correspondence with an anti-Semitic agitator who tried to recruit Nietzsche – and "Zarathustra" too, as Nietzsche says with disgust[4] – into his camp.

Here are a few illustrations. In the *Genealogy* Nietzsche says of the anti-Semites:

> This hoarse, indignant barking of sick dogs, this rabid mendaciousness and rage of "noble" pharisees, penetrates even the hallowed halls of science. (I again remind readers who have ears for such things of that Berlin apostle of revenge, Eugen Dühring, who employs moral mumbo-jumbo more indecently and repulsively then anyone else in Germany today: Dühring, the foremost moral bigmouth today – unexcelled even among his own ilk, the anti-Semites.)
>
> (*GM* III 14, pp. 559–60)

> "This is our conviction: we confess it before all the world, we live and die for it. Respect for all who have convictions!" I have heard that sort of thing even out of the mouths of anti-Semites. On the contrary, gentlemen! An anti-Semite certainly is not any more decent because he lies as a matter of principle.
>
> (*AC* 55, pp. 640–1)

> Meanwhile they [the Jews] want and wish rather, even with some importunity, to be absorbed and assimilated by Europe;

they long to be fixed, permitted, respected somewhere at long last, putting an end to the nomads' life, to the "Wandering Jew" . . . to that end it might be useful and fair to expel the anti-Semitic screamers from the country.

(BGE 251, pp. 377–8)

Since Wagner had moved to Germany, he had condescended step by step to everything I despise – even to anti-Semitism.

(NW, p. 676)

To Overbeck:

This accursed anti-Semitism . . . is the reason for the great rift between myself and my sister.

(BW III, p. 503)

And to his sister:

You have committed one of the greatest stupidities – for yourself and for me! Your association with an anti-Semitic chief expresses a foreignness to my whole way of life which fills me again and again with ire or melancholy . . . It is a matter of honor with me to be absolutely clean and unequivocal in relation to anti-Semitism, namely, opposed to it, as I am in my writings. I have recently been persecuted with letters and anti-Semitic Correspondence Sheets[5]. My disgust with this party (which would like the benefit of my name only too well!) is as pronounced as possible . . . and that I am unable to do anything against it, that the name of Zarathustra is used in every Anti-Semitic Correspondence Sheet, has almost made me sick several times.

(Christmas 1887, *PN*, pp. 456–7)

The intimate texts carry special weight, because they prove that Nietzsche's opposition to anti-Semitism was not merely external and "political" (or "politically correct"), as with many liberals, but penetrated into the deep recesses of his mind. That result might have been reinforced by Nietzsche's intense relations with anti-Semites such as his sister, Wagner, Cosima and perhaps also Jacob Burckhardt.[6] These depth-psychological relations could have served as a lever in providing the energy for overcoming his own early anti-Semitism in the intense way he did, that is, not as liberal rationalist but with all the passion of his being – that is, in a "Nietzschean" way.

THE ANTI-ANTI-SEMITE: QUID JURIS

Even without considering psychology, there are sufficient *philosophical* grounds for Nietzsche's active anti-anti-Semitism. The anti-Semitic movement contains and heightens most of the decadent elements in modern culture which Nietzsche's philosophy has set out to combat:

1 Anti-Semitism is a mass movement, vulgar, ideological, a new form of "slave morality" and of the man of the Herd.

2 As such, anti-Semitism is a popular neurosis, affecting weak people who lack existential power and self-confidence (as opposed to Nietzsche's "Dionysian" person).

3 Anti-Semitism, especially in Germany, served to reinforce the German *Reich* and the cult of *politics* and the *State*, which Nietzsche, as "the last *un*-political German", denounces as "the New Idol".

4 Anti-Semitism, in Germany, was also the lubricant of German *nationalism*, which Nietzsche opposed most insistently (though he did so "from the right").

5 Anti-Semitism also depends on *racism*; yet Nietzsche's philosophy rejects racism as a value distinction between groups (though he does admit of race as a descriptive category). Nietzsche demands the *mixing* of races within the new Europe he envisages.

6 At the ground of all the preceding points lies a common genealogical structure – fear, insecurity, existential weakness and above all *ressentiment* – the malignant rancor against the mentally powerful and self-affirming, and the hatred toward the other which preconditions one's own self-affirmation and self-esteem. The anti-Semite's ardor conceals his/her deep insecurity: he does not start with the celebrating affirmation of his own being, but with the negation of the other's, by which alone the anti-Semite is able to reaffirm his own self – which he does in an overblown, empty and arrogant manner. "They are all men of *ressentiment*, physiologically unfortunate and worm-eaten, a whole tremulous realm of subterranean revenge, inexhaustible and insatiable in outbursts against the fortunate and happy" (*GM* III 14, pp. 559–60).

Here are a few more quotes, illustrating his opposition to nationalism and the cult of politics and the state:

> Is there any idea at all behind this bovine nationalism? What value can there be now, when everything points to wider and

more common interests, in encouraging this boorish self-conceit? And this in a state of affairs in which spiritual dependency and disnationalization meet the eye and in which the value and meaning of contemporary culture lie in mutual blending and fertilization!

(*WP* 748, pp. 395–6)

The whole problem of the Jews exists only in nation states, for here their energy and higher intelligence, their accumulated capital of spirit and will, gathered from generation to generation through a long schooling in suffering, must become so preponderant as to arouse mass envy and hatred. In almost all contemporary nations, therefore – in direct proportion to the degree to which they act up nationalistically – the literary obscenity is spreading of leading the Jews to slaughter as scapegoats of every conceivable public and internal misfortune. As soon as it is no longer a matter of preserving nations, but of producing the strongest possible European mixed race, the Jews are just as useful and desirable an ingredient as any other national remnant.

(*HAH* 475, p. 62)

Culture and the state – one should not deceive oneself about this – are antagonists. . . . All great ages of culture are ages of political decline: what is great culturally has always been unpolitical, even *antipolitical*.

(*TI* "What the Germans lack" 4, pp. 508–9)

On the New Idol

State is the name of the coldest of all cold monsters. Coldly it tell lies too; and this lie crawls out of its mouth: "I, the state, am the people." That is a lie!

. . . every people speaks its tongue of good and evil . . . but the state tells lies in all the tongues of good and evil . . .

Everything about it is false; it bites with stolen teeth, and bites easily. Even its entrails are false.

"On earth there is nothing greater then I: the ordering finger of God and I" – thus roars the monster. And it is not only the long-eared and shortsighted who sink to their Knees.

123

Escape from the bad smell! Escape from the idolatry of the superfluous .... Only where the state ends, there begins the human being who is not superfluous: there begins the song of necessity, the unique and inimitable tune.

(Z I, "On the new idol", pp. 160–3)

Combined, Nietzsche's four negations – of nationalism, of racism, of anti-Semitism and of the cult of the state – also explain why his philosophy is inherently opposed to fascism and Nazism, although these ideologies have abused Nietzsche for their purposes.

THE ANCIENT "PRIESTLY" JUDAISM

Nietzsche's attack on ancient ("priestly") Judaism is as fierce and uncompromising as his assault on anti-Semitism. The Jewish priests have spread the spurious ideas of a "moral world order", sin, guilt, punishment, repentance, pity and the love of the neighbor. Thereby they falsified all natural values. The meek and the weak are the good who deserve salvation; all men are equal in their duties towards a transcendent God and the values of love and mercy He demands. (Nietzsche thus attributes to the Jewish priests a *direct* Christian content, and often describes them as Christian *from the start*.) Yet beneath his doctrine of mercy, the priest's soul was full of malice and *ressentiment*, the rancor of the mentally weak whose will-to-power turns into hostility and revenge against the other, which is his only way to affirm himself. Thereby the Jewish priests – pictured as early Christians – have created the "slave morality" which official Christianity then propagated through the world. Whereas the anti-Semites accuse the Jews of having killed Jesus, Nietzsche accuses them of having *begotten* Jesus.

> The slave revolt in morality begins when *ressentiment* itself becomes creative and gives birth to values: the *ressentiment* of natures that are denied the true reaction, that of deeds, and compensate themselves with an imaginary revenge. While every noble morality develops from a triumphant affirmation of itself, slave morality from the outset says No to what is "outside," what is "different," what is "not itself"; and this No is its creative deed.
>
> (*GM* I 10, pp. 472–4)

Priestly morality is the morality of the existentially impotent, in whom *ressentiment* against the powerful and the self-assured has become a value-creating force. The existential "slaves" take vengeance on their "masters" on an ideal plane, in that they succeed in imposing their own values on the masters, and even cause them to interiorize those new values, and thereby subjugate them. Henceforth the powerful person sees himself/herself as sinner not only in the other's eyes but in his/her self-perception as well, which is the ultimate form of subordination and also corruption.

Nietzsche thereby places the critique of ancient Judaism at a crucial junction of his philosophy. It is grounded in *ressentiment*, a key Nietzschean category, and is responsible for the corruption of Europe through Christianity. However, his critique does not serve Nietzsche in fighting against contemporary Jews, but against contemporary Christianity and the "modern Ideas" he sees as its secular offshoots (liberalism, nationalism, socialism, etc.). For modern Jews, after they go out of the ghetto and become secularized, Nietzsche has far-reaching prospects, whereas the modern anti-Semite is analyzed as the genealogical cousin of the ancient Jewish priest, whose properties the anti-Semite has inherited, but on a lower level still, since he lacks the value-creating power which the Jewish priests have demonstrated, and since, in order to feel that he is somebody, he requires the fake security of mass culture and the "togetherness" of a political movement.

Nietzsche's analysis, like Socrates' dialectic, ends in an ironic reversal. While the anti-Semite is the ancient Jewish priests' relative, the modern Jew is their complete opposite (or "antipode"). As such modern Jews are candidates for helping to create a new Dionysian culture and redeem Europe from the decadence instilled by their forefathers.

Rhetorically, too, the anti-Semite learns that, at bottom he has the same psychology as his worst enemies in their worst period, and this is supposed to shock the anti-Semite into disgust – perhaps at himself. However, by using anti-Semitic images ostensibly against themselves Nietzsche is playing with fire.

It follows that Nietzsche holds two rather univocal positions: against modern anti-Semitism and against ancient priestly Judaism, which are linked by the same genealogical root, *ressentiment*. Nietzsche's ambivalence derives from the combination of these two positions, which look contradictory but are not so in effect. From a logical or systematic point of view there is no contradiction between rejecting both anti-Semitism and the moral message of ancient Judaism, yet this combination creates a strong psychological tension which ordinary people find hard to sustain. Hence the need to transcend ordinary psychology and cultivate an *uncommon*, noble character capable of holding on to both positions despite the tension they create. In other words, what is needed in order to maintain the two tense positions is not only a common link between them (the opposition to *ressentiment*) but a special *personality* whose mental power allows it to maintain a stance of "nevertheless" and insist on the distinction it involves.

This is nothing new. Almost every important matter in Nietzsche calls for an uncommon psychology. This is true, above all, of *amor fati*, which draws creative power from hard truths, and affirms life despite the demise of all "metaphysical consolations". In Nietzsche one needs anyway to go beyond the limits of ordinary humanity and human psychology, toward a goal which his rhetoric dramatizes under the name of *Ubermench*. Nietzsche's position on Judaism and anti-Semitism is no exception.

In a word, Nietzsche's non-contradictory ambivalence requires holding two (or more) differentiated positions that are logically compatible yet psychologically competitive and hard to maintain together for the ordinary person. This analysis can also help explain why Nietzsche's position has so widely been abused; for the mental revolution which he sought did not take place, while his ideas were generalized, vulgarized and delivered to a public in which the old psychology prevailed.

At the same time, we noticed on several occasions that Nietzsche himself exploits anti-Semitic feelings and images which exist in other people (or whose traces persist in his own mind) and manipulates them in a dialectical technique, as a rhetoric device to insult the anti-Semites or hurt Christianity. For example:

> Consider to whom one bows down in Rome itself today, as if they were the epitome of all the highest values – and not only in Rome but over almost half the earth ... three Jews, as is known, and one Jewess (Jesus of Nazareth, the fisherman Peter, the rug weaver Paul, and the mother of the afore-mentioned Jesus named Mary).
>
> (*GM* I 16, p. 489)

As I said before, Nietzsche in this and similar cases is playing a dangerous game; his meaning can be twisted against his intention, his irony misunderstood and his words may enhance that which he actually opposes. The irony of speaking ironically to the vulgar is that the speaker himself may end up the victim of an ironic reversal, by which his intent is undermined and his discourse is taken at face value. Nietzsche as a master of the art should have anticipated the ironic fate of ironizers.

THE THREE PHASES OF JUDAISM

We have also seen that Nietzsche does not attribute to Judaism a constant essence or genealogical pattern, but distinguished three periods or phases within it.

(1) In Biblical times (the Old Testament) Nietzsche perceives Dionysian greatness and natural sublimity that arouses his reverence. He does not accept the content of the biblical figures' religious belief, but admires their attitude to life and religion because it was vital, natural, this-worldly and was built on self-affirmation rather than self-recrimination.

> In the Jewish "Old Testament," the book of divine justice, there are human beings, things, and speeches in so grand a style that the Greek and Indian literature have nothing to compare with it. With terror and reverence one stands before these tremendous remnants of what man once was.
>
> (*BGE* 52, pp. 255–6)

> At the time of the kings, Israel also stood in the right, that is, the natural relationship to all things. Its Yahweh was the expression of a consciousness of power, of joy in oneself, of hope for oneself: through him victory and welfare were expected; through him nature was trusted to give what the people needed above all, rain. Yahweh is the god of Israel and therefore the god of justice: the logic of every people that is in power and has a good conscience.
>
> (*AC* 25, p. 594)

(2) The second temple and its priests are the object of Nietzsche's harsh and merciless attack. Here the "slave morality" revolution was performed, the major de-naturation and reversal of values that led to Christianity, as analyzed before.

127

To have glued this New Testament to make one book, as the "Bible," as "the book par excellence" – that is perhaps the greatest audacity and "sin against the spirit" that literary Europe has on its conscience.

(*BGE* 52, pp. 255–6)

The concept of God falsified, the concept of morality falsified: the Jewish priesthood did not stop there. The whole of the history of Israel could not be used: away with it! These priests accomplished a miracle of falsification.... With matchless scorn for every tradition, for every historical reality, they translated the past of their own people into religious terms, that is, they turned it into a stupid salvation mechanism of guilt before Yahweh, and punishment.

(*AC* 26, p. 595)

On such utterly false soil, where everything natural, every natural value, every reality was opposed by the most profound instincts of the ruling class, Christianity grew up – a form of mortal enmity against reality that has never yet been surpassed.

(*AC* 27, p. 598)

(3) Diaspora Jews again arouse Nietzsche's admiration, because they have demonstrated the power of affirming life in the face of suffering and drawn force from it. Moreover, Diaspora Jews have the merit of having rejected Christ and served as a constant critic and counterbalance to Christianity.

In the darkest times of the Middle Ages ... it was Jewish free-thinkers, scholars, and physicians who clung to the banner of enlightenment and spiritual independence in the face of the harshest personal pressures and defended Europe against Asia. We owe it to their exertions, not least of all, that a more natural, more rational, and certainly unmythical explanation of the world was eventually able to triumph again.

(*HAH* 475, pp. 61–2)

The Jews, however, are beyond any doubt the strongest, toughest and purest race now living in Europe; they know how to prevail even under the worst conditions) even better than under favorable conditions), by means of virtues that today one would like to mark as vices – thanks above all to a resolute faith that need not be ashamed of "modern ideas."

(*BGE* 251, pp. 377–8)

CONTEMPORARY JEWS AND THE
CLOSING OF THE CIRCLE

As a result of their hard and long schooling and invigorating experience, the Jews reached the modern era as the strongest and most stable people in Europe, and could have dominated it, though they did not wish to do so. However, once they decided to mingle with the other European nations, then because of their greater existential power they would naturally, without intending to, reach a dominant position, in the sense of determining the norms and the new values in Europe. If however, the Jews continued their seclusion, Nietzsche grimly predicted they would "lose Europe" (that is, emigrate or be expelled) as their ancestors had left or been driven from Egypt. Nietzsche advocates the first alternative. The Jews must pour their gifts and power into a new Europe that will be free of the Christian heritage: *the forebears of Christ must work today in the service of the modern anti-Christ (i.e. Nietzsche-Dionysus), and thereby pay their debt to Europe for what their priestly ancestors had done to it.*[7]

For this to happen, European society must open up to the Jews and welcome them, and the Jews must end their voluntary seclusion and involve themselves with all European matters *as their own:* in this way they will, inevitably, attain excellence and end up determining new norms and values for Europe. Nietzsche welcomes this prospect with enthusiasm, because he sees the Jews as allies and levers in the transition to a higher human psychology and culture. If the Nazis considered the Jews as *Untermenschen,* to Nietzsche they were a possible catalyst of the *Ubermensch.*

Nietzsche thus assigns a major role to the Jews *as Jews* within his new Europe. He opposes a nationalist (or Zionist) solution, because he wants the Jews to mix with the other European peoples. At the same time he also opposes the usual, passive and imitative, Jewish assimilation. His solution is *creative assimilation,* in which the Jews are secularized, excel in all European matters and serve as catalysts in a new revolution of values – this time a curative, Dionysian revolution – that will overcome the Christian culture and the "modern ideas" born of it (the Enlightenment, liberalism, nationalism, socialism, etc. (and, if living to see it, fascism as well). The Jews' role is thereby a transitory one, for it will abolish itself when successful.

It should be noted that Nietzsche's admiration for Diaspora Jews is not aimed at them as bearers of a *religious* culture, but as displaying the human, existential element which he needs for his revolution. Nietzsche, of course, is as opposed to the Jewish *religious* message as he is to any other transcendent religion. The Jews' role is certainly not to "Judaize" Europe in a religious sense. But *Nietzsche seems to believe that their existential qualities can be extracted regardless of the content of their belief.* Nietzsche would rather expect them to *secularize* and practice creative assimilation in the framework of an atheistic Europe.

I must also emphasize that Nietzsche's pro-Jewish attitude does not derive from liberalism. Just as his attack on nationalism and racism is coming, so to speak, "from the right",[8] so his defense of the Jews derives from Nietzsche's own (Dionysian and anti-liberal) sources. Also, the Jews are supposed to enhance that same Nietzschean philosophy of life – a task which many Jews, who were and are liberals, can hardly welcome.

Nietzsche's enthusiasm for the vocation of modern Jews is not merely theoretical; it derives also from a classic problem confronting any revolutionary: where is the lever *within* the existing system by which to revolutionize it? Who are the forces uncontaminated by the system? The existence, in the form of the Jews, of a human group he considers more powerful than the others and free of Christian culture is a practical asset which Nietzsche badly needs in order to make his revolution look less utopian in his and in others' eyes.

In any case, my study shows that the Jewish issue was far more central to Nietzsche's thought and project than is usually recognized. The former corrupters of European culture and its designated redeemers, the Jews are placed by Nietzsche at two of the critical junctures in his philosophy. It is thus noteworthy that he always attributes some decisive historical role to the Jews, whether negative or positive, corrupting or redeeming. In this ironic sense he continues to regard them as a kind of "chosen people" – or the secular, heretical Nietzschean version of this concept!

This closes the circle of our analysis. Nietzsche as anti-anti-Semite (and the "Dionysian" admirer of modern Jews) complements Nietzsche as critic of ancient Judaism, within *the same* basic conception and *a single* philosophical project. Using these distinctions, we have delineated the structure of Nietzsche's ambivalence and the relation between its ingredients. The analysis found a fairly consistent thought behind it. Beyond the contradictions, flashes of brilliancy, dubious historical examples and arbitrary statements which Nietzsche's pen often ejects, we discovered at bottom a uniform way of thinking, applied to a central philosophical theme.

APPENDIX: NIETZSCHE AND HIS ABUSES

Here the question must arise: why was Nietzsche abused more than other philosophers? What was it that attracted his abusers? There seem to be at least four reasons for this: his special mode of writing; the non-ordinary psychology required by his position; the "right-wing" origin of his sensibilities; and his political impotence.

(1) Nietzsche's mode of writing is one major reason. His rhetoric is deliberately often wild and paradoxical, intended to arouse and provoke rather than to simply argue and inform; Nietzsche is at times ironic, at times bombastic, and both tonalities are traps for the naive reader; for Nietzsche's irony is not easy to decipher and his fanfare produces overstated effects which others might take at face value. Another factor in his writing is the often deliberate use of contradiction, which he used for several reasons, including his "experimental" way of philosophizing which shuns final, dogmatic truths and tries to undermine its own authoritative tone.

(2) Another reason for abuse is that Nietzsche's philosophy puts a strain on ordinary mentalities and often breaks the usual "packaging" of intellectual strands; it requires a person to hold on *at the same time* to positions which are usually considered psychologically incompatible. There is always some narrow path Nietzsche traces within the cruder ordinary distinctions, a path which cannot always be defined conceptually but requires, he says, a certain *personality* to locate and identify. Such narrow paths are dangerous, however, in philosophy no less than in mountaineering; one can easily take a deep fall and imagine one drags the author along.

(3) Several of Nietzsche's sensibilities, criticisms, etc., when taken in isolation, may invoke the joy of recognition in a rightist reader. Because of this partial, local affinity he finds with a Nietzschean idea or sentiment, such a reader then sweeps the *whole* of Nietzsche into his own camp, no matter how many unsurpassable obstacles he has to jump or ignore. This is bad, intellectually corrupt, historically unjust, but very common and all too human. Today there is also a left-wing appropriation of Nietzsche, which makes him the father of pluralism (even of tolerance in a "post-modern" sense),[9] the liberator from "hierarchic" rationalism and the "oppressive" Enlightenment.

This abuse is no better, intellectually, than the right-wing one, though politically it seems less ominous.

(4) Finally, Nietzsche attracted abusers because of what I call his political impotence – the vacuum he left in political theory. I know this is not the common view today, but I think Nietzsche's protests against politics are borne out by a marked lacuna in his thinking – the lack of a positive philosophy of the "multitude". Politics is not about the happy few, but about those ordinary people, the modern mass or "herd" which Nietzsche did not care about and did not make the topic of any positive philosophical reflection. This invites abuse, because when ordinary people are supposed to act in *extra*ordinary ("Dionysian") ways, or when a patrician message intended for a minority is generalized – that is, vulgarized – into a mass political movement, the result is not only intellectually grotesque but a political profanation and possible catastrophe, quite opposed to Nietzsche's aspirations, yet an outcome he should have foreseen.[10]

ABBREVIATIONS

AC Nietzsche, Friedrich, *The Antichrist*, in *The Portable Nietzsche*, ed. and tr. Walter Kaufmann, New York: Viking Press, 1954.

BGE Nietzsche, Friedrich, *Beyond Good and Evil*, in *Basic Writings of Nietzsche*, ed. and tr. Walter Kaufmann, New York: Random House, 1966.

BW Nietzsche, Friedrich, *Nietzsche Briefwechsel Kritische Gesamtausgabe*, ed. Giorgio Colli and Mazzino Montinari, Berlin: de Gruyter, 1975.

GM Nietzsche, Friedrich, *On the Genealogy of Morals*, in *Basic Writings of Nietzsche*, ed. and tr. Walter Kaufmann, New York: Random House, 1966.

HAH Nietzsche, Friedrich, *Human, All Too Human*, in *The Portable Nietzsche*, ed. and tr. Walter Kaufmann, New York: Viking Press, 1954.

NW Nietzsche, Friedrich, *Nietzsche Contra Wagner*, in *The Portable Nietzsche*, ed. and tr. Walter Kaufmann, New York: Viking Press, 1954.

PN Nietzsche, Friedrich, *The Portable Nietzsche*, ed. and tr. Walter Kaufmann, New York: Viking Press, 1954.

TI Nietzsche, Friedrich, *Twilight of the Idols*, in *The Portable*

Nietzsche, ed. and tr. Walter Kaufmann, New York: Viking Press, 1954.

WP Nietzsche, Friedrich, *The Will to Power*, tr. Walter Kaufmann, New York: Random House, 1968.

Z Nietzsche, Friedrich, *Thus Spoke Zarathustra*, in *The Portable Nietzsche*, ed. and tr. Walter Kaufmann, New York: Viking Press, 1954.

NOTES

1 *Hegel and Nietzsche on Judaism* (Hebrew; Tel Aviv: Schocken, 1996; English edition in preparation).

2 In a paper published in 1988 (M. Duffy and W. Mittelman, "Nietzsche's attitude toward the Jews", *Journal of the History of Ideas* 49 (1988): 301–17) the authors attribute to Nietzsche a threefold division very much like mine, which they say they couldn't find in any former publication. Had they looked more attentively they would have seen a short paper of mine, "Perspectives nouvelles sur Nietzsche et le judaïsme", *Revue des etudes juives* 88 (1979): 483–5, which suggests almost exactly the same division. That paper was a summary of public lectures given first at the Israel Academy of Sciences and Humanities and later at the Paris Societé des Etudes Juives (materials from that summary are included in the present chapter). This oversight also has a reassuring side, because if others have independently reached the same thesis, then there must be something in the material which strongly calls for it. The threefold division suggested in my *REJ* paper is recognized and debated in another French paper by D. Bechtel, "Nietzsche et la dialectique de l'histoire juive", in D. Bourel and J. le Rider, *De Sils-Maria à Jérusalem* (Paris: Cerf, 1991), pp. 67–9.

3 This section and the next are drastically shortened summaries. For a more complete discussion, see Yirmiyahu Yovel, "Nietzsche, the Jews, and *ressentiment*", in R. Schacht (ed.), *Nietzsche, Genealogy, Morality* (Berkeley: University of California Press, 1994), pp. 214–36.

4 This indicates, by the way, that Nietzsche was aware of already being abused in his lifetime, hence his protests and indignation.

5 Nietzsche seems to refer to the Fritsch affair mentioned above.

6 There is no doubt Nietzsche considered Burckhardt an anti-Semite (though he was perhaps less extreme than the others).

7 This analysis is chiefly based on *Daybreak* 205 (tr. R. J. Hollingdale, Cambridge: Cambridge University Press, 1982), which Nietzsche considered most representative of his views about Diaspora Jews (he referred others, like the anti-Semitic Fritsch, to it). Its length does not allow quoting it in this summary.

8 From an aristocratic ethics of virtue and excellence and a Dionysian ethics of power.

9 This makes no sense, because Nietzsche does not tolerate all forms of life – some he would have abolished completely – and because there is

no principle of *right* behind his allegedly "pluralistic" position (indeed no principle at all) which is incompatible with the left-wing politics.

10 I think he did, but was unable to cope with it – except by indignant protests, as in the Fritsch affair.

Part II
NIETZSCHE'S JEWISH RECEPTION

7

NIETZSCHE, KAFKA AND LITERARY PATERNITY

Stanley Corngold

What things do we copy, writing and painting, we mandarins with Chinese brushes (*mit chinesischem Pinsel*), we immortal-izers of things that can be written . . .?

(Nietzsche[1])

Nothing of that, slanting through the words there come vestiges of light.

(Kafka[2])

Aut liberi aut libri.

(old saying)

I raise the question of Kafka as a reader of Nietzsche in order to focus on the topic of *literary paternity* – the relation of the producer of literature to his products as male parent to offspring. It is not so much some hypothetical paternal relation between Nietzsche and his reader Kafka that is at stake: Kafka's literary personality did not, at any rate, come of Nietzsche as, let us say, his story "The judgement" came out of him, "like a regular birth."[3] I am concerned, instead, with Nietzsche's and Kafka's own views on literary paternity – and the relation that might be said to exist between them on the basis of their views.

Now, to be willing even to consider "literary paternity" of a "regular" or legitimate kind is of course to strike a defiantly modern stance, for this stance is radically anti-Platonic, and, in Nietzsche's words, modernity is "the fight against Plato."[4] Literary paternity, the conjunction of male acts of writing with live proper offspring, joins what Plato's Socrates put asunder, even if this figure remains, of course, well within the orbit of his influence.

The metaphor of literary paternity is of Socratic origin, but the notion of a proper literary paternity is for Socrates untrue or incomplete. Plato's translator and commentator Jowett sums up the relevant portion of the *Phaedrus*:

> Writing is inferior to speech. For writing is like a picture which can give no answer to a question, and has only a deceitful likeness of a living creature. It has no power of adaptation, but uses the same words for all. It is a sort of bastard and not a legitimate son of knowledge, and when an attack is made upon this illegitimate progeny, neither the parent nor anyone else is there to defend it. . . . The living is better than the written word . . . the principles of justice and truth when delivered by word of mouth are the legitimate offspring of a man's own bosom, and their lawful descendants take up their abode in others.[5]

The text of the *Phaedrus* actually succeeds less well in distinguishing the proper offspring of speech from the bastards of script. It describes the "right man," certainly, as one "who thinks that in the written word there is necessarily much which is not serious" but as one who also holds that

> only in principles of justice and goodness and nobility taught and communicated orally and *written in the soul, which is the true way of writing*, is there clearness and perfection and seriousness; and that such principles are like legitimate off-spring (my italics).[6]

To suppose the contrary, that both Nietzsche and Kafka care for writing because writing might entail legitimate reproduction, is to second their fight against Plato. I repeat this point: *might* entail legitimate reproduction; it is by no means a settled matter.[7]

Let us look now at these actual, complicated cases, beginning with the view of a recent reader of Nietzsche, Alexander Nehamas. In *Nietzsche: Life as Literature*, Nehamas argues that Nietzsche actually succeeded, through effects of writing, in fathering a human personality. For Nietzsche's books amount neither to a philosophical system nor to a collection of aperçus but rather to the production of a "character." "In engaging with [Nietzsche's] works," Nehamas writes,

> we are not engaging with the miserable little man who wrote them but with the philosopher who emerges through them, the magnificent character these texts constitute and manifest, the

agent who, as the will to power holds, is nothing but his effects – that is, his writings.[8]

Even acknowledging, as Nehamas does, that "the parallel between life and literature is" (to say the least) "not perfect," nonetheless his formulation more or less meets the conditions of paternity: the empirical Nietzsche does indeed produce ("constitutes and manifests") a personal being ("a magnificent character"), it being, for the moment, of only secondary importance that the person fathered by "this miserable little man" Nietzsche was actually *himself*. The dwindling empirical personality produces, through acts of writing, another self, its deep self – it reproduces itself, becoming the self it was. Odd as this formulation may sound, we have no choice, on Nehamas's view, but to call Nietzsche's literary persona a human self, so clearly marked is it by the customary attributes: it is a speaking (or echoing) subject, stylized into a character of depth, variousness and complexity, recognizable through its many appearances, endowed with moods, modulating its identity through the effects it imaginatively produces on its audience. This state of affairs can be confidently characterized as "literary paternity" – indeed at the very least as "literary" paternity, since it appears to verge closely on real paternity.

If, though, we are willing to entertain this view of Nietzsche as a father – and, indeed, as the father of himself – what are we to make of Nietzsche's insistence on the difference between life and literature, in, for instance, *Ecce Homo*: "I am one thing, my writings are another matter"?[9] For this difference stipulates decisively the very distinction between real and artificial reproduction, from which there follows nothing less than the impossibility of literary paternity and hence the profoundly abusive character of this metaphor. For even if Nietzsche's life (or so-called "experience") is literally and deeply entangled in his literature (or so-called "rhetoric"), nonetheless, "paternity" remains one of those knifeblade words mercilessly distinguishing literal and figurative meanings without further recourse: nation-states, for example, have traditionally required fathers to feed, clothe and shelter their offspring but not their "offspring," i.e. their literary effects.[10] Nietzsche himself excerpted with interest this cautionary sentence: "Paternity [is] not something self-evident but rather a legal institution achieved only late."[11]

As it springs from Nietzsche's pen, the tense distinction between reproduction in life and literature produces some highly charged results. Toward the end of *Beyond Good and Evil*, Nietzsche writes: "This 'work,' whether of the artist or of the philosopher, invents the man who has created it, who is supposed to have created it: 'great man,' as they are venerated, are subsequent pieces of wretched minor fiction."[12] Consider, then: artistic "paternity" in this instance is but a bad fiction, a type of the minor fiction of so-called personal "creation." In fact, it is the offspring who retrospectively "invents" the personality of its supposed begetter. Nietzsche's key words here are "invents" (*erfindet*), not "creates" (*schafft*), "pieces of wretched minor fiction" (*kleine schlechte Dichtungen*), not truly "great men" (*große Männer*). The destructive force of this passage cannot be confined to a chiastic reversal of direction of the paternity metaphor. On the contrary, the passage annihilates the paternity metaphor purely and simply by degrading it to a wretched minor invention.[13]

In *On the Genealogy of Morals* we find a more revealing example of Nietzsche's attack on the paternity metaphor. Nietzsche famously writes:

> One should guard against confusion through psychological *contiguity*, to use a British term, a confusion to which an artist himself is only too prone; as if he himself were what he is able to represent, conceive, and express. The fact is that *if* he were it, he would not represent, conceive, and express it: a Homer would not have created an Achilles or Goethe a Faust. Whoever is completely and wholly an artist is to all eternity separated from the "real," the actual; on the other hand, one can understand how he may sometimes weary to the point of desperation of the eternal "unreality" and falsity of his inner-most existence – and that then he may well attempt what is not forbidden him, to lay hold of actuality (*ins Wirkliche über-zugreifen*), for once actually to *be*. With what success? That is easy to guess.[14]

It is not so easy to guess. It might be easy to guess that the outcome would be disastrous, but our power to envision this disaster fails on account of our necessarily weak understanding of what it might mean "to lay hold of actuality, for once actually to be." It does seem immediately plausible to grasp this "*typical velleity* of the artists" as moving toward an act modeled on the sexual incursion that could father a child (the German suggests, along with "a laying hold," "a forced entry") and in so doing forge a fetter binding the artist to "the real." On this view, Nietzsche resists the fall from artistic askesis into the sexual reality of the woman – into what is termed, in the critique of Wagner immediately following, the world of the "woman in need."[15]

This reading is pertinent. The image of sexual transgression arises immediately afterwards in this essay (though in a displaced way). We need to feel, as the argument unfolds, the heady ambivalence of Nietzsche's attraction to *and* contempt for the act of "laying hold of actuality." It is crucial, for one thing, that the artist who is exemplary for caving in to the temptation "actually to be" is his beloved adversary, the aging Wagner – and the fruit of his lapse, *Parsifal.* What kind of offspring – legitimate or bastard – is this?

A more nearly illegitimate one. The artist, Nietzsche writes, does violence to his own nature in becoming a kind of priest and metaphysician – a deluded propagator of ethical ideals. (One could say, he becomes "the wretched fiction" of a propagator of ideals.) According to Nietzsche, Wagner's late, dubious achievement is to "utter *ascetic ideals*," an act, however, which is not even original with Wagner but one for which he had to gain "*courage* [from] ... the prop provided by Schopenhauer's philosophy." This appropriation of influence is altogether improper, for, according to Nietzsche, Schopenhauer's philosophy itself has no designs on "'the real,' the actual," being the work of "a genuinely independent spirit ... a man ... who had the courage to be himself, who knew how to stand alone."[16] (We should reflect on this "standing alone," on a way of being that is not *actually* a way of being.) Wagner's use of Schopenhauer is a perversion; he turned Schopenhauer's private system into a public spectacle.

What drives Wagner to this violence? It is the force of his desire to "lay hold of actuality." It made him vulnerable to poisonous influences, and it overrode even his loyalty to himself – the loyalty his earlier aesthetic position required from him, for (here I quote Nietzsche):

> There exists a complete theoretical contradiction between his earlier and his later aesthetic creed – the former set down, for example, in *Opera and Drama*, the latter in the writings he [Wagner] published from 1870 onward. Specifically, he ruthlessly altered ... his judgment as to the value and status of *music*; what did he care that he had formerly made of music a means, a medium, a "woman" who required a goal, a man, in order to prosper – namely, drama![17] He grasped all at once that

with the Schopenhauerian theory and innovation *more* could be done *in majorem musicae gloriam* – namely, with the theory of the *sovereignty* of music as Schopenhauer conceived it. . . . With this extraordinary rise in the value of music that appeared to follow from Schopenhauerian philosophy, the value of *the musician* himself all at once went up in an unheard-of manner, too: from now on he became an oracle, a priest, indeed more than a priest, a kind of mouthpiece of the "in itself" of things, a telephone from the beyond – henceforth he uttered not only music, this ventriloquist of God – he uttered metaphysics: no wonder he one day finally uttered *ascetic ideals*.[18]

In the new system, representing a "complete theoretical contradiction" of the old, the ascetic priest plays the dominant, displacing the artist-mediator – read: procurer – whose music drama arose from a sexual coupling. Wagner, the ascetic priest, does not grasp, however, that in this way he himself becomes an invader of boundaries,[19] an implicitly sexual transgressor of what is forbidden in reality.

In both cases, Nietzsche sexualizes Wagner's theoretical *mise-en-scène* of opera: explicitly, in the first case, as a scene of sexual intercourse – the masculine Word of drama impregnates music figured as Need; implicitly, in the second, as a scene of violation, in order that music, and with it the musician, "prosper" (*gedeihen*) – which means, reproduce.[20] I draw this reproductive conclusion with the help of other passages, e.g. from *Thus Spoke Zarathustra*: "Everything about women is a riddle, and everything about women has one solution: that is pregnancy."[21] (It is no secret that Nietzsche has more interesting things to say about women – who, in at least one instance, we are meant to believe is Truth, and as such no longer the riddle but its solution.)[22]

At this point it is clear that Nietzsche, with Schopenhauer's help, has rejected the association of art with sexual reproduction. Yet we do not want to leave Nietzsche's argument without noting an important swerve – namely, it will soon be Schopenhauer's turn to be excoriated. For, like Wagner, he too abuses art in his aesthetics by instrumentalizing it as a palliative against sexual desire. The contrary figure to Schopenhauer, for Nietzsche, is now Stendhal (as the contrary figure to Wagner was Schopenhauer) – Stendhal, who does indeed acknowledge the power of art to "arouse" the will, for art is most truly a scene of sexual excitation.[23] But this sort of sexual charging can be safely preferred to Wagner's early aesthetic of impregnation, because it appears to identify art with male arousal or, better, masculinizes aesthetic excitation in opposing it to woman's desire for reproductive fulfillment.

Nevertheless, a number of Nietzsche's texts are regularly cited as erasing this opposition. Sarah Kofman, for example, concludes from her reading of the *Genealogy of Morals* that "because the birth of a work of art is also the birth of a gifted child, Nietzsche uses the same economic hypothesis to understand it [and thus 'the work of art draws on all the reserves and supplements of the force and vigor of animal life']."[24] A work of art is like "a gifted child"? One is reluctant to criticize so progressive an idea. But this sort of intervention arises from what Benjamin, in his *Elective Affinities* essay, terms "lightly-assumed liberalism (*gespielter Freisinn*)."[25] I know of no sentence in which Nietzsche identifies the work of art with the birth of a gifted child. Indeed, in the preceding aphorism Nietzsche has the opposite to say about children – gifted or otherwise: "Every philosopher would speak as Buddha did when he was told of the birth of a son: Rahula has been born to me, a fetter has been forged for me [Rahula here means 'little demon']."[26] Why would it also not be important that books precisely not be such little devils in any way whatsoever?

A couple of famous aphorisms from *The Gay Science* also suggest an intimate link between authorship and male parturition. "Constantly," writes Nietzsche, "we [philosophers] have to give birth to our thoughts out of our pain and, like mothers, endow them with all that we have in us of blood, heart, fire, pleasure, passion, agony, conscience, fate, catastrophe."[27] The same book, however, also offers an opposed account: "Spiritual pregnancy produce[s] the character of the contemplative type, which is closely related to the feminine character: it consists of male mothers." Note, however that the value for Nietzsche of "the contemplative type," let alone "the male mother," hardly goes uncontested. For the excursus on spiritual pregnancy is preceded by the qualification: "Pregnancy has made women kinder, more patient, more timid, more pleased to submit";[28] we recall that in just the same way "spiritual pregnancy produce[s] the character of the contemplative type," etc. The sexual charge on art is not improved by its dissipating into a submissive body.

Should one, then, be as sad as Laurence Rickels, who, noting Heidegger's misappropriation of Nietzsche, remarks: "Here we traverse an uncanny and barren landscape, one in which everything recalls to us that Nietzsche died without having had children"?[29]

Did Nietzsche want to have children?

The stage has been set for the conclusive proclamations of *Ecce Homo*:

> The good fortune of my existence, its uniqueness perhaps, lies in its fatality: I am, to express it in the form of a riddle, already dead as my father, while as my mother I am still living and becoming old.[30]

Nietzsche thereafter develops the conceit differently, shrinking from his feminization: "At another point as well," he writes, "I am merely my father once more and, as it were, his continued life after an all-too-early death."[31] To the extent that Nietzsche's riddle is thinkable, his literary reproduction was confined to his incessantly reproducing himself as his father. Everything points to Kierkegaard, in *Fear and Trembling*: "The one who will not work fits what is written about the virgins of Israel: he gives birth to wind – but the one who will work gives birth to his own father."[32] Nietzsche kept on fathering his father whose task it was to father him. The point goes back to the earliest years of Nietzsche's writing, to *Human, All Too Human*: "If one does not have a good father, one should furnish oneself with one"; and things are always so, for "in the maturity of his life and understanding a man is overcome by the feeling his father was wrong to father him" (translation modified).[33] And so Nietzsche had, so to speak, to give birth continually to himself. Recall the prohibition against the artist's attempt "for once actually to *be*." As his already dead father, Nietzsche had his father's work to do – and did, a work without conclusion.

At this point, it might be observed, we have put forth claims bordering on Nehamas's – namely, that Nietzsche reproduced his genuine self in his writing and that in this sense Nietzsche's work crosses the divide between literature and life: but note the important difference in our conclusion. Nietzsche does not reproduce himself so much as he perpetually produces himself for the first time in the one form he wants to be. This is not quite an affair of becoming the "philosopher" or "character" who transcends the "miserable little man" who writes. His task is more fundamental still. He writes in order to be – or not to be – a ghost.[34] This is not reproduction but a movement incessantly repeating an inconclusive birth. Nietzsche had to locate the task of generation further back; he had first to set his genealogy to rights, then strive to be the being he never yet was.

Something of this argument is present even in the triumphalist

rhetoric of *Thus Spoke Zarathustra*. In "On child and marriage,"
Nietzsche writes:

> You are young and wish for a child and marriage. But I ask
> you: Are you a man *entitled* to wish for a child? Are you the
> victorious one, the self-conqueror, the commander of your
> senses, the master of your virtues? This I ask you. Or is it the
> animal and need that speak out of your wish? Or loneliness?
> Or lack of peace with yourself?
>
> Let your victory and your freedom long for a child. You shall
> build living monuments to your victory and your liberation.
> You shall build over and beyond yourself, but first you must
> be built yourself, perpendicular in body and soul. You shall not
> only reproduce yourself, but produce something higher! (*Nicht
> nur fort sollst du dich pflanzen, sondern hinauf!*). May the
> garden of marriage help you in that![35]

"On child and marriage" distinguishes the reproduction of a child
in marriage (*sich fortpflanzen*) from another sort of action which may
be sexual but is not reproductive at all (*sich hinaufpflanzen*). This
action suggests an arousal of the will and hence artistic excitement.
But for all his instinctualization of the act of writing, the view is not
the Freudian one which considers such work as "substitutive [sexual]
gratification" (especially if the scene of gratification be conjugal and
its tendency reproductive). In urging the instinctual character of
writing, Nietzsche means, on the one hand, to elude the pitfalls of
sublimation and the eternal series of reverse valorizations the concept
engenders (the sublimated product, the artwork, is "finer," but
it is also "meeker" – and hence, decadent). On the other hand,
Nietzsche wants the act of writing to be the immediate – read
Dionysian – *discharge* of an affect, hence, more nearly a squandering:
this means, he wants to give away whatever there is of himself now.
Perhaps *he* is preserved in a particulate way in this scattering of word-
charges (but "A living thing seeks above all to *discharge* its strength
... self-preservation is only one of the indirect and most frequent
results").[36] But there is certainly no suggestion here of reproduction,
let alone a welcome acknowledgement of his verbal offspring for
containing the contribution of any other mother's charge (I am
thinking of Paul Rée, who dedicated a work to Nietzsche thus: "To
the father of this text, most gratefully, its mother").[37] Nietzsche's
main concern is to resist any intervention or injury to his narcissism
but his own – a narcissism that, by the way, is always only just about

STANLEY CORNGOLD

to glimpse itself. It feels itself as the will to the shattering that could being it into being for the first time. And so it strives to accumulate its erotic charge around a point of possibly productive self-scattering.

What task, now, was laid on Kafka, whose father would have very likely found it superfluous that Kafka give birth to him, being already superabundant in life?[38] The answer – Kafka's sense of the demand for reproduction – was shaped by Nietzsche's conclusion: this is the main point of this chapter.

The story of Kafka's actual reception of Nietzsche begins in 1900 with the attempt to seduce a girl by the name of Selma Kohn with passages from *Thus Spoke Zarathustra*.[39] Kafka's earliest, strongest experience of reading Nietzsche is therefore marked by sexual desire, irresolution, misogyny – and, of course, writing, for Selma was the daughter of the chief postman. There is nothing further in Kafka's reading relation to Nietzsche that can be specified in a positive way aside from the recollections of friends that Kafka took part in discussions on Nietzsche while at the university. In all his journals and correspondence Kafka never once mentions Nietzsche by name; except for Selma Kohn's letter to Max Brod, there are no hard data bearing on Nietzsche's importance for Kafka.[40] This state of affairs has led to a general agreement that, like Thomas Mann in *Doctor Faustus*, Kafka did not need to mention Nietzsche by name since he is everywhere in the work, like salt in seawater.[41]

I can agree with this to the extent that I am interested in pursuing one line of salt tears, and that is Kafka's sorrow over paternity.

Maurice Blanchot surmises that Kafka's ordeal of writing takes place inside a (Jewish) religious conflict.[42] The drama runs as follows: Kafka cares inordinately for writing, and the measure of the inordinateness of his concern is his readiness to test God with it: "God doesn't want me to write," Kafka wrote, "but I, I must."[43] This struggle is also the measure of writing's antithetical character, which, at the order of religion, means its diabolism. This association was never far from Kafka's mind. The act of writing may be devilish; the wager, in writing, is for nothing less than salvation – the failure, nothing less than damnation.

Here (in Blanchot's own words) is Kafka's predicament:

Kafka needed more time, but he also needed less of the world. The world was first his family, whose constraint he bore with difficulty, never being able to free himself from it. It was next his fiancée and his fundamental desire to observe the law which

146

requires man to fulfill his destiny in the world, have a family, children, and take his place in the community. Here the conflict assumes a new aspect, enters a contradiction which Kafka's religious position makes especially strong.

Blanchot proceeds to describe the difference in intensity between the predicaments of Kafka and Kierkegaard (to Kafka's disadvantage) and concludes:

> Kafka seemed to identify with the exigency of the work of art that which could bear the name of his salvation. If writing condemned him to solitude, made his existence that of a celibate, without love, without bonds, if however writing seemed to him ... the sole activity which could justify him, it was because, at all events, solitude was a threat to him within and without, it was because the community was nothing more than a phantom and because the law which still speaks through it (the community) is not even the forgotten law but the feigned forgetting of the law. Writing becomes once more, then ... a possibility of fulfillment, a path without a goal perhaps comparable to that goal without a path which is the only one that must be reached.[44]

But the matter cannot be put (nor does Blanchot finally put it) so victoriously. A good deal of Kafka's work and imagery in the years following his first broken engagement suggests an intention to straddle both positions by producing a literary progeny pleasing to God. Kafka did imagine a *literary* paternity.

If an undistorted disgust of reproduction colors *The Boy who Sank out of Sight* (*Der Verschollene*), there is the ecstatic breakthrough of "The judgment," which Kafka likened to a real birth. (Some readers have seen the breakdown of the writing machine in "In the penal colony" as a mark of Kafka's despair of ever again producing a story as quick and vital as "The judgement".) In March 1917 Kafka wrote the extraordinary story "Eleven sons," which is supposed to code in the narrator's eleven children eleven stories that Kafka was writing. Scholars in acknowledging this allusion have mostly focused their efforts on aligning the right story with the right son, without raising the basic question underlying this connection.

Max Brod concludes that "Eleven sons" amounts to a powerful proof of the idea that Kafka craved – and, more, achieved – paternity. "In a story like 'Eleven Sons,'" he writes,

STANLEY CORNGOLD

this high esteem for ... the patriarchal way of life ... stands
out clearly.... The prose piece "Eleven Sons" is, in my
opinion, to be understood as a wishful picture of fatherhood,
of founding a family, which can be held up against the father's
example as something of equal value, that is to say, something
just as magnificent and patriarchal.... This explanation is not
contradicted by the fact that Franz once said to me, "The
Eleven Sons' are quite simply eleven stories I am working on
this very moment." After all, stories were his children. In his
writing he was accomplishing on a remote territory, but
independently, something which was analogous to his father's
creative power – I am following Franz's conception of this
point, not my own – and which could be set alongside it.[45]

Yet I am not satisfied that Max Brod has accurately reproduced
Kafka's mood. "I am following Franz's conception of this point, not
my own," Brod writes immediately after having written the phrase
"in my opinion." The comfortable affirmation of literary paternity,
in which a "wishful picture" soon appears as an "accomplishment,"
stands in uneasy proximity with the lightly assumed liberalism of
Sarah Kofman's view on Nietzsche (that is the "gifted child" view).
The question missing from Brod's account of Kafka's position is
whether this act of autonomous reproduction could be regarded as
legitimate paternity, since it is a paternity obtained without the
advantages or (let us speak plainly in the case of Nietzsche and Kafka)
the deficits of natural paternity, namely, sexual and social intercourse
with a women.[46]

Wouldn't such paternity amount, in Kafka's case, to outwitting
the Jewish God by a trick, wouldn't his offspring seem a monstrous,
a devilish brood, and his skill at fraud, taken to an extreme, allow
him to come forward as a false messiah?

In any case, Kafka never allowed the fantasy of paternity to get to
this point, though the question continued to torment him. In the
months before his death, Kafka certainly had reason to brood over
the sorrow of being

without forebears, without marriage, without heirs, with a
fierce longing for forebears, marriage and heirs. There is an
artificial, miserable substitute for everything [he continues
pointedly], for forebears, marriages and heirs. Feverishly you
contrive these substitutes, and if the fever has not already
destroyed you, the hopelessness of the substitutes will.[47]

148

Nonetheless, for several years, Kafka gave himself fully to the design of one distinguished substitute – to writing. The distinction of this substitute is heightened by a set of later aphorisms, which place the ordeal of paternity in a metaphysical light. This light can be called Gnostic and shines especially strongly after 1918.

In January 1918 Kafka wrote in the series "Reflections on sin, Suffering, Hope and the True Way," "There is nothing besides a spiritual world; that we call the world of the senses is the Evil in the spiritual world." Ergo, there is a spiritual world, which might be augmented, while the sensory world, including the material creation and its Demiurge, remains evil. In 1920, Kafka wrote: "In one of our ancient scriptures it is said: 'Those who curse life and therefore think not being born, or subjugating life, is the greatest or the sole non-deceptive happiness must be right, for the judgement concerning life. . . .'"[48] The text breaks off, as if to mark the Sisyphean labor of believing in this scripture.[49]

In 1920 Kafka also composed a second series of aphorisms called "He." In January he wrote:

> All that he does seems to him, it is true, extraordinarily new, but also, because of the incredible spate of new things, extra-ordinarily amateurish, indeed scarcely tolerable, incapable of becoming history, breaking short the chain of generations, cutting off for the first time at its most profound source the music of the world, which before him could at least be divined. Sometimes in his arrogance he has more anxiety for the world than for himself [note the destructibleness of the world].[50]

In February 1920 he wrote:

> He does not live for the sake of his personal life; he does not think for the sake of his personal thoughts. It seems to him that he lives and thinks under the compulsion of a family, which, it is true, is itself superabundant in life and thought, but for which he constitutes, in obedience to some law unknown to him, a formal necessity.[51]

His family obligation has become an affair of occupying a certain "formal" position, which could point to the formal operation of writing. This formal position has in it all the closeness to family he can and must endure.

A thesis on the transmission of a certain attitude toward paternity from Nietzsche to Kafka now begins to define itself: Kafka's Gnostic turn was informed by a reminiscence of the Zoroastrianism of *Thus Spoke Zarathustra*, a recollection which repeats the religious-historical connection of Zoroastrianism to Gnosticism. This influence would be reinforced by the fact that in the first decades of the twentieth century, in Prague and elsewhere in Central Europe, Zoroastrianism was very much in the air.[52]

Zoroastrianism, as it backgrounds Nietzsche's *Zarathustra*, became a privileged marker for Kafka of a suicidal moral dualism – and the possibility of its overcoming. The way to that overcoming depends on the observance of a (barely readable) law or formal necessity and not, certainly, on any direct augmentation of "the world of the senses," which is idolatry. In this perspective, writing slides out from under the paternal, the reproductive metaphor: it has another purpose.

This context of purposes can be summed up as follows: Kafka must first of all be understood in a Jewish framework, in the Judaism of Jehovah after the covenant with Abraham. The problematic of paternity of a literary or indeed of any other kind is connected for Kafka with this religious frame. But as long as he stays within it, the problem for him *as a writer* is insoluble, for he is torn between two unacceptable positions. One is to be the father of Jewish children – but he cannot be this; because, two, he must write; but yet again writing might be only a gesture of diabolical defiance or a miserable substitute for Jewish paternity.

Kafka needs a thought model that no longer demands bodily reproduction. A Gnosticism entirely consonant with the Judaism of the Old Testament *before the covenant* gives him this other frame. The Persian-Manichean strain, for example, is ascetic in the sense of being quite literally opposed to reproduction: in holding the soul to be a particle of light, it deplores reproduction, an act by which these particles of light are further shattered and "world harmony" destroyed.[53]

As a Gnostic, Kafka is relieved of the burden of supposing his writing is only a miserable substitute, since that for which writing is only a miserable substitute is itself only a miserable simulacrum of the divine. In turning to Gnosticism he accomplishes a turnabout within, or upon, his own dilemma. Accordingly, the defects of the second position, which advocates writing (the objection being that writing is a diabolical presumption or a miserable substitute) are chiastically attached to the first position: it is actually fathering a sensuous child that is a diabolical presumption and a miserable substitute. Writing is now freed to perform its task of the negative.

Consider, now, Nietzsche's Zoroastrian Gnosticism, as it is spelled out in *Ecce Homo*. It contains the two familiar moments: Zoroaster was the greatest dualist; Zoroaster's dualism is a moral one, consisting of the two opposed moments: Good and Evil, Ormazd and Ahriman. Because Zoroaster was, for Nietzsche, "the first to consider the fight of good and evil the very wheel in the machinery of things, the transposition of morality into the metaphysical realm, as a force, cause, and end in itself," Zoroaster became "the first moralist."[54] In *Thus Spoke Zarathustra*, however – thus Nietzsche in *Ecce Homo* – *his* fictitious Zarathustra negates and overcomes the principles of his historical predecessor. "Zarathustra created this most calamitous error, morality: consequently", writes Nietzsche, "he must also be the first to recognize it."[55]

Thus Spoke Zarathustra, I am arguing, remains for Kafka an indelible reading experience, which stamps and shapes his Gnostic position. For Kafka's Gnosticism, too, is a metaphysical dualism which, in the absence of an indubitable Gnosis, is capable, perhaps of being overcome by one type of sensory practice – that is, of course, artistic practice. "The heavens assault Kafka's bodily ego," writes Harold Bloom, *"but only through his own writing"*[56]: writing is therefore also the place where the heavens can be resisted – or joined. The task of the negative might be accomplished through the sole covenant in which Kafka trusted: the covenant of writing. He turns to a "Hebrew variant of *Kunstreligion*"[57] – thus Walter Sokel – a mode of transcendence, an artistic practice, that is moral not because it attempts to discern Good and Evil, the spiritual and the sensual worlds, and hence "speak ascetic ideals," but because as an autonomous activity it is the sole appropriate form of a striving for purity and truthfulness. Nietzsche wrote: "Am I understood? – The self-overcoming of morality, out of truthfulness; the self-overcoming of the moralist, into his opposite – *into me* – that is what the name of Zarathustra means in my mouth."[58] Kafka wrote on 25 September 1917: "I can still have passing satisfaction from works like *A Country Doctor*, provided I can still write such things at all. . . . But happiness only if I can raise the world into the pure, the true, and the immutable."[59]

Both Nietzsche and Kafka strove to put down the torments of failed paternity, either by thinking of their books as offspring – a wretched minor fiction they were too scrupulous to avow for long –

STANLEY CORNGOLD

or by finding an intellectual, moral and feeling frame in which not having children would be pardonable. They imagined they had found such a frame, and Nietzsche helped Kafka to this discovery. The frame that pardons them implies at the same time the unheard-of freedom of producing the self by an artistic will to destruction of the created world.[60] Nietzsche jubilantly proclaims this freedom on the brink of insanity. Kafka, lucid to the end, could not welcome this freedom except with a tremor of anxiety, "sometimes ... fearing more for the world than for himself."[61]

NOTES

1 Friedrich Nietzsche, *Beyond Good and Evil*, in *Basic Writings of Nietzsche*, tr. Walter Kaufmann (New York: Random House, 1968), 296, p. 426.
2 Franz Kafka, *Dearest Father*, tr. Ernst Kaiser and Eithne Wilkins (New York: Schocken, 1954), p. 261.
3 *The Diaries of Franz Kafka, 1910–1913*, ed. Max Brod, tr. Joseph Kersh (New York: Schocken, 1948), p. 278.
4 Nietzsche, *Beyond Good and Evil*, Preface, p. 193.
5 *The Works of Plato*, tr. B. Jowett (New York: Tudor, n.d.), p. 368.
6 Ibid., pp. 446–7.
7 We should not leave this fight against Plato without distinguishing, though, the early modern stance of Nietzsche and Kafka from the late modern associated with Derrida precisely through his deconstruction of the *Phaedrus* (Jacques Derrida, "Plato's Pharmacy," in *Dissemination*, tr. Barbara Johnson (Chicago: University of Chicago Press, 1981), pp. 61–171).
   The elicitation of a post-modern literature, which Derrida seems to sponsor in disassembling Plato's valorization of speech over writing (literature being, in this sense, the post-modern as such), occurs not with a view to reversing the prestige and propriety of speech over writing, a reversal which gives exterior writing the vital predominance over self-reflective speech. Rather, Derrida's deconstruction proceeds in a spirit of (quietly maniacal) irony that makes it impossible to assert either Plato's seeming value judgement against writing – or the reverse. That is because, for Derrida, the topics of speech and writing are snarled in an infinite Greek, Egyptian and western textuality, whose ruling order, as he says, cannot be grasped in a perception, but only unraveled by an interminable reading that must needs delay the appearance of any conclusion having the form of progeny. A sharp interpreter of such procedures, Edward Said, remarks on the superannuated logic of "classical" writing:

   The classical novel contained the molestations of psychology and language in the pattern of procreation and generation found in the genealogically imagined plot, the family, and the self. But such a pattern cannot properly begin or order writing once the human subject is no longer given as capable of such procreation, once as a subject its major feature is not the author's faith in it but the fact that it, and its author, are fictions together being produced during the writing.

(*Beginnings* (New York: Basic Books, 1975), p. 157)

But if the argument against the procreative power of writing has to rest on the view that the human self is a fiction, then the argument cannot be grounded on either Nietzsche or Kafka (for neither is the self a fiction). (See Stanley Corngold, "Self and subject in Nietzsche" and "The author survives on the margin of his breaks: Kafka's narrative perspective," in *The Fate of the Self* (New York: Columbia University Press, 1986), pp. 95–128, 161–79.) This problem is a ready marker, if you will, between early and late modern.

8 Alexander Nehamas, *Nietzsche: Life as Literature* (Cambridge, Mass.: Harvard University Press, 1985), p. 234.

9 Friedrich Nietzsche, *Ecce Homo*, in *Basic Writings*, "Why I write such good books"1, p. 715.

10 There is a fine sardonic formulation of this distinction in Dostoevsky's *Notes from Underground*, where it takes the form of polemic. The Underground Man says, to conclude:

Why we don't even know where the living lives today, or what it is, or what its name is. Leave us on our own, without a book, and we shall instantly become confused and lost – we shall not know what to join, what to believe in, what to love and what to hate, what to respect and what to despise. We even feel it's too much of a burden to be men – men with real bodies, real blood *of our own*. We are ashamed of this, we deem it a disgrace, and try to be some impossible "generalhumans." We are stillborn; for a long time we haven't even been begotten of living fathers, and we like this more and more. We have developed a real taste for it. We'll soon invent a way of somehow getting born from an idea. But enough; I do not want to write any more "Notes from Underground".

(Dostoevsky, *Notes from Underground*, tr. Mirra Ginsburg (New York: Bantam, 1983), p. 153)

Here, Dostoevsky is conjuring a condition contrary-to-fact, whose rhetorical force is chiefly comminatory, meaning to warn against any deeper immersion into the book-madness of modern life. Kafka and Nietzsche are not infected with this despair: both have a good deal to say about the benefits of a disappearance of living fathers.

11 *Nachgelassene Fragmente* (8/6), *Kritische Studienansgabe*, vol. 10, p. 326, cited in Klaus Goch (ed.), *Nietzsche uber die Frauen* (Frankfurt am Main and Leipzig: Insel, 1992), p. 228.

12 Nietzsche, *Beyond Good and Evil* 269, p. 408.

13 Importantly, the passage leaves open the question of whether personality can ever be assigned to a work of art; on the other hand, it rules out the

possibility of assigning any comparable (greatness of) personality to the so-called "creator." Hence, since reproduction implies production in kind, there is no kinship in this relation of author to book beyond the illusion of kinship, an illusion which can be seen through in the way that the factitiousness of the wretched minor fiction can be seen through.

14 Friedrich Nietzsche, *On the Genealogy of Morals*, in *Basic Writings*, III 4, p. 537.

15 Compare these lines from *Twilight of the Idols*:

> If there is to be art, if there is to be any aesthetic doing and seeing, one physiological condition is indispensable: frenzy.... What is essential in such frenzy is the feeling of increased strength and fullness. Out of this feeling one lends to things, one *forces* them to accept from us, one violates them – this process is called *idealizing*.
> (*The Portable Nietzsche*, tr. Walter Kaufmann (New York: Viking, 1969), "Skirmishes of an untimely man" 8, p. 518)

16 Nietzsche, *Genealogy of Morals* III 4, p. 538.

17 It it is true that the act previously conjured – of "laying hold of actuality" (*das Übergreifen ins Wirkliche*) – adumbrates a sexual clasp and incursion, then Wagner will already have scandalously displaced this scene of violence into the interior of the music drama.

18 Nietzsche, *Genealogy of Morals* III 4, p. 539.

19 Like the upstart in Kafka's *The Castle*, also a "Landvermesser."

20 Compare the similar conclusion that Geoff Waite comes to, after taking a different route of reflection – namely, Nietzsche's reflections on Baudelaire:

> It seems, in any case, that the music of Wagner, now as mediated by Baudelaire, possessed for Nietzsche the quasi-sexual, and certainly phallocentric, power not merely to *disseminate* but also to *re/produce* the (semiotic and illocutionary, if not also physio-logical) *tools* of dissemination.
> (Geoff Waite, "Nietzsche's Baudelaire, or the sublime proleptic spin of his politico-economic thought," *Representations* 50 (Spring 1995): 22)

21 *Thus Spoke Zarathustra: A Book for All and None*, in *Portable Nietzsche*, "On little old and young women," p. 178. I owe this reference to Peter Burgard's introductory essay – "Figures of excess" – in Peter Burgard (ed.), *Nietzsche and the Feminine* (Charlottesville and London: University Press of Virginia, 1994), p. 7.

22 "Supposing truth is a women – what then?" (*Beyond Good and Evil*, Preface, p. 192).

23 Cf. Nietzsche, *Twilight of the Idols*, p. 518.

24 Sarah Kofman, "A fantastical genealogy: Nietzsche's family romance," in Burgard (ed.), *Nietzsche and the Feminine*, p. 49.

25 The phrase is assigned sardonically to Gundolf, Goethe's hagiographer, in "Goethes Wahlverwandtschaften," *Gesammelte Schriften*, ed. Rolf

Tiedemann and Hermann Schweppenhaüser, vol. 2 (Frankfurt am Main: Suhrkamp, 1972), p. 199. Walter Benjamin, "Goethe's elective affinities," tr. Stanley Corngold, in *Works*, ed. Michael Jennings and Marcus Bullock (Cambridge, Mass.: Harvard University Press, forthcoming).

26 Nietzsche, *Genealogy of Morals* III 7, p. 543.

27 Friedrich Nietzsche, *The Gay Science*, tr. Walter Kaufmann (New York: Vintage, 1974), Preface for the 2nd edn, 3, pp. 35–6.

28 Ibid., II 72, p. 129.

29 Laurence Rickels (ed.), *Looking After Nietzsche* (Albany: SUNY Press, 1990), p. xv.

30 Nietzsche, *Ecce Homo*, "Why I am so wise" 1, p. 678.

31 Ibid., 5, p. 684.

32 Søren Kierkegaard, *Fear and Trembling/Repetition*, ed. and tr. H.V. and E.H. Hong (Princeton: Princeton University Press, 1983), p. 27. Cited in a senior thesis by Ioannis Mentzas, *Volume I: Onans* (Princeton University, June 1994).

33 Friedrich Nietzsche, *Human, All Too Human*, tr. R.J. Hollingdale (Cambridge: Cambridge University Press, 1986), 381, 386, p. 150.

34 On Nietzsche's fear of being a ghost, Henry Staten, in *Nietzsche's Voice* (New York: Cornell University Press, 1991), p. 184, writes aptly of *Ecce Homo*:

> Has there ever been a more cunning project of self-representation? Nietzsche does not say "here I am, look at me, I display my portrait to you"; he leaves everything to be inferred from hints, allusions, tones of voice, from the structure of the masks he wears when he speaks, not the man himself but his traces. And yet these traces project the strange illusion of a being of infinite pathos whose pathos is that he cannot quite become real, a being of flesh and blood. He remains a kind of phantasm or ghost who does not inhabit the text but *haunts* it: "Example: one reaches out for us but gets no hold of us. That is frightening. Or we enter though a closed door. Or after all the lights have been extinguished. Or after we have died" (*GS* 365). What makes this phantasm disturbing is that it seems to be the "real" Nietzsche, the only Nietzsche that ever managed to come into being, as though this were not only all that is left of him but also all there ever was.

35 Friedrich Nietzsche, *Thus Spoke Zarathustra*, in *Portable Nietzsche*, "On child and marriage," pp. 181–3.

36 Nietzsche, *Beyond Good and Evil* I 13, p. 211.

37 Jochen Hörisch, "Die Armee, die Kirche und die alma mater: Eine Grille über Körperschaften," *Merkur* 44(7) (July 1990): 553.

38 Johannes Urzidil recalls that while out walking one day, he met Kafka, who asked, "What are you pulling in that little wagon?" while pointing to an apparatus of black steel and glass.

> "It's an enlarger," said Urzidil.
> "What is it used for?" Kafka asked.
> "I take photographs, and I enlarge them."

STANLEY CORNGOLD

"Whom do you photograph?"
"O, my sister, my mother, my father."

For a moment Kafka was still. "And you want to *enlarge* them?" This story was told by Urzidil to the German poet, Reinhard Paul Becker, and Becker told it to me.

39 Peter Mailloux, Kafka's American biographer, is certain that the section of *Thus Spoke Zarathustra* that Kafka read aloud to Selma Robitschek née Kohn was the "Dionysus dithyrambs," that is, hot seductive inducements. For my part, I am fairly confident that the text that Kafka recited was "On child and marriage" (Nietzsche's anti-conjugal thesis), because, as we know from Selma Robitschek's letter to Max Brod, Kafka tried very hard to induce her to study at the university. Franz Kafka, *Briefe 1902–1924*, ed. Max Brod (Frankfurt am Main: Fischer, 1958), p. 495. Kafka owned a copy of *Also Sprach Zarathustra*. In his description of Kafka's library, Jürgen Born records

> Item 180: **Nietzsche, Friedrich**: *Also Sprach Zarathustra*. Ein Buch für Alle und Keinen. Von Friedrich Nietzsche. (= *Nietzsche's [sic] Werke*. Erste Abteilung, Bd. VI). 38., 39. u. 40. Tsd. Leipzig: Verlag von C.G. Naumann, 1904. 531 S.
> (*Kafkas Bibliothek: Ein beschreibendes Verzeichnis* (Frankfurt am Main: Fischer, 1990), p. 119)

40 Kafka also subscribed to *Die Kunstwart*, a journal with a Nietzschean presence, from 1900 to 1904, and a year before his death put Ernst Bertram's *Nietzsche: Versuch einer Mythologie* on a list; see Jürgen Born, *Kafkas Bibliothek*, p. 183. But these are fugitive signs. Significantly, Steven E. Aschheim, in *The Nietzsche Legacy in Germany: 1890–1990* (Berkeley: University of California Press, 1993), has nothing to say about Kafka's reception of Nietzsche, for his is the historian's view.

41 On the relation of Nietzsche's and Kafka's thought generally, Gerhard Kurz asserts: "Having discovered him while in Gymnasium, Kafka remained faithful to Nietzsche's thinking until his death" ("Nietzsche, Freud, and Kafka," tr. Neil Donaghue, in Mark Anderson (ed.), *Reading Kafka: Prague, Politics, and the Fin de Siècle* (New York: Schocken, 1988), p. 138). This approach also has its own rigor: witness the study by Jacob Golomb, "Kafka's existential metamorphosis," *Clio* 14 (1985): 271–86.

42 Maurice Blanchot, "The diaries: the exigency of the work of Art," tr. Lyall H. Powers, in Angel Flores and Homer Swanders (eds), *Franz Kafka Today* (Madison: University of Wisconsin Press, 1964), pp. 195–220.

43 Frank Kafka, *Letters to Friends, Family, and Editors*, tr. Richard and Clara Winston (New York: Schocken, 1977), p. 10.

44 Blanchot, "Dairies," pp. 197–8.

45 Max Brod, *Franz Kafka: A Biography*, tr. G. Humphreys Roberts (New York: Schocken, 1947), pp. 139–40.

46 Bernhard Böschenstein's independent analysis of "Eleven sons" comes to a comparable conclusion. Böschenstein argues that the rhetoric of the

156

father-narrator is designed to seize possession of his children by confining their *being* to a few marked sensory attributes. The result is that "every assertion about the eleven sons contains judgments by Kafka the author on his eleven stories and at the same time cancels out these very judgments in denying the legitimacy of the father's procedure" (Bernhard Böschenstein, "Elf Söhne," in Claude David (ed.), *Franz Kafka: Themen und Probleme* (Göttingen: Vandenhoeck & Ruprecht, 1980), pp. 136–51).

47 *The Diaries of Franz Kafka, 1914–1923*, ed. Max Brod, tr. Martin Greenberg (New York: Schocken, 1949), p. 207.

48 Kafka, *Dearest Father*, p. 291.

49 "This feeling of those who have no children: it perpetually rests with you, whether you will or no, every moment to the end, every nerve-racking moment, it perpetually rests with you, and without results. Sisyphus was a bachelor" (Kafka, *Dairies*, p. 205).

50 Franz Kafka, *The Great Wall of China*, tr. Willa and Edwin Muir (New York: Schocken, 1960), pp. 263–4.

51 Ibid., p. 269.

52 According to Klaus Wagenbach, Kafka heard a number of lectures by Rudolf Steiner in Prague in 1911 employing such expressions as "Ahrimanian forces." "I remember noticing," reported Berta Fanta, in whose mother's house the event took place, "how during the lectures Kafka's eyes flashed and gleamed and a smile lit up his face" (Klaus Wagenbach, *Franz Kafka: Eine Biographie seiner Jugend, 1883–1912* (Berne: Francke, 1958), p. 175).

53 Michael Schreiber, "*Ihr sollt euch kein Bild – ...*": *Untersuchungen zur Denkform der negativen Theologie im Werk Franz Kafkas* (Frankfurt am Main: Peter Lang, 1988), p. 92. See further Walter Sokel, "Between Gnosticism and Jehovah: the dilemma in Kafka's religious attitude," *The South Atlantic Review* 50 (January 1985): 3–22.

54 Nietzsche, *Ecce Homo*, "Why I am a destiny" 3, pp. 783–4.

55 Ibid., p. 784.

56 Harold Bloom, "Introduction," in *Modern Critical Interpretations: Franz Kafka's The Trial* (New York: Chelsea House, 1987), pp. 17, 4.

57 Sokel, "Between Gnosticism," p. 10.

58 Nietzsche, *Ecce Homo*, "Why I am a destiny" 3, p. 784. On the distinction between truth and truthfulness in Nietzsche, see Jacob Golomb, "Nietzsche on authenticity," *Philosophy Today* 34 (1990): 243–58.

59 Kafka, *Dairies, 1914–1923*, p. 187.

60 Kafka evokes "a living magic or a destruction of the world that is not destructive but constructive" (*Dearest Father*, p. 103).

61 Kafka, *Great Wall of China*, pp. 263–4.

8

NIETZSCHE AND THE MARGINAL JEWS*

Jacob Golomb

How was Nietzsche received by Germany's *Grenzjuden*? I address the question of the marginal Jews in the *deutschen Sprachraum* the question of the marginal Jews in the *deutschen Sprachraum* and the German *Kulturbereich* by documenting the enthusiastic reception given to Nietzsche by two of their representatives. The identity crisis experienced by these individuals was the main factor precipitating their passionate interest in Nietzsche. Both the marginality of the *Grenzjuden*, and Nietzsche's congeniality to the need for personal authenticity aroused by this marginality, contributed to the irresistible attraction his works has for these Jews.

I am not claiming that the marginal Jews were the first or only contemporary admirers of Nietzsche. The Japanese, English and Russians were, perhaps, among the first to recognize his importance.[1] Nonetheless, it is well known that as early as 1875, members of the Austrian Pernerstorfer circle – which included such Jewish luminaries as Gustav Mahler and Viktor Adler – were profoundly inspired by Nietzsche.[2] Further, the first popular lectures on Nietzsche were given in 1888 by Morris Kohen (alias Georg Brandes),[3] some of the pioneering references to Nietzsche's genius as a German writer came from the pen of Leo Berg,[4] and Gustav Landauer was an early fan of Nietzsche, while Max Nordau was an early critic.[5] My interest here, however, is the manner in which Nietzsche's thought touched upon the central identity problems many of the *Grenzjuden* shared. They did not simply read Nietzsche, but, as Thomas Mann put it, keenly and deeply "experienced" him.[6] Nietzsche both diagnosed the agonies the *Grenzjuden* were undergoing, and prescribed means for relieving them.

THE *GRENZJUDEN*

By the term "marginal Jews", I refer to something more specific than that "problematic sector" which, according to Grunfeld, "produced most of those artists and intellectuals who helped to create the most turbulent period in the spiritual history of Germany".[7] Grunfeld uses the term to refer to such prominent Jewish women and men of letters as Else Lasker-Schüler, Arthur Schnitzler, Jakob Wassermann, Lion Feuchtwanger, Stefan Zweig, Alfred Döblin, Franz Kafka, Franz Werfel, Theodor Lessing, Kurt Tucholsky, Walter Benjamin, Carl Sternheim, Karl Kraus, Ernst Toller, Sigmund Freud and many others. All were *Grenzjuden* in that they had lost their religion and tradition, but had not been fully absorbed into secular German or Austrian society. For some, hatred of their ancestral roots led to self-destruction and breakdown.[8] These individuals tragically lacked an identity: they rejected any affinity with the Jewish community but were nonetheless unwelcome among their non-Jewish contemporaries. Jakob Wassermann describes them from within as: "religiously and socially speaking floating in the air. They no longer had the old faith; they refused to accept a new one, that is to say, Christianity . . . the physical ghetto has become a mental and moral one."[9] According to Gershom Scholem, "because they no longer had any other inner ties to the Jewish tradition, let alone to the Jewish people", these marginal Jews "constitute[d] one of the most shocking phenomena of this whole process of alienation".[10] Yet despite their desperate attempts to be accepted by the Germans as Germans, most recognized the traumatic truth that "for a Jew, especially in public life, it was impossible to disregard the fact that he was a Jew."[11]

The German Jews in general attempted a wide spectrum of solutions to this unbearable state of uprootedness, from full assimilation, even conversion to Christianity, to identification with some definite ideological or political cause, such as socialism (Ernst Bloch, Kurt Tucholsky and Ernst Toller) or Zionism (Martin Buber, Gershom Scholem, Nahum Goldman and Max Nordau). My concern, however, is limited to a subgroup of *Grenzjuden*: those who, in spite of the existential pressure, remained in a state of suspended identity – neither opting for socialism or Zionism nor embracing, like Alfred Döblin, some form of Catholicism.

These marginal Jews preferred to forego an identity rather than adopt a ready-made one. Nietzsche taught them that given the death of God all the ideological and political "isms" that had emerged in the nineteenth century were but residual shadows. Werfel poignantly expressed this sentiment: "socialism and nationalism are political *ersatz* religions." Continuing, he then pondered on his Jewish brethren:

> What way of escape do they have? The way of liberalism? Who would not be ashamed of its superficial and false cheapness? The way of nationalism? Self-deceit and self-destruction! One becomes a Hebrew nationalist in order not to have to be a Jew any longer! The way of orthodoxy? There is no retreat from life into fossilization, even if it be the holiest fossilization. The way to Christ? . . . There is no way out![12]

Nietzsche's attractiveness to them is rooted in his inspiring call to become a genuine free spirit and to search for one's *own* self and personal authenticity. Nietzsche urged his readers to create their own selves and lives just an as artist creates his works of art.[13] And creative the *Grenzjuden* certainly were, as their determination to shun all dogmatic ideology opened up "infinite perspectives" for them, echoing Nietzsche's anti-dogmatism and his plea to live creatively even "on the verge of an abyss".

As they solved their identity problems one way or another, the marginal Jews ceased to refer to Nietzsche, and freed themselves from his spell. But at the beginning of their tortuous searches for personal authenticity, many young, sensitive and vulnerable Jewish intellectuals were excited by the possibilities Nietzsche held out to them. While at the *Gymnasium* or university, these marginal Jews were often euphoric about Nietzsche, seeing in him a sustaining companion in their existential search. A case in point is that of Martin Buber, who, after adopting a kind of pacifist Zionism and existential Judaism, made strenuous efforts to free himself of the influence Nietzsche had exerted on him in his younger days, as he admits in his writings and letters.[14] The same is true of Alfred Döblin, after he became a Catholic,[15] and Ernst Toller after he decided to embrace revolutionary socialism.[16] Only Stefan Zweig, and those who, like him, never subscribed to any final definite identity, continued to write enthusiastically on Nietzsche and his ideas.

THE RECEPTION OF NIETZSCHE BY THE "PROPHETS WITHOUT HONOUR"

There were misunderstood geniuses among the Jews, prophets without honor, men of mind who stood up to an astonishing degree – for the great spirits among the German themselves.[17]

Due to considerations of space, I will not cite even the most typical personal responses to Nietzsche by some of the prominent Jewish "prophets" who, unable or unwilling to find honour in adopting a ready-made identity, conferred much honour on Nietzsche. These responses to Nietzsche's writings remind one of Nietzsche's own statement:

> There are books that have opposite values for soul and health, depending on whether the lower soul, the lower vitality, or the higher and more vigorous ones turn to them: in the former case, these books are dangerous and lead to crumbling and disintegration; in the latter, herald's cries that call the bravest to their courage.[18]

The passionate reaction of many of the marginal Jews to Nietzsche's books reflected the latter attitude – they appeared to agree with Robert Weltsch that "preoccupation with Nietzsche would make Jews stronger than a forced return to a ritual in which we do not believe".[19]

To be sure, these highly intellectual and well-educated Jews read voraciously, everything from the classics to contemporary German writing, in fact, they read European literature in general and not just Nietzsche, as Stefan Zweig testifies in his autobiography.[20] Their writings make frequent reference to Spinoza, Goethe, Heine, Ibsen, Strindberg, Dostoevsky, Rilke, Gerhart Hauptmann, Hugo von Hofmansthal, Schopenhauer and others, but generally, such references are far less emotional than those to Nietzsche.

Indeed, the personal manner in which the *Grenzjuden* hailed Nietzsche, as expressed in their writings, including their autobiographical reports and memoires, is unparalleled. Many describes their first encounter with Nietzsche's writings as a revelation: an "emotional shock", a "shaking" experience which they endured "breathlessly" or as an "invasion".[21]

I will mention in passing just two salient examples. First is Stefan Zweig, one of the most versatile representatives of *Exil Literatur* written by German Jews after they were forced to flee the Nazis. Zweig is one of those humanists who, unwilling to commit themselves to any ideology, perfectly exemplify my definition of the "marginal Jews". Hence, it is not surprising that throughout his life, Zweig showed great respect, even admiration, for Nietzsche, and often expressed characteristically Nietzschean sentiments and ideas in his writings.

JACOB GOLOMB

As early as 1904, in his doctoral dissertation on *"Die Philosophie des Hippolyte Taine"* he refers approvingly to Nietzsche's ideal of authentic existence, namely, that which harmonizes "Art with Life".[22] In *Die Welt von Gestern*, from 1942, Zweig tells of his *Gymnasium* days, in which, he "read Nietzsche" under his desk while his teacher delivered "time-worn", boring lectures.[23] He describes how, in Vienna's coffeehouses, he and his friends heatedly and incessantly discussed "Nietzsche, who then was still scorned".[24]

Zweig's fascination with Nietzsche cannot be disputed. Not only do we have several essays he wrote on Nietzsche,[25] but he also frequently refers to his greatness and genius in his letters.[26] However, most significantly, even after Hitler's rise to power, Zweig's affection for Nietzsche did not diminish. On the contrary, as we learn from his pre-war essay,[27] letters[28] and his novel *Ungeduld des Herzens* from 1939. In this novel, speaking of Nietzsche's aversion to pity (*Mitleid*), Zweig continues to refer to him as to "the most brilliant man of the last century".[29]

In a letter to Romain Rolland, Zweig admiringly portrays Nietzsche as an independent *"Prinz Vogelfrei"* and as *"den ersten Europäer"*.[30] Clearly, the Nietzschean notion of "the good European" deeply influenced Zweig, for whom, as for Nietzsche, Europe was a spiritual homeland. When he lost it, he put an end to his life.[31]

Another good example of Nietzsche's attractiveness for the *Grenzjuden* who did not adopt any definitive identity is Wassermann. In his 1921 autobiography he depicts the tragic predicament of a marginal Jew for whom the German language is the essence of his creative life though the people who use this language reject him:

The language is the breath of life to me. To me it is far more than a means of communication ... its words and rhythm constitute my innermost life. It is the building-material for a spiritual world for the fashioning of which I feel a vital urge, though the power is not yet mine.[32]

Wassermann asks, in this imaginary dialogue between himself as a Jew and a fictitious friend – himself as a German – the classical question of an assimilated Jew: "what does it mean for me to be a Jew? Why do I still consider myself to be one?" To resolve this unbearable dilemma Wassermann "sought a precedent and an example" (*My Life*, p. 96) and looked for some exemplary teacher to assist him in his fight "for self-liberation and self-realization, for purification and exaltation, that is, for objectives of a moral nature"

162

(ibid., p. 130). And indeed, he finds such a mentor in Nietzsche, who reveals to him his "beatific mission ... in this world" (ibid., pp. 203, 170–1). Nietzsche's name is one of only a few mentioned in Wassermann's autobiography. He refers to Nietzsche as one who "stressed again and again" that "without the devotion and infallible enthusiasm of the modern Jew, art would have been but sorrily understood and received in the last fifty years", and refers to him as one of the few "to whom *Antisemiterei*, as he called it, was a horror and an abomination; nay, more – an indignity".[33] He even goes so far as to replace the Jewish belief that the Jews are "the chosen people" with the Nietzschean idea of "the chosen individual" (*der auserwählte Einzelne*).[34]

The long list of early Jewish admirers of Nietzsche can, of course, be further expanded to include such names as Walter Benjamin,[35] Carl Sternheim,[36] Franz Rosenzweig,[37] Arnold Zweig,[38] Lion Feuchtwanger,[39] Franz Kafka,[40] Sigmund Freud,[41] or Karl Kraus, a pre-eminent example of marginality, who converted to Catholicism in 1911 and left the Church in 1923.[42] Other prominent Jewish women and men of letters who should be mentioned include Else Lasker-Schüler (1869–1945),[43] Hermann Broch (1886–1951),[44] Kurt Tucholsky[45] and Franz Werfel (1890–1945).[46] It should suffice to note that out of the 480 items located by Richard Frank Krummel,[47] about seventy titles were written by these I defined above as "marginal Jews". The proportion is almost the same in the first volume of Hillebrand's *Nietzsche und die deutsche Literatur* in his collection of "*Texte zur Nietzsche-Rezeption 1873–1963*". This is extremely significant, since Jews comprised less than 1 per cent of the population of Germany in the nineteenth and twentieth centuries. The *Grenzjuden*'s preoccupation with Nietzsche became so intensive that the pro-Nietzsche anti-Semites actually blamed them for monopolizing his thought and influence.[48]

How can we explain the *Grenzjuden*'s fascination with Nietzsche? Apart from the clearly philo-Semitic and sympathetic attitude he expressed now and then towards Jews and ancient Hebrews, as I have documented in several articles,[49] what was so magnetic in his writings?

THE FASCINATION WITH NIETZSCHE

Nietzsche's thought performed a number of vital functions for the marginal Jews. It acted variously as catalyst and impetus, as apology and justification, and as explanation. It provided Jewish scholars such as Theodor Lessing with an explanatory framework for understanding anti-Semitism and Jewish self-hatred (*Selbsthass*), helping them withstand the wrenching existential predicament of marginality. But, above all, Nietzsche functioned as a force enticing them to embark upon the arduous task of creating their authentic selves.

Authenticity

The crucial question was articulated by Wassermann: "But what can the Jews do?"[50] Solutions ranged from baptism *en masse* to "*Los von Europa*" – "Away from Europe". However, between the polar solutions of embracing Christianity and embracing Zionism, the marginal Jews who affirmed their marginality found an inspiring guide in Nietzsche, who provided a third solution: the personal authenticity of the "free spirit" amid the "good European" cultural framework.

The *Grenzjuden*'s longing for personal authenticity was inspired, among other things, by the Nietzschean aesthetic model of the spontaneously created self and life. This desire for authenticity is touchingly expressed by Toller:

> Go your own way, even though the world persecutes you and obstructs you. I died/Was reborn/Died/Was reborn/I was my own mother.... Once in his life every man must cast adrift from everything, even from his mother; he must become his own mother.[51]

What was it the marginal Jews found in Nietzsche that so echoed their longing for personal authenticity?

Nietzsche did not use the term "authenticity" explicitly, but it is possible to detect its presence in the recurrent distinctions he makes between *Wahrheit* (truth) and *Wahrhaftigkeit* (truthfulness).[52] One of the basic intuitions of Nietzsche's thought is the concept of complete immanence, formulated in sections 108–125 of *The Gay Science*. There are no transcendental entities or supranatural powers, there is no "pure reason", no other world, no domain different from or superior to our own. After the "Death of God" one must adopt for oneself the God-like role of originator of truth and of one's own self. The absence of a "pre-established harmony" between our cognitions and reality permits us to shift our attention to the creation of our own genuine selves.

We are true to life only if we accept it in all its harshness and complete immanence. The individual who is prevented from genuinely creating and expressing his self experiences deepening alienation between himself, his civilized acts and his civilization. The goal of Nietzsche's philosophy is to assist us in overcoming culture's repression and to entice us into uncovering and reactivating our own creative powers. Nietzsche employs the metaphor of art and artistic creation. The search for authenticity is the wish to express one's indeterminacy by the spontaneous choice of one of many possible ways of life. The individual is akin to the artist who freely shapes his self as a work of art. To become what we are is not to live according to our so-called "innate nature", but rather to create ourselves freely. To that end we must know ourselves, in order to distinguish what we can change in ourselves and in the external circumstances which have shaped us from that which we have to accept as inevitable. This we must do in the heroic manner of *amor fati* and of "self-overcoming".

The purpose of this self-overcoming is to attain maturity, authenticity and power. In this respect the will to power is of a piece with the quest for authenticity – it is the will to become the free author of one's own self. The optimal will to power is expressed by the ideally authentic *Übermensch*. If the will diminishes in quality, the tendency to escape from the task of creating one's self and to identify with the "herd" will intensify. One endowed with a will to power of higher quality and greater vitality will manifest the "master morality" and authentic life patterns, in contrast to the "slave morality" typical of those possessing lesser power or *Macht*. The latter, however, may be endowed with greater physical force or *Kraft*. Nietzsche's distinction between *Kraft* and *Macht*[53] represents his philosophical emphasis on the transition from sheer physical force and brutal violence (*Gewalt*) to spiritual-creative power, a transition which is necessary if one is to attain authenticity.

Nietzsche was aware of the strong pressure exerted by social convention and education. Hence the road to authenticity and spontaneous creativity requires the stages described by Nietzsche's Zarathustra: "the spirit becomes a camel; and the camel, a lion; and the lion, finally, a child" (Z 137). "The lion" must liberate himself from "the camel", i.e., from the external layers imposed on him by cultural and institutional conditioning. Only then, after attaining a childlike state of "innocence" (Z 139), can he proceed to a second stage, in which he consciously adopts and assimilates moral norms.

These norms may reflect the traditional values discarded in the first stage; but it is not their content that matters, but the unconstrained *manner* in which they are adopted.

This teaching appealed to marginal and creative Jews who sought to shed their traditional Jewish heritage to become what Toller called their own mothers – authors of their new lives. They were drawn by Nietzsche's ultimate vision of a creative and authentic life in a world without dogmatic beliefs. The death of dogmas does not lead to disintegration of the self, but rather liberates the individual's creative resources. It opens up new horizons which function as life-enhancing "perspectives". The *Grenzjuden* regarded Nietzsche's philosophy as he himself had regarded it: as a means, "a mere instrument", to entice them into forming their authenticity.

Nietzsche's enticing writings however, being merely a path, were naturally abandoned by many of the *Grenzjuden* once the destination had been reached. Nietzschean philosophy became, for them, a sort of temporary scaffolding, or provisional "hypothesis". It was a metaphoric structure in the original meaning of the term *meta-phora*, to be abandoned once it had served its purpose.

Nietzsche's basic idea of the "transfiguration of all values" does not call for radical abolition of all inauthentic life patterns, but for a gradual approximation of authenticity. This process is constantly taking place "within a *single* soul" (*BGE* 260) vacillating between opposed modes of living. Nietzsche thus describes the internal pathos of the *Grenzjuden* who experienced such fluctuating sentiments.[54]

As acutely felt inward experience, the sentiments, emotional states and types of pathos of the individual personality require no metaphysical and ideological commitments; they are thus the elements in the lives of the "marginal Jews" who, shunning all ready-made identities, prefer to persist in their uprootedness as authentic "free spirits".

Atheism

For the religiously uprooted Jews, in the midst of the process of secularization, the problem of faith and direction in matters of belief was acute.[55] The simplicity and difficulty of Nietzsche's atheistic solution thus fascinated them.

His plea to embrace the idea of complete immanence and to do away with all Gods appealed to marginal Jews who desperately needed support in passing safely through the "twilight of the idols", the journey away from their ancient tradition. The impotence of metaphysics and religion felt so keenly by Jewish intellectuals at the turn of the century attracted them to Nietzsche, who against the religious gospels of salvation from the hardship of life posited their antithesis: salvation from the transcendental doctrines of salvation by inciting readers to create authentic selves and live a healthy atheistic life.[56]

"Beatific mission"

It is not enough, of course, to abandon God, for one has to fill the vacuum left by this traumatic loss. This need cannot be satisfied by another God or a shadow of the former God, for these have also lost their credibility with the death of the Almighty God in one's heart. Nietzsche provides the marginal Jews with what Wassermann calls a "beatific mission" in the framework of a higher, rejuvenated, European humanity, a more authentic vital culture.[57] Nietzsche directed the intellectual elite of the *Grenzjuden* to a higher calling and bestowed upon them a vital role in the Europe of the future. In view of the positive psychological qualities Nietzsche found in the Jews, especially their "strong instinct" and abundance of power, he predicts that the Jews and the Russians will be "the provisionally surest and most probable factors in the great play and fight of forces" (*BGE* 251). He does not imply Jewish political domination over Europe, but rather alludes to the Jews' spiritual role in the future when their creative resources will flow "into great spiritual men and works . . . into an eternal blessing for Europe" (*D* 205).

Echoing the Old Testament prophecy about Israel's magnificent future and its spectacular salvation, Nietzsche claims that the Jews will once again become the "founders and creators of values". The creation of values is the most significant task in Nietzsche's philosophy, which always returns to the "transfiguration of values" and the transfiguration of the nature of our culture, in which the Jews are to play the major role as well as to serve as catalysts. Nietzsche's hope of mobilizing European Jewry to assist him in this transfiguration of values is the background for his emotional exclamation: "What a blessing a Jew is among Germans!" (*WP* 49).

These words, and the mission entrusted by Nietzsche to the German *Grenzjuden*, came at the right time. Indeed, the Jewish intellectuals responded eagerly, helping bring about what is still considered to be one of the most creative periods in German culture, parallel to and even embracing what Buber called "the Jewish Renaissance". Nietzsche's philosophy provided the godless Jewish intellectuals with legitimization to participate in and contribute to the broad framework of German humanist culture. If Nietzsche killed God (and incidentally, as is well known, he adopted the leitmotif of the "Death of God" from Heinrich Heine, one of the greatest German *Grenzjuden*) and if he attempted to foster the *Übermensch*, so too the *Grenzjuden*, having put an end in their hearts to their religion, sought, in a sense, to become *Überjuden*. Stefan Zweig, for example, willingly adopted the cultural task assigned by Nietzsche to the Jewish writers, and spoke in his autobiography about the idea that had "become central to [his] life: the intellectual unification of Europe", an idea which gave him "the satisfaction of having lived·the life of a European for at least one decade according to one's own free will and with complete interior freedom". His suicide in 1942 was the outcome of his desperate realization that, "Europe, our home, to which we had dedicated ourselves, had suffered a destructon that would extend far beyond our life".[58]

Overcoming the antiquarian historical consciousness

For modern Jews to become an effective and creative agent in the coming European renaissance, they had to overcome their traditional Talmudic patterns of learning, which could not be incorporated within European culture. Thus they considered orthodoxy, in the words of one of their eloquent spokesmen, Werfel, to be a "holiest fossilization". Jewish renaissance demanded that the Jew overcome his antiquarian-Rabbinic consciousness, around which he had structured his Jewish identity in the Diaspora, and instead adopt a "monumental" approach centring around the grandeur of his glorious days in ancient Israel. This incitement to "monumental history" is expressed in Nietzsche's essay, "On the uses and disadvantages of history for life", in which he asserts that "monumental" historical consciousness lends support to the creative and powerful individual who seeks an existence that expresses his inner power. It makes possible an emphathetic identification with exemplary figures, and reassures those who aspire to greatness by showing them that "the greatness that once existed was in any event once *possible* and may thus be possible again".[59] The ambitious man is encouraged to reject any gnawing uncertainties and to pursue the path of glory and creation. And who among these *Grenzjuden* did not harbour such ambitions? It is small wonder, then, that the better-known historical novels and dramas of many Jewish writers described the glorious past of their people and tried to foster in their secular readers the aspiration to recreate their monumental ancient history.[60]

De-Spiritualization

Martin Buber, in his article on the "Jüdische Renaissance",[61] argued that the two thousand years in the Diaspora forced the Jews to transform their physical energy into purely spiritual energy. This effected their alienation from nature and a loss of balance between their physical and spiritual being. Buber called upon modern Jews to liberate themselves from the "fettered spirituality" (*unfreie Geistigkeit*) and regain a "completely harmonious sense of living". This call for the de-spiritualization of Jewish life also echoed Nietzsche's teachings.

Already in *The Birth of Tragedy* Nietzsche claimed that the dominance of the Apollonian-rational element in human beings over their Dionysian drives diminished the vitality of their creative powers. The spiritual asceticism, he claimed, is caused by excessive repression of instincts and mental spiritualization ("*Vergeistigung*", *GM* II 16). To reverse these destructive tendencies Nietzsche advocates returning to the vitality of the senses and a full sensual life.

Marginal Jews, acutely aware of their anomalous existence, and longing for healthy and natural life outside the ghetto's walls, responded to this directive enthusiastically. Rejecting the repressive patterns of traditional life, they virtually exploded with astonishing creative drive, markedly enriching the Weimar Republic.

Psychologization

Another important aspect of Nietzsche's philosophy that attracted the marginal Jews was its psychology. To help them cope with extreme identity crises, many of the *Grenzjuden* needed self-analysis. They sought consolidation of their souls and reactivation of the inner cores of their personalities which had been lost in the tug of war between polar foci of identity. Many of the Jewish writers were, like Wassermann, immersed "in sincere self-analysis" (*My Life*, p. 91). Hence the intimate bond between the psychoanalytic movement and the marginal Jews: the first Psychoanalytic Society in Vienna, apart from Jung, consisted primarily of Jewish intellectuals and physicians. The prospect of therapy offered by psychoanalysis had great appeal for all those *Grenzjuden* who, like Freud, wavered between Rome and Jerusalem, between the German culture and the Jewish tradition of their forefathers.

Indeed, Freud frequently emphasized the intimate relation between his psychoanalysis and the Jewish *Geist* and genius.[62] Marthe Robert was thus quite right to connect the emergence of the psychoanalytic movement with the psychosocial patterns of Freud and his followers, who, like all the *Grenzjuden* discussed here, were suspended "between two histories, two cultures, two irreconcilable forms of thought".[63] The marginal Jews, led by Freud and his followers, drew frequent analogies between Freudian teachings and Nietzschean psychology, which in many instances had anticipated many of Freud's major "discoveries" and concepts.

The Jewish psychoanalysts were especially attracted by Nietzsche's genealogical methods of "unmasking". Nietzsche used these methods to attain a solid sense of selfhood and individual identity by freezing one's motivation to uphold any religious, metaphysical and social ideologies that had previously provided ready-made and inauthentic identities. Following the death of the Father – the Jewish God – and the decline, in the typical Jewish family, of the authority of the father, who was responsible for bringing his sons to the schizoid state they were now in, the *Grenzjuden* sought to establish firm and authentic identities which would not draw their content from faith and tradition, but would derive it solely from the individual's own mental resources. Nietzsche encouraged this process by showing how psychologization could liberate the individual from dependence on mechanical internalizations, habits of thought and hereditary conventions.

Nietzsche served as a model of penetrating self-analysis of an acute neurosis, and also demonstrated, before Freud, the therapy needed to overcome this neurosis. According to Nietzsche's testimony, his neurosis, to which Freud frequently referred,[64] facilitated his psychological insights, and helped him grasp such contrasts as good and evil as opposed to good and bad. Only those, like many of the marginal Jews, who had experienced and overcome such neuroses possessed an "inborn fastidiousness of taste with respect to psychological questions" (*GM* Preface 3) and were able to "go inside". This ability to "go inside" and overcome states of negative pathos is regarded by

Nietzsche as a major indicator of an individual's positive power – his ability to explicate the darkest recesses of his soul for the sake of health and vitality. Many of the creative *Grenzjuden* dared "go inside" and used such self-overcoming to produce masterpieces which were informed by this psychological enlightenment. Nietzsche served them as both guide to and monumental model of this creative process.

Self-hate and anti-Semitism

The fascination Nietzsche had for the marginal Jews was also fuelled by his psychology, which helped them understand one of the most troublesome phenomena they experienced in their daily lives: their own poisonous *Selbsthass* (self-hatred), and the hatred of the Aryan anti-Semites. Thus, for example, Theodor Lessing (1872–1933), a disciple of Nietzsche who dedicated several writings to his philosophy,[65] wrote a comprehensive treatise on *Der Jüdische Selbsthass*, which he tried to understand using Nietzschean concepts.[66] In this book Lessing describes the Jews in the Diaspora as people who have been forced to live unnatural lives. After separation from their land, they turned to an excessively spiritual life which they live "together with their dead ones". Lessing claims, in language that is definitely Nietzschean, that in their internalized lives, as the result of external pressure and out of fear of their hostile surroundings, the Jews began to direct their spiritual resources against themselves, manifesting self-doubt, insecurity and self-torture. This agonizing state of affairs was so unbearable that they attempted to liberate themselves from it by despising anything that had to do with Judaism and Jewishness, especially themselves. Lessing ends his essay with a call to these Jews: "*Sei was immer du bist.*"[67]

We should recall that the existential motto of Nietzsche's autobiography, *Ecce Homo*, which appears in its subtitle, is "*Wie man wird, was man ist*" ("How one becomes what one is"). In Nietzschean terms, Lessing is calling upon these Jews not to betray their fate, but to love it in the manner of *amor fati*, that is, not in the sense of resignation and passive submission to wretched conditions, but by accepting their genuine selves and approving their organic roots. Lessing calls upon them to reactivate their mental resources in courageous acts of self-overcoming with respect to whatever threatens this identity and authentic selfhood. In a lecture he delivered three months before his murder by a Nazi agent in

Marienbad, in August 1933, Lessing appeals to these Jews to assert their "*Machtwille*" and return to "*Natur und Erde*".[68]

To understand Lessing's enigmatic message one must turn briefly to the second part of Nietzsche's *Genealogy of Morals*, where he deals with the phenomena of *ressentiment* and *Verinnerlichung*. The powerful "masters" are responsible for the phenomenon of "internalization", in which most of man's instincts are turned "inward" against "man himself"; they evoke in the "weak" the feeling of *ressentiment* which characterizes the first stage of the "slave morality", becoming "bad conscience" in the second stage, when the "instinct for freedom [is] pushed back and repressed ... [and is] finally able to discharge and vent itself only on itself" (*GM* II 17). As a result, the intimidated individual becomes a schizoid personality in constant internal strife, fighting himself out of sheer impoverishment and self-hatred and being prevented from attaining inner harmony by this struggle.

This exposition can, of course, also be applied to the anti-Semite, who is a weak and psychologically unstable individual with the character of a "slave". The phenomenon of anti-Semitism, which Wasserman rightly asserted was a "horror and an abomination" for Nietzsche, can be elucidated with reference to the psychological patterns of the weak and impoverished personality, described in Nietzsche's main writings, beginning with *The Gay Science*.[69] Lacking personal power, and as a result of *ressentiment* and mental impoverishment, the anti-Semite is dependent upon certain external surroundings for self-determination. He needs acts of violence and cruel exploitation of others to enhance his feeble sense of power (*GS* 359). He is a vengeful and reactive person who uses his hatred, a hatred in which "there is *fear*" (*GS* 379), to attain some sort of security and self-identity. It follows that the anti-Semite is actually the "slave" and not the "master". This insight, of which the marginal Jews were in tremendous need, clearly encouraged them to follow Nietzsche's attitude.

Richard Maximilian Cahen, who, writing under the name Richard Maximilian Lonsbach, published *Friedrich Nietzsche und die Juden* in 1939, was one of those who were heartened by this attitude. He explained why Nietzsche regarded the rising tide of anti-Semitism as a new revolt of the slave-man and fought it bitterly.[70] Anti-Semitism was for Nietzsche the viewpoint not of a people or a class but of the vile and worthless individuals who had been worsted in the struggle for existence. Nietzsche coined a new word to designate them: *die*

Schlechtweggekommenen. Anti-Semitism was the revolt of those who were poor in spiritual values and it indicated an envious and cowardly personality, against which Nietzsche's philosophy of power was directed. And thus, Lonsbach crowns these ruminations with one of Nietzsche's last utterances: "I want all anti-Semites shot."[71]

Wasserman's description of anti-Semitism seems also to be derived from Nietzsche's analysis: "Greed and curiosity are involved here, blood thirstiness and the fear of being lured or seduced ... and scanty self-esteem ... it is a peculiarly German phenomenon. It is a German hatred" (*My Life*, p. 64). Some of the *Grenzjuden* responded to this "German hatred" with a hatred of the Germans, a hatred which they lacked either the courage or the desire to express directly. Instead, they turned once again to Nietzsche.

Nietzsche on Germans

Nietzsche's sharp criticism of Germany and its drive for power (*Kraft*) was another reason for the marginal Jews' attraction to his writings. These Jews, deeply ambivalent about their relations to Germany, dared not make explicit the reservations they obviously had concerning the contemporary German scene, despite their tireless efforts to be assimilated into German society and counted among its legitimate members. Nietzsche, as one of the most brilliant representatives of this non-Jewish German society, gave vent, in his harsh critique of the Germans, to the *Grenzjuden*'s feelings of bitterness and frustration toward the Germans. This ambivalence towards German was, therefore, yet another factor that made Nietzsche attractive to the *Grenzjuden*.

Two striking examples suffice to illustrate Nietzsche's criticism of Germans.

> Whoever reads me in Germany today has first *de-Germanized* himself thoroughly, as I have done: my formula is known, "to be a good German means to de-Germanize oneself"; or he is – no small distinction among Germans – of Jewish descent. – Jews among Germans are always the higher race – more refined, spiritual, kind. – *L'adorable* Heine, they say in Paris.[72]

Another famous example is included in a section of *Götzen-Dämmerung* entitled "What the Germans lack":

> One pays heavily for coming to power: power *makes stupid.* The Germans – once they were called the people of thinkers:

do they think at all today? The Germans are now bored with the spirit, the Germans now mistrust the spirit; politics swallows up all serious concern for really spiritual matters. *Deutschland, Deutschland über alles* – I fear that was the end of German philosophy.[73]

Jewish intellectuals, who always mistrusted violent political *Kraft*, and were victims of its uglier manifestations, drank in these words, indeed were virtually intoxicated by their spirit.

After promulgation of the Nüremberg Racial Laws in 1935, all efforts at spiritual fusion of Germans and Jews yielded to strict segregation of the two groups. The slogan "German *and* Jew" was replaced by the implacable "German *or* Jew". Baptism no longer admitted Jews to the ranks of the Germans, and marriage between Jews and Germans was banned as *Rassenschande*, racial defilement.

In spite of the Nazification of Nietzsche's thought, the *Grenzjuden* were not taken in by it and remained grateful to Nietzsche for his naive advocacy of the mating of Prussian nobility and Jewish intelligentsia as a desirable means of hastening the evolution of a superior and authentic type of humanity.

CONCLUSION

By way of summary, let me recapitulate the main element in Nietzsche's thought that made it a magnetic source of inspiration and encouragement for the *Grenzjuden*.

The marginal Jews urgently felt the need to overcome their unbearable identity crisis and the conflict between their heritage and their present culture. Nietzsche excelled at describing their predicament. Although his analyses dealt with western ethics in general, they were specifically relevant to and valid for the *Grenzjuden*, who had become the main victims of the culture which they had been so instrumental in growing and fostering. Nietzsche claimed that traditionally, that is, according to accepted morality, man "*divides* his nature and sacrifices one part of it to the other" and thus "treats himself not as *individuum* but as *dividuum*" (*nicht als individuum sondern als dividuum*, *HAH* I 57, emphasis in original). When the prevalent ethical systems demand personal schism and repression of important elements of the self, this precludes attaining personal harmony and expressing one's character as a whole. Hence Nietzsche rejects such repressive morality and seeks to go "beyond good and evil". The internally torn Jewish individual was especially susceptible to the Nietzschean ideal of self-overcoming and attracted by Nietzsche's "transfiguration of all values", his transition from the universal morality of tradition to personal authenticity. Nietzsche calls upon us to overcome all elements alien to our inner, organic personality, all elements that preclude authentic creativity and firm selfhood. The *Grenzjuden*, who felt such alien elements in their beings intensely, were especially responsive to this call, for they felt it might provide some succour for the unbearable tension they experienced. Under Nietzsche's guidance they tried to overcome both the traditions of their Jewish forefathers and their ultra-Germanism and self-hatred. They aspired to a harmonious synthesis between Berlin and Jerusalem, and to accept their marginality in an *amor-fati* manner not as their inevitable fate but as their own authentic, creative accomplishment.

ABBREVIATIONS

AC   Nietzsche, Friedrich, *The Antichrist*, in *The Portable Nietzsche*, ed. and tr. Walter Kaufmann, New York, 1954.

BGE   Nietzsche, Friedrich, *Beyond Good and Evil*, tr. Walter Kaufmann, New York, 1966.

BT   Nietzsche, Friedrich, *The Birth of Tragedy*, tr. Walter Kaufmann, New York, 1967.

D   Nietzsche, Friedrich, *Daybreak*, tr. R.J. Hollingdale, Cambridge, 1982.

EH   Nietzsche, Friedrich, *Ecce Homo*, tr. Walter Kaufmann, New York, 1969.

GM   Nietzsche, Friedrich, *On the Genealogy of Morals*, tr. Walter Kaufmann, New York, 1967.

GS   Nietzsche, Friedrich, *The Gay Science*, tr. Walter Kaufmann, New York, 1974.

HAH   Nietzsche, Friedrich, *Human, All Too Human*, tr. R.J. Hollingdale, Cambridge, 1986.

TI   Nietzsche, Friedrich, *Twilight of the Idols*, in *The Portable Nietzsche*, ed. and tr. Walter Kaufmann, New York, 1954.

UM   Nietzsche, Friedrich, *Untimely Meditations*, tr. R.J. Hollingdale, Cambridge, 1983.

WP   Nietzsche, Friedrich, *The Will to Power*, tr. Walter Kaufmann, New York, 1968.

Z   Nietzsche, Friedrich, *Thus Spoke Zarathustra*, in *The Portable Nietzsche*, ed. and tr. Walter Kaufmann, New York, 1954.

JACOB GOLOMB

NOTES

* This study was supported by the *Forschungsreisestipendium* of the Fritz Thyssen *Stiftung*. Researched at the *Deutsches Literaturarchiv* in Marbach am Neckar it could not have been completed without the unfailingly informed and helpful assistance of Reinhard Tgahrt and his staff. I am grateful to them all.

1 See, e.g., Hans Joachim Becker, *Die frühe Nietzsche-Rezeption in Japan (1893–1903)* (Wiesbaden, 1983); David S. Thatcher, *Nietzsche in England: 1890–1914* (Toronto, 1970); Bernice Glatzer Rosenthal (ed.), *Nietzsche in Russia* (Princeton, 1986). Admitting his indebtedness to Nietzsche, in a letter dated 28 November 1949, Gottfried Benn declares: "He has anticipated and formulated everything ... we poke around in – what else have we done these last fifty years but trot out and vulgarize his gigantic thoughts and suffering?" (cited in J.P. Stern's "Nietzsche's heirs and the justification through art", in Volker Dürr, Reinhold Grimm and Kathy Harms (eds), *Nietzsche: Literature and Values* (Madison, Wis.: 1988), p. 137. Stern describes the heritage of which Benn speaks, as "second to none. Nietzsche's influence ... becomes a European phenomenon well before his death in 1900" (p. 137).

   Incidentally, Benn was not exactly an admirer of the Jews. His 1934 essay "Lebensweg eines Intellektualisten", in his *Doppelleben* (Wiesbaden, 1950), pp. 9–73 has strong racist undertones. However, referring to some of the *Grenzjuden* mentioned here, Benn writes, *after* World War II, that they have been "Der Glanz des Kaiserreichs, sein innerer und äußerer Reichtum", "*Doppellebon*", p. 82. Cf. Bruno Hillebrand, "Gottfried Benn und Friedrich Nietzsche", in Bruno Hillebrand (ed.), *Nietzsche und die deutsche Literatur*, vol. 2 (Tübingen, 1978), "Forschungsergebnisse", pp. 186–211 and Michael Hamburger, *A Proliferation of Prophets: Essays on German Writers from Nietzsche to Brecht* (New York, 1984), pp. 58–61, 207–8, 240–1. Hamburger states that "Nietzsche also holds the key to twentieth-century German literature ... his problems were the problems of almost every later writer who matters" (ibid., p. 46). This is especially true of the marginal Jewish German writers.

2 See William J. McGrath, *Dionysian Art and Populist Politics in Austria* (New Haven and London, 1974).

3 See his 1888 essay "Friedrich Nietzsche: Eine Abhandlung über Aristokratischen Radikalismus", in George Brandes, *Menschen und Werke: Essays* (Frankfurt am Main, 1895), pp. 137–213. In this second edition Brandes adds in a footnote a passage from a letter from Nietzsche dated 2 November 1887, in which Nietzsche states: "Der Ausdruck 'aristokratischer Radikalismus' dessen Sie sich bedienen, ist sehr gut. Das ist, mit Verlaub gesagt, das gescheuteste Wort, das ich bisher über mich gelesen habe" (p. 137). English edn.: *Friedrich Nietzsche: An Essay on Aristocratic Radicalism* (London, 1914).

4 As early as 1889, the Jewish journalist and critic, Leo Berg (1862–1908) writes: "Man mag einst über Nietzsche denken, wie man will, über den Schriftsteller in ihm wird es bald keinen Zweifel mehr geben. Er ist der

größte Virtuos der deutschen Sprache", in "Friedrich Nietzsche", *Deutschland* (Berlin) 9 (1889), pp. 148–9; 168–70. For other aspects of Nietzsche's writing see Berg's early essays on Nietzsche: "Friedrich Nietzsche: Ein Essay", *Die Gesellschaft* 6 (1890): 1415–28; "Friedrich Nietzsche und seine Zeit" (1900) in his *Neue Essays* (Oldenburg and Leipzig, 1901), pp. 284–90; "Heine und Nietzsche", in *Heine-Nietzsche-Ibsen: Essays* (Berlin, 1908), pp. 13–27; "Nietzsche Freundschaft-stragödien", ibid., pp. 31–62; and finally his book *Der Übermensch in der modernen Litteratur* (Paris, Leipzig and Munich, 1897). Cf. Berg's review of various works on Nietzsche: "Nietzsche-Schriften", in *Das litterarische Echo* 2 (1899/1900): 1702–7 and his own overall review in *Das litterarische Echo* 3 (1900/1): 1535–9.

5 See, e.g., Landauer's essay "Religiöse Erziehung" in *Freie Bühne* 2 (1891): 134–8 where he refers to Nietzsche's "Zarathustra" as "des genialen Weisen". In his 1893 novel *Der Todesprediger* (Dresden), his main hero, the shoemaker Adam Starkblom, declares that *Also sprach Zarathustra* "ist ein wundersames Buch" (in the 3rd edn, Köln a. R., 1923, p. 92). Cf. Landauer's "Der neue Gott", in *Die Gesellschaft* 15(4) (1899): 119–22, and the following letters in Martin Buber (ed.), *Gustav Landauer: Sein Lebensgang in Briefen* (Frankfurt am Main, 1929): vol. 1: 12 August 1899 (p. 37); 16 June 1903 (p. 117); 21 December 1909 (p. 274); 18 January 1910 (p. 291); 15 September 1910 (p. 323); 17 September 1910 (pp. 324–5); 8 December 1910 (p. 331); and 25 July 1912 (p. 411). Landauer's more critical attitude to Nietzsche is expressed later in his lecture "Friedrich Hölderlin in seinen Gedichten", in his *Der werdende Mensch: Aufsätze über Leben und Schrifttum*, ed. Martin Buber (Potsdam, 1921), pp. 155–88 and in *Beginnen: Aufsätze über Sozialismus*, ed. Martin Buber (Cologne, 1924), p. 9. On Nietzsche's influence upon Landauer, see Charles B. Maurer, *Call to Revolution* (Detroit, 1971), esp. pp. 153–4. A more detailed analysis can be found in Eugene Lunn, *Prophet of Community: The Romantic Socialism of Gustav Landauer* (Berkeley, 1973).

As to Max Nordau, see, from his pre-Zionist phase, *Entartung*, vol. 2 (Berlin, 1893), esp. Book 3, ch. 5: "Friedrich Nietzsche", pp. 272–357, where Nordau discusses Nietzsche at length, seeing in him a symptom of *fin-de-siècle* degeneration. However, this largely unjustified criticism of Nietzsche (see the concluding chapter of my *Nietzsche's Enticing Psychology of Power* (Ames, 1989)) does not invalidate my thesis here, as is claimed by Aschheim in an otherwise superb analysis: see Steven E. Aschheim, "Nietzschean moment in Jewish life (1890–1939)", *Leo Baeck Institute Yearbook* 37 (1992): 189–212. An integral part of any significant reception is also "unbridled" rejection, which surely indicates that the figure under attack is regarded as one to be reckoned with, and one worthy of lengthy rebuttal. Nordau's ambivalence toward Nietzsche at such an early stage is in fact evidence in favour of my argument here. However, I am indebted to Aschheim for his comments on the earlier (Hebrew) version of the present article (in *Jerusalem Studies in Jewish Thought* 4 (1985): 97–143) which led me to soften some of the claims I make here.

JACOB GOLOMB

6 Thomas Mann, *Reflections of a Nonpolitical Man*, tr. Walter D. Morris (New York, 1983), p. 13.

7 Frederic V. Grunfeld, *Prophets without Honour* (London, 1979), p. 17.

8 Cf. Solomon Liptzin, *Germany's Stepchildren* (Philadelphia, 1944), p. 195.

9 *The Maurizius Case* (London, 1930), p. 297. In his telling autobiography, Wassermann declares: "In a sense I was a Moses descending Mount Sinai, but without any recollection of what he had seen there and of what God had told him" (*My Life as German and Jew*, tr. S.N. Brainin (New York, 1933), p. 31). Wassermann's identity as a Jew was thus negative: "Precisely speaking, we were Jews only in name and in the hostility, remoteness or aloofness of the Christians about us. . . . Why, then, were we still Jews, and what did it mean?" (ibid., p. 17). Such questions, with which most of the marginal Jews were preoccupied, served as catalysts for their passionate search for personal authenticity. Wassermann's feeling of estrangement was the background for his yearning

> to be not merely a guest, to be regarded not as a stranger. Not as an invited guest, nor as one tolerated out of pity and kindliness, nor worst of all, as one admitted because his hosts have consented to ignore his race and descent. (ibid., p. 24)

10 Gersham Scholem, "Jews and Germans", *Commentary* (November 1966) p. 35.

11 My translation from Arthur Schnitzler's *Jugend in Wien*, ed. Therese Nickl and Heinrich Schnitzler (Wien, 1968), p. 328: "Es war nicht möglich, insbesondere für einen Juden, der in der Offentlichkeit stand, davon abzusehen, dass er Jude war." See also "The Jew in me and my works: confessions of literary luminaries on their intimate attitude toward the Jewish complex: I spurn the Dodge of Baptism", *The American Hebrew* 15 (20 August 1926): p. 407. Little wonder that in Schnitzler's eyes the most important of his writings was his first, unfinished and lost drama "Der ewige Jude" (*Jugend in Wien*, p. 74). On anti-Semitism in Schnitler's Vienna see ibid., pp. 78, 329.

12 Franz Werfel, *Between Heaven and Earth*, tr. Maxim Newmark (London, 1947), "Foreword" (written in 1944), p. viii; "Theologoumena", p. 141.

13 On the Nietzschean aesthetic model of authentic life see my "Nietzsche on authenticity", *Philosophy Today* 34 (1990): 243–58, and *In Search of Authenticity from Kierkegaard to Camus* (London, 1995), ch. 4.

14 In an autobiographical piece, Buber writes that at age 17, when still hesitating as to his way as a Jew and a Zionist, he was so attracted to Nietzsche's *Also Sprach Zarathustra* that he decided to translate it: "This book worked on me not in the manner of a gift but in the manner of an invasion which deprived me of my freedom, and it was a long time until I could liberate myself from it." In a footnote he adds: "I was at that time so taken by the book that I decided to translate it into Polish and had even translated the first part" (Autobiographical fragments: Martin Buber", in P.A. Schilpp and M. Friedman (eds), *The Philosophy of Martin Buber* (La Salle, Ill., 1967), pp. 12–13.

15 However, before his conversion to Catholicism in 1941, Döblin was very much under the spell of Nietzsche. He reports on his first acquaintance with "Dostojewski ... Heinrich von Kleist ... Schopenhauer ... Hölderlin" but notes that "In der Prima oder schon vorher die Begegnung mit Nietzsche: die '*Genealogie der Moral*', die ich mit Zittern und atemlos las" (Alfred Döblin, *Autobiographische Schriften und letzte Aufzeichnungen*, ed. Edgar Pässler (Olten, 1977), p. 90). Döblin's uprootedness was vividly portrayed in his memoirs. He first describes his existential predicament:

> And what about Judaism? I had been told at home in Stettin that my parents were of Jewish origin and we were a Jewish family. That was about the only thing concerning Judaism that I noticed about our family. ... As for the religious teaching – I read it and listened to it. It was, and remained, superficial to me. It did not affect me emotionally, I felt no connection to it. ... My mother could read Hebrew, and it was touching to see her, she who worked so hard and cared for us and hardly had time to read a newspaper, sitting off quietly to one side of a room on the high holidays. She would hold one of her books in her hand and read Hebrew for a while, softly out loud. (*Destiny's Journey*, ed. Edgar Pässler, tr. Edna McCown (New York, 1992), pp. 105–6)

This passage is followed by a relatively long entry on Nietzsche, whose discovery he sees as a revelation:

> At the beginning of my university studies in Berlin in 1902 ... I stumbled across ... Nietzsche. I was then twenty-four years old and studying medicine. ... I remember sitting in my room, having read the *Genealogy of Morals*, and laying it aside, covering it with a notebook, literally shaking, shivering. ... I remember standing up in my room and walking up and down, beside myself. ... I didn't know what had happened to me, what had been done to me. ... Then a lightning bolt fell from heaven, struck right in front of me, and in its blinding light I saw something I had never seen before ... the *Genealogy of Morals*. ... Nietzsche ... didn't know much about the natural sciences, but he knew what to make of what he did know. I followed what he wrote breathlessly and thought about his ideas. ... I let them have their effect on me. It brought enlightenment and emotional shock to me. (ibid., pp. 107, 109).

In his *Schriften zu Asthetik, Poetik und Literatur* (Olten, 1989) there are seventeen references to Nietzsche and his writings; some of Nietzsche's key concepts, like that of the *Übermensch*, are frequently referred to. Döblin's preoccupation with Nietzsche began as early as 1902–3, with two unpublished essays: "Der Will zur Macht als Erkenntnis bei Friedrich Nietzsche" (in Bruno Hillebrand (ed.), *Nietzsche und die deutsche Literatur* (Tübingen, 1978), vol. 1: *Texte zur Nietzsche-Rezeption: 1873–1963*, pp. 315–30) and "Zu Nietzsches Morallehre" (from 1903, ibid., pp. 331–58). Cf. his other Nietzschean essays, one

JACOB GOLOMB

entitled "Dionysos" and written under the pseudonym Linke Poot in
Die neue Rundschau 2 (1919): 885–93, and the other, "Krieg und
Frieden" in *Der neue Merkur* 4 (1920): 193–207. Also see his more critical
remarks on Nietzsche in *Wissen und Verändern* (Berlin, 1931), esp. pp.
72ff., 168, 169. Blunt rejection of Nietzsche's biological ideas – partially,
perhaps, in an attempt to shed his fascination with Nietzsche before
World War II and his conversion – can be found in his "Die literarische
Situation", in *Schriften zur Politik und Gesellschaft* (Olten, 1972), pp.
423–38. Compare, however, his more positive attitude to Nietzsche in
his 1938 essay "Prometheus und das Primitive" (*Schriften*, pp. 346–68),
and in a book, first published in 1933 by S. Fischer in Berlin before
Döblin fled Germany, *Unser Dasein* (Olten, 1964), esp. pp. 191ff., 231.
As far as I know, there is no comprehensive comparative study of
Nietzsche and Döblin, though there are some comparative remarks in
Erwin Kobel, *Alfred Döblin* (Berlin, 1985); Wolfgang Kort, *Alfred
Döblin* (New York, 1974), esp. p. 34; Ernst Ribbat, *Die Wahrheit des
Lebens im frühen Werk Alfred Döblins* (Münster, 1970), pp. 88ff.;
Monique Weyembergh-Boussart, *Alfred Döblin* (Bonn, 1970), esp.
pp. 89–92; Adalbert Wichert, *Alfred Döblins historisches Denken*
(Stuttgart, 1978).

16 Toller's grandfather still studied the Talmud, but Toller became a leader
of the Bavarian Soviet Republic of 1919. His flight from Judaism led him
first to ultranationalism and superpatriotism, then to socialism and
cosmopolitanism, and finally to his suicide on 22 May 1939. In his
autobiography from 1933, Toller provides us with a retrospective
account of how he "worshipped false gods and believed in false
prophets" ("Introduction", *I was a German*, tr. Edward Crankshaw
(New York: Paragon, 1990)). Using Nietzschean language, he describes
how he has "killed the Lord God dead" by destroying the *mezuzah* on
the door of his family home, (ibid., p. 20). His flight into marginality
and flirtation with different identities is touchingly portrayed: "I don't
want to be a Jew. I don't want the other children to run after me shouting
'Dirty Jew!'" (ibid., p. 23). Before embarking on his journey in search
of personal identity, Toller became engrossed with the teachings and
figure of Nietzsche and recounts how he and his fellow students in the
"German Students' Union" at the University of Grenoble "used to
discuss Nietzsche" (ibid., p. 47). In his autobiography, he relates how a
sense of self and authenticity awakened in him while reading Nietzsche:
"I would have to reckon with a new self of whose existence I had been
entirely unaware. . . . I began reading Nietzsche" (ibid., p. 51). Cf.
Toller's first play (*Die Wandlung*, Potsdam, 1919), which reflects his
break with Jewish tradition and his desire to be fully accepted as a
German citizen.

To my knowledge, as in the case of Döblin, no authoritative study has
yet been made of Toller's relations to Nietzsche. See, however, some
passing remarks in René Eichenlaub, *Ernst Toller et l'expressionisme
politique* (Paris, 1980), esp. pp. 58–61, where the author, analysing
Toller's play *Aufrüttelung* and his hero Friedrich, claims that in it one
"can discern Nietzsche's ideas" (p. 61).

17 Scholem, "Jews and Germans", p. 37. See also Wasserman's testimony
in *My Life*, where he describes the Jews' function in regard to Germany's
geniuses, referring, among others, to Nietzsche in this context: "Jews
were their discoverers and their receptive audience, Jews proclaimed
them and became their biographers, Jews have been and still are the
sustaining pillars of almost every great name" (pp. 200, 203). Therefore
it is not surprising that in the recently published diaries of Scholem we
find many laudatory references to Nietzsche and his works. See *Gershom
Scholem Tagebücher*, ed. Karlfried Gründer and Friedrich Niewöher
(Frankfurt am Main, 1995), esp. pp. 46, 51–2, 65, 80.

18 *BGE* 30, pp. 42–3.

19 Quoted by George L. Mosse, in *Germans and Jews* (New York, 1970),
p. 96. Of course Nietzsche's effect on the *Grenzjuden* does not in any
way minimize his great influence on many German-Aryan intellectual
figures, writers and poets. See, e.g., Michael Hamburger, *Reason and
Energy: Studies in German Literature* (London, 1957), p. 216: "I should
like to add the name of Nietzsche, whose shattering effect on almost all
the German poets writing in 1912 can hardly be exaggerated." For a
detailed description see Steven E. Aschheim, *The Nietzsche Legacy in
Germany: 1890–1990* (Berkeley, 1992).

20 Stefan Zweig, *The World of Yesterday* (New York, 1943), esp. ch. 2.

21 See note 15 on Döblin and note 14 on Buber. Another enthusiastic fan,
Arthur Schnitzler, frequently uses superlatives to refer to Nietzsche and
his works: "Nietzsche! Bei keinem hab ich noch so tief emfunden, dass
er etwas gibt, was ich *nicht* werden kann." (*Arthur Schnitzler Tagebuch:
1879–1892* (Wien, 1987), p. 342 (entry from 21 July 1891))

Nietzsche's impact on Schnitzler was so strong that he occasionally
reports dreams related to Nietzsche. Thus, for example, in his diary he
describes a dream from 4 April 1915 in which "Someone asks me what
book I had put on my chair. I answer 'An exchange of letters between
Nietzsche and Faust'." He notes parenthetically that he was reading
"Nietzsche's letters" at the time (*Arthur Schnitzler Tagebuch:
1913–1916* (Wien, 1983), p. 186, my translation). See also a note on
another dream from 7 September 1920 (*Arthur Schnitzler Tagebuch:
1920–1922* (Wien, 1993), p. 84).

Schnitzler's admiration for Nietzsche was not uncritical. He notes
aspects of Nietzsche's philosophy which he considers dubious, for
example, the eternal recurrence of the same (*Arthur Schnitzler Tagebuch:
1917–1919* (Wien, 1985), p. 60; and see his *Tagebuch: 1920–1922*, p. 95).

However, earlier, in a letter to Hugo von Hofmansthal dated 27 July
1891, Schnitzler writes:

Gelesen wird manscherlei Burckhardt, Cultur der Renaissance,
Goethe ... etc. Besonders Nietzsche – zuletzt hat mich sein
Schlußcapitel und das Schlußgedicht zu Jenseits von Gut und Böse
ergriffen – Erinnern Sie sich? Nietzsche Sentimentalität! –
Weinender Marmor [a weeping marble]!
(*Briefe 1875–1912*, ed. Thérèse Nickl and Heinrich Schnitzler
(Frankfurt am Main, 1981), p. 120)

JACOB GOLOMB

In a letter from 21 June 1895 he proclaims:

> Ich kann mir selbst große Künstler denken, die Nietzsche nicht
> kennen, auch solche, die ihn kennen u. nicht lieben. Misverstehen
> Sie mich nicht: ich kenne ihn und liebe ihn. Daß er kein Philosoph,
> im Sinn der systemat. Philosophie ist, bringt ihn mir nur noch
> näher. . . . Ich sehe heute alles Schöne und Große wie ich es vorher
> gesehn habe. . . . Ich verehr ihn hoch – (in gewissen Abständen)
> neben Goethe, neben Beethoven, neben Ibsen, neben Maupassant
> – neben Michelangelo – ich habe einen Genuß mehr seit Nietzsche
> – aber ich habe keinen Genuße anders als ich ihn gehabt habe. –
> Es ist gewiß wahrscheinlich, daß die moderne Production auch in
> bedeutenderen Werken von einem so großen Geist nich wird
> unbeeinflußt bleiben können.

(ibid., p. 262)

Some comparative studies of Nietzsche and Schnitzler have been
undertaken. See, for example, Roland Duhamel, "Schnitzler und Nietz-
sche" *Amsterdamer Beiträge zur neueren Germanistik* 4 (1975): 1–25;
B. Ewing, "The politics of nihilism: Schnitzler's 'Last Man'", *Journal of
the International Arthur Schnitzler Research Association* 5 (1966): 4–16;
Herbert W. Reichert, "Nietzsche and Schnitzler", in Herbert W.
Reichert and Hermann Salinger (eds), *Studies in Arthur Schnitzler*
(Chapel Hill, 1963), pp. 95–107; Herbert W. Reichert, "Nietzsche's
Geniemoral and Schnitzler's ethics", in Herbert W. Reichert, *Friedrich
Nietzsche's Impact on Modern German Literature* (Chapel Hill, 1975),
pp. 88–116. See also G.K. Schneider's dissertation: "Arthur Schnitzler
und die Psychologie seiner Zeit, unter besonderer Berücksichtigung der
Philosophie Friedrich Nietzsches" (Ann Arbor, Michigan: University
Microfilms, 1969).

22 Zweig's unpublished Ph.D dissertation submitted for the University of
Vienna on 7 April 1904, one copy of which can be found in the *Deutsches
Literaturarchiv* in Marbach am Neckar, states: "Ihn [Taine] erfüllte, wie
seinen Freund und Jünger Nietzsche der Traum jener Griechentage, da
Kunst und Leben harmonie war" (p. 107). Perhaps Zweig was aware
that, as Hamburger put it, "Nietzsche remained virtually unread – except
by a few friends or disciples and one or two distinguished foreigners like
Taine, Brandes and Strindberg – before his collapse" (Hamburger,
Proliferation of Prophets, p. 25).

23 Zweig, *World of Yesterday* p. 39.

24 Ibid., p. 40, and see also pp. 44, 165, 351.

25 See his "Friedrich Nietzsche" in *Der Kampf mit dem Dämon* (Leipzig,
1925), pp. 231–322 (this is the second volume of his *Die Baumeister der
Welt*, tr. Eden and Cedar Paul as *Master Builders* (New York, 1939), pp.
441–530); "Nietzsche und der Freund" (Franz Overbeck), *Neue Freie
Presse* (Wien), 21 December 1916, pp. 1–5, reprinted in *Insel Almanach
auf das Jahr 1919* (Leipzig, 1919), pp. 111–23 and in Knut Beck (ed.),
Menschen und Schicksale (Frankfurt am Main, 1981), pp. 114–23. Also
see his 1932 lecture "Der europäische Gedanke in seiner historischen
Entwicklung", in S. Zweig, *Die Monotonisierung der Welt* (Frankfurt

182

am Main, 1976), pp. 47–71, and his 1909 article, heavily inspired by Nietzsche, "Das neue Pathos", *Das literarische Echo* 11 (1909): 1701–7.

26 See, for example, *Romain Rolland–Stefan Zweig: Briefwechsel 1910–1940*, ed. Waltrand Schwarze (Berlin, 1987), which contains at least eighteen significant pre-1933 references to Nietzsche, the general tone of which can be summarized by the phrase "der große Nietzsche" (from a letter dated 28 March 1930, in vol. 2, p. 366). Cf. his *Briefwechsel mit Hermann Bahr, Sigmund Freud, Rainer Maria Rilke und Arthur Schnitzler*, ed. Jeffrey B. Berlin, Hans-Ulrich Lindken and Donald A. Prater (Frankfurt am Main, 1987), and his *Briefe an Freunde*, ed. Richard Friedenthal (Frankfurt am Main, 1978), where, in a letter dated 12 January 1924, he prays: "Gott schenke uns ... einen neuen Nietzsche, einen einzigen großen *Jasager* zum eben!" (p. 149). Zweig's correspondence with the Nietzsche-Archiv is still unpublished and is to be found in the Goethe-Schiller-Archiv in Weimar. See *Stefan Zweig: An International Bibliography*, compiled by Randolph J. Klawiter (Riverside, Calif., 1991), p. 507.

27 "Mater Dolorosa: Die Briefe von Nietzsches Mutter an Overbeck", *Neues Wiener Tageblatt*, 21 December 1937, pp. 2–3, reprinted in Knut Beck (ed.), *Zeiten und Schicksale: Aufsätze und Vorträge aus den Jahren 1902–1942* (Frankfurt am Main, 1990), pp. 317–24.

28 See, e.g., the second volume of his *Briefwechsel* with Romain Rolland, especially letters from his exile in London, for example, that dated 10 June 1934, where he refers to Nietzsche and quotes his existential formula of "*amor fati*" (p. 569), and that of 4 October 1934, where he mentions that "der geniale Nietzsche" had predicted the beginning of the end of Christendom (p. 582). Also see his letter of 13 January 1936 (p. 618).

29 Zweig, *Beware of Pity*, tr. Phyllis and Trevor Blewitt (New York, 1939), pp. 205, 208. Thus the English title of this novel is well chosen. Cf. Adrian Del Caro, "Stefan Zweig's *Ungeduld des Herzens*: a Nietzschean interpretation", *Modern Austrian Literature* 14 (1981): 195–204.

30 See the letter from 4 May 1925 to Romain Rolland, where Zweig, referring to his essay on Nietzsche in *Der Kampf mit dem Dämon*, writes: "My whole essay is a hidden polemic against the attempt ... to claim Nietzsche for Germany, for war, for the 'good cause of Germany', he who was the first European, our ancestor ... le superbe 'sans-patrie'" (cited by Donald A. Prater, in *European of Yesterday: A Biography of Stefan Zweig* (Oxford 1972), p. 149). Cf. Klaus Bohnen, "Europäisches Bewußtsein in der Krise: Unveröffentlicher Briefwechsel zwischen Stefan Zweig und Georg Brandes", *Orbis Litterarum* (Copenhagen) 33 (1978): 220–37.

31 Interestingly enough, despite Zweig's amply documented preoccupation with Nietzsche, the subject has not yet been adequately researched. See, however, Del Caro, "Zweig's *Ungeduld des Herzens*", remarks by Hermann Bahr in "Der Kampf mit dem Dämon", *Neue Freie Presse*, 21 May 1925, and in Ulrich Weinierl (ed.), *Stefan Zweig – Triumph und Tragik* (Frankfurt am Main, 1992), pp. 28–33. See also an essay by Leon Botstein, "Stefan Zweig and the illusion of the Jewish European" in

Marion Sonnenfeld (ed.), *Stefan Zweig* (Albany, 1983), pp. 82–110, esp. 89–90.

32 Wassermann, *My Life*, p. 81. And see Julie Wassermann's sensitive account of her husband's dilemmas regarding his Judaism in "Biographical notes", in *The Letters of Jakob Wassermann to Frau Julie Wassermann*, ed. V. Grubwieser, tr. Phyllis and Trevor Blewitt (London, 1935), pp. 7–33.

33 Wassermann, *My Life*, p. 203.

34 Ibid., p. 93. The wide use of Nietzschean notions in Wassermann's early writings suggests that Nietzsche exerted considerable influence on him. Thus, for example, in "Faustina: Ein Gespräch", from 1907, Wassermann writes: "Der Liebende ist Augenmensch; seine Leiden sind wirklich, seine Freuden sind *dionysisch*; der andere, der die Liebe nur ahnt wie ein Nachtgänger das *Morgenrot*" (*Imaginäre Brücken: Studien und Aufsätze* (Munich, 1921), p. 55); and in his *Rede an die Jugend über das Leben im Geiste* (Berlin, 1932) delivered (in January, 1932) at the University of Basel, where Nietzsche once taught, Wassermann, speaking of the "europäische Gestalt", refers once again to him (p. 37). For Nietzsche's influence on Wasserman, see Anne-Liese Sell, *Das metaphysich-realistische Weltbild Jakob Wassermans* (Marburg, 1932); the chapter on Nietzsche's influence on Wassermann in Walter Goldstein's *Wassermann: Sein Kampf um Wahrheit* (Leipzig and Zürich, 1929), pp. 309ff. and cf. Walter Goldstein, *Jakob Wassermann: Der Mann von sechzig Jahren* (Berlin, 1933), which elucidates many Nietzschean motifs in Wassermann's writings; see esp. pp. 27ff. Ironically – and tragically – the book, published in the same year as Hitler's seizure of power, contains the following sentence: "Der Weg des deutschen Juden von Heine zu Wassermann ist der Weg von der Unsicherheit zu neu errungener Sicherheit" (p. 37).

35 There are at least twenty references to Nietzsche in Walter Benjamin's *Briefe*, ed. Gershom Scholem and Theodor W. Adorno (Frankfurt am Main, 1966). And see his "Nietzsche und das Archiv seiner Schwester" from 1932, in *Walter Benjamin Gesammelte Schriften*, vol. 3, ed. Hella Tiedemann-Bartels (Frankfurt am Main, 1972), pp. 323–6.

It is interesting to note that "Scholem was often 'utterly surprised to find a liberal dash of Nietzsche' in Benjamin's utterances" (Hamburger, *Proliferation of Prophets*, p. 286). Hamburger claims that for Benjamin, "Nietzsche was the very prototype of the experimental, non-systematic thinker" (ibid., p. 287). Cf. Peter Pütz, "Nietzsche im Lichte der Kritischen Theorie", *Nietzsche-Studien* 3 (1974): 175–91; H. Pfotenhauer, "Benjamin und Nietzsche", in B. Linder (ed.), *Links hatte noch alles sich zu enträtseln ...: Walter Benjamin im Kontext* (Frankfurt am Main, 1978), pp. 100–26; G. Franck, "Walter Benjamin e i paradossi di Zarathustra", in F. Rella (ed.), *Critica e storia* (Venice, 1980), pp. 117–36.

36 See, e.g., his letter from November 1906 and other references to Nietzsche in *Carl Sternheim Gesamtwerk*, ed. Wilhelm Emrich, vol. 7, (Neuwied am Rhein, 1967), pp. 847–8, 854–5, and his essays "Morgenröte?" (1919), "Berlin oder Juste milieu" (1920) and "Tasso oder Kunst

des Juste milieu" (1921), in vol. 6 (1966), pp. 101–2, 105–71, 177–201 (esp. pp. 125, 142, 159, 199). See also his essay "Das Arbeiter – ABC" (1922), pp. 240–55 (esp. p. 248) and his 1932 autobiographical piece "Vorkriegseuropa im Gleichnis meines Lebens", in ibid., vol. 10 (1976), esp. pp. 189, 258–9. Cf. Herbert W. Reichert, "Nietzsche und Carl Sternheim", *Nietzsche-Studien* 1 (1972): 334–52 and his *Nietzsche Impact*, pp. 29–50 and in Hillebrand (ed.), *Nietzsche und die deutsche Literatur*, vol. 2, pp. 11–35.

37 See Robert A. Cohen, "Rosenzweig vs. Nietzsche", *Nietzsche-Studien* 19 (1990): 346–66; Steven E. Aschheim, "Nietzsche and the Nietzschean moment", p. 202 and H. Liebeschütz, *Von Georg Simmel zu Franz Rosenzweig: Studien zum Jüdischen Denken im deutschen Kulturbereich* (Tübingen, 1970), p. 172.

38 See his *Bilanz der deutschen Judenheit: Ein Versuch* (Amsterdam, 1934; Leipzig, 1990) pp. 236–8, and articles in a journal, *Orient*, edited and published by Arnold Zweig and Wolfgang Yourgrau in Haifa, Palestina, when he was living there; and, for example, an interesting essay by Paul Riesenfeld, "Übermensch und Untermensch", *Orient* 12 (June 1942): 11–14. Cf. Arnold Zweig's essay on the occasion of Freud's eightieth birthday, 6 May 1936, which bears the Nietzschean title "Apollon bewältigt Dionysos". Zweig declares there that Freud was the "greatest psychologist since Nietzsche", *Das neue Tage-Buch* (Paris and Amsterdam, 1936), vol. 18, reprinted in *Text und Kritik* (Munich), *Heft 104: Arnold Zweig* (October 1989): 3–8.

Also see his letters to Freud: dated 2 December 1930, where he speaks about his wish to write an essay "about [Freud's] relationship to Nietzsche" (Ernst L. Freud, *The Letters of Sigmund Freud and Arnold Zweig*, tr. Elaine and William Robson-Scott, 9th edn (New York, 1970), p. 23); dated 28 April 1934, where he speaks of his plans to write "a novel about Nietzsche's madness", stating that Nietzsche was an "idol of [his] youth" to whom he has "come close again, because in [Freud he] recognized the man who has carried out all that Nietzsche first dreamt of" (ibid., pp. 74ff.); and dated 6 June 1934, where once again he claims that "F.N. was a youthful love of mine, admired as a prose writer and as a thinker too" (ibid., pp. 80–1; cf. a letter dated 8 July 1934, ibid., pp. 83–4). Compare Freud's letter to Arnold Zweig dated 11 May 1934 (ibid., pp. 76–9), advising him not to write his novel about Nietzsche. This advice influenced Zweig, who reluctantly gave up his project of writing on Nietzsche but not before eulogizing this "sensitive nostalgic seeker" who was devoured by "the Germany of Bismarck and the Nazis, everything he despises" in a letter written in Haifa, and dated 12 August 1934 (ibid., p. 88).

In any event, Nietzsche is also mentioned in Zweig's 1936 eulogy of a Jewish German Nietzsche scholar: "Theodor Lessing, ermordet am 31. August 1933", in Arnold Zweig, *Ausgewählte Werke in Einzelausgaben*, vol. 16 (Berlin, 1967), pp. 83–91. Nietzsche is also mentioned by A. Zweig several times in course of his correspondence with another famous *Grenzjude*, Lion Feuchtwanger. See Harold von Hofe (ed.), *Lion Feuchtwanger/Arnold Zweig Briefwechsel 1933–1958*, 2 vols (Berlin and

JACOB GOLOMB

Weimar, 1984), particularly letters Zweig wrote from Haifa dated 7 May
1945 (vol. 1, p. 336); from Berlin dated 25 August 1951 (vol. 2, p. 143);
from Berlin dated 11 December 1951 (vol. 2, p. 150) and from Berlin on
4 February 1957 (vol. 2, p. 370). Cf. references in note 39 below and
Georg Wenzel (ed.), *Arnold Zweig 1887–1968: Werk und Leben in
Dokumenten und Bildern* (Berlin and Weimar, 1978).
   Little comparative work has been done. None is noted in the
comprehensive *Bibliographie Arnold Zweig* compiled by Maritta Rost,
vol. 2: *Sekundärliteratur* (Berlin und Weimar, 1987). See however, Bernd
Hüppauf, "Assoziationen", *Text und Kritik* (Munich), *Heft 104:
Arnold Zweig* (October 1989): 38–55, esp. section 2, "Zweig und
Nietzsche"; and Manuel Wiznitzer, *Arnold Zweig: Das Leben eines
deutsch-jüdischen Schriftstellers* (Königstein, 1983).

39 In von Hofe (ed.), *Briefwechsel*. Also see two letters by Feuchtwanger:
from 30 March 1945 (ibid., vol. 1, p. 323) and 25 September 1951 (ibid.,
vol. 2, p. 144). Cf. Hamid Ongha, *Geschichtsphilosophie und Theorie des
historischen Romans bei Lion Feuchtwanger* (Frankfurt am Main, 1982),
esp. the section on "Nietzsche und Feuchtwanger", pp. 129–32. See also
Feuchtwanger's "Über *Jud Süss*", in his *Centum Opuscula* (Rudolstadt,
1956), pp. 388–91, where Feuchtwanger maintains that *Jud Süss* was
intended to show the path of European man from Buddha to Nietzsche.

40 See, e.g., Ralf R. Nicolai, "Nietzschean thought in Kafka's 'A report to
an academy'", *Literary Review* 26 (1983): 551–64; Wiebrecht Ries,
"Kafka und Nietzsche", *Nietzsche-Studien* 2 (1973): 258–75; Gerhard
Kurz, *Traum-Schrecken: Kafkas literarische Existenzanalyse* (Stuttgart,
1980); Patrik Bridgwater, *Kafka und Nietzsche* (Bonn, 1974); Reinhold
Grimm, "Comparing Kafka and Nietzsche", *German Quarterly* 52
(1979): 339–50 and my "Kafka's existential metamorphosis: from
Kierkegaard to Nietzsche". *Clio* 14 (1985): 271–86.

41 See, e.g., Paul-Laurent Assoun, *Freud et Nietzsche* (Paris, 1980); Bruce
Mazlish, "Freud and Nietzsche", *The Psychoanalytic Review* 55 (1968):
360–75; Friedrich Tramer, "Friedrich Nietzsche und Sigmund Freud",
Jahrbuch für Psychologie, Psychotherapie und Anthropologie 7 (1960):
325–50; Richard Waughman, "The intellectual relationship between
Nietzsche and Freud", *Psychiatry* 36 (1973): 458–67. Also see my
Nietzsche's Enticing Psychology of Power; "Freudian uses and misuses
of Nietzsche", *American Imago* 37 (1980): 371–85; and "Jaspers, Mann
and the Nazis on Nietzsche and Freud", *Israel Journal for Psychiatry* 18
(1981): 311–26.

42 See Kraus's article in his *Die Fackel*, announcing Nietzsche's death "Zu
Friedrich Nietzsches Tod" 2(51) (1900): 19–22, where he eulogizes
Nietzsche's suffering to attain authentic life in terms of the "freiwilligen
Leiden der Wahrhaftigkeit" (p. 19) (reproduced in Heinrich Fischer
(ed.), 39 vols (Munich 1968–73), vol. 3). Also see other articles from *Die
Fackel*: 2(52) (1900): 14–16 and 23 (577/582) (1921): 61–6, as well as his
Die dritte Walpurgisnacht (1933), ed. Heinrich Fischer (Munich, 1952),
pp. 59–65.
   Comparative remarks on Nietzsche and Kraus are few: see Joachim
Stephan, *Satire und Sprache* (Munich, 1964), esp. pp. 137–8; Gerald Stieg,

Der Brenner und die Fackel (Salzburg, 1976); William M. Johnston, *The Austrian Mind: An Intellectual and Social History 1848–1938* (Berkeley, 1972), pp. 4, 206 (and see on p. 137 his comparison between Nietzsche and Mahler).

43 See, e.g., her 1932 "Der kleine Friedrich Nietzsche", in her *Gesammelte Werke*, ed. Friedhelm Kemp, vol. 2 (Munich, 1962), pp. 721–3; cf. Jakob Hessing's *Else Lasker-Schüler* (Munich, 1987), pp. 67ff.

44 See, e.g., the letters from 21 November 1932 and from 1 May 1935 in his *Briefwechsel*, ed. B. Hack and M. Kleiß (Frankfurt am Main, 1971), pp. 408, 632, and a letter from 17 February 48 in Hermann Broch, *Briefe von 1929 bis 1951*, ed. Robert Pick (Zürich, 1957), pp. 285–6. Cf. Endre Kiss, "Brochs Stellung zu Nietzsche", in Richard Thiebergerin (ed.), *Hermann Broch und seine Zeit* (Berne, 1980), pp. 88–96; and his "Über Hermann Brochs Ehrgeiz . . .", in *Hermann Broch: Werk und Wirkung*, ed. Endre Kiss (Bonn, 1985), pp. 65–86; Uwe Dörwald, *Über das Ethische bei Hermann Broch* (Frankfurt am Main, 1994); Karl Menges, *Kritische Studien Zur Wertphilosophie Hermann Brochs* (Tübingen, 1970), esp. pp. 121–3; Dominick La Capra, "Broch as cultural historian", in Stephen D. Dowden (ed.), *Hermann Broch: Literature, Philosophy, Politics* (Columbia, SC, 1988), pp. 42–53.

45 See, e.g., his "Zarathustra und Appelschnut", in *Die Schaubühne* 9(42) (1913): 1011, reprinted in *Gedichte*, ed. Mary Gerold-Tucholsky (Reinbek bei Hamburg, 1983), pp. 56–7; "Kartengruß aus dem Engadin", in *Die Weltbühne* 22(30) (1926): 151, reprinted in *Gedichte*, pp. 503–4; "Fräulein Nietzsche", in *Die Weltbühne*, 28(2) (1932): 54–9, reprinted in *Gesammelte Werke*, ed. Mary Gerold-Tucholsky and Fritz J. Raddatz, vol. 10 (Reinbek bei Hamburg, 1975), pp. 9–15; and his "Pfiff im Orgelklang" (a reply to "Offener Brief an Nietzsche" by Hans Flesch in *Die Weltbühne*, 26 January 1931, pp. 125–9) in *Die Weltbühne* 28(5) (1932): 164–5, reprinted in *Gesammelte Werke*, vol. 10, pp. 22–4.

46 See, e.g., his essay "Der Snobismus als geistige Weltmacht", in *Jahrbuch des Paul Zsolnay-Verlages* (Berlin, Wien and Leipzig, 1928), pp. 9–34, esp. pp. 21ff. This is a chapter from an unpublished book, *Die Krizis der Ideale*, on Nietzsche's *Ecce Homo*.

Many of the aphorisms in his "Theologoumena" (*Between Heaven and Earth*, pp. 94–176) are unmistakably Nietzschean, and Nietzsche's name is explicitly mentioned several times, e.g., on pp. 129, 151. And cf. Lothar Huber, "Franz Werfel's *Spiegelmensch*: an interpretation", in Lothar Huberin (ed.), *Franz Werfel: An Austrian Writer Reassessed* (Oxford, 1989), pp. 65–80. See also Peter Stephen Jungk, *Franz Werfel*, tr. Anselm Hollo (New York, 1990), esp. p. 28, where the biographer describes how Werfel and his friends, among them Kafka, Brod, etc., were "immersed in discussions" of Nietzsche in the Café Arco in Prague. See the reference on p. 63, to how in April 1918 Werfel compared his book of poems *The Last Judgment* to Nietzsche's *Zarathustra*, and that on p. 90 which describes how he began to compose music and set Nietzsche's poem 'Venice' to a tune.

47 Richard Frank Krummel, *Nietzsche und der deutsche Geist* (Berlin, 1974).

48 For references see Aschheim, "Nietzsche and the Nietzschean moment",
    p. 191, n. 14. Ironically, Nietzsche was also cited, though of course not
    monopolized by Germans opposing these forces. In the work toward
    post-war political reconciliation, *Die Umschau: Internationale Revue*
    (Mainz), published, in its first 1946 volume, "Friedrich Nietzsche über
    die Juden" (p. 317). (This is the well-known section 475 of the first
    volume of *Human, All Too Human*, where Nietzsche thanks the Jews
    for providing humanity with "the noblest human being [Christ], the
    purest sage [Spinoza], the mightiest book and the most efficacious moral
    code in the world" (*HAH*, p. 175). Of special interest in this context is
    a double issue of the Parisian *Acéphale* published in January 1937.
    Written by such prominent French intellectuals as Georges Bataille,
    Pierre Klossowski, Jean Wahl, etc., it was devoted, as the subtitle –
    "Réparation a Nietzsche" – implies, to fighting the distortion and
    Nazification of his thought by the "intellectuals" of the Third Reich.
49 See my "Nietzsche on Jews and Judaism", *Archiv für Geschichte der
    Philosophie* 67 (1985): 139–61; and a more extended version, "Nietz-
    sche's Judaism of power", *Revue des études juives* 147 (1988): 353–85.
50 Wasserman, *My Life*, p. 233.
51 Toller, *I was a German*, pp. 99–100. Cf. Werfel's Nietzschean ex-
    clamation there: "Man, be yourself!"(p. 157). Jethro Bithell in his
    Modern German Literature 1880–1950 (London, 1959), p. 423, correctly
    points out that "This call to man: to thine own self be true! is the very
    message of Franz Werfel".
52 *D* 73, p. 73; cf. *GS* 357; *BGE* 1.
53 The distinction between *Kraft* and *Macht* is crucial to any understanding
    of Nietzsche's mature doctrine of power; see my *Nietzsche's Enticing
    Psychology of Power*, pp. 179–221.
54 See e.g., *GS* 317, p. 252; *BGE* 257; *EH*, p. 296.
55 As Arthur Schnitzler puts it:

> The problem of religion occupied me more . . . than ever before
> . . . it had to flow together with the basic questions of philo-
> sophy. . . . It is nonsense to say "As God wills". We will, God
> has to.
> (*My Youth in Vienna*, tr. Catherine Hutter (New York: Holt &
> Winston), pp. 77–8)

See also Wassermann's *My Life*, where he confesses that "The Jewish
God was a mere shadow [for him]" and hence he "sought to grasp the
God-concept" (p. 19); and Werfel's announcement that "the real crux
lay not between Right and Left, but between Above and Below"
(*Between Heaven and Earth*, p. viii).
56 The Spinozistic model of salvation which proffered a metaphysical and
    rationalistic *amor dei intellectualis*, was a worthy, though anachronistic,
    rival of the Nietzschean *amor fati* (see the chapter on "Spinoza and
    Nietzsche" in vol. 2 of Yirmiyahu Yovel's *Spinoza and Other Heretics*
    (Princeton, 1989); Joan Stambaugh, "Amor dei and *Amor fati*: Spinoza
    and Nietzsche", in James C. O'Flaherty *et al.* (eds), *Studies in Nietzsche
    and the Judaeo-Christian Tradition* (Chapel Hill, 1985), pp. 130–41).

Indeed both names appear frequently in the writings and memoirs of the marginal Jews. One notable example is Döblin:

> Früh merkte ich, daß ich der Metaphysik verfallen war – und suchte mich zu entziehen. Ich las unheimlich viel, wenigen "schöne literatur" als Philosophie (noch in meiner Gymnasialzeit, als bis 1906), Spinoza, Schopenhauer und Nietzsche. Am intensivsten Spinoza.
> (*Autobiographische Schriften und letzte Aufzeichnungen*, p. 440)

Wassermann also describes how "the works of Spinoza . . . had a curious fascination" for him (*My Life*, pp. 21–2, 85, 101). Cf. Werfel's *Between Heaven and Earth*, pp. 41, 78, and p. 116, where Werfel, speaking about the "stupid" notion of an "impersonal God", refers to "senile pantheism", alluding, of course, to Spinoza's teaching.

It was easier to identify with Spinoza, the most prominent early Jewish heretic, since he too had emerged from the same tradition from which the *Grenzjuden* now felt completely estranged. But in the twentieth century it seemed far too late to turn to metaphysics, one of the dead God's shadows. Nietzsche, who went radically beyond the "metaphysical crutch" and tried to inspire modern humanity to rely solely on its own resources by living creatively in a completely immanent world, thus had far greater appeal for modern secular Jews, and hence decisively won the ideological battle with Spinoza, at least in the hearts of the marginal Jews. His model allowed liberation from the constraints of all the various doctrines of metaphysical salvation and thus was more relevant to their existential concerns than Spinoza's still too-traditional model of salvation, which was already powerless to sustain them in the abysses of modernity.

57 Wasserman, *My Life*, pp. 170–1, 203.
58 Zweig, *World of Yesterday*, pp. 326–8, 436. That this "destruction" of his European "homeland" actually ended Zweig's life can be directly deduced from Zweig's last "Declaration", written in Petropolis, Brazil on 22 February 1942, a few hours before his and Lotte Zweig's suicides:

> Every day I have learnt to love this country better and nowhere would I have more gladly rebuilt my life all over again, now that the world of my native tongue has perished for me, and *Europe, my spiritual home*, is destroying itself.
> But one would need special powers to begin completely afresh when one has passed one's sixtieth year. And mine are exhausted through the long years of homeless wandering . . .
> I greet all my friends! May they live to see the dawn after the long night is over! I, all too impatient, am going on alone.
> (My italics, tr. Christobel Fowler in Hanns Arens (ed.),
> *Stefan Zweig: A Tribute to his Life and Work* (London, n.d.),
> p. 4. The original German letter is to be found in the
> Department of Manuscripts and Archives of the National
> and University Library in Jerusalem)

Zweig's unwavering European humanism is nicely described in Berthold Viertel's "Farewell to Stefan Zweig" (ibid., pp. 151–7):

> But where was Stefan Zweig's own Europe? At this point I seem to hear again Peter Altenberg's dictum: "A women has only one world: the world of love. A man has only one love: love of the world." Lotte Zweig had no desire to survive the extinction of her world, since Stefan Zweig was incapable of surviving the extinction of his. For his world was Europe, his country as he called it, in his dignified farewell letter. (ibid., pp. 152–3)

Cf. Zweig's dispute with his friend, Abraham Schwadron, an ardent Zionist, to whom he writes, probably in 1917, commenting on his "Jeremiah", written during World War I: "For me the glory and greatness of the Jewish people is to become the only people with a spiritual home, an eternal Jerusalem only ... instead of striving for the real Palestine" (my translation from Zweig's letter, found in the National and University Library in Jerusalem). And cf. Wassermann's admission:

> I am European, full to the brim with European destiny, moulded by the European spirit.... I recoiled from what they called the Jewish nation.... The ideal nation surviving in the Jewish diaspora appeared to me finer, nobler, more fruitful than any reality. (*My Life*, pp. 280, 195)

59 In *UM*, p. 69 (emphasis in original) and cf. *BGE* 30.
60 We can detect an echo of Nietzsche's disparagement of the "antiquarian conciousness" in Stefan Zweig's story "Buchmendel". The hero of this story, a Galician Jew and second-hand book dealer named Jacob Mandel, is described as an obsessive genius who "studied catalogues and tomes ... as Jewish boys are taught to do when reading the Talmud". However, his "antiquarian memory" was "in the last analysis unproductive and uncreative" and actually impaired his vitality and interest in the real grimy life. When the grimy realities of the external world beyond "the remote calm atmosphere of his bookish world" exploded in his face, during World War I, he died and vanished into "oblivion" (in Stefan Zweig's collection, *Kaleidoscope*, tr. Eden and Cedar Paul (New York, 1943), pp. 235, 239, 255, 261).
    Actually Zweig's "Zwölf historische Miniaturen", portrayed in his *Sternstunden der Menschheit* (Stockholm, 1943), were written from the Nietzschean perspective of "monumental history": namely the "great moments in the struggle of the human individual" which "constitute a chain [that] unites mankind across the millennia like a range of human mountain peaks" ("On the uses and disadvantages of history for life", *UM* p. 68). These dramatic events and moments constitute the "republic of genius of which Schopenhauer once spoke" (ibid., p. 111). In his "Vorwort" to the *Sternstunden der Menschheit*, Zweig uses the same notions and images when he speaks of "die sublimen, die unvergeßlichen Momente" (Frankfurt am Main, 1987, pp. 7–8). Such dramatic Jewish "moments" were vividly portrayed in Zweig's play *Jeremias: Eine*

Dramatische Dichtung in Neun Bildern (Frankfurt, 1917; Stockholm, 1939; tr. as *Jeremiah* by Eden and Cedar Paul, New York, 1929) and in his 1936 legend "Der begrabene Leuchter" ("The buried candelabrum", in *Jewish Legends*, tr. Eden and Cedar Paul with a new introduction by Leon Botstein (New York, 1987), pp. 3–143) where he pays tribute to the heroism and the unfaltering faith of Jews in Roman times. (Compare the other legends in that collection.)

Not incidentally, the series in which Zweig included his chapter on Nietzsche had a definitely "monumental" title: *Master Builders: The Typology of the Spirit* (New York, 1931; the chapter on Nietzsche – from 1925 – is on pp. 443–530). See also Feuchtwanger's *Der jüdische Krieg* (1932); *Der Tag wird kommen* (1945); *Die Jüden von Toledo* (1955); *Jefta und seine Tochter* (1957) and his short biblical dramas in two volumes, *Kleine Dramen* (1950–6); Jakob Wassermann's *Alexander im Babylon* (1905); Franz Werfel's *Paulus unter den Juden* (1926), where the writer announces that "With fear and trembling I present this Drama to the public.... For I wished to portray nothing less momentous than that decisive hour in which Christianity separated itself from its mother-environment" ("The argument" in *Paul among the Jews: A Tragedy*, tr. Paul. P. Levertoff (London, 1928)); Alfred Döblin's *Babylonische Wanderung* (1934); and Lasker-Schüler's *Hebräische Balladen* (1920), in her *Gedichte 1902–1943*, ed. F. Kemp (Munich, 1959), pp. 291–311.

61 *Ost und West* 1 (1901): 7–10.

62 Note, for example, Freud's admission:

> Because I was a Jew I found myself free from many prejudices which restricted others in the use of their intellect; and as a Jew I was prepared to join the opposition and to do without agreement with the "compact majority". ("Address to the Society of B'nai B'rith", in *The Standard Edition of the Complete Psychological Works*, vol. 20 (London and New York, 1953–74), p. 474).

Cf. ibid., "An autobiographical study", pp. 9ff.

63 Marthe Robert, *From Oedipus to Moses: Freud's Jewish Identity*, tr. Ralph Manheim (New York, 1976), pp. 11–12.

64 See *GM*, Introduction 3; H. Nunberg and E. Federn (eds), *Minutes of the Vienna Psychoanalytic Society* (New York, 1967); and Ernst Jones, *Sigmund Freud: Life and Work*, vol. 2 (London, 1955).

65 Theodor Lessing, *Schopenhauer, Wagner, Nietzsche: Einführung in moderne deutsche Philosophie* (Munich, 1908), and his "Anzeigen" of this work in *Die Zukunft* 15 (Berlin), 12 January 1907, p. 75; also his *Nietzsche* (Berlin, 1925) and an epilogue: "Ein Doppel-Portrait", by Rita Bischof (Munich, 1985). Cf. the Nietzsche-inspired work written by Lessing during World War I: *Geschichte als Sinngebung des Sinnlosen oder die Geburt der Geschichte aus dem Mythos* (Hamburg, 1962), in which Nietzsche is frequently quoted.

66 Theodor Lessing, *Der Jüdische Selbsthass* (Berlin, 1930; reprinted in Munich, 1984, with an introduction by Boris Groys). Cf. his *Deutschland und Seine Juden* (Prague, 1933); and Lawrence Baron, "Theodor Lessing: between Jewish self-hatred and Zionism", in *Leo Baeck*

Institute Yearbook 26 (1981): 323–40, whose author claims that "although Lessing admired Nietzsche's anti-positivism and insights into the genesis of morality, he opposed the idea of an *Übermensch* who was beyond good and evil".

67 Lessing, *Der Jüdische Selbshass*, p. 51. In another essay he urges the assimilated Jews: "Werde, der Du bist. . . . Deutscher bleibe Deutsch. . . . Und Jude sei Jude", *Deutschland und Seine Juden*, p. 23.

68 Lessing, *Deutschland und Seine Juden*, p. 14.

69 See my *Nietzsche's Enticing Psychology of Power*, chs 4, 5, 6.

70 Richard Maximilian Lonsbach, *Friedrich Nietzsche und die Juden: Ein Versuch* (Stockholm, 1939; reprinted and ed. Heinz Robert Schlette Bonn, 1985).

71 Lonsbach, *Nietzsche*, p. 55: "Ich will alle Antisemiten erschießen lassen." This is the last sentence of Nietzsche's last postcard to his loyal friend Overbeck, from 6 January 1889, translated by W. Kaufmann as "I am just having all anti-Semites shot", in *The Portable Nietzsche*, ed. and tr. Walter Kaufmann (New York, 1968), p. 687.

72 These words were intended to be included in "Why I write such good books" 2, *Ecce Homo*, n. 1 of Walter Kaufmann's commentary (New York, 1969), p. 262. It was discarded but their spirit nevertheless remains in innumerable other published passages. See, e.g., *EH*, p. 245.

73 *Portable Nietzsche*, p. 506.

9

FREUD IN HIS RELATION TO NIETZSCHE

Peter Heller

GENERAL REMARKS

My initial resistance to seeing Freud's relation to Nietzsche in the context of "Jewish culture" takes the form of questioning the legitimacy of such an undertaking. Is there a characteristically Jewish attitude toward Nietzsche? If being a Jew meant belonging to a religious faith or a way of life determined by a religious tradition, a common denominator might be assumed, which even the assumption of a merely national identity renders questionable. There has been something like a "German" – that is: an aggressively national-istic – Nietzscheanism. Mercifully this was not adopted by all Germans. One need only think of Overbeck or Thomas Mann. And if being a Jew meant merely belonging to an ethnic or "racial" group, could or should ways of thinking be related to such affiliation? Was Spinoza – as Nietzsche apparently thought (see *NSW*, vol. 11, p. 319) – a typically Jewish pantheist? Jesus of Nazareth a typically Jewish founder of a religion? Moses, whom Freud considered to be an Egyptian (*FGW*, vol. 16, pp. 114ff.), a typically Jewish leader and law-giver? If so, in what sense?

In his aggressive atheism, his anti-nationalistic cosmopolitanism, his turn against cover-ups of convention and in his positive faith in the objectivity and truth of science, Freud felt himself to be a modern continuer of the most essential Jewish tradition. His last book suggests he even might have thought of himself as the Moses of the twentieth century. In his relationship to Nietzsche, which he was at some pains to understate or deny altogether, he certainly did not consider himself a Nietzschean, that is, the follower of a thinker who, by virtue of his multiperspectivism, did his best to make it difficult

193

to assume such a posture. (Would-be followers of Nietzsche always had to make a selection from Nietzsche in keeping with their own bias.) Again the question arises whether Freud may be treated as representative of "Jewish culture" in his attitude toward Nietzsche.

Yet an inquiry into how Jews looked upon or came to terms with Nietzsche is hardly illegitimate; and once this is granted, the thought recurs – as counterclaim to reservations above – that there may be a common denominator in the Jewish reception of Nietzsche. Even a man like Freud, who did not associate himself with a Jewish national or religious community, was not one to minimize what Lessing's Sultan Saladin refers to as "the accident of birth" (*Nathan the Wise*, v. 1846). In fact, Freud did acknowledge his Jewish identity with some pride, if without the defensive sensitivity which, in the wake of the Nazi genocide, inclined some of us to label every Jewish self-criticism a symptom of Jewish "self-hatred".

There are, after all, variable physical and mental characteristics of peoples and races, whether due to genetic inheritance, cultural traditions or sociohistorical conditions. In the circles of Jewish "assimilationists," who were decisive in terms of Jewish contributions to German culture from the eighteenth to the twentieth century, there even existed something like a dominant intellectual tradition. For they mostly sympathized with the Enlightenment which liberated the Jews from the ghettos. In the German language orbit most of us "assmilationists" or Jews marked, at least, by the imprint of assimilationism, shared in an ideology derivable from *Nathan* and the Lessing–Mendelssohn epoch. Even that, however, cannot be maintained without reservations, e.g., for the subsequent Romantic phase, the later Mendelssohns and Veits, the late Romantic aspect of Heine, or, in the twentieth century, for Kafka or Buber. The working-through of the Romantic heritage in particular is characteristic also for Freud. His entire work of discovery and system of metaphors is dedicated to research into what the Romantics called the "night-side" of human nature. Indeed, the younger Freud still admits to this rebellious sympathy with "Lucifer-Amor" (letter to Fliess, 7 July 1900) and suggests it at least in the motto to the *Interpretation of Dreams* ("Flectere si nequeo superos/acheronta movebo"; "if I cannot bend the superior powers, I shall set the underworld in motion"). Later on, he will prefer a stylization in keeping with a rational realism, such as the Faustian project envisaged in the *New Introductory Lectures*: "Where Id was, there Ego shall be" (*FGW*, vol. 15, p. 86).

This attempt to combine a rationalistic, positivistic and anti-metaphysical mentality with a Romantic heritage, to blend in the case of Freud – Diderot and Helmholtz, so to speak, with E.T.A. Hoffmann, and to transcend them thereby, has its analogue in Nietzsche. For neither can Nietzsche be associated simply with a late Romantic conception of the Dionysian, which may still predominate in *The Birth of Tragedy*; nor can he be reduced to a skeptical, quasi-positivistic and rationalistic dialectic which comes to the fore in the middle phase of his movement of thought. Spreading enlightenment about the Enlightenment, combining the latter, including nineteenth-century Positivism, with perspectives of German Idealism, a "Romantic" dynamic and a transvaluation of the drive-like Will of Schopenhauer, he seeks to arrive at a new image and model of man.

Freud certainly had a more enduring affinity to the sobering perspectives of Enlightenment and Positivism than Nietzsche, though the latter concerned himself with the instinctual and "irrational" above all where they find a sublimated expression, that is, as critic and philosopher of culture. Freud, on the other hand, made it his main concern to turn to impulses and manifestations which were suppressed by culture or civilization (a distinction he refused to make). Yet it is readily understandable that Freud's positive relation to Nietzsche concerns primarily Nietzsche's sober, critical, psychological insights rather than his ecstatic Dionysian modes and moods, let alone the preaching Nietzsche of Zarathustra who is accused by Freud of having proclaimed an illusionary "Soll" ("Thou Shalt), instead of staying with what "is," which is to say, with mere reality (see below, p. 203). And yet it may be argued that Freud himself, though he denied this, proclaimed, almost as emphatically as Nietzsche, an – equally biased – dogma of salvation, and indeed a kind of religion of the earth.

An important delimitation of Freud's relation to Nietzsche is suggested by a sentence from his correspondence in old age with Arnold Zweig. In his youth, he wrote in a letter of 11/12 May 1934, Nietzsche meant to him a nobility which he could not attain.[1] The remark is not to be understood as positive endorsement of Nietzsche's ideal. Freud considered himself an ethical human being. As the member of an elitist, bourgeois society of "high culture" prior to its collapse into a state of twentieth-century barbarianism, he was of the somewhat smug and unjustified opinion that the claims of decency were self-evident and their observance to be taken for granted.

Though Nietzsche's ideal of nobility may have impressed Freud greatly in his youth, it did not appeal to him in his later years. He found the "positive" Nietzsche – especially the prophet of master races and of superman – not merely inaccessible. Even prior to the excessive use made of them by the Nazis, Freud disapproved of these postulates, while he shared with – and may have found in – Nietzsche the term and concept of sublimation as a psychological basis for his faith in culture and civilization.[2]

Marx, Nietzsche and Freud, the three most influential religious atheists of "Modernism" share, of course, some basic features. In a positive sense these consist in their emphatic atheism itself: the renunciation of a "beyond," or of any guiding power superior to man and not merely dwelling within him; and in the exclusive concentration of all hope on the shaping of a terrestrial existence, in short: on a religion of the earth. With respect to their negative, critical side, they share a type of multilayered approach. For in spite of, or rather within the frame of their ideal of civilization and culture, their emphasis is upon the guiding power of "low" and basic forces or conditions. Using a Marxist notion in a somewhat enlarged sense, one may say that this emphasis finds its expression in a comprehensive critique of ideologies, as well as of civilized man and his society. Nothing is accepted simply as what it appears to be. Everything is treated as a symptom of some underlying, basic need, drive or conflict, which is both disguised and revealed in the manifest content or phenomenon. At the same time, these thinkers acknowledge that the motivation or causation by the basic guiding force or condition may remain unconscious. This is less apparent in Marx. However – to give an example – when he conceives of the declaration of human rights as an ideological superstructure of the mentality and conditions of free, capitalist trade, he certainly does not mean to say that the ideologians of the French Revolution were conscious of striving merely for free enterprise in business. With Nietzsche the assumption of unconscious motivation is dominant – whether in his critique of Christianity, Epicureanism or German Idealism *et al.* In Freud it is proclaimed as an almost unheard-of *novum* and used in multiple ways: thus for example in his interpretation of dreams, the manifest dream is seen as due to unconscious thought in accordance with the Primary Process and as a product of secondary elaboration transforming the latent dream thoughts. Moreover, he distinguishes between "conscious" and "preconscious" (as distinct from "unconscious"), etc. In polemical opposition to the notion of "higher" worlds posited by Idealism, Marx conceives of the existence and the history of mankind as determined by socioeconomic conditions and a class struggle fuelled by material interests. Nietzsche likewise points to "vital" interests or instincts which achieve a more or less disguised or sublimated expression; and the same applies to Freud. Nietzsche focuses predominantly on a notion of aggression which dominates, as diagnosis of *ressentiment* (a form of inverted aggression), his most comprehensive critique of Christianity; though he does acknowledge sexuality as well as co-determinant even in the most spiritual achievements of man. Freud first conceived of sexuality as the prime hidden agent, suppressed to a large extent by civilization from its very inception. Only the later Freud introduces the dualism of aggression and sexuality, or Eros and Thanatos, as an antimetaphysic and pseudo-biological schema. In comparison to Nietzsche, Freud's findings with regard to our deception about our unconscious motivations and his critique of illusions remain within the confines of psychology. Science, according to Freud, does not deceive us. This positivistic scientism belongs to the unshakeable, exoteric ideology of Freud. This is true, even if he intimates occasionally – as he does in *Beyond the Pleasure Principle* – that the terms of "depth psychology" – indispensable for the description and the very perception of "corresponding" phenomena – belong to a language of "images" or metaphors which would be improved if physiological or chemical terms could be substituted for them, though these in turn belong as well to a "language of images" or metaphors, but to one more familiar to us by now, and perhaps also simpler (*FGW*, vol. 13, p. 65). Nietzsche pursues analogous observations about the deception predominating in our consciousness concerning our true motivations. However, he does so more radically, as a philosopher. Like Freud he starts out, in some of his aphorisms, from considerations about the factors inducing dreams, but arrives at the suggestion that we, in fact, always deceive ourselves about the impulses which move us. Do we not always ascribe by an interpretation to a stimulus or sensation, *ex post facto* a cause which included them? Thus we make appear what was first, namely the stimulus or sensation, as consequent of a putative antecedent which we made up or added by way of interpretation.[3] Indeed, it is one of Nietzsche's perennial theses that we are always and necessarily enmeshed in error, a world of illusions which includes our science and cognition, however necessary they are to us. This is a conclusion alien to Freud, even though nothing but a phenomenon of the psyche, thus coming close to a pan-psychism in at least one of his later aphorisms.[4] The conviction of his daughter Anna that all that is essential takes place "within,"[5] was certainly not alien to this psychologist, even though it clashed with the realism and objectivism he preached.

The differences between the three are no less apparent. From Marx to Nietzsche interest shifts from society – state, people, community – to the individual. Nietzsche's perspectivism envisages all matters in terms of his concern for the individual. Basically, he hardly credits any other concern. Freud's psychology also remains a psychology of the individual insofar as he constructs every extension to society and history or prehistory from the vantage point of a genetic psychology of the individual. However, unlike Nietzsche, he emphasizes, above all, the family as proto-community. This is true even of the psycho-analytic movement founded by him. With its innumerable, intimate and quasi-incestuous crossings or networks it constituted a kind of superfamily or super*mishpoche*. In this emphasis on the community of family extending to a clan, one might even recognize a traditional Jewish trait, characteristic at least for the Jews of the Diaspora who, for centuries, were in fact nearly stateless, or certainly did not belong with any degree of assurance to a larger national community, and were thus dependent on clan and family.

NIETZSCHE IN FREUD'S "COLLECTED WORKS"

Such comparisons could be and have been extended much further. Before I touch on some attempts of this kind, I should, however, like to consider Freud's explicit remarks on Nietzsche.[6]

The index to his *Collected Works* (*FGW*, vol. 18) lists fifteen references to Nietzsche, sixteen to Schopenhauer.

In the *Interpretation of Dreams* Freud uses the expression "trans-valuation of all values," namely between the (assumed) latent mater-ial of a dream and the manifest dream (*FGW*, vols 2/3, p. 335; cf. p. 667). However, he uses the expression in a reverse sense than Nietzsche who wanted to attain a higher degree of veracity by way of his transvaluation, while in Freud the transvaluator, that is, the manifest dream, disfigures and conceals the underlying truth. In accordance with Nietzsche's sense Freud uses a quote from *Human, All Too Human* I (aphorism 13) concerning the "archaic heritage" of mankind which can be inferred from the dream (*FGW*, vols 2/3,

p. 554). In the *Psychopathology of Everyday Life* (*FGW*, vol. 4, p. 162), as well as in the case of the Rat-Man (*FGW*, vol. 8, p. 497), Freud likewise acknowledges Nietzsche's insight into unconscious motivation; here of forgetting, motivated by a defense against displeasure. No one had been able to illustrate this as impressively as Nietzsche: "This I did, says my memory. This I cannot have done, says my pride, and remains adamant. Finally – memory yields" (*Beyond Good and Evil* IV 68).

Freud mentions Nietzsche-Zarathustra's hymn "Before sunrise" (*Zarathustra* III) in the discussion of Schreber's paranoia, to support his interpretation that the sun stands for the father. "Nietzsche too," he notes "had known his father only as a child" and thus, presumably, longed for him (*FGW*, vol. 8, p. 290). However, while this may confirm Freud's acquaintance with Nietzsche's best-known work, it does not indicate Nietzsche's influence on Freud.

The question of such influence, which was brought up again and again, was summarily dismissed in Freud's essay of 1914, "On the history of the psychoanalytic movement": he had little taste, he claimed, for philosophical readings in his earlier years. In a later period he had denied himself the high pleasure of reading Nietzsche's works, with the conscious motivation that he did not want to be hampered in his own work by any preconceptions. In return he had to be prepared – and was so gladly – to surrender any claims to priority in the many instances in which insights gained by laborious psychoanalytical research could only confirm the intuitive insights of the philosopher (*FGW*, vol. 10, p. 53). Freud's awareness that prior to him others, such as Schopenhauer and Nietzsche, had recognized and described "repression," a phenomenon of decisive importance for Freud's entire system, provides a context for these remarks. They are made in the spirit of the politics of the Psychoanalytical Movement, to support the attempt to establish psychoanalysis as a legitimate science.

The truth of the matter is quite different. Actually, as Freud himself pointed out elsewhere, he took a passionate interest in philosophical issues in his youth to which he returned in his old age, if, in fact he ever gave it up.[7] It is probable that he read Nietzsche early on, and certain that he heard a lot about Nietzsche as a young man. For his close friend Joseph Paneth, who contributed a section to the Nietzsche biography of Nietzsche's sister, reported in letters to Freud about Nietzsche, whom Paneth met in Nizza in the early 1880s.[8] In a letter to Fliess of 1 February 1900, Freud mentions that he had "acquired Nietzsche" in the hope to find there "words for much that remains mute in me," but had "not opened him yet" because he was "too lazy for the time being." Later on, Freud learned about Nietzsche through Lou Salomé, an intimate friend of Nietzsche's who had a profound knowledge of his works and thought. Whether due to forgetfulness or deliberate concealment and denial, the failure to acknowledge sources and stimulating ideas which influenced him was frequent with Freud.[9] The self-stylization of a thinker and author, who often worked with the boldest of hypotheses and intuitions, as the laboriously advancing research scientist in contrast to the purely "intuitive" Nietzsche – a philosopher who was, after all, quite capable of systematic thought – is a gross simplification.

Even where Freud – treating of "various character types" – acknowledges (see *FGW*, vol. 10, p. 391) that Zarathustra's speech "On the pale criminal" (*Zarathustra* I) describes a type of "criminal motivated by a sense of guilt" that is prior to the criminal deed which serves to rationalize it, he points out that a friend brought this priority of Nietzsche to his attention, so as to suggest that he made the same discovery in his scientific work as therapist without the help of the intuitive philosopher.

In the later Freud the skeptical rejection of Nietzsche's ideal of nobility comes to the fore. In *Beyond the Pleasure Principle* (*FGW*, vol. 13, p. 44) he criticizes the "faith" in a human drive for perfection which had raised man to the present height of mental achievements and ethical sublimation, and might be expected to take care of our development to "superman." "I can see no way," he observes, "to spare this agreeable illusion." (That Nietzsche envisaged this remote possibility of perfection for none but the very few is not taken into account by Freud in this context.)

In his treatise on *Group Psychology and the Analysis of the Ego*, where Freud treats of the "father of the primal horde" (*FGW*, vol. 13, p. 138) as a strong, self-reliant leader, he observes: "At the inception of the history of mankind, he was the superman, expected by Nietzsche only from the future." Again the implication is negative. For, as Freud remarks, "even today" the individual members of the masses (*Massenindividuen*) need the pretence and delusion (*Vorspiegelung*) "that they are loved equally and in a just manner by their leader, while the leader himself needs to love no one else," but may rather be of the "nature of a master" (*von Herrennatur*), "absolutely narcissistic, but sure of himself and independent."

Via Groddeck, and, in a sense also via Nietzsche, Freud borrowed the term "the Id" (*das Es*) as "grammatical expression for the impersonal and natural necessity in our being" (*The Ego and the Id: FGW*, vol. 13, p. 261). The expression, Freud claimed, was quite usual in Nietzsche,[10] which is not the case. Moreover, the systematic use he made of the term – while somewhat in keeping with Groddeck's use of it – went far beyond anything intended by Nietzsche.[11]

Freud's "self-portrait" (*An Autobiographical Study: FGW*, vol. 14, p. 86) repeats – with reference to Schopenhauer and Nietzsche – the half-truth that he had always remained in such intimate contact with the analytical material that he had been careful to avoid any approximation to philosophy proper, even when he had distanced himself from direct empirical observation. And indeed, a "constitutional incapacity" had greatly facilitated such "abstention" on his part.[12]

In *The Future of an Illusion* (*FGW*, vol. 14, p. 338) Freud compares the natural powers, elevated into gods and thereby anthropomorphized and made somewhat accessible, to "violent supermen" which one could attempt to implore, pacify, bribe, etc. The term is again used in a pejorative sense.

The last remark is to be found in Freud's obituary for Lou Salomé (*FGW*, vol. 16, p. 270) who had "dedicated the last twenty-five years of her life to psychoanalysis":

> One knew of her that she had maintained a relationship of intense friendship with Nietzsche, founded upon a deep understanding for the bold ideas of this philosopher. The relationship came to an abrupt end, when she refused his proposal of marriage.

FREUD'S PATHOGRAPHY OF NIETZSCHE

A survey of this sort creates the impression that Freud's enduring awareness of Nietzsche remained quite marginal. However, the *Minutes of the Vienna Psychoanalytic Society* of 1906 to 1918 indicate that Freud's circle was intensely and continuously concerned with Nietzsche. In 1908 two sessions, on ascetic ideals (the third essay of the *Genealogy*) and on the autobiography *Ecce Homo*, were dedicated to Nietzsche (see *PS*, vol. 1, pp. 334–9; *PS*, vol. 2, pp. 22–9). In the course of the discussions Freud developed some hypotheses which can be connected and combined.

Nietzsche, he thought, who lost his father in childhood, "killed" him a second time in his autobiography (*PS*, vol. 2, p. 27). Implied is that he killed him the first time – in his mind – as a child, after the father's early death. "Growing up in a family of women" (*PS*, vol. 2, p. 27) the boy – under the pressure of his sense of guilt via-à-vis the deceased father – soon finds, like other "great thinkers and discoverers," his main theme, the origin of evil (*PS*, vol. 1, p. 339), that is, the analysis of morality. Freud refers here to the treatise which Nietzsche wrote at age 13.[13]

However, according to Freud, Nietzsche's personality was an enigma – a point he was to repeat to Zweig decades later in a letter of 15 July 1934. A human being could only be understood if one had a notion of his psychosexual constitution, which in the case of Nietzsche remained uncertain, even if some sexual abnormality was certain (*PS* vol. 2, p. 27). Jung, whose uncle, Otto Binswanger, a noted psychiatrist, treated Nietzsche as his patient in a clinic at Jena in 1889–90[14] – claimed, according to Freud, to have learned that Nietzsche had acquired his syphilitic infection in a homosexual brothel (*PS*, vol. 2, p. 27).[15]

In the Vienna Psychoanalytic Society the opinion predominates that Nietzsche was homosexual. However, in addition to the claim of Nietzsche's friend Deussen that Nietzsche never "touched a woman" (*nullam feminam attigit: PS*, vol. 2, p. 25), there is mention of rumors concerning Nietzsche's occasional visits to – heterosexual – brothels, and to his intensely erotic flirtation with Lou Salomé (*PS*, vol. 2, p. 25), who did write that in the course of her wanderings with Nietzsche through moonlit Rome, their sightseeing of classical antiquities had been subject to some interruptions, due to his presence.[16]

Be that as it may, Nietzsche, who, according to Freud, showed no trace of neurotic suffering (*PS*, vol. 2, p. 27), had achieved a unique introspective insight into his own psyche, which was unlikely ever to recur again in any human being (*PS*, vol. 2, p. 28). Freud offered several observations to explain this phenomenon. Since for him homosexuality – an attraction to one's own sex, and thus to a kind of *alter ego* – was connected with narcissism, the following remark is quite understandable: "Nietzsche," he said, "completely cut off from life by his sickness, turns to the only subject of research which remained to him and was anyway close to him as a homosexual: namely, his own self" (*PS*, vol. 2, p. 27).

He begins with great acumen to gain insight, by way so to speak
of endopsychic perception, into the layers of his self. He makes
a number of brilliant discoveries on his own person. But now
the sickness intervenes: He is not satisfied with guessing
correctly these interconnections which he discovered in himself, but projects them as vital imperative to the outside world.

(*PS*, vol. 2, pp. 27f.)

An editorial footnote explains: "With the insane, the external world
is, after all, the copy of his internal world" (*PS*, vol. 2, p. 28).

On his [Nietzsche's] psychological insight supervenes the di-
dactic, pastoral element, which remained part of him from his
[early] ideal of Christ [later reversed, according to Freud, into
an ideal of the "Anti-Christ" (cf. *PS*, vol. 2, p. 27)]. In this way
arise the confusing results of Nietzsche's views, which, are
however, basically correct. This formula, he had concocted for
himself for the case of Nietzsche.

(*PS*, vol. 2, p. 28)

Similarly, that is: by way of the projection of entities (*Sub-
stanzen*) perceived through endopsychic perception, all of
mankind had created for itself a moral world of shadows. An
introspection such as Nietzsche attained, was never attained by
any man before and probably would never be attained again.
What disturbs us, is that he transformed what "is" into what
"ought" to be. Any "ought" (*Soll*) is, however, alien to science.
He still remained a moralist in this respect, he did not get rid
of the theologian.

(*PS*, vol. 2, p. 28)

However to all this, the essential element is still to be added,
namely the role of the paralysis in Nietzsche's life.

(*PS*, vol. 2, p. 28)

Nietzsche's late phase does not merely show characteristic symptoms
of the paralytic, such as the "beautifully" (i.e. fully) developed
euphoria (*PS*, vol. 2, p. 27) observable in *Ecce Homo*. What empowered Nietzsche for "the quite uncommon achievement to recognize the drives through all the strata" of the psyche, was the "process
of loosening up through paralysis. Thus he put his paralytic disposition (*paralytische Anlage*) into this service to science" (*PS*, vol. 2,
p. 28). Through the falling away of inhibitions, characteristic of this
disease, he could see through the otherwise concealed layers of his self.

PETER HELLER

Freud's hypothesis postulates the coming together of a number of factors, namely: Nietzsche's early sense of guilt about the death of his father which led him to the analysis of morality; his sickness and a homosexual narcissism which made his own "ego" the sole object of his studies (projected, to be sure, onto the outside world); and the paralytic "enlightenment" through the falling away of inhibitions. This unique conjunction enabled Nietzsche to achieve unique knowledge of himself and thus of the human psyche. However, unable to shed the theologian, he proclaimed his essentially correct insights in form of a moralistic "Thou Shalt."[17]

Added to these considerations is Freud's conception of the "abstract" ways of philosophy generally, which he declares to be profoundly unattractive to him (*PS*, vol. 1, p. 338; *PS*, vol. 2, p. 303). What he rejects is not only metaphysics – which he reduces summarily to "projection of endopsychic perceptions" (*PS*, vol. 1, p. 140). His blanket statements, such as "every philosophy is a paranoia" (*PS*, vol. 2, p. 335) imply also his objection to an unrestrained striving for – and unwarranted postulation of – some comprehensive unity. He considers this characteristic of philosophers (including Nietzsche), and derives it from an infantile narcissism, that falsifies reality for the sake of a species of wishful thinking.[18]

Claims for a connection between genius, abnormality, disease or insanity are familiar. (Freud says specifically with reference to Nietzsche: "Where paralysis befell great spirits, extraordinary achievements have been accomplished, until shortly before the outbreak of the disease" (*PS*, vol. 2, p. 27).) Freud's attempt to explain Nietzsche's psychological genius largely in terms of pathology should not be read as mere devaluation. He subjected other "great men" – such as Leonardo and Dostoevski – to similar and similarly hypothetical psychoanalytic derivations and explanations. Nonetheless, the manner of the psychologist in trying to explain Nietzsche for himself, does suggest the way he holds himself aloof from the figure he has in mind. Freud's Nietzsche is a narcissist, driven by his defense against a phantasized patricide to the attempt to overcome morality. He proceeds as do all philosophers, reduced as they are to variants of narcissistic and wishful thinking instead of a scientific recognition of reality. However, he is motivated in addition by a disease, reducing him to his self as the only object of study. And if he is, at the same time, empowered to unique clarity of intuitive vision by the falling away of all barriers in the euphorias of paralysis, he is decisively impaired as well by symptoms of the same affliction, such as his euphoric megalomania and the erroneous projection of endopsychic insights. In no way, Freud suggests, is he to be confused with this narcissist, motivated by his father-complex and isolated intellectually within his own self; a man who – whether as homosexual, frequenter of brothels or semi-ascetic – had, for all his need of friendships, never formed a lasting emotional tie to a love-object; and who was aided decisively in the achievement of his astonishing insights by a supervening physical pathology culminating in his insanity. By contrast, he, Freud, had arrived – as he suggested to his circle and the world at large – at his insights and science modestly, laboriously, not by means of his pathology, but in a legitimate – "scientific" – manner, a normal, healthy way, oriented toward reality.

For all the sterile recognition which Freud displays toward Nietzsche, it is evident again in this context how vigorously he fends off the suspicion that he owed anything of major significance to his works. And the same applies to Freud's attitude toward the notion that there exists some affinity between his and Nietzsche's personalities. He later on sharply rejected Zweig's attempt to conceive of Freud as the thinker who fulfilled and perfected what Nietzsche initiated and intended. The only "real bond" between him and Nietzsche, he told Zweig, was Lou.[19]

COMPARISONS AND JUXTAPOSITIONS

Freud derives philosophy from – and accuses it of – infantile, wishful thinking and thus of an unwarranted intellectual optimism conditioned by such wishful thinking. In a section of her diary entitled "Freud and philosophy,"[20] Lou Salomé reports a conversation with Freud about his resistance to pure philosophy as objection to the profoundly anthropomorphic need of philosophers to find an ultimate unity in all things. "Afterwards," she writes, "we talked about the sadness which more and more accompanies our life and experience even when fortune is favorable, about the diminution of our euphoria," and about Freud's horror at the "Hymn to life" (written by Lou Salomé), "which he must have read in Nietzsche's musical version."

> Might there not be a connection between the two, the diminished longing for unity and the diminished euphoria? Freud acknowledged that this striving for unity has its ultimate source

PETER HELLER

in narcissism. But according to his own view that is also the ultimate source of our love of life.

Surely it is bold of the man of thought to presuppose his unity with all things or even just to "suppose" it. But is it not still bolder of him to live as a human being?

Moreover, she continues, are not "scientific activities" also "undertaken on behalf of man's euphoria – only by a detour from the 'pleasure principle' by way of the 'reality principle' and back to pleasure – to use Freud's words?" Later in the diary,[21] she will oppose affirmation of life to banality, which, she says, results from a negative attitude toward life; and quotes Nietzsche: "Denn alle Lust will Ewigkeit" which – with the loss of the dual meaning of "Lust" as pleasure and desire – may be rendered as "All pleasure wants eternity."

Lou thus argues against Freud in favor of the – "tragically" – optimistic "Hymn to Life" which he had rejected. Accordingly, Freud might actually appear as a depressive character. For, according to Lou, every mentality focusing on isolation of the individual led to banality and depression, while the striving for unity (and thus for fusion) led to a consolation.

These thoughts, in turn, recall somewhat analogous considerations of C.G. Jung in his *Critique of Psychoanalysis* and his *Memoirs*.[22] The reductive "causal" determinism of Freudian psychology corresponds, he observes, to the (then) dominant mode in the natural sciences. It is applicable in psychology for the treatment of the sick who suffer from their past, and are thus determined by it. However, it is insufficient as general psychology. For it offers no idea of an aim, and therefore none of a future dimension, which is why the Freudian psychology has basically a depressive, disillusioning effect. Its anti-idealistic (quasi-biologistic, or materialistic) determinism makes it a passive psychology. Without devaluating the deficient Freudian schema, which remains applicable to a pathological aetiology, Jung proposes rather to include it, but to enrich it by adding its missing – and better – half. He offers his own psychology which recognizes a positive, creative, future-oriented, active, teleological and mythopoeic (transrational) or "symbolic" dimension and perspective in contrast to the psychology of Freud, that is based merely on the reductionism of the natural sciences.

It is but a step from these observations to another set of more aggressive antitheses. These will confront a quasi-soulless, rational-

206

istic, materialistic or deterministic and essentially negating Jewish mentality, disintegrating all that is positive by a nihilistic lack of faith, with an active, positively "idealistic," transrationally or "irrationally" heroic, tragic, and, at any rate, creative Aryan spirit. Whether such a perspective was implicit in Jung's own views may be debatable. However, it is Nietzsche in whose name Jung proclaims the better or positive half of his psychology. For it was Nietzsche who as supertheologian, projected in the image of superman a future ideal for mankind, or at least for the few in the master races who could be capable, in autonomous self-creation, of striving toward this exalted goal or guiding symbol. No wonder, some Freudians would argue, that this appealed to Jung who, as Freud himself pointed out, hailed from a theological Christian tradition, much as Freud had reminded his circle in reference to Nietzsche, the Christian as Anti-Christian, that "we are far too little aware of the difference between our own emotional life and that of a Christian" (*PS*, vol. 2, p. 27).[23]

Pursuing these lines of thought and considering that even in Nietzsche's *Birth of Tragedy* the active, tragic mentality of the Aryan is contrasted with the passive and negating Semitic spirit (*NSW*, vol. 1, p. 69), one might now conclude that Freud knew only of the "reactive" aspect of the psyche: reacting, that is, pathologically to a trauma. He could *analyze* the psychology of *ressentiment* but could not comprehend the affirmative aspect of the psyche corresponding to abundant vitality and positive power. Indeed, this was naturally so, and in keeping with Nietzsche, who, in addition to many positive remarks about the Jews (notably their intelligence), also found them to be "the people of the *ressentiment par excellence*" (*Genealogy* I 16) and leaders of all movements of *ressentiment*, that is: of the "slave rebellion in morals" (*Beyond Good and Evil* 195), including Christianity.[24] The Jew could penetrate with his insight only the reactive psyche determined by *ressentiment* (injury, weakness, sickness, decadence) in the sense of the slave's morality of good and evil but could not attain to the nobility of an amoral ethos of "good" and "bad" and the creative aspects of the psyche in keeping with the plenitude of power in the master races. The psychology of the Aryan Nietzsche, who understood both types of morality and psychology, proclaiming, among other things, the struggle of Rome against Judaea (*Genealogy* I 16), was related to the psychology of Freud, the Jew, as the whole is to one of its parts, and indeed to the lesser, sick and worse part. And similar considerations also induced Ludwig Klages to claim of Freudian psychoanalysis that it consisted of one-sided distortions and exaggerations, isolating some of Nietzsche's psychological insights and discoveries.[25]

A closer look at Nietzsche's prejudiced confrontation of herd and slave morality with the ethos of their masters might, to be sure, also lead beyond it. Nietzsche did suggest on occasion that the conflict between the two types of morality occurred in every man. As for Freud, he, arguably, did not restrict his research altogether to traumata but also pointed out positive transformations of the libido or Eros. And was not "the spirit" or intellect itself treated by Nietzsche – among other things – as a product of *ressentiment* or reactive defense against and internalization of a sadism inverted to masochism? The semi- or pseudo-scientific phantasies about the origin of morality, civilization or culture in Nietzsche and Freud were, in fact, strikingly similar in kind as well as in their arbitrary and intuitive structure and subjective vehemence. Hence anyone inspired by all too positive intentions might now, in turn, approximate the two once more to one another. The question remains, however, whether their respective thoughts would become clearer or more convincing in the process.

It is not the purpose of this essay to unravel these well-worn and tangled webs of thought and prejudice. However, contrasts between Freud and Nietzsche have been stressed also in the psychoanalytic camp.

The analyst Didier Anzieu, for example, developed a notion of the creation of psychoanalysis as defensive measure against depression: Freud began his self-analysis, from which psychoanalysis emerged, in order to combat his own depressive tendencies, and established his theories as "obsessional defences against his depressive anxiety."[26]

Allow me to add here also as an aside that an unresolved "father complex," which Freud postulated in Nietzsche, has been diagnosed, ever since the somewhat eccentric book by the Nietzschean Charles E. Maylan, and with compelling arguments, in the case of Freud as well.[27]

Have we, then, safely arrived in an orbit of perspectives which set Nietzsche off elevating himself into a kind of superpositive mania against a negating and depressive Freud? By no means, for, lo and behold! Anzieu draws from his findings the opposite conclusion: Freud, trusting in the superiority of the positive vital drives over the death drives distinguished himself precisely by this from Nietzsche who was preoccupied with aggression. Not in Freud, but in Nietzsche's thought and life did self-destruction prove the stronger force.

Of what value are such mirror-inverted mirror-writings? They serve as reminders both of attempts to oppose Nietzsche and Freud to one another, and of attempts to harmonize or even equate them, which have been more in fashion in recent decades.

Configurations of thought can be turned and twisted like waxen noses until they closely resemble one another. But are those noses, after they have been treated cosmetically and shaped to conform to a norm, still the same they were before, when left alone within the contexts of their respective faces?

The attempt has been made[28] to equate Nietzsche's thought of the eternal return of the same – resting, as it very nearly does, on the hypothesis that nothing at all recurs, except everything in its inalienable, unchangeable uniqueness – with Freud's hypothesis of the repetition compulsion in the service of Thanatos. In this attempt, the other cosmic power in Freud's dualistic phantasy, namely Eros, which is opposed to the repetition compulsion and seeks to create ever new fusions, must needs be neglected. Nonetheless, it is possible that Freud was influenced by Nietzsche's formula, which he quotes in introducing the repetition compulsion doing its work in *Beyond the Pleasure Principle*. After his fashion, Freud might well have translated Nietzsche's notion from the realm of philosophical abstraction into the domain of his psychology. For, as noted above, he did believe that Nietzsche's intuitions, justified as endopsychic perceptions, had been projected illegitimately by him upon the external world or into existential imperatives. The hypothesis of eternal recurrence of the same, which made its appearance as a physicometaphysical hypothesis and an existential imperative, could be conceived as a psychological perception of the "conservative" character of drives which Nietzsche, exaggerating it by way of radical abstraction, projected upon both the universe and his own ideal of vitality. In this kind of Freudian translation the specific character of Nietzsche's hypothesis would be lost. The conservatism of drives or repetition compulsion would have little in common with the concept called by Nietzsche the hardest of thoughts. For what would keep repeating itself endlessly would not be one's entire existence but merely similar events or processes within one existence or life-span or between similar existences. Neither Nietzsche's conception of the eternal recurrence as cosmological hypothesis nor his notion of it as the hardest of existential imperatives or challenges, which in truth is hardly separable from his cosmological hypothesis,[29] would still pertain. And yet it is conceivable that a translation into Freudian psychology could still interpret the silent operation of the repetition compulsion as the "hardest of thoughts," since nothing may be more depressing for a human being than the insight that he cannot escape some of his perennial tendencies, or indeed, his unalterable character.

CONCLUSIONS

Other attempts to see Nietzsche and Freud together are justified. An example is Jacob Golomb's perspective which conceives of Nietzsche and Freud as proponents of psychological interpretations and therapies for the individuals and the societies of a sick civilization. Admittedly, the two therapists proceed in different ways. Except for the middle phase of his movement of thought. Nietzsche engages early and late in a polemic against the "Socratic" attempt to drag unconscious motivations into the – quasi-permanent and inhibiting – daylight of critical consciousness.[30] He considers this effort which arises from an insecurity and disorientation with regard to one's own instincts and impulses, to be a symptom of decadence. In this way he anticipates the *bon mot* of Karl Kraus who said of psychoanalysis that it was a symptom of the disease which it pretended to cure. Moreover, Freud's faith in the sobering procedures and *Weltanschauung* of science is treated by Nietzsche time and again as an ascetic illusion in opposition to those vital illusions whose affirmation he claims to consider a sign of health. Yet it is true that he is himself constantly engaged in a Socratic uncovering of unconscious motivations; and one can always quote – along with his polemic against, and very denial of, "truth" – his saying that the strength of a human being is measured by the amount of truth he can stand (see *Beyond Good and Evil* 39; *Ecce Homo*, Preface 3).

With respect to their lives and mentalities, the two are quite far apart. The lonely thinker and poet, who struggles with his euphoria against the physical torments of sickness and against his own weariness of life, constantly provokes his readers. The professional therapist, profoundly bourgeois as *pater familias* and head of an ever-increasing, bickering, worshipful tribe, disguises his boldest inventions and flashes of thought as empirical scientific observations.

However, such reservations miss the essential point of an attempt to harness Nietzsche and Freud in the service of our age on the basis of their shared ethos of culturally productive sublimation. To be sure, where no inspiration "from above" is allowed, since God and idealistic metaphysics are no longer thought to be viable, the only alternative left for those who have faith in culture would seem to be the productive, ennobling transformation of the instinctual potential of man – the given "lower" forces – if such a term or indeed the distinction between "lower" and "higher" domains of the human psyche are still held to be appropriate. Yet this does not argue against but confirms the atheistic faith in culture which Freud and Nietzsche do have in common.

Thomas Mann spoke with regard to Freud of contributions or "building blocks" for a future anthropology,[31] a future image of man. This perspective, more applicable to their modes of thought than their results, applies to both the dogmatizing manner in which Freud carried forward his bold labors of discovery and to Nietzsche's emotionally experimenting style of thinking and writing. Both are enlargers of the image of man, liberators of a desire to question and of a pleasure in exploring even and especially the questionable and unpleasing. They are protagonists of a new kind of veracity – even if, in keeping with the usual pathos of apostles of truth, they themselves were self-disguisers, adept at concealment; and even though Freudians, much like Nietzscheans, did their best to narrow down or undo their veracity. In thinking with these two prot- agonists, the Nietzschean imperative "Don't follow me!" is always to the point. In a somewhat different sense from the one intended at the end of Goethe's Faust, it can be said of both: "Das Unzulängliche, hier wird's Ereignis!" Both of these explorers and experimenters may be seen in closest proximity to one another, when they are under- stood and appreciated, not as teachers of a terrestrial recipe for salvation, or rather especially as such, in both the validity or inevitability and the insufficiency of their inchoate, tentative and inspiring thoughts and works.

ABBREVIATIONS

FGW Freud, Sigmund, *Gesammelte Werke*, 18 vols, London: Imago, 1942ff. and Frankfurt am Main: S. Fischer, various dates.

NSW Nietzsche, Friedrich, *Sämtliche Werke (Studienausgabe)*, 15 vols, Munich: dtv and Berlin: de Gruyter, 1967ff.

PS *Protokolle der Wiener Psychoanalytischen Vereinigung, 1906–1918*, 4 vols, Frankfurt am Main: S. Fischer, 1976ff. (first published in English translation as *Minutes of the Vienna Psychoanalytic Society*, New York: International Universities Press, 1962ff.).

PETER HELLER

Freud's letters to Wilhelm Fliess of 1897–1904 (*Briefe an Wilhelm Fliess*, Frankfurt am Main: S. Fischer, 1986) and to Arnold Zweig (Sigmund Freud and Arnold Zweig, *Briefwechsel*, ed. Ernst Freud, Frankfurt am Main: S. Fischer, 1986; English translation: *The Letters of Sigmund Freud and Arnold Zweig*, tr. Elaine and William Robson-Scott, New York: Harcourt Brace Jovanovich, 1970) are cited by their respective dates.

NOTES

1 The sentence ("In meiner Jugend bedeutete er [Nietzsche] mir eine mir unzugängliche Vornehmheit" (Freud and Zweig, *Briefwechsel*, p. 89), correctly translated by Ernest Jones (*The Life and Work of Sigmund Freud*, vol. 3 (New York: Basic Books, 1957), p. 460) and Paul-Laurent Assoun (*Freud et Nietzsche* (Paris: Presses Universitaires de France, 1980), p. 35; "Il representait pour moi une noblesse qui, ajoute le Freud de 1934, était hors de ma portée"), is mistranslated in The Letters of Sigmund Freud and Arnold Zweig, p. 78, as "In my youth he was a remote and noble figure for me."

2 The term occurs in the first aphorism of Nietzsche's *Human, All Too Human* I (1878). Its first appearance in Freud may be in a letter of 2 May 1897, to Fliess. In his works it occurs as early as 1905 in *Three Essays on Sexuality* (*FGW*, vol. 5, p. 55), and in the case history of "Dora" of the same year.

3 For this progression in Nietzsche's interpretation of dreams (as archaic thought, wish fulfillment, etc.), see *Human, All Too Human* I 5, 12, 13; *Dawn* 119 which takes the further step to suggest "Erleben ist ein Erdichten" ("to experience is to invent"); the further elaborations in *Twilight of the Idols* ("The four great errors" 4); and my commentary in *"Von den Ersten und Letzten Dingen": Studien und Kommentar zu einer Aphorismenreihe von Freidrich Nietzsche* (Berlin: de Gruyter, 1972), pp. 11–115, 148–52, esp. pp. 153–62.

4 See the notes of June 1938, e.g.:

> 22.VIII. Spatiality (*Räumlichkeit*) may be the projection of the extension of the psychic apparatus. No other derivations probable. Instead of Kant's a priori conditions of our psychic apparatus. Psyche is extended, doesn't know anything about that. (*FGW*, vol. 18, p. 152)

5 "[A]lles Wirkliche geschieht doch immer innen" ("everything real always takes place within"): letter to Eva Rosenfeld, 6 July 1930, in P. Heller (ed.), *Anna Freud's Letters to Eva Rosenfeld* (Madison: International Universities Press; 1992), p. 145.

6 Most of the primary source material considered in this section, as well as the material drawn from the *Minutes of the Vienna Psychoanalytic Society* in "Freud's pathography of Nietzsche," below, is presented and

discussed at some length – if from a different perspective – in the introduction and the first part of Paul-Laurent Assoun's thorough study of *Freud et Nietzsche*, pp. 5–76.

7 Peter Gay, *Freud: A Life for our Time* (New York: Norton, 1988), pp. 118f., quotes pertinent passages to show that "in reality, 'philosophical' questions were never far from [Freud's] awareness." In a letter of 2 April 1896, when he was 40, Freud wrote to Fliess concerning his youth: "I knew no longing other than that for philosophical insight, and I am now in the process of fulfilling it, as I steer from medicine over to psychology." In another letter of 1 January 1896, he told Fliess, "I see how you, through the detour of being a physician, are reaching your first ideal, to understand humans as a physiologist, just as I most secretly nourish the hope of reaching my original goal, philosophy." See also further passages relating to Freud's early interest in philosophy in Gay, *Freud*, pp. 25, 28, 29, 31.

In view of the incompatibility of Freud's remarks on this subject, Gay claims that this "inconsistency is more apparent than real." Freud

in true Enlightenment fashion . . . denigrated the philosophizing of metaphysicians as unhelpful abstractions. He was equally hostile to those philosophers who equate the reach of the mind with consciousness. *His* philosophy was scientific empiricism as embodied in a scientific theory of the mind. (Gay, *Freud*, pp. 118f.)

These remarks, though echoing Freud's ideology, do not resolve the issue. It makes little sense to attribute to "scientific empiricism" such speculations as Freud's postulate of a dualism between Eros and Thanatos or libido and aggression, or, for that matter, the therapeutic ethos of "Where Id was there Ego shall be." As for Freud's rejection of mere wishful thinking, it would surely be shared by idealists and empiricists alike, while the philosophical striving for intellectual "unity," to which he objected so strenuously (see below, p. 215), might be compatible with some modes of "scientific empiricism," etc.

8 See letter from Freud to Arnold Zweig (11/12 May 1934) in Jones, *Life and Work*, vol. 3, p. 460: "A friend of mine, Dr. Paneth, had got to know him in the Engadine and he used to write me a lot about him." The excerpts from Joseph Paneth's letters published in Elisabeth Förster-Nietzsche, *Das Leben Friedrich Nietzsches* vol. 2, section 2 (Leipzig: C.G. Naumann, 1904), pp. 479–93, indicate that Paneth did not meet Nietzsche in the Engadine, but in Nizza, and not in 1885, as Jones assumes, but between December 1883 and March 1884.

9 A well-known instance is his failure to acknowledge the influence of W. Fliess regarding the concept of bisexuality, which led to the extended quarrel involving Swoboda and Weininger's philosophical best-seller on gender and character (cf. my essay "A quarrel over bisexuality," in Gerald Chapple and Hans H. Schulte (eds), *The Turn of the Century: German Literature and Art, 1890–1915* (Bonn: Bouvier, 1983), pp. 87–116). Other instances are his failure to acknowledge the priority of Jung with respect to the notion of a collective unconscious, implied in one form or other in some of Freud's later writings both with respect to

civilized mankind and specifically to the Jews in their relation to Moses. Similarly, the notion of basic aggression is adopted by Freud without reference to Adler's priority. (Note in this connection that the *Index* (*FGW*, vol. 18) listing both direct and indirect references to Nietzsche, fails to include one of Freud's remarks on the fundamental Nietzschean notion of the "Will to Power," of which he says that it appears in Adler as "masculine protest" (*FGW*, vol. 10, p. 98). As for parallels between Nietzsche and Freud, they are far too numerous to be dealt with here in detail. Jones (*Life and Work*, vol. 3, pp. 283f.) points out, for example, a "truly remarkable correspondence between Freud's conception of the super-ego and Nietzsche's exposition of bad conscience" as internalized aggression in the *Genealogy*. For detailed discussions of many points of intersection see the second part of Assoun's *Freud et Nietzsche* and Jacob Golomb, *Nietzsche's Enticing Psychology of Power* (Ames: Iowa State University Press, 1989).

10 Similarly, Freud wrote in the *New Introductory Lectures* (*FGW*, vol. 15, p. 78): "Following Nietzsche's usage, and due to a suggestion of G. Groddeck, we call it [i.e. the domain of the psyche alien to the ego] henceforth the Id."

11 See Herbert Will, "Das Es bei Groddeck und Freud," in *Groddeck Almanach* (Basel: Stroemfeld/Roter Stern, 1986), pp. 192–6. The Nietzsche passage mentioned in this context occurs in *Beyond Good and Evil* (*NSW*, vol. 5, pp. 30f.).

12 A similar disclaimer of his interest in philosophy and a similar justification of his avoidance of Nietzsche is to be found in Freud's letter of 28 June 1931 to Lothar Bickel (typescript copy, by permission of Sigmund Freud Copyrights, Wivenhoe), quoted by Gay, Freud, p. 46: "Lacking talent for philosophy by nature," he wrote in 1931, looking back, "I made a virtue of necessity": he had trained himself to "convert the facts that revealed themselves to" him in as "undisguised, unprejudiced, and unprepared" form as possible. The study of a philosopher would inevitably enforce an unacceptably predetermined point of view. "Hence I have rejected the study of Nietzsche although – no, because – it was plain that I would find insights in him very similar to psychoanalytic ones." – Freud also makes essentially the same points in meetings of the Vienna Psychoanalytic Society. See *PS*, vol. 1, p. 338; *PS*, vol. 2, p. 28.

13 See *Genealogy*, Preface 3, "Memorabilia"; *NSW*, vol. 8, p. 505: "Saw God in his glory as a child. – First philosophical writing about the origin of the devil (God thinks himself; can do this only through the conception (*Vorstellung*) of his opposite"; and *Beyond Good and Evil* 129.

14 *The Freud/Jung Letters*, ed. William McGuire (Princeton: Princeton University Press, 1974), p. 24, n. 1.

15 The added sentence: "However, this was of no account" – whether in reference to homosexuality or to the presumed infection, seems incongruous. Freud's hypotheses on Nietzsche rely on both of these data. When the elder Freud repeated the rumor to Arnold Zweig and again referred to Nietzsche's personality as unknowable, he did so in the context of his persistent effort to discourage Zweig's project to write a

novel in which he would explain Nietzsche in terms of his childhood
and the rebellion against his family, notably the women who brought
him up and surrounded him. In a letter of 15 July 1934, Freud told Zweig:

> It is impossible to understand anyone without knowing his sexual
> constitution, and Nietzsche's is a complete enigma. There is even
> a story that he was a passive homosexual and that he contracted
> syphilis in a male brothel in Italy. Whether this is true or not –
> quien sabe? Secondly, he had a serious illness and after a long
> period of warning symptoms, he suffered a general paralysis.
> Everyone has conflicts. With a general paralysis the conflicts
> recede into the background of the aetiology.

16 Sigmund Freud and Lou Andreas Salomé, *Briefwechsel* (Frankfurt am
Main: S. Fischer, 1980), p. 140.
17 This thesis stands in pointed – and possibly intentional – contrast to the
self-estimate of Nietzsche-Zarathustra whose basic sermon is one on
overcoming the dragon of "Thou Shalt" (*Zarathustra* I, "On the three
metamorphoses"). 〕*NB*
18 In connection with the remarks on Freud's attitude toward philosophy
in this section, see also *FGW*, vol. 14, p. 123 (philosophy as a kind of
"singing in the dark" to overcome one's anxiety); *FGW*, vol. 14, p. 217
(the defense of the piecemeal empirical labor of psychoanalytic science
contrasted with the presumed origin of philosophical systems); *New
Introductory Lectures*, Lecture 35 (translated as "The question of a
Weltanschauung"); esp. *FGW*, vol. 15, pp. 189f. (rejection of philosophy
and philosophical sophistry as unscientific) and in *FGW*, vol. 15, p. 173,
Freud's favorite quote from Heine about the philosopher: "Mit seinen
Nachtmützen und Schlafrockfetzen/Stopft er die Lücken des
Weltenbaus" ("with his nightcaps and the tatters of his dressing-gown,
he patches up the gaps in the structure of the universe"), directed once
more against philosophy's illusory pretense to offer a comprehensive
explanation of our universe and condition. Less sweeping, but perhaps
no less important for Freud's discomfort with philosophy as he sees it,
is his opposition to any monistic interpretation. "No monism," he
observes, "can bridge the opposition (*Gegensatz*) between mental
representations (*Vorstellungen*) and their objects" ("Den Gegensatz
zwischen den Vorstellungen und ihren Gegenständen gleicht kein
Monismus aus," *PS*, vol. 4, p. 129). In this connection Freud observes
that if he had to choose among the *Weltanschauungen* of the philosophers,
he would have to characterize himself as a dualist (*PS*, vol. 4, p. 129).
Having based his psychology on the irreducibility of mental phenomena
– rather than on processes reducible to terms of physiology, as he
attempted to do at an early stage – Freud apparently felt he could not side
with the quantifying Positivism of the Helmholtz-Brücke School which
he had largely endorsed at one time, nor, of course, with systems of
Idealism (such as those of Romantic *Naturphilosophie*, etc.). In a sense,
his "dualism" resembles a secularized version of Spinozism, acknowledging as irreducible both Mind and "Reality" *qua res extensa*, the two
"attributes" of the unfathomable recognized in Spinoza, but remaining

in Freud, so to speak, without their attribution to the one and only Spinozan substance of God.

19 Letter to Arnold Zweig of 11 February 1937, quoted by Ernest Jones, *Life and Work*, vol. 3, p. 213.

20 *The Freud Journal of Lou Andreas Salomé* (New York: Basic Books, 1964), pp. 104–6.

21 Ibid., p. 117.

22 For the following, see, for example, C.G. Jung, *Critique of Psycho-analysis* (Princeton: Princeton University Press, 1975), esp. pp. 209–11, 217, 221, 236) and his *Memoirs, Dreams, Reflections*, recorded by Aniela Jaffé (New York: Vintage Books, 1965).

23 "Wir werden uns überhaupt viel zu wenig des Unterschieds bewusst, der zwischen unserem Gefühlsleben und dem eines Christen besteht" (*PS*, vol. 2, p. 27).

24 For a summary on this topic, see my essay on "Nietzsche and the Jews," in *Nietzsche Heute*, ed. S. Bauschinger *et al.* (Berne: Francke, 1988), pp. 149–60.

25 See Ludwig Klages, *Die Psychologischen Errungenschaften Nietzsches* (Leipzig: Barth, 1926) and P. Heller, *"Von den Ersten und Letzten Dingen": Studien und Kommentar Zu einer Aphorismenreihe von Friedrich Nietzsche* (Berlin: de Gruyter, 1972), p. 159.

26 Didier Anzieu, *Freud's Self-analysis* (London: Hogarth Press and the Institute of Psycho-Analysis, 1986), p. 581.

27 See Charles E. Maylan, *Freuds Tragischer Komplex: Eine Analyse der Psychoanalyse*, 2nd edn (Munich: E. Reinhardt, 1929), a work referred to by C.G. Jung in his *Critique of Psychoanalysis*, p. 217, n. 2) and Marianne Kruell, *Freud und sein Vater: die Entstehung der Psychoanalyse und Freud's ungelöste Vaterbindung* (Freud and his Father: The Origins of Psychoanalysis and Freud's Unresolved Father-fixation) (Munich: Beck, 1979).

28 See, for example, Daniel Chapelle, *Nietzsche and Psychoanalysis* (Albany: SUNY, 1993).

29 According to Nietzsche the thesis of the eternal recurrence of the same is the hardest of thoughts, capable of devastating most humans and of elevating only the very few who could affirm the option of living their life over again in all its specificity. However, unless one thought the cosmological thesis of the eternal recurrence of the same to be, at the very least, a probable hypothesis about the way things are, it would immediately lose its force. For why should anyone feel compelled to believe in an improbable As-If? The compelling and challenging weight of the hypothesis of Eternal Recurrence depends entirely on the acceptance of the belief in either the certainty or the probability that one would be enclosed in his individual temporal existence in all eternity without change or alteration. (Even this, though, might hardly cause a ripple in some who feel quite smug and comfortable with themselves and their lives.)

30 For Nietzsche's Anti-Socratism (in contrast and conjunction with his – avowed – proximity to Socrates), see *The Birth of Tragedy* and the section on "The problem of Socrates" in *Twilight of the Idols*.

31 See the conclusion of Mann's essay on "Freud's position in the intellectual history of modern times" ("Die Stellung Freuds in den modernen Geistesgeschichte"), in *Das Essayistische Werk*, vol. 1 (Frankfurt am Main: Fischer Bücherei, 1968), p. 385.

10

MAHLER AND THE VIENNA NIETZSCHE SOCIETY

William J. McGrath

In June 1877 Friedrich Nietzsche received a letter from his friend Erwin Rhode mentioning that he had recently met a young man who was "a member of a Nietzsche Society in Vienna. He is tremendously enthusiastic about you and says he has sent you his book, *Prometheus Unbound*."[1] The young man to whom Rhode referred was Sigfried Lipiner, and Nietzsche responded enthusiastically to his book, describing it as the work of a "veritable genius."[2] Nietzsche had adorned the title page of his first major work, *The Birth of Tragedy*, with a drawing of the unbound Prometheus to express his ideal of a heroic humanity independent of the gods, and Lipiner's title was but one of many indications of his intellectual debt to Nietzsche's philosophy. Nietzsche was sufficiently impressed or flattered to accept Lipiner's overture, and the correspondence which ensued brought the philosopher into contact with a group of young intellectuals who were to play a major role in disseminating his ideas to the culture of *fin-de-siècle* Vienna.

The Nietzsche Society to which Rhode referred was not formally organized as such, but was rather a group of university students, known as the Pernerstorfer circle, whose members had assumed intellectual leadership of the most influential student organization at the University of Vienna, the Leseverein der deutschen Studenten Wiens. Their first overture to Nietzsche had been made a year earlier in April 1876, when one of their number, Joseph Ehrlich, wrote to Nietzsche to express his appreciation of the philosopher's *Untimely Observations*; in that letter Ehrlich had declared that he spoke, "in the name of your enthusiastic admirers" at the university.[3] During the mid-1870s, the members of the Pernerstorfer circle sponsored a series of lectures and discussions aimed at instructing their fellow students in the radical critique of contemporary values to be found in Nietzsche's writings.

The circle with which Nietzsche established contact had been formed a decade earlier by a group of *Gymnasium* students, and when most of them went on to study at the University of Vienna, their enthusiasm for German nationalism and social reform made them active participants in the political activities of the *Leseverein*. The group counted among its members a number of young men who went on over the next half-century to play an important role in the political, intellectual and artistic life of Austria and Germany. Some of the long-standing members included: Victor Adler, the founder of the Austrian Socialist party; his close political associate, Engelbert Pernerstorfer; Heinrich Friedjung, a prominent historian; and Heinrich Braun, an important figure in the German socialist movement and a contributor to the development of modern sociology.[4] Later in the 1870s the group was joined by the writer Sigfried Lipiner, as well as the composer Gustav Mahler, and during this period Joseph Paneth, a medical student who was a close friend of Sigmund Freud, was also associated with the circle for a time.[5] Despite the fact that most of the circle's members were Jewish, they cheerfully associated themselves with a German nationalist movement which had not yet turned anti-Semitic, and they looked with admiration to figures such as Nietzsche and Wagner whose works seemed to promise a rebirth of German culture from a long period of stagnation.

NB

After Nietzsche responded favorably to Lipiner's overture, the members of the Pernerstorfer circle decided to take the occasion of the philosopher's birthday (18 October 1877) to send him a collective letter expressing not only their admiration but also their dedication to the particular ideas found in his writings. Referring to themselves as "a small band of young men, who have long desired an opportunity to express to you their sincere respect and heartfelt gratitude," they conveyed their good wishes for the occasion, and then declared:

> We believe we are acting entirely on your principles when, instead of trying to describe in words how deeply your writings have moved us, we rather give you the assurance that this emotion has strengthened in each of us the firm resolve to follow you as our luminous and transporting guide.[6]

This reference to taking Nietzsche as a "transporting guide" was not intended to be mere celebratory rhetoric; it alluded to specific ideas found in the third volume of his *Untimely Observations*, and the authors of the letter went on to make explicit their acceptance of these concepts. They promised "to strive like you with the most powerful will, selflessly and honestly for the realization of that ideal which you have delineated in your writings, particularly your *Schopenhauer as Educator*."[7] This book, which Nietzsche published in 1874, has much in common with his first important philosophical work, *The Birth of Tragedy*, but it also elaborates on concepts which anticipate the idea of self-overcoming that became the focus of his later writings. It was the germ of this idea that seems to have been particularly attractive to the members of the Pernerstorfer circle.

In *Schopenhauer as Educator*, Nietzsche continued the sharp criticism of his time and culture that chararcterized all of his early works. He placed somewhat greater emphasis than before on the economic weaknesses of the existing order, but as before, he saw this as part of a larger cultural development. He writes,

> Nowadays almost everything is determined by the crudest and the worst forces, by the egotism of the money-makers and the military despots. The state, in the hands of the latter, makes the attempt, as does the egotism of the money-makers, to organize everything anew from itself outward.[8]

Nietzsche foresaw a destructive but inevitable "atomistic revolution," the expectation of which, along with "the greedy exploitation of the moment, brings out every form of cowardice and selfish drive of the soul."[9]

In response to what he saw as the degrading economic and social values of his time, Nietzsche prescribed a remedy that could come from within each individual. He referred to the need for inspiring "images of man" which would move the individual to transcend his base motivations for a more noble ideal, and he held up the life of Arthur Schopenhauer as an example of such a noble image. The importance of these noble images to Nietzsche's outlook is seen in his assertion that

> Only he who has given his heart to some great man receives the *first consecration of culture*. The sign of this is shame without self-loathing, hatred of one's own narrow and shriveled nature, sympathy with the genius who tears himself away from our dullness and dryness.[10]

Both the word "consecration" and the description of the "sign" betray the spiritual nature of the individual's devotion to such a noble image, and this religious dimension was deeply rooted in Nietzsche's concept of a culture community. In *The Birth of Tragedy* he had explored the religious-artistic bases of the ancient Greek cultural community, and in his *Schopenhauer as Educator* he attempted to draw out the consequences of this example for the contemporary individual:[11]

> Here I have come to the point of answering the question of whether it is possible to reach the great ideal of Schopenhauerian man through one's own regular activity. Above all, it is certain that these new duties are not the duties of the isolated individual; rather one belongs to a mighty community which is held together not by external forms and laws but by a fundamental *idea*. This is the fundamental idea of *culture*.

The spiritual nature of Nietzsche's conception of culture can be seen not only in this capacity for drawing men together, but also in what he referred to as the "metaphysical meaning of culture."[12] He argued that

> Just as nature needs the philosopher, so she also needs the artist for a metaphysical purpose, namely for her own self-enlightenment so that she may at last see as a clear and distinct image what she never sees in the flux of becoming – and thus reach self-knowledge.[13]

So through his participation in the cultural community, man would learn to serve nature's deepest purposes.

On the individual level, the cultural community would give its members the desire and the strength for self-transcendence:

> Everyone who possesses culture is, in fact, saying: "I see something higher and more human than myself above me. Help me, all of you, to reach it, as I will help every person who recognizes the same thing . . . so that finally the man may again come into being . . . who with all his being is part of nature."[14]

Nietzsche's ideal of the cultural community thus demanded of the individual an almost religious devotion to the task of overcoming his own egoistic existence to achieve a measure of unity with nature and his fellow man. This idea of culture "sets but one task for each of us: *to further the production of the philosopher, of the artist and of the saint within us and outside us, and thereby to work at the consummation of nature*."[15] To the extent that the cultural community

221

could bring forth such examples of genius it would provide further impetus to self-transcendence through imitation of these noble images. The genius thus occupied a central position in Nietzsche's cultural religion,

> for the genius longs more deeply for holiness because he has seen, from his watchtower, further and more clearly into the reconciliation of knowledge and being, into the realm of peace and the negated will, over to the other shore of which the Indians speak.[16]

Nietzsche regarded Schopenhauer as such a genius, who could serve as educator through the example of his life as well as through his ideas.

Nietzsche's ideal of a cultural community carried a number of important implications for those who shared his outlook. In addition to the first consecration of culture in which the individual devoted himself to some noble image of man, he also envisioned the possibility of groups organizing to further the work of the consecrated.

> They themselves want, by means of a strong organization, to prevent themselves from being swept away and dispersed by the crowd ... and all who take part in the institution shall be concerned, through a continual purification and mutual care, with the birth of the genius and the fruition of his work.[17]

The community of the consecrated would answer the inner cry of men everywhere: "Come, help, complete, combine that which belongs together! We have an immeasurable longing to become whole!"[18] In addition to the inner labor of self-transcendence, the individual had to go through a second consecration of culture: "Culture demands from him not only inner experience ... but finally and chiefly, action. This means fighting for culture and being hostile to the influences, laws and institutions in which he does not recognize his goal: the production of genius."[19] Throughout *Schopehauer as Educator* Nietzsche emphasized the role of uniting thought with life and action, the ideal of the heroic life of a man who "fights against very great odds for what it beneficial to all."[20]

When the members of the Pernerstorfer circle sent their collective letter to Nietzsche subscribing to the ideas of his *Schopenhauer as Educator* they clearly thought of themselves as ready for membership in this new cultural community. After declaring their acceptance of the ideals expressed in this work, they went on to emphasize their

full consciousness of the heavy responsibility which we thereby take upon ourselves, for none of us would endure the
thought of any sort of desire or action which would make us
ashamed before an image such as yours which lives within us
as a mighty presence.[21]

With these words they took upon themselves the "first consecration
of culture" by pledging to look upon Nietzsche himself as an
inspiring image of man whom they would emulate in order to lift
themselves up to a higher cultural community. In a separate personal
letter commenting on the fact that the collective letter had only six
signatures (Lipiner, Max Gruber, Pernerstorfer, Heinrich Braun,
Victor Adler and his brother Sigmund) Lipiner told Nietzsche that
"It is intended very seriously. We could have had many signatures
if we had taken it less strictly."[22] Nietzsche responded to the letter
with words of encouragement which seemed to indicate that he had
accepted his disciples.

In addition to accepting Nietzsche's first consecration of culture,
with its commitment to aim at a higher cultural community through
individual self-overcoming, the members of the Pernerstorfer circle
also acted in the spirit of his second consecration by their efforts as
a group to translate his ideas into actions. In criticizing the greed and
avarice of *laissez-faire* liberalism, Nietzsche's writings struck a
responsive chord in a circle whose members had already become
increasingly aware of the high social costs of Austrian liberalism's
new economic order. His warnings about an "atomistic revolution"
that would destroy any sense of social wholeness reinforced their
determination to solve the "social question," by emphasizing a
communitarian outlook. Their political activities pursued this goal
of community not only in the form of a reunited German *volk* but
also as part of a more unified and equitable social order, and this
combination of nationalism and social reform was widely accepted
within the powerful student movement led by the *Leseverein*.[23]
Moreover, the circle used the extensive format of lectures and
discussions sponsored by the *Leseverein* to achieve the widest
possible dissemination of the ideas Nietzsche put forth in his
Untimely Observations.[24]

Although Nietzsche's criticism of the political, social and economic values of nineteenth-century liberalism served primarily to
reinforce the existing political views of the Pernerstorfer circle and
the Leseverein, his particular conception of culture and his emphasis

on fostering the spirit of genius as a way of creating a higher cultural community offered the members of the circle a new philosophical perspective that strongly influenced their outlook. In particular, the idea that self-overcoming led to participation in a higher cultural community provided a philosophical basis for the admiration of German culture felt by the Jewish members of the circle. Having grown up during the brief period when ascendant Austrian liberalism seemed to offer the prospect that Jews would no longer be confronted with various kinds of discrimination, most of these young men had embraced the assimilationist ideals of their time. During a period when German identity was defined primarily by language and culture rather than race, they were eager to regard themselves as German and to participate in what they saw as a higher, more cosmopolitan culture than that of their ancestors.

The enthusiasm they felt about this process of assimilation into German culture is conveyed in a letter Victor Adler wrote in 1872 describing how he had met and become acquainted with Joseph Ehrlich, who shortly thereafter became a member of the circle. After reporting that the young man was a poet who had written a play entitled *Jokobo Ortis*, Adler wrote, "The whole thing is mystic philosophy – Jakob Böhme – and it is thrilling." He went on to add that Ehrlich was a "a Polish Jew who first learned high German at fifteen and began his drama at twenty."[25] Adler himself came from a wealthy, thoroughly assimilated, Jewish family, and his description of Ehrlich conveys the feeling of rich opportunity that he associated with learning German and becoming a contributor to the German cultural tradition.

Another insight into the attractiveness of Nietzsche's thought to the Jewish members of this circle is provided by the testimony of Joseph Paneth. Paneth, who belonged to the circle in the mid-1870s, was one of the members who lectured on Nietzsche's work to the Leseverein, but he eventually left the group out of annoyance that he had not become close to its leaders.[26] He was not among those who signed the collective letter to Nietzsche, but he met and formed a friendship with the philosopher some years later while travelling in France, near Nice.

Paneth wrote several detailed letters describing his conversations with Nietzsche, and one of these involved the subject of anti-Semitism. After expressing his rejection of anti-Semitism, Nietzsche asked Paneth about the ideals and hopes cherished by Jews. Paneth wrote:

I then told him that I, and those who thought as I did, did not want to be seen as Jews, as a race, but rather as individuals. . . . I alluded to the fact that Jews who thought as I did had lost their Jewish traditions.[27]

When Nietzsche suggested that such liberated individuals were dangerous, Paneth agreed that they were indeed dangerous to conventional values and replied that, "They are free spirits (*freien Geister*) in your sense." He then went on to argue in the spirit of Nietzsche's *Untimely Observations* that "to be free only means to be free of the traditional and conventional; every individual will indeed realize what interests and forces within himself are enduring. Expressing these, he will bind himself and give himself laws."[28] Here Paneth took the traditional German idea of freedom under self-imposed law and related it to Nietzschean self-overcoming. The free individual threw off the conventional beliefs of his time (and in this context the traditions of his Jewish ancestors as well) in order to affirm enduring values discovered within. Paneth concluded that "All this applies to the moral as well as to the intellectual. And thus a free spirit possesses a strong will to live." According to Paneth, Nietzsche seemed to be in agreement with all of this.[29] For Jewish members of the circle such as Adler or Paneth the process of assimilation was seen as a way of deciding within oneself to reject inculcated traditions in order to enter a higher cultural community of the sort described in Nietzsche's philosophy.

The injunction in Nietzsche's *Schopenhauer as Educator*, to cultivate genius as a way of creating the higher cultural community, also had a strong impact on the Pernerstorfer circle. The importance of this idea to Nietzsche personally can be seen in his reaction to reading Lipiner's *Prometheus Unbound*, the event that began his brief period of contact with the circle. In describing the author as a "veritable genius," he apparently intended the term in the sense conveyed by his *Untimely Observations*. He must have believed that he had encountered one of those gifted individuals who had the capacity to recognize the emptiness of contemporary values and lift himself up to the higher cultural community through his creative work. The prestige Nietzsche accorded to genius may also account for the surprising amount of influence Lipiner exercised within the circle. As one of its youngest and newest members, he could not otherwise have been expected to take on the leading role that he assumed within the discussions of the *Leseverein* and in the circle's correspondence with Nietzsche.

Similar considerations about the importance of genius (with far more justification) seem to have been involved in the Pernerstorfer circle's relationship with Gustav Mahler. Mahler became a member toward the end of the 1870s when he was brought into the circle through his friendship with Lipiner.[30] At about the time Mahler joined the group, it was undergoing important changes in its activities and outlook. When the government dissolved the *Leseverein* to curb its advocacy of radical German nationalism, the circle was forced to redirect its political activities from a student environment to the tasks of party organization and mass movements.[31] At the same time, the circle's relationship with Nietzsche suffered when the philosopher took offense at Lipiner's awkward attempts to establish a close personal friendship.[32] Although Nietzsche continued to wish his Viennese followers well – from a careful distance – and most of the circle's members remained committed to his ideas, the circle increasingly shifted its focus from philosophical discussion to the practical tasks of realizing its political and cultural goals.

That the members of the circle took seriously their goal of fostering genius is revealed, in Mahler's case, by the fact that Victor Adler went to the expense of buying the best piano he could find so that the impoverished Mahler could practice. He also set about locating pupils for the hours of piano instruction that constituted Mahler's chief livelihood while he was a student at the Vienna Conservatory.[33] Mahler returned the favor by providing the piano accompaniment for the nationalist songs that the group performed at its political gatherings.[34] With respect to Mahler's exposure to Nietzsche's thought, the evidence suggests that although the moment of the circle's closeness to Nietzsche had passed, Mahler's association with the group gave him a general knowledge and admiration of the philosopher's outlook that was expanded to a detailed understanding of Nietzsche's work at a later time.

For most members of the Pernerstorfer circle, the encounter with Nietzsche's thought they experienced as university students significantly influenced the accomplishments of their mature years, but it was in the work of Gustav Mahler that the philosopher's ideas achieved their fullest artistic realization. In his Third Symphony, which was composed during the two successive summers of 1895 and 1896, Mahler gave expression to a metaphysical conception of reality that was deeply influenced by Nietzsche's philosophy. Mahler used a poem from Nietzsche's *Thus Spoke Zarathustra* as the text for the fourth movement of the symphony, and at one point he told one of his friends, "I will call the whole thing *My Joyous Wisdom (Meine fröhliche Wissenschaft)*," an allusion to Nietzsche's book, *The Gay Science (Die fröhliche Wissenschaft)*.[35] Various comments in Mahler's letters reveal that in the early 1890s the interest in Nietzsche aroused in his student days took on new importance as he explored the grand vision to be realized in his Third Symphony. For example, in an 1894 letter, he wrote of his revived study of Nietzsche's philosophy: "Also in these recent weeks I have finished such remarkable readings that they indeed appear to be exercising an *epoch-making* influence on my life."[36] Unfortunately, Mahler's letters and comments do not reveal the particular works by Nietzsche that produced this epoch-making impression, but the evidence of the Third Symphony shows that the Nietzschean conceptions expressed in that composition derived at least as much from early works such as the *Untimely Observations* and the *Birth of Tragedy* as from his later writings.

Mahler's Third is a most unusual symphony in that it has a unifying philosophical theme which is carefully developed and elaborated from the first through the sixth movements, the theme of self-overcoming. Nietzsche had advanced this concept most explicitly in such works as *Thus Spoke Zarathustra*, which is why Mahler drew the text of his fourth movement from that work, but the idea of self-overcoming was implicit in both the *Birth of Tragedy* and *Schopenhauer as Educator*.

In the *Birth of Tragedy*, self-overcoming resulted from that interaction of Apollonian and Dionysian forces to which Nietzsche attributed the genius of Greek drama and culture. He argued that, in the great tragedies, the Apollonian force of rationality, individuation and form that manifested itself in the plastic arts came to be synthesized with the Dionysian force of emotion, community and dissolution that was expressed in dithyrambic music. In the dramatic festivals of the Greek city-states the individual citizen was so powerfully moved by the Dionysian music of the chorus that his sense of self dissolved into an all-embracing community of feeling and will. Then, as the drama proceeded, the Apollonian elements of form projected this communal feeling of oneness into the individuated mythic world presented on the stage. The mythic world of the drama thus represented the synthesis of the two forces. The various myths were individuated – they were specific stories about particular gods, goddesses and heroes – but they were invested with a universal significance that bespoke the community of humanity and nature.

The idea of self-overcoming, then, applies to the experiences of the individual citizens who made up the audiences for these dramatic festivals. As spectators they were aesthetically transported beyond any sense of themselves as individuals to a consciousness of belonging to the community that found political expression in the city-state. In the third of his *Untimely Observations* Nietzsche updated this idea of self-overcoming to make it applicable to the conditions of his own "atomistic" time. With no political equivalent for the community of the Greek city-state, he emphasized a more individual approach in which those capable of understanding the higher meaning of culture would employ the inspiring images of philosophers or artists or saints as models for life, and thereby lift themselves up to join a higher cultural community.

In the Third Symphony Mahler created a Nietzschean framework to convey an idea of community that is expanded to embrace not only all of humanity but all levels of being in the world of nature. The symphony is divided into a long first movement which performs the role of the ancient Greek chorus by evoking the tremendous power of Dionysian emotion, and this is followed by an Apollonian vision in which movements two through six reveal how the hierarchy of being reflects the inner relationship between the underlying Dionysian unity and the particular forms in which life appears.[37] The tentative titles which Mahler assigned to these movements in his early programs reveal his underlying purpose. The music of the first movement, "Summer marches in," expresses the power of the life force as it triumphs over the deadness of winter, and this life force was at one with the unconscious Dionysian element at work in nature, culture and the individual human being. Hans Redlich, a music critic who was a contemporary of Mahler, recognized the Dionysian spirit of this first movement in one of his comments. He wrote, "For Mahler the 'people,' the 'mass,' is naturally a Dionysian one. Where Mahler, as in the first movement of the Third Symphony, creates from a profound Dionysian fervor for the masses, the communal forming (*Gemeinschaftbildende*) effect . . . is the strongest."[38] The march which concludes the first movement creates a powerful sense of humanity united in common feeling and action.

The Apollonian section of the symphony which follows is presented as a dream vision inspired by the emotional intoxication of the first movement, and in this vision all of nature finds a voice and speaks its inner secrets. The second movement is entitled, "What the flowers in the meadow tell me"; the third, "What the animals in the forest tell me"; the fourth, "What the night tells me (the man)"; the fifth, "What the morning bells tell me (the angels)"; and the sixth, "What love tells me."[39] As Mahler explained to a friend, he could also have entitled the sixth movement "What God tells me."[40] The six movements of the symphony present the life force or will in ascending order though the different levels of the great chain of being, from tortured birth out of inanimate nature to final apotheosis in divine oneness.

From the point of view of the audience listening to Mahler's symphony, the music was intended to lead them through the process of self-overcoming by revealing, on both an emotional and a rational level, how their innermost beings were related to the life force manifested in all aspects of nature. The fourth movement was particularly important to this goal, because it dealt with the human level in the chain of being, and Mahler used this movement to offer his audience philosophic instruction. What separated humanity from all the lower orders of being was its consciousness of self, and this rational faculty was, in the tradition of Schopenhauer, Wagner and Nietzsche, as much a curse as a blessing.

To convey the movement of the life force or will to this rational level, Mahler employs the human voice for the first time in the symphony, and he says of the transition from the previous "animal" movement, "The adagio follows upon it as a confused dream is followed by an awakening – or rather a gentle coming to consciousness of oneself."[41] The words of the movement, in close interaction with the musical theme representing the life will, suggest that rational consciousness is limited to a surface world of appearance where life is filled with conflict and woe, but at the very end of the movement Mahler's music departs from Nietzsche's tragic view to hint at the possibility of redemption. Mahler hoped his audience would realize the limitations of egoistic reason and the need to balance this uniquely human faculty with the emotional, Dionysian, life force that he saw at work in all of nature. With that realization, individuals previously divided from each other by competition and selfish egoism might come together in harmonious community. As he observed of the final movement, "in the adagio everything is resolved in peace and being; the Ixion's wheel of appearance is finally brought to rest."[42]

One of Mahler's final finishing touches on the Third Symphony involved its opening theme, which was taken from a German nationalist song with particular meaning to the university students of Mahler's generation. The words of the song, "We had built a stately house," expressed the determination of university student organizations to resist government attempts to ban their political activities on behalf of German unity,[43] and it would have reminded Mahler of his own student days when he shared the German nationalist aspirations of the Pernerstorfer circle. Mahler's musical allusion to the song gains particular significance, however, in light of the fact that when the government dissolved the *Leseverein der deutschen Studenten Wiens* in 1878 the members of the society had gathered together one last time to sing the song as an act of defiance against the government action.[44] Mahler's friends in the Pernerstorfer circle had used the *Leseverein* as their primary instrument for spreading the ideas that Nietzsche had put forth in his early writings, so it was highly appropriate for Mahler to quote this student song at the beginning of his Nietzschean symphony. Mahler referred to this opening theme as a "walking call" (*Weckruf*), by which he meant that it awakened the dormant life force from the dead of winter,[45] and by alluding to this student song he could recall the student movement which had popularized Nietzsche's waking call to cultural rebirth. He could acknowledge the way his circle of friends had embraced Nietzsche's vision of a cultural community and had attempted to realize that vision by reaching beyond the limits of their own parochial traditions to something higher.

It also seems particularly appropriate that, having made the final changes involving the opening theme of the Third, Mahler set out to visit Sigfried Lipiner, the friend who had introduced him to the circle which first popularized Nietzsche's ideas in Vienna.[46] Mahler's new composition owed much to the ideas and aspirations that he and Lipiner had shared in their student days, and like Lipiner he had given those ideas his own particular interpretation and development. Drawing on the German cultural tradition that had inspired the assimilationist hopes of so many members of his generation, Mahler created a symphony that moved beyond any kind of cultural nationalism to a vision of community that embraced all of humanity and all of nature.

NOTES

1 *Briefe an Friedrich Nietzsche Januar 1875–Dezember 1879*, in *Kritische Gesamtausgabe, Nietzsche Briefwechsel* (hereafter *KGB*, ed. Georgio Colli and Mazzino Montinari (Berlin and New York: de Gruyter, 1975–93), II 6/1, p. 595.

2 *KGB* II 5, p. 278.
3 *KGB* II 6/2, p. 314.
4 See William J. McGrath, *Dionysian Art and Populist Politics in Austria* (New Haven and London: Yale University Press, 1974), chs 1, 2.
5 Ibid., pp. 62, 89. For Paneth's association with the circle see Aldo Venturelli, "Nietzsche in der Berggasse 19: Uber die erste Nietzsche-Rezeption in Wien," *Nietzsche-Studien Internationales Jahrbuch für Nietzsche-Forschung*, ed. Ernst Behler *et al.*, 13 (1984).
6 *KGB* II 6/2, p. 737.
7 Ibid.
8 Friedrich Nietzsche, *Schopenhauer as Educator*, tr. James W. Hillesheim and Malcolm R. Simpson (Chicago: Henry Regnery Company, 1965), p. 39.
9 Ibid., p. 40.
10 Ibid., p. 61.
11 Ibid., p. 56.
12 Ibid., p. 79.
13 Ibid., p. 56.
14 Ibid., p. 61.
15 Ibid., p. 56.
16 Ibid., p. 28.
17 Ibid., p. 81.
18 Ibid., p. 62.
19 Ibid., p. 62.
20 Ibid., p. 45.
21 *KGB* II 6/2, p. 737.
22 *KGB* II 6/2, p. 740.
23 McGrath, *Dionysian Art*, pp. 35–8.
24 Ibid., pp. 61–4.
25 Venturelli, "Nietzsche in der Berggasse 19," p. 449.
26 Ibid., p. 450.
27 Ibid., p. 471.
28 Ibid.
29 Ibid.
30 McGrath, *Dionysian Art*, p. 89.
31 Ibid., ch. 6.
32 Venturelli is particularly good in tracing Nietzsche's changing attitude toward Lipiner ("Nietzsche in der Berggasse 19," pp. 456–60).
33 McGrath, *Dionysian Art*, p. 89.
34 Ibid.
35 Natalie Bauer-Lechner, *Erinnerungen an Gustav Mahler* (Leipzig, Vienna and Zürich: E.P. & Co. Verlag, 1923), pp. 19–20.
36 Gustav Mahler, *Briefe 1879–1911*, ed. Alma Maria Mahler (Berlin: Paul Zsolnay Verlag, 1925), p. 151.
37 McGrath, *Dionysian Art*, pp. 137–40.
38 Hans Redlich, *Gustav Mahler, Eine Erkenntnis* (Nuremberg: Verlag Hans Karl, 1919), p. 29.
39 Bauer-Lechner, *Erinnerungen*, p. 20.
40 Mahler, *Briefe*, p. 161.

41 Bauer-Lechner, *Erinnerungen*, p. 118.
42 Ibid., pp. 50–1.
43 William J. McGrath, "Mahler and Freud: the dream of the stately house," in *Beiträge '79–81 Gustav Mahler Kolloquium 1979 Ein Bericht*, ed. Rudolf Klein, Österreichischen Gesellschaft für Musik (Kassell, Basel and London: Bärnreiter, 1981), pp. 44–5.
44 Ibid., p. 45.
45 Paul Stefan, *Gustav Mahler* (Munich: R. Piper & Co. Verlag, 1920), pp. 125–6; Paul Bekker, *Gustav Mahlers Sinfonien* (Berlin: Schuster & Loeffler, 1921), p. 113.
46 Bauer-Lechner, *Erinnerungen*, p. 55.

11

ZARATHUSTRA'S APOSTLE

Martin Buber and the Jewish renaissance

Paul Mendes-Flohr

BUBER AS A DISCIPLE OF NIETZSCHE

In the winter of 1893, while yet a lad of 14, Martin Buber (1878–1965) – destined to be one of the towering figures of modern Jewish thought – visited a cousin in the Polish city of Pinsk. While strolling home along the city's stately promenade, Buber pointed vaguely to the other side of the street, a gesture which his younger companion greeted with the sophomoric comment, "So, Beyond Good and Evil!" Surprised by his cousin's erudition, Buber asked, "Have you also read Nietzsche?" No, was the embarrassed reply. "But have you?" "Oh, two or three years ago, I was a passionate Nietzschean, but now I see him just . . ."[1]

This disarmingly precocious exchange would suggest that Buber's interest in Nietzsche was but episodic. But this was hardly the case. An unpublished essay, "Zarathustra,"[2] written several years after the peripetetic colloquy with his cousin,[3] indicates that he soon overcame his youthful reservations about Nietzsche. Written in an autobiographical voice, the essay was intended as a primer for a proper understanding of Nietzsche's teachings. He tells that *The Birth of Tragedy* was his first encounter with Nietzsche. "This book made me a disciple of Nietzsche, a sick disciple." He accepted Nietzsche's thought uncritically, and hence the essay bears the subtitle, "A history of an illness, and the recovery and redemption therefrom." Nietzsche appealed to Buber's romantic discontent: ". . . a raging hatred of the entire nauseating [world] in which I lived, a wrathful aversion against the official morality, the official education, the conventional smiles, whinning, and chatter." But it was

Nietzsche's celebration of Wagner in *The Birth of Tragedy* that led Buber to regard the the latter as the "apotheosis" of the new, anti-bourgeois man. In his "naïveté," the younger Buber became an inebriated Wagnerian. Thus when he later read Nietzsche's critique of the prophet of Bayreuth, he sided with the latter. Feeling that Nietzsche had betrayed his own system, Buber ceased to read him. Then he chanced to read *Thus Spake Zarathustra* once again and discovered anew the myth of "the eternal return." Buber now understood Nietzsche's words not as a doctrine but rather as a poetic demand for a radical skepticism of all systems.

> And this his "most profound thought" of the eternal return is precisely only poetic.... One of Nietzsche's principal objectives is ... the awakening of mistrust of all and everything ... of even his own words, and silence. Not the Superman-fantasy, but the arduous way to truth is Nietzsche's true, great idealism.

Turning to Nietzsche, then still alive, he confesses: "This was my illness. I did not believe in you, but rather I believed you" (*nicht glaubte ich an dich, sondern glaubte ich dir*) – I followed your teachings as *ex cathedra* doctrine, but not your personal example of the true philosophical quest.[4]

Buber was so taken by his new understanding of Nietzsche that he undertook to render *Zarathustra* into Polish. The 17-year-old student completed the translation of the first part of the book, when he learned that a prominent poet already had a contract for the project.[5] Years later a former classmate at the Polish gymnasium of Lvov (Lemberg) recalled that Buber would appear each day in class with a copy of Nietzsche's *Zarathustra* in hand.[6] His enthusiasm for Nietzsche would not wane, and, indeed, traces of his influence could be found in all stages of Buber's evolving thought.[7]

About the same time that he penned his Zarathustra essay, Buber joined the nascent Zionist movement, founded by Theodor Herzl in 1898. Buber would soon introduce a Nietzschean perspective into Zionist affairs. His message to his fellow Jews was anticipated in his very first German essay, published in December 1900, a eulogy for Nietzsche, who had died several months earlier. Entitling his article "A word about Nietzsche and life values" ("Ein Wort über Nietzsche und die Lebenswerte"),[8] Buber claims it would be amiss to evaluate Nietzsche's legacy under any of the given vocational rubrics, for he was neither a philosopher, nor a poet, nor an artist, nor a psychologist, nor a founder of a new society. Rather he was the embodiment of a new vision of what it means to be a human being. Nietzsche, Buber exults, is "the emissary of life";[9] he was a "creator" (*Schöpfer*)[10] – a heroic figure who "created" himself and thus surpassed himself.[11] What made Nietzsche's teaching so powerful was that he shared in the endemic sickness of the age. Hence what he proclaimed was not his "own being but a longing for [true] being":[12]

> That the sick one taught a new health – [Buber cites Nietzsche] "a stronger, wittier, more tender, more daring, a more joyful individual" – that the silent thought-poet (*Gedanken-Poet*), devoted to contemplating the innermost things, glorified the will to power and the rebirth (*Wiedergeburt*) of the instinctual life, this seems to us to be a crystallization of our own tragedy.[13]

The tragedy or illness of the age was, Buber averred, ever so much more acute among his fellow Jews, and thus their urgent need to heed Nietzsche's healing message.

Zionism had come to assume the task of the long-awaited Messiah and "liberate" the Jews from the Diaspora, a condition that was interpreted not only politically but spiritually. This was in consonance with the traditional Jewish understanding of Israel's millenial sojourn in exile; the Zionists, however, tended to view Jewry's spiritual torment in radically secular terms, as generally pointing to the deformations of Jewry's inner life.[14] Nietzsche's analysis of the spiritual maladies of bourgeois civilization appealed to many Zionists, for it offered them insights into what they regarded as being the spiritual corruption and desiccation attendant on two thousand years of exile, in which Israel was denied the normal conditions of healthy, life-affirming existence in tune with the creative forces of the people. Buber was hence one of a veritable battalion of Nietzsche's desciples among the ranks of the Zionists.[15] His distinction was that among German-speaking Zionists, he quickly took center-stage, and provided a vocabulary about which others would organize their commitment to a Nietzschean renewal of Israel's spiritual and creative life. In 1901 he published, in the central organ of the World Zionist Organization, *Die Welt*, to which Herzl had just appointed him to serve as editor-in-chief, a poem in which he encapsulated his vision of a reawakening of Israel's long-slumbering life-force:

Lord, Lord, shake my people,
Strike it, bless it, furiously, gently,
Make it burn, make it free,
Heal your child

God, give the lost glow
Back to my weary people,
In wild, intoxicated flames
Bestow on them your happiness.

See, only a fever can save it
And raging exuberance,
Awaken it, and, Father, lead the throng
To Jordan's field.[16]

The Nietzschean inflections of this pathetic cry are unmistakable, as they are in an essay he published a month earlier, "Jüdische Renaissance."[17] This essay was to have an seminal impact on Zionist and twentieth-century Jewish discourse in general.

THE JEWISH RENAISSANCE

Buber notes that the renewal of the Jewish people, which Zionism seeks to sponsor, is part of a general "cultural germination" (*Kulturkeime*)[18] then experienced by various peoples in Europe. For the Jews, however, one should perhaps better speak of a "resurrection" (*Auferstehung*)[19] – a spiritual rebirth that is a sheer wonder. "The Jewish people are about to experience a resurrection from a half of life to a full one."[20] Hence, a cultural "awakening" will be for them far more difficult than it is for other people. For the Jews are shackled to an inner "*ghetto* and *golus* [exile]" – the *ghetto* of "unfree spirituality" due to "the compulsion of a tradition divested of sensuality"; and the *golus* that enslaved the Jews to "unproductive" occupations and "a hollow-eyed homelessness that vitiates all unity of will."[21] Obliquely arguing against Herzl's political conception of Zionism – which set as the movement's pre-eminent objective the attainment of political sovereignty, preferably in Israel's ancient homeland – Buber argued that the restoration of Zion must be preceded by its rebirth in the soul of the Jew. It is thus incumbent upon Zionism to requicken "the life-feeling (*Lebensgefühl*) of the Jews."[22] Therefore, he remarked in a subsequent essay, the Jewish Renaissance is, like its earlier renowned namesake, more than a mending of torn threads. Nor does it mean a return – and this must again be emphasized – but rather a rebirth (*Wiedergeburt*) of the whole man .... A new type of Jew is gradually emerging.[23]

To launch this program for a creative, life-affirming Jewry, Buber, together with the graphic artist Ephraim Mose Lilien (1874–1924), organized an art exhibition of contemporary Jewish art at the Fifth Zionist Congress, which took place in Basel in December 1901. The exhibit featured works by Jehudo Epstein, Jozef Israels, Eduard Bendemann, Isidor Kaufmann, Lessery Ury, Samuel Hirzenberg and by Lilien himself.[24] At the plenum of the congress Buber delivered an address "On Jewish art," in which he explained that:

Zionism and art are two forms of our rebirth .... [Jewish art] signifies for us first of all a great educator. An educator for a vital perception (*Anschauen*) of nature and human beings – a vital feeling (*Empfinden*) of all that is strong and beautiful. This perception and feeling, which we have lacked for so long, will be restored to us by our artists. And it is of utmost importance for us that our people regain this vital perception and feeling. For only full human beings can be full Jews, who are capable of and worthy of achieving for themselves a homeland.[25]

The promotion of Jewish art was, then, not a question of cultural enrichment and edification. Rather it was to revitalize the sensibilities of the Jews and to re-empower them to live fully and creatively.

Buber's address, delivered with "fiery" pathos,[26] was greeted with enthusiasm,[27] which helped him overcome the determined opposition of Herzl to various cultural programs he and his colleagues placed before the Congress for endorsement. Herzl, nonetheless, succeeded in blocking Buber's request for sizable allocations in support of the founding of a publishing house. Buber was undaunted, however. The following year, he and his friends succeeded in collecting the requisite funds from independent resources in order to found the Jüdischer Verlag, which until its closure by the Nazis published a remarkable series of books and journals.[28] In the foreword to its first publication, the poet and Buber's close collaborator Berthold Feiwel (1875–1937) presented the ambitious program of the press:

We wish to achieve a measure of Jewish cultural work by faciliating the establishment of a central platform for the promotion of Jewish literature, art and scholarship. Next to the ethical-Jewish ideal that a Jewish person will be once again a solid entity, reflecting national and personal self-confidence, an aesthetic-Jewish ideal is to arise. The new Jewish view of life should be suffused with something profound and soulful (*Seelenvolles*), with a new power, a new beauty.[29]

With its bold *Zarathustrastil* (a style that is reminiscent of the diction and tonality of Nietzsche's *Zarathustra*), enhanced by most refined artistic detail, the Jüdischer Verlag transformed the cultural landscape of Central European Jewry.

The Jewish renaissance was well under way. The term itself was immediately and widely adopted, and became the rallying call for numerous artists and writers within and without the Zionist movement bent on revitalizing Jewish life. The votaries of the Jewish renaissance, of which one spoke until the Third Reich, soon forgot it was Buber who coined the term. While not begrudging Buber's contribution, the publicist and at the time Nietzsche-disciple Nathan Birnbaum (1864–1937) argued that the movement the term came to denote was rather a groundswell of gushing energy that had no pedigree other than the immense yearning of the Jewish people for renewal.

This entire Renaissance movement – the regeneration of language, cultural transformation, the process of searching for oneself and discovery – is made and led by no one. All the persons and groups, whom we see entering this movement, in no way prescribe its way.

Birnbaum further explains that the Jewish renaissance must by its very nature remain leaderless and amorphic. For it is the task of the movement

first to arouse the people, and to track out a thousand paths in order to bring from a thousand sources new nourishment to the people's spirit and body ... so that it might adapt to the new times in which we live and in which to live is a joy.[30]

In his own writings, Buber did not tire of indicating that Nietzsche was the *Wegbereiter* – the forerunner – who by creating "new life values and a new feel for existence (*Weltgefühl*)"[31] forged the most promising path for the Jewish renaissance.[32]

ZIONISM AND THE AESTHETIC
EDUCATION OF THE JEWS

Buber was one of the principal architects of the Democratic Fraction, which sought to organize within the ranks of the Zionist movement oppositions to what they deemed to be Herzl's autocratic, undemocratic rule. A coalition of East and West European Zionists, the Democratic Fraction also sought to promote itself as an alternative to Herzl's political program, inspired by the teachings of Ahad Ha'am (Asher Ginsberg; 1856–1927), a Hebraist from Odessa, who even before the formal establishment of Herzl's movement, advocated what was to be known as spiritual or cultural Zionism. Whereas Herzl's political Zionism was presented as a solution to anti-Semitism – what he called the *Judennot* (the distress of the Jews) – Ahad Ha'am spoke of the *Not des Judentums* (the distress of Judaism).[33] The modern world, he argued, confronts Judaism as a system of religious knowledge and practice with a severe, if not fatal challenge. Neither the defensive posture of East European rabbis nor the apologetic religious cosmetics of western Jewry are adequate to the task. If Judaism is to survive in the contemporary world, he taught, it must accept the premises of modernity – which he identified with science and humanism – and radically reconstitute itself as a national, secular culture. Grounded in a modernized Hebrew as the spoken and written tongue of the "Jewish nation," this culture would draw from the traditional sources of Judaism values and ideas that led themselves to a reinterpretation in the light of rational humanistic civilization.

Through his association with cultural Zionism Buber has often been cast as the German Achad Ha'am.[34] This is a misleading characterization. First, Achad Ha'am's struggle against Nietzsche's influence on East European Zionists should alert us to a profound difference between the two. Affectionately called by his admirers as an "agnostic rabbi,"[35] Achad Ha'am found Nietzsche's concept of a "transvaluation of values" far too radical, for when applied to Judaism it could well lead to an utter break with the "ethical and spiritual" foundations of Judaism, serving the modern Jew from the primal sources of his or her identity. Nietzsche, especially in the hands of overly exhuberant youth, threatened the continuity that

Acad Ha'am sought.[36] While sharing his Russian colleague's commitment to Jewish spiritual continuity, Buber evaluated Nietzsche's teachings in a far more nuanced fashion.

For Achad Ha'am Nietzsche evoked the specter of a nihilistic anarchism. For Buber he represented the possibility of regeneration of Jewish cultural and spiritual life. Ultimately the difference between Achad Ha'am and Buber – and their respective understanding of Nietzsche's significance for Zionism – lies in their differing conceptions of culture. Following the positivistic doctrines then popular among certain liberal Russian circles, Achad Ha'am regarded culture – and thus cultural continuity – in essentially formal terms: language, literature and governing ideas. Buber, on the other hand, was beholden to the romantic traditions which also informed Nietzsche.[37] He thus viewed culture as primarily the realm of inner aesthetic and spiritual sensibility. The *locus classicus* of this conception of culture is Friedrich Schiller's epistolary essay of 1795, *On the Aesthetic Education of Mankind.*[38] There he speaks of culture as serving the ideal of the "finely tuned soul,"[39] which by virtue of learning to appreciate beauty – sensuously and not just intellectually – dwells in the realm of true freedom. For beauty is untouched by the contingencies and imperious interest-laden claims of one's external environment; as such beauty, or rather the inner, subjective experience of beauty, is the ground of true autonomy and freedom. "[I]t is only through Beauty that one makes his way to Freedom."[40] Further, within the dominion of beauty one is "immune from all human arbitrariness,"[41] and is thus allowed the possibility of self-perfection, an aesthetic education then projects as it were a utopia of the soul, which anticipates the ideal of humanity and the self-perfection of the individual.[42] The practical lesson that Schiller drew from this thesis was "all improvement in the political sphere must proceed from the ennobling of character."[43]

This conception of culture was mediated to Buber through the neo-romanticism of the fin-de-siècle Germany, and especially the teachings of the *spiritus rector* of his youth, Nietzsche. Indicatively, within Zionist discourse, he consistently spoke of *Kulturpolitik*, the preparation of the Jews for the envisioned political and social transformation through the transfomation of their aesthetic and spiritual sensibilities. While the leadership of the Zionist movement was negotiating with Great Britain for what is now known as the Balfour Declaration, issued in 1917 and hailed as a crowning victory for political Zionism, Buber warned that Zion could only be redeemed through *Kulturpolitik*: "Palestine can only be built through a life-affirming activity that stems from the spirit and the effect of a Judaism attuned and bound to the spirit."[44] Earlier he defined his conception of Zionist politics:

a transvaluation (*Umwertung*) of all aspects of . . . the life of the people to its depths and very foundations. It must touch the soul . . . . We must unlock the vital powers of the nation and let loose its fettered instincts.[45]

Nietzsche's imprint on both the tonality and diction – not to speak of the content – of Buber's message is manifest, and undoubtedly explains the enormous resonance it enjoyed among a generation of Zionists who, like innumerable non-Jewish contemporaries, were inspired by Zarathustra's lonely quest for a life of integrity, disciplined passion and creativity.

NOTES

1 A. Eliasberg, "Aus Martin Bubers Jugendzeit," *Blätter des Heinebundes* 1(1) (April 1928): 1f.
2 "Zarathustra" (handwritten manuscript), *Martin Buber Archives*, Jerusalem, *Varia* 320, B/7.
3 On the dating of this essay, see my *From Mysticism to Dialogue: Martin Buber's Transformation of German Social Thought* (Detroit: Wayne State University Press, 1989), p. 147, n.2.
4 Towards the end of his life, Buber also recalled his encounter with Nietzsche's *Zarathustra* from the perspective of seventy years:

[When I was about seventeen] a book took possession of me, a book that was, to be sure, the work of a philosopher but was not a philosophical book: Nietzsche's *Thus Spake Zarathustra*. I say "took possession of me," for here a teaching did not simply and calmly confront me, but a willed and able – utterance stormed up to and over me.
(Buber, "Autobiographical fragments," in P.A. Schilpp and M. Friedman (eds), *The Philosophy of Martin Buber: The Library of Living Philosophers* (LaSalle, Ill.: Open Court, 1967), p. 12)

5 Ibid., p. 13.
6 Letter from Withold O. to Buber, 27 July 1962, in *The Letters of Martin Buber: A Life of Dialogue*, ed. Nahum N. Glatzer and P. Mendes-Flohr (New York: Schocken, 1991), p. 648.
7 See my *Mysticism to Dialogue*, pp. 49–82, *passim*; also see M. Friedman, *Martin Buber's Life and Work*, vol. 1 (New York: Dutton, 1981), pp. 31–2, 39, 44, 111, 137; and G. Schaeder, *The Hebrew Humanism of*

Martin Buber, tr. N.J. Jacobs (Detroit: Wayne State University Press, 1973), pp. 31–7, 244f.

8 *Die Kunst im Leben* 1(1) (December 1900): 12–13.
9 Ibid., p. 13.
10 Ibid., p. 12.
11 Ibid., p. 13.
12 Ibid.
13 Ibid.
14 See Arnold Eisen, *Galut: Modern Jewish Reflections on Homelessness and Homecoming* (Bloomington: Indiana University Press, 1983).
15 See B.E. Ellerin, *Nietzsche among the Zionists* (unpublished Phd Dissertation, Cornell University, 1990), and his "Nietzsche et les Zionistes; tableau d'une reception," in D. Bourel and J. Le Rider (eds), *De Sils-Maria à Jérusalem: Nietzsche et le judaïsme: les intellectuels juifs et Nietzsche* (Paris: Editions du Cert, 1991), pp. 111–19; and D. Ohana, "Zarathustra in Jerusalem: Nietzsche and the 'New Hebrews,'" in Robert Wistrich and David Ohana (eds), *The Shaping of Israeli Identity: Myth, Memory and Trauma* (London: Frank Cass, 1995), pp. 38–60; also Steven E. Aschheim, *The Nietzsche Legacy in Germany: 1890–1990* (Berkeley: University of California Press, 1992), pp . 93–112.
16 "Das Gebet" (1990), *Die Welt* 5 (10) (8 March 1901): 13, tr. in Friedman, *Life and Work*, vol. 1, p. 42.
17 *Ost und West* 1(1) (January 1901): cols 7–10; Buber, *Jüdische Bewegung: Gesammelte Aufsätze und Ansprachen*, first series, 1900–14 (Berlin: Jüdischer Verlag, 1916), pp. 7–16.
18 Ibid., p. 7.
19 Ibid., p. 9.
20 Ibid.
21 Ibid., p. 12.
22 Ibid., p. 13.
23 "Renaissance und Bewegung" (1903), in Buber, *Jüdische Bewegung*, first series, p. 99.
24 *"Eine neue Kunst für ein altes Volk":* Die Jüdische Renaissance in Berlin *1900–1924*, exhibition magazine (exhibit at Martin-Gropius-Bau, Berlin, from 25 September to 15 December 1991), conception and text by Inka Betz (Berlin: Jüdisches Museum/Abteilung des Berlin Museums, 1991), p. 4.
25 "Von jüdischer Kunst," in *Jüdische Bewegung*, first series, pp. 64f.
26 Letter to his wife, Paula, 26 December 1901, in Glatzer and Mendes-Flohr (eds), *Letters*, p. 81.
27 Friedman, *Life and Work*, vol. 1, p. 55.
28 Revived in the early 1970s, the Jüdischer Verlag is presently part of Suhrkamp Verlag, Frankfurt am Main.
29 *Jüdisches Almanach* (Berlin: Jüdischer Verlag, 1902); cited in H. Kohn, *Martin Buber: Sein Werk und Seine Zeit: Ein Beitrag zur Geistesgegesichte Mitteleuropas: 1890–1930*, 2nd expanded edn (Cologne: Joseph Melzer Verlag, 1961), pp. 42f.
30 Mathias Acher (= N. Birnbaum), "Die jüdische Renaissance-bewegung," *Ost und West* 2 (1902): 577, 584.

31 Cited in Kohn, *Buber*, p. 36.
32 "Ein Wort über Nietzsche und die Lebenswerte," *Die Kunst im Leben* 1(1) (December 1900). This was the inaugural essay in a series entitled "Wegbereiter der neuen Kultur." Buber also wrote an introductory essay for the entire series.
33 See Ahad Ha'am, "The transvalution of values" (1898), in *Nationalism and the Jewish Ethic: The Basic Writings of Ahad Ha'am*, ed. and intro. Hans Kohn (New York: Schocken, 1962), pp. 165–87.
34 Jehuda Reinharz, "Achad Ha'am und der deutsche Zionismus," *Bulletin des Leo Baeck Instituts* 61 (1982): 4–27.
35 Arthur Hertzberg (ed. and intro.), *The Zionist Idea: A Historical Analysis and Reader* (New York: Atheneum, 1969), p. 247.
36 See Ben Halpern, *The Idea of the Jewish State* (Cambridge, Mass.: Harvard University Press, 1961), pp. 25–7.
37 Avraham Shapira, "Buber's attachment to Herder and 'Volkism,'" *Studies in Zionism* (Tel Aviv University), 14(1) (Spring 1993): 1–30.
38 Schiller, *On the Aesthetic Education of Man*, tr. and ed. E.M. Wilkinson and L.A Willoughby (Oxford: Clarendon Press, 1967).
39 Ibid., p. 219.
40 Ibid., p. 9.
41 Ibid., p. 55.
42 See Klaus L. Berghahn, *"Gedankenfreiheit from Political Reform to Aesthetic Revolution in Schiller's Work,"* in E. Bahr and T.P. Saine (eds), *The Internalized Revolution. German Reactions to the French Revolution, 1789–1989* (New York and London: Garland Publishing, Inc., 1992), p. 113.
43 Schiller, *On the Aesthetic Education of Man*, p. 55.
44 "Bericht über den ausserordentlichen Delegiertentag der Zionistischen Vereinigung für Deutschland (25. und 26. Dezember 1916)," *Jüdische Rundschau*, (5 January 1917), p. 10.
45 "Zionistische Politik" (1903) in *Jüdische Bewegung*, first series, pp. 113ff.

12

DIASPORAS

Gary Shapiro

Once again this fall I was teaching my beloved *On the Genealogy of Morals*, this time to the frosh in my Core Course "Exploring human experience."[1] Just in college for two weeks, and with no warning or preparation we were asking them to think about masters and slaves, to entertain this insidious assault upon their rather vague Christianity. If Nietzsche imagined that one day wars would be fought in his name (and I don't think he meant culture wars), the professor within him also fantasized that a chair would eventually be established for the teaching of *Zarathustra*. But when he prophesied that Europe would one day survive in the form of thirty or so imperishable books, I don't suspect he was thinking that historically Baptist institutions, such as the one where I teach, would include the *Genealogy* as part of the multicultural spectrum of texts with which every first-year student must wrestle along with Lao Tzu, the Qur'an and Don DeLillo's *White Noise*. And once again, a student asked "What does Nietzsche really think about the Jews?" temporarily frustrating my attempt to steer the discussion towards the opposition between guilt cultures and shame cultures, the brilliant explanation of the origins of civilization, bad conscience and western religion, and the rank order of forms of asceticism (artists are best, followed closely by philosophers, all the way down to historians, with – surprise! – priests squarely in the middle). In my inspired answer, as I recall (all praise to active forgetfulness), I said that in keeping with Nietzsche's lapidary maxim that "only that which has no history can be defined," there was no essence of the Jew or of Judaism in his perspective. He admired the warrior kings and other towering figures of the Hebrew Bible. I could have quoted *Beyond Good and Evil*: "With terror and reverence one stands before these tremendous remnants of what man once was, and will have sad thoughts about ancient Asia and its protruding little peninsula Europe" (*BGE* 52). But after their political and military defeat, the priests took over from the warriors, exploiting the split which was always already there in the ethos of the masters. It's that defeated, priestly people of ancient times who become the masters of *ressentiment*, and eventually hatch Christianity, the greatest outrage of history. So, I underline the point pedagogically, it's not a question of comparing Jews unfavorably to Christians; as for modern anti-Semitism, Nietzsche finds it to be a virulent form of plebeian *ressentiment*, and when given a racial formulation by German ideologues, a grotesque absurdity, since the Jews are a stronger, better race than the mongrel Germans, who would do well to learn some wit and *esprit* from the Jews among them. I could have gone on to speak of how Nietzsche's writings become increasingly friendly toward the Jews, as he begins to think of his future readers and the way in which his thought will be propagated. One might do a very subtle analysis of Nietzsche's construction of his "friend Georg" Brandes, in the light of Nietzsche's ambition for his work, his difficult notion of friendship and his ambiguous praise of contemporary Jews as actors and logicians.[2]

That class occurred between Rosh Hashanah and Yom Kippur. I absented myself from teaching on the day of atonement, practicing a religion (in the sense of *religio*, a binding) that had more to do with asserting my difference from the prevailing and all too homogeneous culture, than with the fasting, repentance and communal worship that are ritually prescribed. Given the occasion, the student's question and perhaps especially that other anniversary of Nietzsche's one hundred and fiftieth birthday that I was being called on to celebrate in all too many venues, my thoughts on this holy day turned to my own peculiar genealogical relation to Nietzsche, a relation as indefinable as all things historical. My text for the day was not the Bible or the Talmud, but Nietzsche's notebooks and letters and what he has to say there about Jews and sometimes to them. The early notes and letters are full of bits of conventional anti-Semitism, as when Nietzsche complains about having to share a carriage or a hotel with Jews; many are written during the high point of his Wagner enthusiasm, although even in 1874–5 Nietzsche is expressing reservations about the vulgarity of Wagner's anti-Semitism and suggesting that Wagner and "the Jews" are mirror-images of one another in their oversimplified views of causality.[3] Eventually, one finds speculations that the Jews could serve as the European ruling caste (of which Nietzsche thinks we are sorely in need) and characterizations

of them as Europe's *Über-Rasse*.[4] And when Nietzsche says that
whoever reads him in Germany must have *entdeutscht* (de-
Germanized) himself or be a Jew, alongside the pronouncement that
a Jew is a "*Wohltat unter deutschen Hornvieh*" ("a blessing among
German cattle"), such a reader feels that Nietzsche wants him, that
the Jewish reader might just be a primary case of the "all and none"
to whom Nietzsche's texts are directed. While the Germans oppose
men, he says, the Jews show a *delicatesse* in their reception of me.[5]

I wonder if Nietzsche's own displacements led to some sympathy
and understanding for those chronically displaced Jews, who might
become his readers. Nietzsche resigns his teaching position because
of ill health, travels back and forth across Europe (mainly in Italy
and Switzerland), becoming increasingly estranged from the Company of Wagner and the Reich. He enters into the postal system, he
is a man without a fixed address, to be reached by general delivery.
The Jews, as he sees them, are a tough and mobile bunch, who have
had to make their way in a variety of circumstances, generally
inhospitable. They're free, he suggests, of an unthinking identification with the identification with the national state.

If I'm being seduced here, maybe I want to be seduced. Does the
German philosopher, German despite his own phantasy of being
Polish, want me for a friend, the way that he wanted and enjoyed
Georg Brandes, Helen Zimmern, Paul Rée and others? Or was I
seduced a long time ago? Has Nietzsche very artfully constructed a
way of drawing his readers in, encouraging them, leading them on
with promises, such as the thought that anyone who could understand six sentences of *Zarathustra* would stand head and shoulders
above all modern men? The "old philologist" as he describes himself,
who asks us to consider the long third essay of the *Genealogy* as the
exegesis of a single sentence from *Zarathustra*, might have a special
appeal for those who come from a culture of the book, who have a
taste for close and ingenious readings of texts. Consider the Talmudic
and kabbalistic temptation of the invitation to decode a book which
is said, as Nietzsche subtitles *Thus Spoke Zarathustra*, to be written
"*For All and None*." There is an aphorism in *The Gay Science* that I
read as part of Nietzsche's strategy to seduce the Jewish reader. He
writes there that scholars tend to reproduce the habits of thought of
their fathers or ancestors in their work: the sons (and daughters, we
would say now) of craftspersons take pride in a completed piece of
work, with all of the footnotes in order; the children of bureaucrats
(like Kant?) are satisfied when they have a system of categories and

classifications into which everything can be fitted; the progeny of advocates or lawyers are happy when they can make a strong and compelling argument that seems to demolish some opposing position. But Jews are different: because no one listens to them simply because of their status or ancestry, they need to rely on logic; that is, they must appeal to some medium that offers the possibility of a relatively non-parochial persuasion. And because of their business talents, tested and refined in the conditions of the diaspora, they are not limited to a single, narrow method of scholarship or reading (*GS* 348). Of course the very next aphorism qualifies this one, because it suggests that Spinoza's view that every being strives to preserve itself is simply a generalization from his own consumptive condition; life is on the whole excess and squandering, Nietzsche insists in this aphorism which is also devoted to the character of scholars, and the scholarly or philosophical reader of Nietzsche should take this to heart.

Nietzsche sometimes thematizes seduction as well as practicing it, as in this aphorism from "The free spirit" section of *Beyond Good and Evil*:

> A new species of philosophers is coming up: I venture to baptize them with a name that is not free of danger. As I unriddle them, insofar as they allow themselves to be unriddled – for it belongs to their nature to *want* to remain riddles at some point – these philosophers of the future may have a right – it might also be a wrong – to be called attempters, seducers, or experimenters [all of these are possible translations of *Versucher*]. This name itself is in the end a mere attempt (*Versuch*) and, if you will, a temptation (*Versuchung*). (*BGE* 42)

It is perhaps something of this project of seduction that we hear in some of Nietzsche's letters, where as Geoff Waite suggests, he formulates the battle plans for his assault on European pieties. Writing of Helen Zimmern, a British Jew whom he befriended, he writes "it is incredible (*toll*) how much this race now has intellectuality (*Geistigkeit*) in Europe in its hands." And he writes with pleasure of having heard of one of his Jewish readers who was so excited by his books that he could not sleep.[6]

When did the seduction begin for me, and did it have something to do with my own displacement, and my need for a certain kind of logic? Nietzsche appeared for me first in St Paul, that is, in the Minnesota city named for the odious founder of Christianity (just as

GARY SHAPIRO

Paul was simply a Jew named Saul before his conversion, so St Paul
was called Pig's Eye in the rough old days of the earlier dispensation
before the sober and pious citizens decided that it needed a more
respectable designation). The house I grew up in in St Paul had just
a few books; there was no atmosphere of Talmudic scholarship that
might have prepared me to be a more sensitive reader of the history
of philosophy. But among these few, there was a group of ten or
fifteen that stood out, more at first for their appearance than for their
contents. There were older, leather-bound volumes of Dumas, a fine
edition of Oscar Wilde's *The Ballad of Reading Gaol* and pebbly-
grained Modern Library books from the 1920s or early 1930s, the
latter including *Beyond Good and Evil* and *The Genealogy of Morals*.
I think that Wilde's *Ballad* was the first of these I read, and its words
were subversive enough for a 7 or 8-year-old in the 1940s:

> Yet each man kills the thing he loves,
> By each let this be heard,
> Some do it with a bitter look,
> Some with a flattering word,
> The coward does it with a kiss,
> The brave man with a sword!

For a number of years I thought Reading was pronounced like the
verb reading, but I discovered early that gaol was jail. As it turns out,
"reading jail" would be a good description of this little cache of
books among a number of mediocre novels of the time. For these
were the books, I was told some years later, that my grandfather
Leon Gleckman had read during his two periods of incarceration in
the federal penitentiary at Leavenworth, Kansas. Leon was a boot-
legger in Minneapolis and St Paul and had some power behind the
scenes in local politics.[7] I treasure the idea of his reading Nietzsche
in Leavenworth, especially these two books, as a way of understanding and resisting his imprisonment. Leon could have read the
savagely brilliant denunciation of St Paul in *Daybreak*:

> Paul had become at once the fanatical defender and chaperone
> of this god and his law, and was constantly combating and on
> the watch for transgressors and doubters. . . . And then he
> discovered in himself that he himself – fiery, sensual, melan-
> choly, malevolent in hatred as he was – *could* not fulfill this law
> . . . his *mind* suddenly became clear: "it is *unreasonable*,"
> he says to himself, "to persecute precisely this Christ! For here

248

is the way out, here is perfect revenge, here and nowhere else
do I have and hold the *destroyer of the law*!"

(D 68)

I would like to think that Leon could have anticipated the wordplay
of some contemporary academics and so have read it as an indictment
of the hypocritical moralism of his city, of Prohibition and of the
smug mix of Christianity and civic virtue that it served. Perhaps he
read H.L. Mencken, the sage of Baltimore, who found Nietzsche an
exhilarating tonic against similar forms of stupidity. Leon had found
a way of living within the interstices of American society, of making
transgression marketable; if his reading list suggests that there is
indeed a deep connection between Nietzsche and transgression, then
perhaps what I and other philosophers who write about Nietzsche
have done is to institutionalize that relationship within the academy.
In *The Closing of the American Mind* Allan Bloom said that the
American university has become totally possessed by Nietzschean
ideology, imported originally by a few radical professors.[8] This
diagnosis wildly exaggerates Nietzsche's presence in the academy
and it neglects the fact that Nietzsche was read for very good reasons
by people like my grandfather who had never set foot inside a
university.

When I was 10, my parents divorced and my mother moved to
Miami Beach with me, my younger brother and her father's books.
Split off from the extended family in St Paul, and not feeling at ease
in the atmosphere of a resort, I turned more and more to reading,
and like many adolescents in analogous circumstances I turned to
those books that offered a delicious thrill of the forbidden, unmasking the claims of religion, morality and the state. Nietzsche has the
amazing attraction for a certain younger reader of making you
believe that you alone, for the first time, have understood something
hidden from the world at large. As older scholars, jaded by years of
close reading and literary theory, we are able to analyze the artful
way in which Nietzsche encodes this seduction in his texts. Consider,
for example, *The Birth of Tragedy* which, as Giorgio Colli suggests,
is structured like the initiation into a Greek mystery religion, the cult
of Dionysus.[9] From the very beginning Nietzsche appeals to his
reader to share his sense of what it is to dream or to be intoxicated,
and by the end he is appealing to the reader as a "friend" who is among
the happy few to join him in a sensitivity to the deeper effects of
music and musical drama (Wagner). I had been displaced and felt that

I was living in exile; Nietzsche, along with the cult of science fiction and the first news of Sartre, Jack Kerouac and Allen Ginsberg, furnished me with the conviction, full of illusions as it was, that I had an identity higher and better than these surroundings in which I temporarily found myself. Finding myself among other Jews, I directed some of my resentment against them, ironically taking some of my justification from Nietzsche's portrait of priestly *ressentiment* in the *Genealogy*. My rebellion already took a rather intellectual form; in addition to reading I became a high school debater, a role that encourages the development of two talents that Nietzsche speaks of as particularly characteristic of Jews, acting and logic.

When I went off to college at Columbia, in New York City, I smuggled the two volumes of Nietzsche out of the house. My mother and I had a running controversy about this theft until, well after I'd become something of a Nietzsche scholar, she gave me the books. At Columbia I realized with something of a shock that lots of other people, certainly the faculty and a few students, had been reading Nietzsche too, and that in addition to my youthful and unfocused enthusiasm, there were some serious philosophical, literary and political interpretations of his work to contend with. He was said to be complicit in the rise of Nazism, to have celebrated irrationalism, to be a friend of the blond beast. I had very mixed feelings upon discovering that my subversive author was part of the reading list for the required freshman course in Contemporary Civilization. Marx, Nietzsche and Freud were said to be the three greatest influences on twentieth-century thought: two heretical German-speaking Jews and a German with a complex and seductive attitude toward just those Jews who might feel attracted to Marx or Freud. In his forthcoming book *Nietzsche's Corps/e*,[10] Geoff Waite suggests, not without some justification, that the aim of Nietzsche's writing is to seduce leftists away from communism, and that the Nietzsche industry has been remarkably successful in achieving this goal with which it has been subliminally infected.

In any case, the seduction was proceeding apace. The summer after my freshman year was a time for new forms of independence and exploration, as well as for reading Nietzsche at greater length; I didn't realize at the time how all of these pursuits were intensifying one another. I devoured every word of Walter Kaufmann's *The Portable Nietzsche* and his *Nietzsche: Philosopher, Psychologist, Antichrist*.[11] Kaufmann was a German with one Jewish parent; when his book was first published in 1950 it helped to dispel many misconceptions. His study aimed at making Nietzsche safe for liberal democracy; he persuasively sorted out what the texts actually said from what the philosopher's sister, or Nazis like Alfred Bäumler had tried to make him say. If there was indeed a sentence in *Human, All Too Human* to the effect that the young stock exchange Jew is perhaps the most repulsive specimen of humanity, a line amplified and repeated by the Nazi Nietzscheans, Kaufmann restored it to its context which is full of praise for the Jews and in which they are seen as a counterweight to the stupidities of all nationalisms (*HAH* 475).[12] For myself, I had already decided that I didn't want a career in the stock exchange, or any of its metaphorical equivalents, so I could sympathize with Nietzsche's distaste while feeling myself flattered by his observations about Jewish resourcefulness, spirituality and intelligence. When it came time to write a paper for my first class in philosophy, at summer school, I chose to compare Spinoza and Nietzsche, on a topic that I dimly remember as having to do with ideas of power and virtue, *conatus* and will to power. I had been inspired, I suppose, by some of Nietzsche's praise of Spinoza for having anticipated him in rejecting pity, the dualism of mind and body, and in his principle that everything which increases our power is good. I'm sure that I did not consciously think about Spinoza's Jewishness as part of this project. Of course I was aware that Spinoza had been excommunicated and I understood why his thought was reprehensible to the orthodox. But Spinoza had renamed himself Benedictus; if his ancestors had been expelled from Spain, and if he could continue to feel blessed living the philosophical life while excommunicated within the diaspora (a kind of double diaspora), thinking about him could be a model (as Nietzsche assured me) of how one might work within the philosophical tradition in a Nietzschean spirit. I would not be a stock exchange Jew (although I have since radically changed my acquiescence in or repression of the ugliness of Nietzsche's remark); I would be a philosopher, perhaps a historian of philosophy who could reread the tradition with something of the excitement with which Nietzsche read Spinoza. Whether one was displaced by being separated from one's initial community (like Spinoza from Spain and the Amsterdam Jews or myself from St Paul) or self-exiled and constantly on the move (like Nietzsche who loathed the Germans and spent his time shuttling back and forth between Swiss mountains and Italian resorts), philosophy was something one could hold on to.

Yet once I had used Nietzsche to get into philosophy, a curious or not so curious repression of his work set in. In 1960 serious students

of philosophy did not do Nietzsche; this was something I absorbed
from the atmosphere at Columbia, where one might immerse oneself
in Wittgenstien's puzzles about the possibility of a private language
(with the bright young professors) or in Whitehead's speculative
metaphysics (with the respectable older guard).[13] I had digested my
Nietzsche for the time being. I would be a logician and actor,
working with the materials provided by my academic environment.
Just recently I was struck by Nietzsche's wondering, parenthetically, in *Twilight of the Idols* whether Plato went to school with the
Jews in his visit to Egypt (*TI*, "What I owe to the Ancients" 2). So
if I was indeed exemplifying Nietzsche's account of the Jewish
intellectual, I was perhaps also part of a "western" tradition that was
implicitly (always already, as Jacques Derrida would say) in thrall to
the spirit of those intellectuals. I suppose that Nietzsche, sophisticated philologist that he was, was thinking not only of the Jewish
dualism between God and the world, but perhaps even primarily of
those scholars who anticipated the great culture of Alexandria and
had established forms of pedagogy and discussion that might have
served as models for the Academy.

If Nietzsche's name came up among philosophers during my
undergraduate and graduate years at Columbia, he was mentioned
as a more lyrical and literary predecessor of what was then called
existentialism, meaning mainly Sartre and Heidegger. And while I
was tempted to choose a dissertation topic in that general area, I
ended up working on the philosophy of Charles Peirce. Peirce, a
scientist, logician and speculative metaphysician, seems to be very
distant from Nietzsche. For me he promised a third way between the
extremes of Anglo-American linguistic analysis and continental
thought; his logic and his insistence on the irreducibility of intentional or rule-obeying behavior linked him with the former, while
his ambitious phenomenology, evolutionary cosmology and belief
in an ultimate community of inquiry that seemed like a secularized
form of Hegel's absolute spirit gave him an affinity with the latter.
Peirce also illustrated, although I scarcely thought about this at the
time, Nietzsche's shrewd observation that the ideal of the scientific
life as developed in the nineteenth century was genetically derived
from and structurally analogous to Christian ascetisicm. As Peirce
formulated it, science required the virtues of faith, hope and charity;
the scientific inquirer must have faith in the ultimate attainment of
the truth (by the ultimate community if not by her or himself), hope
that inquiry will progress, and charity in the form of a willingness to

abandon any specific hypothesis of the inquirer's own when confronted with conflicting evidence or a better explanation. I seemed to have come a long way from Nietzsche, even if his inspiration had helped to get me there. Since then, it's occurred to me that Nietzsche and Peirce are in some ways reversed images of one other, illustrating the different roads one might take from the various philosophical crises of their century. Nietzsche was also a scientist, that is a philologist, who emphasized the diversity of languages and their imbrication with power. Both would have subscribed to the hierarchy of the normative sciences that Peirce formulated explicitly: logic is a form of conduct, and so is subordinate to ethics, while ethics must be for the sake of intensely desirable qualities of feeling and so must be governed by aesthetics. Of course the contents of these different norms would differ drastically for the two and each could point to the other as a terrible example of what happens when one pursues a Christian or anti-Christian path.

When I finished my work at Columbia I took my first full-time teaching position at the University of Kansas. Seen from New York Kansas had an almost mythical status as the ultimate form of diaspora; it was not just that I did not expect to find many Jews there, but is was, for New Yorkers, a synonym for everything provincial, a black hole where there were no delis, no subways, no theaters, no intellectual life. My mother was aghast at the idea that I would take up residence there, and it only gradually dawned upon me that her main association with the state was her father's incarceration there in the 1930s. She had visited him in jail and she must have retained a sense of a desolate place that served as a backdrop for the giant penal colony of Leavenworth. Since the teaching position at Kansas was the only one I was offered in 1970 that seemed to have much of a future, my official reasons for going there were impeccable. But in retrospect I think that my desire to start anew, to say goodbye to some of the personal and political chaos of the radical politics in which I'd become involved in the 1960s, might also have masked a need to lose myself, perhaps to pursue a certain form of abjection far from the Jewish intellectual world of New York. Was it a coincidence that I headed for the site of the family's shame and the scene of Nietzschean self-instruction?

As it turned out, Kansas was a real place and not simply a surrogate for fantasies. What appeared as a blank slate from the eastern coast of the United States had its own topography, traditions and structures. There was a hardy group of Jews there, but there was also a strong current of mid-American self-righteousness and suspicion of anything that appeared different. If I was in one of the further reaches of the diaspora I now proceeded, largely unconsciously, and with Nietzsche's help, to re-create something of the diasporal structure within my situation at the University of Kansas. I had been hired, in part, because I had taken the advice of one of my professors concerning the job interview. Having run into Robert Paul Wolff in a Broadway supermarket on the eve of my trip to Kansas for that interview, Wolff gave the invaluable suggestion to tell the prospective department that I could teach anything. Was this advice, I now wonder, coming from that same ancient source that Nietzsche described in his assimilation of the Jew and the actor? In any case I sailed forth, played my assigned role and received the offer of a position. The department thought it would be good for me to teach nineteenth-century philosophy and aesthetics in my first semester as well as a course in American pragmatism. The first two served as forums for introducing Nietzsche into my teaching. But I had contracted a passion for Hegel, who was the continental version of Peirce, and it took some years before the transition from Hegel to Nietzsche was effected, even as I frequently relied on Karl Löwith's book to explain that movement in its nineteenth-century form.[14] While I was conducting my self-education in public, at least through the publicity of the classroom, I was coming to have less and less in common with my colleagues in philosophy. And while this is a common enough experience as one develops one's own intellectual perspective, it has a weightier significance out on the American Great Plains, where the distances between universities are measured in hundreds of miles, than in New York, where you can jump on the subway to meet someone with compatible interests just a few stops away.

While on one level my move towards Nietzsche had to do with my continuing work with Kierkegaard, Sartre and Heidegger, and then later with "literary theory" (actually French philosophy in disguise), there was no doubt also a strong appeal being exercised by Nietzsche's denunciations of German stupidity and provinciality, which I understood subliminally as directed toward the environment in which I found myself. While the central Midwest seems ethnically quite bland, it is historically, and in a certain way phenomeno-logically, rather German. If the condition of understanding Nietz-sche is that one be *entdeutscht* as he says, then the condition of my reading him was to distance myself from my surroundings and my colleagues, the former being a surrogate for what he disliked about Bismarck's *Reich*, and the latter being largely committed to the use of reason as it manifested itself to Anglo-American philosophy of recent decades. By 1976 I had begun to formulate a program to understand philosophy in terms of a set of literary and rhetorical strategies; if the spirit of this was Nietzschean, the specific categories with which I was working then were derived from Hegel's lectures on poetry. But I had deformed Hegel in a Nietzschean direction by understanding those categories not as ways in which poetry moved beyond itself to religion and finally to the transparency of the *Begriff*, but as ways in which philosophy necessarily testified to its own failure to rise beyond the figurative and the rhetorical. It goes without saying that such a project was destined, if not designed, to raise the hackles of my philosophical colleagues in Kansas, who believed themselves to be in the position of having to defend philosophy as a genuine and serious intellectual enterprise in an environment that they perceived as indifferent or hostile to sustained inquiry and reflection. The odd direction that my thinking had taken could only reinforce the forces of darkness who were waiting for an excuse to curtail superfluous studies like philosophy.

Off in my isolation in Kansas, I was only vaguely aware that a number of French thinkers had already developed a number of very sophisticated critiques of philosophical language and had articulated close readings of philosophical texts that paralleled what I was beginning to do in my more naive fashion. A crucial turning point was the year 1976–7 that I spent as a fellow of the School of Criticism and Theory at the University of California at Irvine. Now I not only received a massive dose of Foucault, Derrida, de Man and others, but I came to see that Nietzsche's texts were inspirations for a large part of what the literary people called "theory" (an odd term, since philosophy seemed to deal with nothing else); his writings were important sites for fighting again and mapping out what Plato's Socrates had called the "ancient quarrel" (*diaphora*) between philosophy and poetry. What I thought that I had been doing off in the wilderness by myself, with what Nietzsche might describe as a dogged Jewish persistence and patience, turned out to be one minor variant on what was quickly becoming the most important new movement in literary studies. The first essay that I wrote and published on Nietzsche, "The rhetoric of Nietzsche's *Zarathustra*," was a product of that year at Irvine. It drew on the tropology that I had picked up there from Hayden White, himself a careful reader of

Nietzsche who seemed to have absorbed the latter's analysis and transformation of ancient rhetoric.

Back in Kansas, I was restless and felt the constraints of the diaspora more strongly than I had before. I began to travel more frequently and acquired a passion to be on the move. I discovered that in some of his discarded versions of a preface for *Daybreak* Nietzsche had written that his aphoristic works were themselves designed to be read on the move, since modern readers travelled and were subject to endless distractions. And he says in number 454 of the published text, it would be a mistake to read the book straight through; that would produce confusion and surfeit. Rather, one should stick one's head briefly into the aphorisms and then out in order to get their full force and to juxtapose them with one's own experience. Nietzsche, in his wanderings, had come to think about what it means to be in a place; I imagined that by following what Gilles Deleuze called his nomad thought I could become cosmopolitan, not simply a Jew exiled to the diaspora.[16] At the same time something was leading me to think more seriously about Nietzsche's relation to Judaism and Christianity. I came to believe that *The Antichrist*, so often dismissed as a work already deformed by the author's impending madness, had a much more rigorous structure than it had been credited with, and that much of this derived from Nietzsche's sustained engagement with Julius Wellhausen's work on the history of Israel (already in evidence in *On the Genealogy of Morals*) and with the writers of various lives of Jesus (D.F. Strauss, Ernest Renan) who had attempted to explain Jesus's relation to the Jewish context. What I argued was roughly what I told the curious student this semester: Nietzsche' understanding of the Jews has to be understood genealogically, semiotically and archaeologically (in Foucault's sense). There is no essence of the Jew of Judaism, but only formations that emerge in specific places, times and circumstances. Jesus, on the other hand, turns out to be something like a blank sign, a floating signifier, such that there is nothing about him which is able to resist the interpretations put on him by other forces; of these the most powerful turn out to be those of *ressentiment*, as embodied in St Paul.[17] What I also rediscovered for myself was Nietzsche's anti-anti-Semitism, which seemed to me to be a key to his unrelenting hostility to Ernest Renan, whom he described as his "antipodes" (*BGE* 48). The latter, whose *Life of Jesus* was one of the phenomenal best-selling books of this time, argued that the contemporary hatred for Jews was continuous with the attacks they experienced in the

Roman Empire and was based on a rational perception: "The Jew . . .
retained his own status; he wished to have the same guarantees as
everybody else, and, over and above that, his own exceptions and
special laws. No people has ever been able to tolerate this."[18] Renan
wrote a history of Christianity as the story of an organic and
continuous development in which the genuine Christian spirit
gradually and definitively disentangles itself from its somewhat
accidental origins in Judaism, so that:

> Entirely Jewish in its origins, Christianity has thus in time
> succeeded in throwing off all its family characteristics, so that
> the view of those who consider it the Aryan religion *par
> excellence* is in many respects true. For centuries we have
> infused in it our modes of feeling, all our aspirations, all our
> good qualities, all our qualities. The exegesis according to
> which Christianity was inwardly molded in the Old Testament
> is the falsest of all. Christianity was the rupture with Judaism,
> the abrogation of the Torah. St. Bernard, Francis of Assisi, St.
> Elizabeth, St. Theresa, Francis of Sales, Vincent de Paul,
> Fenelon, Channing, have no trace of Judaism. They are people
> of our own race, feeling with our hearts and thinking with our
> brains. Christianity was the traditional theme on which they
> wove their poem; but its genius is their own.[19]

While Nietzsche affirms the discontinuity of the Jewish and Christian bibles, he does so in a totally different tone, one that is full of
admiration for the figures of Hebrew narrative and disdain for
Christian vulgarity and sentiment. Writing an essay on Nietzsche
and Renan had a purgative value for me, allowing me to vent my
spleen on all of the smarmy and weakly Hegelian readings of the
Jewish–Christian relation that continue to proliferate. An ironic
footnote to this study was the realization that many of the racist, anti-
Semitic and pro-German misinterpretations of Nietzsche may owe
something to the suggestion by Nietzsche's Jewish "friend Georg"
Brandes that he and Renan were surprisingly close in their thought.
It was Renan, however, not Nietzsche, who had flirted with the idea
of a race of technological supermen, probably German, who would
achieve an absolute mastery of the earth.[20]

I pursued the same line of thought in a talk that I gave at Baylor
University in Waco, Texas at a conference on "Nietzsche and the
Judaeo-Christian tradition," in 1991. Just two years later Waco was
the site of David Koresh's version of Armageddon, the slaughter and

suicide of the Branch Davidians with the assistance of the United States government, which combined elements of Jewish and Christian apocalypse in a perverse stew. I began in a deconstructive vein by saying that I would like to speak of the hyphen in the conference title, that is, to reflect on the facile assimilation of the two religions, and even their submergence in the rather watery notion of a "tradition." Instead, it would be worthwhile to reflect precisely on the distinctions that Nietzsche draws between the two, distinctions that could lead to a clearer sense of the genealogy of religion. In *The Antichrist* Nietzsche defines "tradition" precisely as that which forbids genealogical thinking. It is the last step of a process in which the leaders of a people "declare the experience in accordance with which the people are to live – that is, *can* live – to be fixed and settled." A twofold wall is erected against all experimentation, consisting first of a revelation credited to divine authority, and second of "*tradition*, that is, the assertion that the law has already existed from time immemorial, that it is impious, a crime against the ancestors, to call it in question" (*AC* 57). Nietzsche's deconstruction of the Judeo-Christian tradition proceeds then in two stages: first by attacking it as a whole, thus mimicking its own totalizing and apocalyptic tendencies and, second, by dissolving, complicating and pluralizing the presumed concept itself. In place of the single narrative that tradition tells of itself, we would see many (as Wellhausen and the higher criticism did in the case of both Jewish and Christian bibles); philologists are described (in *The Antichrist*) as "destroyers of every belief based on books." But the philosopher, Nietzsche urges in *Beyond Good and Evil*, should make use of religions (decidely in the plural), and this may lead to such nuanced judgements as his praise for the shrewdness of the ascetic priest with his comprehensive system of interpretation and his suspicion of the militant and dogmatic atheist whose passion is simply the reverse of that which he attacks (*BGE* 61).

I'd be surprised to discover that David Koresh or his followers were in the audience in Waco when I commended the anti-apocalyptic and anti-messianic side of Nietzsche's thought (while acknowledging that it has its own apocalyptic dimension, as in the "Decree against Christianity" which was to conclude *The Antichrist* or in the talk about splitting the history of humanity into two parts). I suggested two books that ought to be read in this spirit, Harold Bloom's *The Book of J* and A.G. Mojtabbi's *Blessed Assurance*.[21] Bloom's reading of the J text is strongly Nietzschean

and philological in the sense defined above. On this reading J satirizes
Yahweh as an angry, unpredictable and laughably anthropomorphic
deity; the text comes from and reflects a chaotic period after the
reigns of David and Solomon. If men and the incorrigibly male
Yahweh all come off badly, Bloom argues, it's because the author is
a woman at the post-Solomonic court who is practiced at seeing
through male bluster and pretension. God is dead, but the book lives
on; the spirit killeth, but the letter giveth life. "Now that God is dead,
who is speaking?" Nietzsche asked (*WP* 275); Bloom pursues the
question by taking apart what we presume to be the first story and
turning it into the late product of a sophisticated literary culture from
which we can learn a generalized suspicion of metanarratives. There
are no origins.

The other text that I commended was Mojtabbi's *Blessed Assurance*,
which undermines prophetic thinking from another, more contemporary direction. It deals with the complicity between end-time
thinking, based on the book of *Revelation*, and preparations for
nuclear war. As the Texas audience might have known, and as
Mojtabbi found out to her surprise, Amarillo, Texas was the center
for two activities, one technological and the other religious, which
appeared to be strangely complicit. It is the most active source of
fundamentalist apocalyptic teaching, according to which we are
already in the final days of the world; and it is (or was) the site for
the final assembly of American nuclear warheads by the Pantex
corporation. The same men and women who relished stories of
impending vengeance and judgement on Sundays dutifully trooped
to their jobs on Monday to fabricate the instruments of destruction.

I'm no longer in Kansas, but like many other Jews I've found that I
carry the experience of the diaspora with me. After I left and moved
closer to the east coast of the United States, I thought that I might
also have done with Nietzsche. After all, I had committed the excess
of publishing two books about him, *Nietzschean Narratives* and
Alcyone: Nietzsche on Gifts, Noise, and Women.[22] Perhaps Nietzsche
was a function of the diaspora which I somehow imagined that I was
leaving. But the Nietzsche industry is an infernal machine, as
Nietzsche said of his sister and mother; it is merciless in its demand
for new papers, new talks. Nietzsche wrote to Brandes in his last
series of communications: "To my friend George! Once you discovered me, it was no great feat to find me: the difficulty now is to
lose me" (I still don't know what to make of the fact that this letter

to the Jewish friend is signed "The Crucified"). Did Nietzsche foresee that his campaign to seduce the reader would lead to a legion of Nietzsche scholars perpetuating the various styles of thought, including the Jewish ones, that he described in *The Gay Science*? Or might we say that all these scholars and philosophers, literary theorists and psychoanalysts, have been *entdeutscht*, perhaps even Judaized, by the successful seduction accomplished by his writing? In his notebooks, Nietzsche asks whether one must not be almost a Jew to escape German romanticism, suggesting inevitably that he was almost such a Jew.[23] If Nietzsche was right that we will never have done with reading him (and this is how I understand his letter to Brandes) then there may be something in this of the Jewish attitude toward scripture as requiring constant commentary and reinterpretation. It would be foolish to look for closure in this project. And yet, next to the battered copy of *Beyond Good and Evil* that my grandfather Leon Gleckman read in Leavenworth prison, there is a brand new, leatherbound, expensive edition of the same book, in the old translation by Nietzsche's Anglo-Jewish friend, Helen Zimmern. This edition appeared this spring, at about the time of my mother's death; it appears in a series called "One hundred books that changed the world." I contributed a brief introduction which, if I'd been given space, might be more like this essay. When I showed it to a colleague she quickly and unerringly voiced two Nietzschean thoughts; she asked me "Have you written a sacred book?" and then remarked on a closer examination of the text, "It smells good." I hope that Leon would have approved of the way I've treated his legacy.

ABBREVIATIONS

AC Nietzsche, Friedrich, *The Antichrist*, tr. R.J. Hollingdale, New York: Penguin, 1954.

BGE Nietzsche, Friedrich, *Beyond Good and Evil*, tr. Walter Kaufmann, New York: Vintage, 1966.

D Nietzsche, Friedrich, *Daybreak*, tr. R.J. Hollingdale, Cambridge: Cambridge University Press, 1982.

GS Nietzsche, Friedrich, *The Gay Science*, tr. Walter Kaufmann, New York: Vintage, 1974.

HAH Nietzsche, Friedrich, *Human, All Too Human*, tr. R.J. Hollingdale, Cambridge: Cambridge University Press, 1986.

KSA Nietzsche, Friedrich, *Kritische Studienausgabe*, ed. Giorgio Colli and Mazzino Montinari, Berlin: de Gruyter, 1980.

TI   Nietzsche, Friedrich, *Twilight of the Idols*, tr. R.J. Hollingdale, New York: Penguin, 1968.

WP Nietzsche, Friedrich, *The Will to Power*, tr. Walter Kaufmann, New York, 1967.

NOTES

1 "Frosh" is a recent American, non-gendered expression for first year college or university students; it is an alternative to the more traditional "freshmen." "Frosh" takes the same form in the singular and the plural.
2 But Brandes misunderstood Nietzsche on a crucial point, linking him to Ernest Renan, whom Nietzsche detested, in a way that made plausible a certain racist and pro-German interpretation of the *Übermensch*; see my essay "Nietsche contra Renan," *History and Theory* 21(2) (1982): 193–222.
3 See *KSA* vol. 7, p. 535; vol. 7, p. 765; vol. 8, p. 502; vol. 8, p. 511.
4 *KSA* vol. 11, p. 72; vol. 11, p. 136.
5 *KSA* vol. 14, p. 503; vol. 14, p. 506.
6 Friedrich Nietzsche, *Sämtliche Briefe*, ed. Giorgio Colli and Mazzino Montinari (Berlin: de Gruyter, 1986), letter to Heinrich Koselitz, 20 July 1886, vol. 7, p. 214 and letter to his mother, 19 September 1886, vol. 7, pp. 249–50.
7 Since I wrote this essay a book has appeared that documents the crime scene in St Paul in the 1920s and 1930s; it includes an extensive discussion of the careeer of Leon Gleckman and documents the collusion between criminals and police that eventually led to the intervention of the FBI. See Paul Maccabee, *John Dillinger Slept Here: A Crooks' Tour of Crime and Corruption in St. Paul, 1920–1936* (St Paul: Minnesota Historical Society Press, 1995). I'm grateful to my aunt Lorane Abramson for this reference and for other information about her father, Leon Gleckman.
8 Allan Bloom, *The Closing of the American Mind* (New York: Simon & Schuster, 1987).
9 *KSA* vol. 1, pp. 902–3.
10 Forthcoming from Duke University Press.
11 Walter Kaufmann (ed.), *The Portable Nietzsche* (New York: Penguin Books, 1982) and Walter Kaufmann, *Nietzsche: Philosopher, Psychologist, Anti-Christ* (Princeton: Princeton University Press, 1974).
12 Kaufmann, *Nietzsche*, pp. 289–90.
13 Now it seems to me worth thinking about the importance that Nietzsche certainly had for Wittgenstein, whose debt to Schopenhauer has already been acknowledged; Stephen Toulmin and Alan Janik scarcely mention Nietzsche in their book *Wittgenstein's Vienna* (New York: Simon & Schuster, 1973), while devoting a good bit of attention to figures like Robert Musil who are inconceivable without him. The issues would have to do with language and silence (in the *Tractatus*) and the critique of Cartesianism, and the notion of linguistic practices as forms of life or expressions of the will to power, rather than as mirrors of the world (in

the *Philosophical Investigations*). What Nietzsche meant to secular Jews in *fin-de-siècle* Vienna is worth investigating by itself. The complexity of the relation is exemplified by Freud, who could deny that he had ever read more than half a page of Nietzsche, praise him as the man who had more self-knowledge than anyone else who had ever lived, and quote him to effect once or twice (for example in his monograph on Schreber: "Psychoanalytic notes upon an autobiographical account of a case of paranoia (dementia paranoides)," in Sigmund Freud, *Three Case Histories* (New York: Collier Books, 1973). As for Whitehead, or the twentieth-century American pragmatists, their reception and perhaps to some degree the genesis of their philosophy had much to do with the vitalism in the air around the turn of the century, owing to a *mélange* of Nietzsche, Bergson and others.

14 Karl Löwith, *From Hegel to Nietzsche*, tr. David E. Greene (Garden City, NY: Anchor Books, 1967).
15 Gary Shapiro, "The rhetoric of Nietzsche's *Zarathustra*," *Boundary 2* 8(2) (1980): 165–89.
16 See my essay "Nietzschean aphorism as act and art," in *Man and World* 17(3–4) (1984): 399–429.
17 See ch. 4 of my *Nietzschean Narratives* (Bloomington: Indiana University Press, 1989), pp. 124–41.
18 Ernest Renan, *Antichrist*, in *Oeuvres Complètes*, ed. Henriette Psichari, vol. 4 (Paris, n.d.), p. 1275; in *Renan's Antichrist*, tr. William G. Hutchison (London: Walter Scott, 1899), p. 126. See my essay "Nietzsche contra Renan," in *History and Theory* (1982): 193–222.
19 Renan, *Marc-Aurele*, in *Oeuvres Complètes*, vol. 5, pp. 1142–3; in *Renan's Marcus Aurelius*, tr. William G. Hutchison (London: Walter Scott, 1903), p. 315.
20 See my "Nietzsche contra Renan," pp. 210–15.
21 Harold Bloom, *The Book of J* (New York: Grove Weidenfeld, 1990) and A.J. Mojtabbii, *Blessed Assurance* (Boston: Houghton Mifflin, 1986).
22 *Nietzschean Narratives*, cited in note 17 and *Alcyone: Nietzsche on Gifts, Noise, and Women* (Albany: SUNY Press, 1991).
23 *KSA* vol. 12, p. 485.

BIBLIOGRAPHY

In spite of its length, this bibliography is not intended to be exhaustive. It attempts to offer an extensive and chronologically updated list (from the very first essays on the general subject as well as on the particular subjects treated by the chapter in this book). The reader may also consult notes of these articles that include comprehensive references.

Achad Ha'am, "Nietzscheanismus und Judentum", *Ost und West* 2 (1902): 145–52, 242–54.

Anderson, M. (ed.) "Juifs Dionysiens: Lectures de Nietzsche à Prague, autour de Brod et de Kafka", in D. Bourel and J. Le Rider (eds), *De Sils-Maria à Jérusalem: Nietzsche et le judaïsme: les intellectuels juifs et Nietzsche*, Paris, 1991, pp. 211–26.

Ansell-Pearson, K., "Nietzsche the rebel: *'non legar, non legar'*", *The Jewish Quarterly* 37 (1990): 27–31.

Aschheim, S., *The Nietzsche Legacy in Germany: 1890–1990*, Berkeley, 1992.

—— "Nietzsche and the Nietzschean moment in Jewish life (1890–1939)", *Leo Baeck Institute Yearbook* 37 (1992): 189–212.

Berg, L., "Friedrich Nietzsche über das Judentum", *Allgemeine Zeitung des Judentums* 55 (1892): 282–4.

Berl, H., "Nietzsche und das Judentum", *Menorah* 10 (1932): 59–69.

Bourel, D., "De Lemberg à Jérusalem: Nietzsche et Buber", in D. Bourel and T. Le Rider (eds), *De Sils-Maria à Jérusalem*, pp. 121–30.

Brinker, M., "Nietzsche's influence on Hebrew writers of the Russian Empire" in B.G. Rosenthal (ed.), *Nietzsche and Soviet Culture: Adversary and Ally*, Cambridge, 1994, pp. 393–413.

—— "*Last Jews or First Hebrews*": Appeals for Re-evaluation of all Jewish Values in Modern Hebrew Literature 1881–1922*, New Haven and London, forthcoming.

Cancik, H. and Cancik-Lindemaier, H., "Philohellenisme et antisémitisme en Allemagne: le cas Nietzsche", in *Sils-Maria à Jérusalem*, pp. 21–46.

Chapelle, D., *Nietzsche and Psychoanalysis*, Albany, 1993.

Cogen, H.R., "Das Judentum als Metapher des Widerspruchs bei Nietzsche", in Willi Goetschel *et al.* (ed.), *Wege des Widerspruchs*, Berne, 1984, pp. 149–64.

BIBLIOGRAPHY

Cohen, M., "Nietzsche; Hebreism, Hellenism, *International Studies in Philosophy*, 26 (1994): 46–65.

Cohen, R.A., "Rosenzweig vs. Nietzsche", *Nietzsche-Studien* 19 (1990): 346–66.

Corngold, S., "Nietzsche, Kafka, and the Question of Literary History", in V. Dürr, R. Grimm and K. Harms (eds), *Nietzsche: Literature and Values*, Madison, 1988, pp. 153–66.

—— "Nietzsche's Moods", *Studies in Romanticism* 29 (1990): 67–90.

Coutinho, A. C., "Nietzsche's critique of Judaism", *Review of Religion* 3 (1939): 161–6.

Duffy, M.F. and Mittleman, W., "Nietzsche's attitudes toward the Jews", *Journal of History of Ideas* 49 (1988): 301–17.

Duncan, L., "Heine and Nietzsche," *Nietzsche-Studien*, 19 (1990): 336–45.

Eisen, A.M, "Nietzsche and the Jews reconsidered", *Jewish Social Studies* 48 (1986): 1–14.

Eldad, I., "Nietzsche and the Old Testament", in J.C. O'Flaherty, T.F. Sellner and R.M. Helm (eds), *Studies in Nietzsche and the Judaeo-Christian Tradition*, Chapel Hill, 1985, pp. 47–68.

Gay, P., *Freud, Jews and Other Germans*, Oxford, 1978.

Gilman, S.L., *Nietzschean Parody*, Bonn, 1976.

—— *Inscribing the Other*, Lincoln and London, 1991.

Golomb, J., "Freudian uses and misuses of Nietzsche", *American Imago* 37 (1980): 371–85.

—— "Jaspers, Mann and the Nazis on Nietzsche and Freud", *Israel Journal for Psychiatry* 18 (1981): 311–26.

—— "Nietzsche on Jews and Judaism", *Archiv für Geschichte der Philosophie* 67 (1985): 139–61.

—— "Kafka's existential metamorphosis: from Kierkegaard to Nietzsche", *Clio* 14 (1985): 271–86.

—— "Nietzsche's Judaism of power", *Revue des études juives* 147 (1988): 353–85.

—— *Nietzsche's Enticing Psychology of Power*, Ames, 1989.

Heinemann, I., "Der Begriff des Übermenschen in der modernen Religionsphilosophie", *Der Morgen* 1 (1925): 3–17.

Heller, P., *Studies in Nietzsche*, Bonn, 1980.

—— "Freud as a phenomenon of the *fin-de-siècle*" in P. Heller (ed.) *Arthur Schnitzler and his Age*, Bonn, 1984.

—— "Nietzsche and the Jews" in S. Bauschinger, S. L. Cocalis and S. Lennox, (eds) *Nietzsche heute: Die Rezeption seines Werks nach 1968*, Berne, 1988, pp. 149–60.

Hirsch, L., "Friedrich Nietzsche und der jüdischer Geist", *Der Morgen* 10 (1934).

—— "Beinahe Echt?: Nietzsche under der jüdischer Prometheus", *Central Verein Zeitung*, 14(25) (June 1935).

Holste, C. "Nietzsche vu par Gustav Landauer", D. Bourel and J. Le Rider (eds), *De Sils-Maria à Jérusalem: Nietzsche et le judaïsme: les intellectuals juifs et Nietzsche*, Paris, 1991, pp. 147–77.

Holub, R.C., "Nietzsche and the Jewish Question, *New German Critique*, 66 (1995): 94–122.

Jankolowitz, S., "Friedrich Nietzsche und der Antisemitismus", *Israeli-tisches Wochenblatt* (Zurich), 13 November 1908.

Knodt, E.M., "The Janus face of decadence: Nietzsche's genealogy and the rhetoric of anti-Semitism", *The German Quarterly* 6 (1993): 160–75.

Kofman, S., *Le Mépris des juifs: Nietzsche, les juifs, l'antisémitisme*, Paris, 1994.

Kraus, E., "Wie Friedrich Nietzsche über das Judentum urteile", *Deutsche Zeitung* (Berlin), 1 January 1909.

Kreis, R., "Zur Beantwortung der Frage, ob Ernst Note oder Nietzsche mit dem Judentum 'in die Irre' ging", *Aschkenas* 2 (1992): 293–310.

Kurz, G., "Nietzsche, Freud, and Kafka", in M. Anderson (ed.), *Reading Kafka: Prague, Politics, and the Fin-de-Siècle*, New York, 1988, pp. 128–48.

Lehrer, R., *Nietzsche's Presence in Freud's Life and Thought*, Albany, 1995.

Le Rider, J., "Les Intellectuels juifs viennois et Nietzsche: autour de Sigmund Freud", in *De Sils-Maria à Jérusalem*, pp. 181–200.

Lewis, C., "Morality and deity in Nietzsche's concept of biblical religion" in *Studies in Nietzsche and the Judaeo-Christian Tradition*, pp. 69–85.

Lewkowicz, J., "Fryderyk Nietzsche o żydach i judaizme", in *Z Filozofji Judaizmu*, Warsaw, 1909, pp. 26–46.

Lonsbach, R.M., *Friedrich Nietzsche und die Juden*, Stockholm, 1939; reprinted and ed. by H.R. Schlette, Bonn, 1985.

Mattenklott, G., "Nietzscheanismus und Judentum", in N. Altenhofer and R. Heuer (eds), *Archiv Bibliographia Judaica: Probleme deutsch-jüdischer Identität*, Bad Soden am Taunus, 1985, pp. 57–71.

—— "Nietzsche dans les revues culturelles juives de langue allemande, de 1900 à 1938", in *De Sils-Maria à Jérusalem*, Paris, 1991, pp. 93–110.

McGrath, W.J., *Dionysian Art and Populist Politics in Austria*, New Haven and London, 1974.

—— "Mahler and Freud: the dream of the stately house", in R. Klein (ed.), *Beiträge 79–81 Gustav Mahler Kolloquium 1979 Ein Bericht*, Österreich-ische Gesellschaft für Musik, Kassel, Basel, London, 1981, pp. 40–51.

—— "Les Rêveurs dionysiaques", *Vienna, 1880–1938: l'apocalypse joyeuse*, Paris; 1986, pp. 172–9.

Mandel, S., *We Homeless Ones: A Biography of Nietzsche and the Jews*, Albany, forthcoming.

Mendes-Flohr, P., "Rosenzweig and Kant: two views of ritual and religion", in *Mystics, Philosophers, and Politicians: Essays in Honor of Alexander Altman*, Durham: Duke University Press, 1982, pp. 315–41.

—— *Von der Mystik zum Dialog*, Königstein am Taunus, 1978; tr. as *From Mysticism to Dialogue: Martin Buber's Transformation of German Social Thought*, Detroit, 1989.

—— "Franz Rosenzweig's concept of philosophical faith", *Leo Baeck Yearbook* 34 (1989): 357–69.

—— and Reinharz J., "From relativism to religious faith: the testimony of Franz Rosenzweig's unpublished diaries", *Leo Baeck Yearbook* 22 (1977): 161–74.

Neumann, H., "Superman or last man? Nietzsche's interpretation of Athens and Jerusalem." *Nietzsche-Studien* 5 (1976): 1–28.

—— "The case against apolitical morality: Nietzsche's interpretation of the Jewish instinct", in *Studies in Nietzsche and the Judaeo-Christian Tradition*, Chapel Hill, 1985, pp. 29–46.

Nicolas, M.P., *From Nietzsche Down to Hitler*, tr. E.G. Echlin, New York and London, 1970.

Nobel, N.A., "Friedrich Nietzsche's Stellung zum Judentum", *Die Jüdische Presse* 31 (36, 37, 39) (1900).

O'Flaherty, J.C. "Introduction" to *Studies in Nietzsche and the Judaeo-Christian Tradition*, Chapel Hill, 1985, pp. 3–15.

Roazen, P., "Nietzsche and Freud; two voices from the underground", *Psychohistory Review* 19 (1991): 327–48.

Rose, G., "Nietzsche's Judaica", in *Judaism and Modernity: Philosophical Essays*, Oxford, 1993.

Rotenstreich, N., *Jews and German Philosophy*, New York, 1984.

Sandvoss, E., *Hitler und Nietzsche*, Göttingen, 1969.

Santaniello, W., *Nietzsche, God, and the Jews*, Albany, 1994.

Schrattenholz, J. (ed.), *Anti-Semiten Hammer*, Düsseldorf, 1894.

Seligman, C., "Nietzsche und das Judentum", in *Judentum und moderne Weltanschauung*, Frankfurt am Main, 1905, pp. 69–70, 76–9.

Shapiro, G. "Nietzsche contra Renan", *History and Theory* 2 (1982): 193–222.

—— "The text as graffito: historical semiotics (*The Antichrist*)", in *Nietzschean Narratives*, Bloomington, 1989, pp. 124–41.

Stein, M., "Friedrich Nietzsche und das Judentum", *Allgemeine Zeitung des Judentums* 64 (1900): 451–3.

Steinberg, A., "Nietzsche und das Judentum", *Ost und West* 3 (1903): 547–56.

Stolzing, J., "Friedrich Nietzsche und Judentum", *Deutsche Tageszeitung* (Berlin), 10 January 1909.

Venturelli, A., "Nietzsche in der Bergasse 19: Über die erste Nietzsche-Rezeption in Wien", *Nietzsche-Studien* 13 (1984): 448–80.

Wiley, R.W., *The Bible and Christian Traditions: Keys to Understanding the Allegorical Subplot of Nietzsche's Zarathustra*, New York, 1991.

Waugaman, R., "The intellectual relationship between Nietzsche and Freud", *Psychiatry* 36 (1973): 458–67.

Witkowsky, G., "Nietzsches Stellung zum Zionismus", *Jüdische Rundschau* 2 May 1913.

Yovel, Y., "Perspectives nouvelles sur Nietzsche et le judaïsme", *Revue des études juives* 88 (1979): 483–5.

—— "Nietzsche, the Jews, and *ressentiment*", in R. Schacht (ed.), *Nietzsche, Genealogy, Morality*, Berkeley, 1994, pp. 214–36.

—— *Hegel and Nietzsche on Judaism* (Heb.), Tel Aviv, 1996.

SUBJECT INDEX

absolute, perspective 102–6, 111, 118
absorption, racial 66–7, 120
acquired characteristics *see* inheritance
aesthetics 239–41
aggression 197, 208; channeling 58; *see also* ressentiment
ambivalence 110, 117–34; distinctions 130; to Germans 173; non-contradictory 126; to priestly Judea 38–9; *see also* contradiction
anarchy 240
ancient Judaism *see* priestly Judaea
annihilation *see* genocide
anthropology 64, 211
anti-anti-semitism 4, 7, 21–5, 31, 37–9, 41, 76, 97, 120–4, 25, 130, 163, 171–2, 256; Nietzsche 25, 38, 69, 80, 117–34; *see also* anti-semitism
anti-semitism 3–16, 25, 26, 31, 35, 36, 38, 65, 68, 96–97, 119–20, 171–3, 224, 257; anti-Christian 25–8, 31, 39; Christian 8–10, 22, 24–8, 31, 34–6, 39, 65, 97; cowardly 173; gentle 66–7; identity 172; leaders in 25; mass movement 7; Nietzsche and 6, 8, 21, 24–5, 36, 37, 41, 66, 79, 80, 119, 124–5, 173, 245; opponents of 4, 7, 21–5, 31, 39, 41, 97, 120–5, 130, 163, 171–2, 256; pogroms 78; slave nature 172;

tasteful 66–7, 69; vulgarity of 122, 145; weakness of 122, 172–3; Wagner circle 22
Antichrist 30–1, 33–7, 40, 65, 68, 77, 94–5, 203, 256
Apollonian forces 227–8
archives, Nietzsche 22
art: as birth 143; Jewish 238
"artistes" 106–7
Aryan 21–3, 27, 33, 40, 55, 57, 250; character 64; diminution 61; mythology 33, 35, 65; opposition to 23; origins 63; religion 257; spirit 207; supremacy 33, 42, 43, 64
ascetics 142
assimilation, Jewish 129, 194, 224
atheism 166–7, 196; Freud 196; Nietzsche 196; *see also* humanism
atomistic revolution 220, 223
Auschwitz 10–12; survivors 12–13
authenticity, Jewish 164–6, 175
autochthony, Greece 57, 60
awakening, cultural *see* renaissance

bad 102, 170, 207; conscience 172; days 114; distinct from evil 104, 108, 170; Jew 76; *see also* evil
Balfour Declaration 240
basic forces *see* lower forces
beatific mission 167–8
beauty 240
Beyond Good and Evil 38, 76, 140, 174–5, 210, 233, 244, 247, 258,

267

SUBJECT INDEX

Jewish 78–9
misinterpretation, Nietzsche 127,
140, 257; *see also* distortion
misquotation *see* distortion
misunderstanding see
misinterpretation
misuse, of Nietzsche *see* distortion
mixed: marriages, ban 174; race *see*
race
model race 61, 62, 68
modernity 118, 137, 196, 239
Mongols 55–75
monotheism 102
monumental history 168–9
mother, to be one's own 160, 164,
166
moral: dualism 150; norms 165–6;
purity 151; repression 174; style,
great 103, 113
morality 27, 31–3, 104, 112, 151;
analysis of 202, 204; bourgeois
15, 31, 195, 20; of childlessness
152; Christian 32–3; conflict
208; dubious 106; European 104;
failure of 12; falseness 128;
genealogy *see* Geneology; herd
208; inferior 25; Judaeo-
Christian 32; language of 105;
master 165; and metaphysics
151; official 233; origin of 208;
priestly 124; pure reason 105;
slave 32, 36, 118, 124, 165, 172,
208; tradition 175; world order
124
motivation 209; unconscious 196,
197, 199, 210, 228
multitude *see* masses
murder *see* genocide
music, value of 141–2
musical achievements, cultural 58
mythology, comparative 63

"*Nachlass*" 24, 35
narcissism 202, 204, 206
nation states, European 108–9
national socialism 3, 4, 5, 9, 12, 23,
27, 30, 129; identification with
159
nationalism: dismissal of 4, 7;

German 43, 122, 219, 223, 226,
230; identification with 159–60;
opposition to 23, 123–4, 129
natural selection 63
nature, consummation of 221, 230
Nazi: appropriation of Nietzsche
42, 174; atrocities 16; distortion
22–4, 36, 42–3, 131–2; Germany,
formation of 22; misuse of
Nietzsche *see* distortion; proto-
22, 28, 33; tradition 24
Nazism 3, 5, 11, 12, 21–54;-
Nietzsche link 4, 5, 6, 9, 11, 16,
22, 23, 42, 43, 124, 250
negation 207
neurosis, Nietzschen 170, 202
New Idol 123–4
New Testament *see* Bible
Nietzsche: admirers of 158; anti-
semitism *see* anti-semitism;
archives 22; attention-getting
devices 7; contradictions 6–7, 9,
12, 24, 36, 38, 117–34; discipline
241; distortion 22–4, 36, 42–3,
127, 131–2, 257; Freud in
relation to 170, 193–217; genius
of 158, 162; Germans, opinion
of 173–4; as guide 219; Heine,
reading of 80–94; as inspiration
158; integrity 241; intuitism 200;
Jewish advocate 38, 41, 69, 76,
77, 79, 80, 130; Jewish
identification 37, 40, 41, 245;
Judaism, views on 6, 8, 21, 24,
37–8, 101–16, 117–34, 193, 256;
Kafka and 137–57; and marginal
Jews 158–92; megalomania 205;
Nazi appropriation of 42, 174;
Nazi Germany, role in 22, 23,
43; opponents 22, 28–9;
opposition to anti-semitism 25,
38, 69, 80, 117–34; pathography
of 201–5; provocatism of 131;
psychology of 169–71, 195; as
recluse 41, 79; rise to fame 23;
sexuality 202; sources 62, 80–94;
upbringing 37, 118
Nietzschean movement 3; de-
Nazification 5; politics 11, 16;

NAME INDEX

Achad, H. 239–40
Adler, S. 223
Adler, V. 158, 219, 223–4, 226
Alexander II 78
Amery, J. 13
Anzieu, D. 208
Aschheim, S. 3–20, 43
Auerbach, B. 81–2
Austrian Socialist Party 219

Bartels, A. 7
Barthelemy, A. 91
Baruch, M. 81
Basel, University of 62, 80
Baumler, A. 7, 251
Baylor University 257
Bendemann, E. 237
Benjamin, W. 143, 159, 163
Berg, L. 158
Binswanger, O. 202
Birnbaum, N. 238
Blanchot, M. 146–7
Bloom, A. 249
Bloom, H. 258, 259
Branch Davidians 258
Brandes, G. 23, 40, 158, 245–6, 257, 259–60
Braun, H. 219, 222
Brinton, C. 24, 41
Broch, H. 163
Brod, M. 146–8
Browning, C. 15
Buber, M. 160, 168–9, 194, 233–43
Buddha 143
Burckhardt, J. 121

Cahen, R.M. 172–3
California, University of 255
Cancik, H. 55–75
Caspari, O. 56
Colli, G. 249
Corngold, S. 137–57

Darwin, C. 63
David 259
Deleuze, G. 4, 256
Democratic Fraction
Derrida, J. 11 4, 255
Descartes, R. 101
Diderot, D. 195
Dionysius 127, 129–30, 145, 195, 227–9, 249
Doblin, A. 159, 160
Dostoevsky, F.M. 161, 204
Dühring, E. 21, 25, 27–8, 30–1, 33, 35, 42, 63, 120

Eckart, D. 7
Ehrlich, J. 218, 224
Epstein, J. 237

Feiwel, B. 237
Fergusson, J. 56
Feuchtwanger, L. 159, 163
Feuerbach, L. 85
Fliess, W. 90
Forster, B. 21, 25–6, 33, 38, 67, 80, 94
Forster-Nietzsche see Nietzsche, E.
Foucault, M. 4, 255